The Memory

The Memory
of Tiresias

Intertextuality and Film

Mikhail Iampolski

TRANSLATED BY HARSHA RAM

UNIVERSITY OF CALIFORNIA PRESS
Berkeley   Los Angeles   London

Published with the assistance of the Getty Grant Program

University of California Press
Berkeley and Los Angeles, California

University of California Press, Ltd.
London, England

Library of Congress Cataloging-in-Publication Data

IAmpol'skiĭ, M. B.
  [Pamiat Tiresiia. English]
  The memory of Tiresias: intertextuality and film / Mikhail Iampolski;
translated by Harsha Ram.
     p.   cm.
  Includes bibliographic references and index.
    ISBN 0–520–08529–9 (cloth : alk. paper.) —ISBN 0–520–08530–2
(pbk. : alk. paper)
    1. Motion pictures.   2. Intertextuality.   I.
Title. PN1995.I1813   1998
791.43'01'5—dc21   97–25664

Printed in the United States of America
9 8 7 6 5 4 3 2 1

The paper used in this publication meets the minimum requirements of American National
Standard for Information Sciences—Permanence of Paper for Printed Library Materials,
ANSI Z39.48–1984.

To Annette Michelson

*Man . . . should concentrate mind
and heart on the source of all sources.*

THE ZOHAR

Contents

Acknowledgments

Publication of this book would not have been possible without Ed Dimendberg, whose role in making the book extended far beyond the usual duties of an editor. From the outset he supported a book written in a language as exotic as Russian. His faith, perseverance, and generosity have been extraordinary. The debt that I owe him cannot be wholly expressed here.

I would also like to extend thanks to Harsha Ram for undertaking the difficult task of translating this book.

Introduction

In *Myth and Reality*, Mircea Eliade gives us a general account of the Greek mythology of memory. It reminds us that the goddess Mnemosyne, sister to Cronos and Oceanus, was considered the mother of the Muses. According to Hesiod, Mnemosyne preserved the memory of everything that had been but also knew what was yet to come. The poet, when graced by the Muses, gains access to the knowledge Mnemosyne possesses, the knowledge of sources and originary principles. The Muses sing: beginning with the sources, they recount the origins of the gods and of human beings. From them the poet receives the superhuman memory of Mnemosyne.

Yet precisely because they are linked to the sources, these aspects of the originary reality do not enter the orbit of our present life and instead remain inaccessible to daily experience. For this reason, Mnemosyne seems to draw the poet she endows with superior memory into another world, the world of oblivion and the past, identified with death. Lethe, the river of oblivion that flows through Hades, annihilates the memory of the deceased: indeed, it is this very act that renders them dead.

With the emergence of metempsychosis as a doctrine, however, Eliade notes a change in the mythology of memory. It is now the prior life of the soul that must be recalled rather than the sources or originary principles. From this point on, oblivion no longer symbolizes death but rather a return to life, a return marked by the soul's loss of any memory of its preceding lives. In this context death emerges once again as the return to another world, the world of sources and higher knowledge. The prophets and those favored by the Muses are among the few to have been permitted by Mnemosyne to retain their memory of their previous lives and the originary principles: "They attempt to unite the scattered fragments, insert them into a single chain, in order to grasp the meaning of their own fate."

I

Because taking fragments of history, fragments that in themselves had nothing in common, and unifying them in recollection signified the "coming together of beginning and end."[1]

In trying to make a coherent text out of fragments receding into oblivion, these poets and prophets do the work of culture, a culture that has become scattered, fragmented, dispersed in the invisible archives of many languages, but one that is seeking to gain wholeness, unity, and logic. In essence every text carries these fragments within itself, sometimes openly, sometimes covertly, and strives to order them according to the logic of its story.

Among the prophets whose memories the gods preserved after their death, there is one, named Tiresias, who stands out. While still a young man Tiresias happened to sight the goddess Athena bathing in the fountain of Hippocrene. For this he was blinded but at the same time granted the gift of foresight. Later, while wandering along the slopes of Mount Cyllene he happened to see two snakes copulating and was turned into a woman for many years. The blind androgyne Tiresias was chosen by the gods to bear forever a memory that would not fade.

The blind Tiresias would later meet Odysseus in the underworld. Recognizing Odysseus, Tiresias foretells his future. Alongside the seer Odysseus encounters his own mother, who sees him but fails to recognize him. The blind man, it turns out, can see better, for his blindness has retained the past and its images in the dark. To recognize is to place what you see alongside what you know, alongside what has already been. Odysseus's mother, bereft of her memory, cannot "see" her son. Sight without memory is blind. This opposition of visionary blindness and blind sight is particularly evident in the tragedy *Oedipus,* where the venerable Tiresias also puts in an appearance. In the words of O. Freidenberg: "The peripetia involving a transition from blindness to sight and vice versa is one of the topics of tragedy. It is most clearly seen in the contrast between Tiresias who is blind but can see and Oedipus who can see but is blind."[2]

Vision, sight, seeing, and looking are all concepts connected with spectacle. Many texts confront us culturally as mobile pictures. In the twentieth century, cinema has come to embody this cultural tendency to cultivate spectacle. But the story Homer tells also serves to remind us that seeing without remembering means not understanding. The memory of Tiresias turns out to be a better spectator than the clouded gaze of Odysseus's mother. A spectacle that is not immersed in memory, that has not been granted access to the sources of Mnemosyne, remains a meaningless collection of disjointed fragments. The memory of culture, the memory of Tiresias must be linked up to the individual text for the desired "union of beginning and end" to take place and for history to emerge.

It is no accident that blindness has become a sign of superior vision. It is the very darkness of memory that allows visual images to come loose from their contexts, forming new combinations, superimposing themselves on each other or finding hidden similarities. Metaphoric blindness becomes the condition of reading and insight. It allows us to break away from the persistent presence of the visible text, in order to raise what is known out of the depths and plunge the text back into its sources.

The blind androgyne Tiresias has come out of antiquity to our own time. He figures in the procession of immortal seers in Apollinaire's *L'Enchanteur pourrissant* and resurfaces in the play *Les Mamelles de Tirésias,* also by Apollinaire. He also enjoys a central place in T. S. Eliot's *The Waste Land:*

> At the violet hour, when the eyes and back
> Turn upward from the desk, when the human engine waits
> Like a taxi throbbing, waiting,
> I Tiresias, though blind, throbbing between two lives,
> Old Man with wrinkled female breasts, can see
> At the violet hour, the evening hour that strives
> Homeward, and brings the sailor home from sea,
> The typist home at teatime, clears her breakfast, lights
> Her stove, and lays out food in tins.
> Out of the window perilously spread
> Her drying combinations. . . .[3]

What is Tiresias doing in this "film" of modern life (and some critics have in fact suggested that Eliot's poetry is directly linked to cinematic montage)?[4] He brings together these montage fragments of life as other people have lived them, using his limitless memory to make them one:

> I Tiresias, old man with wrinkled dugs
> Perceived the scene, and foretold the rest—
>   (*The Waste Land*, ll. 228–229)

Eliot himself had noted: "Tiresias, although a mere spectator and not indeed a 'character,' is yet the most important personage in the poem, uniting all the rest."[5] Eliot is here making an essential observation. His point is that only the viewer or the reader can unite a text, using his cultural memory to make it one. The androgynous Tiresias is the ideal reader of any text, as one Eliot critic notes: "Thus, all the men, though individually identified, are one man; all the women one woman; and man and woman meet in Tiresias, the blind seer, who is both a mere spectator and 'the most important personage,' is at the same time pivotal and peripheral."[6] The synchronic nature of the pivotal and peripheral positions that a viewer's memory together brings to bear upon a text is one of the basic themes of the pages to follow.

James McFarlane has called the mode of seeing typical of modern culture "Tiresian." This is how memory sees the fragmented images of the world around us, images that its vision tries to arrange within the vast labyrinth we call culture. The main hero of Elias Canetti's novel *Auto da Fé* can find his way by touch through the huge library that he has hidden in his memory. In becoming blind, the hero is brought into contact with the world's imaginary library.

The memory of Tiresias gives us our bearings; it is the guiding thread that keeps us, however illusory its effects may be, from losing ourselves in the chaos of texts and the chaos of being. It is the ability to unite, juxtapose, and make sense of things. Every reader or spectator has this visionary memory to varying degrees. The memory of Tiresias, it seems to me, might well serve as a symbol for cultural theory today, which is also called upon to unite, juxtapose, and make sense of things.

PART I

Basic Concepts

CHAPTER ONE

Cinema and the Theory of Intertextuality

CINEMA HISTORY AS A TEXTUAL ELEMENT: ICONOGRAPHY AND ICONOLOGY

In 1989, a special issue of the French journal *Hors Cadre* was published. Entitled *Film Theory and the Crisis in Theory,* the issue pointed to an epistemological crisis that had been the object of recent discussion among film critics. This general sense of crisis was expressed by Jacques Aumont:

> The first thing we must do is state the fact: that today there is nothing like a dominant theory, indeed nothing that really appears to be theory at all. Nothing comparable to what semiology was between 1965 and 1970, to the Marx-Freud rapprochement of 1970, to the psychoanalysis of 1975, or even to the kind of analysis of film that provided a refuge to so many of us at the end of the seventies. If there is a scholarly discourse that is dominant today, then we would all have to say that it is the discourse of History: the problematic discourse par excellence, that has great difficulty even defining itself.[1]

Of course Aumont's assertion is difficult to accept as it stands. Theory exists and continues to develop. In recent years the fields of narratology and pragmatics have expanded and feminist film theory and the study of new technologies have produced some interesting work. But none of this, it goes without saying, in any way undermines the general pathos of Aumont's position. "Large-scale" theorization is over, and the resulting vacuum has been filled with historical studies.

In the humanities this kind of scenario generally points to a crisis in method. When a large conceptual paradigm ends, there is a return to empirical investigation, albeit enriched by the experience of the theorizing that came before.

But the relation of theory to history cannot be reduced to the idea of them simply alternating within the social sciences, and still less to the opposition of theoretical to empirical knowledge. To a considerable degree the crisis of theory is the result of its own inability to integrate historical material within itself, thanks to a kind of "innate" resistance that history manifests toward all forms of systematic theorization. This is linked above all to the tendency of theory to create its own "specific" or immanent field in which history, with its huge volume of heterogeneous matter, cannot be contained. Theory traditionally aspires to be synchronic.

Within this scenario, history, the diachronic level of analysis, remains, as Aumont puts it, a "problematic discourse," one that "has difficulty even in defining itself." It is true that the most recent histories of film, particularly in the area of early cinema, have been moving toward a greater sense of scholarly precision and a harmonizing of theoretical approaches with the concrete results of research (this is particularly evident in the attempts to construct a history of systems of representation). An effective conceptualization of history, however, remains unreachable. Michèle Lagny, whose *Histoire et cinéma* is a fairly successful attempt at unifying the historical and theoretical approaches to cinema, is relevant here:

> In fact there is a fundamental incompatibility of spirit between those approaches that are primarily seeking to account for the ways that writing functions as well as for the process by which meaning is produced, and the historical mode of questioning, which is less concerned with the text itself than with that whose trace the text happens to be. Semiotics, nonchronological and comparativist in its essence, does not have the same needs as history, which typically tries to organize particular events along a linear axis of time.[2]

Lagny's observation is very much to the point here. It appears that theory—which studies the production of meaning—and history have no obvious points of contact, although the meaning of a work is linked both to the historical context of its creation and to the position of a given text within the evolution of art. The semantic fullness of any text is surely the result of its ability to establish a connection with the texts that came before it, and occasionally with those that came later.

Writing came about to preserve memory. The same can be said about other durable forms of textualization. For this reason writing, understood in the broadest sense of the word, heightens the relevance of the problem of strengthening tradition. In examining this question, Iurii Lotman reaches a conclusion that is crucial for what it tells us about the history of culture: "For writing to become essential, historical conditions must be unstable, circumstances must be dynamic and unforeseeable, and a need must be felt for various kinds of semiotic translation, a need arising from frequent and prolonged contact with another ethnic milieu."[3]

In other words, the need to consolidate memory is itself the result of an unstable and dynamic cultural moment, one that shows an increasing tendency toward innovation. Modern culture, even as it increases the possible modes of textualization, is involved simultaneously in a constant search for the new. Novelty and tradition enter into a dynamic fusion that is to a large extent responsible for the production of new meanings. In essence the production of meaning is resolved in this "struggle" of memory and the way it is overcome. History is drawn into a text's structure as a semantically productive element.

For a long time the problem of the presence of cultural history within a text was essentially reduced to the question of influence, that of a predecessor over his successor. Influence was considered the principal marker of the presence of tradition within a text. But the very notion of "influence" turned out to be thoroughly vague and posed more problems for scholars than it solved.

To begin with, the notion of influence assumed that the past continued to impinge on the present, while any "choice of influence" was made in the present. The influence of the older text on the present thus appeared as the result of a contemporary author's activity. Could such a means of translating tradition be called *influence*? Even if one were to adopt the psychoanalytic interpretation of influence as the internalization of a certain experience, it would be hard not to conclude that the originary trauma is to a large extent the retroactive construct of subsequent experience. The entire problematics of influence could not escape what Laplanche and Pontalis have called the "phantasm of origins."[4]

The other dominant way of accounting for influence involved a depersonalization of the creative process. According to this perspective, the artist had only a limited say in choosing his material. The latter rather presented itself to him as a kind of lexicon of themes, motifs, construct, in other words a given "artistic language" that allowed for the construction of a new text. Such a position served to demystify the concept of influence. After all, one could hardly speak of the *influence* of language, if the latter was understood as the medium in which a text was formed and continued to exist. This depersonalization of tradition was carried out in the realm of the visual arts by the Vienna school of art history, culminating in the iconographic studies of Erwin Panofsky.

The field of cinema studies can also boast of a great number of quasi-iconographic studies, above all in the area of specific genre films such as the Western, film noir, and so on. There have even been attempts at compiling an exhaustive "symbolarium" of world cinema.

Raymond Durgnat, for example, has produced a "little dictionary of the poetic motifs" that wander, authorless, from film to film. The following motifs find their way into Durgnat's dictionary: blindness, carnivals, prisons, fairs, flowers, mechanized music, mirrors, paintings and posters, railway stations, shop windows, statues, record players, and the underworld. The main defect of Durgnat's thesaurus of symbols and similar lexicons lies in their attempt to affix some kind of univocal and unchanging meaning to a given motif. For example: "The fair is not freedom but an anarchy that generates chaos."[5]

Somewhat less arbitrary are dictionaries of symbols with specific delimitations, where the iconographic forms are defined by a given cinematic opus or a highly codified genre. There have been several attempts, none very successful, to analyze the iconography of D. W. Griffith's melodramas.[6] An iconographic approach to early cinema was advanced by Erwin Panofsky, who believed that a persistently iconographic stage was a necessary moment in the way cinema evolved its semantic strategies. Traditional iconography helps us to understand early cinema. It functions a little like the subtitles in silent movies, which, according to Panofsky, played a role analogous to that of medieval *tituli:*

> Another, less obtrusive method of explanation was the introduction of a fixed iconography which from the outset informed the spectator about the basic facts and characters, much as the two ladies behind the emperor, when carrying a sword and a cross respectively, were uniquely determined as Fortitude and Faith. There arose, identifiable by standardized appearance, behavior and attributes, the well-remembered types of the Vamp and the Straight Girl (perhaps the most convincing modern equivalents of the medieval personifications of the Vices and Virtues), the Family Man, and the Villain, the latter marked by a black mustache and walking stick. Nocturnal scenes were printed on blue or green film. A checkered tablecloth meant, once and for all, a "poor but honest" milieu; a happy marriage, soon to be endangered by the shadows from the past, was symbolized by the young wife pouring coffee for her husband; the first kiss was invariably announced by the lady's gently playing with her partner's necktie and was invariably accompanied by her kicking out with her left foot.[7]

The persistent motifs that Panofsky enumerates here carry a meaning that is immutable and upon which a film or indeed any artistic text can rely. Yet these motifs do not participate in the production of new meaning; rather, they passively transmit significations from the past into the present. Panofsky himself relegated these motifs to the realm of iconography, calling them "secondary" or "conventional." He provides us with an eloquent example when he points out that thirteen men seated in a particular way around a table signify the Last Supper—this is the conventional iconographic signification. Yet da Vinci's painting on this theme signifies something far greater—and this new signification, intrinsic to da Vinci's fresco, Panofsky calls its "inner meaning" or "content": "The discovery and interpretation of these 'symbolical' values (which are often unknown to the artist himself and may even emphatically differ from what he consciously intended to express) is the object of what we may call 'iconology' as opposed to 'iconography.' "[8]

Both the potential and the complexities of an iconological approach to meaning become clearer in the light of the example to follow. I have consciously taken it from the early history of cinema, during which the iconographic layer in films was consistently highlighted. I am thinking of a particular motif in D. W. Griffith's *Intolerance* (1916), the statues of elephants with their trunks raised adorning the main set in the film's Babylonian episode. It is generally believed that Griffith borrowed these elephants from the Italian film *Cabiria* (1914) directed by Pastrone. To be sure, the relationship between Griffith and Pastrone now appears a lot more complicated than a case of the latter influencing the former; yet after B. Hanson's research on the subject, the fact that some borrowing occurred seems beyond dispute.[9] Significantly, this borrowing took place despite Pastrone's fierce resistance to any form of plagiarism: the Italian director had even taken the precaution of having false scenery built for *Cabiria* to prevent any plagiary. Although his deception was largely successful, the elephants were nonetheless stolen, even before Griffith got to them, to appear soon after *Cabiria* in the film *Salammbô*.[10]

The desire to display elephants as a decorative motif in *Cabiria* and *Salammbô* need hardly surprise us if we recall that both films were set in Carthage, a city readily connected to elephants through Hannibal's legendary crossing of the Alps on elephant-back. Yet Griffith's decision to place elephants in Babylon seems somewhat baffling, since there is no traditional link between Babylon and elephants and since Griffith himself was generally quite opposed to such anachronisms. As Griffith's assistant Joseph Henabery remembers:

> Griffith was very keen on those elephants. He wanted one on top of each of the eight pedestals in Belshazzar's palace. I searched through all my books. "I'm sorry," I said, "I can't find any excuse for elephants. I don't care what Doré or any other Biblical artist has drawn—I can find no reason for putting elephants up there. To begin with, elephants were not native to this country. They may have known about them but I can't find any references."
>
> Finally this fellow Wales found someplace a comment about elephants on the walls of Babylon and Griffith, delighted, just grabbed it. He very much wanted elephants up there.[11]

The question then arises: What kind of meaning could this motif have as part of the Babylonian scenery? A brief mention must be made here of the representation of elephants in the iconographic tradition.[12] In general the elephant appears as a wise, pure, and God-fearing creature. It has been endowed with the ability to blush, for which reason it becomes a symbol of chastity. The *Physiologus,* the basic sourcebook for most Christian bestiaries, speaks of the antagonism between the elephant and the dragon. While fleeing from the dragon, the she-elephant gives birth in water. The *Physiologus* compares the male and female elephant to Adam and Eve after they have tasted of the forbidden fruit, while the newly born elephant cub has been seen as Jesus Christ. The dragon, needless to say, is equated with the Devil. Leonardo da Vinci viewed the elephant as an embodiment of honor, prudence, justice, and religious piety, while Bernini deployed the elephant in his celebrated obelisk as a creature of the sun. The notion of the elephant as a solar animal goes back to the nineteenth century and is definitively established in J. Collin de Plancy's *Dictionnaire Infernal.*[13]

Enough has been said for us to realize that the iconographic symbolism of the elephant is difficult to reconcile both with the general context of Babylon and with the specific content of Griffith's Babylonian episode, in which the ancient city is evoked according to its traditional image as the embodiment of sin. In this sense the iconographic tradition throws little light on the meaning of the motif; indeed, the motif now appears even more enigmatic.

Yet the Babylonian scenery in Griffith's film has one other figurative source that is at least as significant as *Cabiria*—namely, the painting *Belshazzar's Feast* (1820) by the English artist John Martin. Griffith, who knew this painting well, included a reproduction of it in the large album of visual material that he put together for the film.[14] It is clear that Griffith's Babylonian scenery follows the broad conception of Martin's painting. *Belshazzar's Feast,* like Griffith's scenery, contains enormous columns; adorning them, however, we find not elephants but snakes. The snake is the primary animal symbol in Martin's painting; it winds around the columns on the left-hand side of the canvas, as well as around the idol standing to the back of the palace. The snake's presence in Martin's painting is doubly motivated. It is the symbol of sin, as well as being a creature from Babylonian mythology called Tiamat, the "dragon of darkness" destroyed by the solar and light-giving Babylonian divinity Marduk. Martin's painting does include some elephants as well, although they function as barely visible ornamental attributes. Martin's elephants stand at the base of Belshazzar's throne with their trunks raised, while snakes, coiled and about to strike, ride on their backs.

It is certainly curious that Griffith should have replaced the elephants with snakes, which were traditionally considered their foes. His choice appears even stranger in the light of the subsequent history of Martin's painting during the nineteenth century. In 1831 H. C. Selous, an epigonal artist of Martin's time, produced an engraving entitled *The Destruction of Babel,* an obvious imitation of Martin that contains four enormous sculpted elephants. Under Martin's influence, Victor Hugo wrote a poem called "Le Feu du ciel" that recounts the destruction of Babylon, Sodom, and Gomorrah. Here, too, we unexpectedly find "granite elephants carrying a gigantic cupola." The poem was illustrated in 1831 by the well-known engraver Louis Boulanger, whose work also clearly indicates the influence of Martin. To the left of Boulanger's print we find an enormous statue of an elephant standing on its hind legs; in the background there is a building in flames, with elephants serving as caryatids and adorning the heads of its columns. Several details in Boulanger's painting, then, closely anticipate Griffith's deployment of the same motif.[15]

Griffith would thus appear to have fallen into a specific iconographic tradition that goes back as far as *Belshazzar's Feast* by Martin and is connected to Babylon rather than Carthage. We might well ask, then, what might have necessitated the insertion of elephants into Griffith's vision of Babylon and its demise.

It should be said that the elephant as a symbol betrays signs of ambivalence quite early in its history. We know that Behemoth, one of the demons from hell, could take on the guise of an elephant.[16] A print by the well-known Franco-Dutch artist Bernard Picard, *The God of Wisdom, Health and Well-Being According to the Sinhalese* (from his series of 1723–1731 entitled *Religious Ceremonies and Customs*), depicts an elephant-headed idol with goat's feet, being worshiped in what closely resembles a Black Mass. Significantly, however, the object of veneration in this rather ambiguous print is still called a god of wisdom and well-being.

It was after the Portuguese discovery of the Elephanta Caves on an island near Bombay in India that the connotations of the elephant as a symbol became markedly more negative. At Elephanta a series of cave temples were uncovered containing innumerable statues of elephants, as well as enormous granite lingams, the striking traces of a phallic cult. This discovery strongly affected the European imagination: it established the link between the elephant as a sculptural motif and the ruination of the idolatrous and sinful city. It was at Elephanta that elephants were found serving as caryatids in close proximity to enclosures containing stone phalluses.[17] By the end of the nineteenth century, we find Felicien Rops depicting an elephant with a phallus-like trunk in his engraving *The Idol*. The entire engraving functions as an allegory of vice. And in his poem "Le Voyage," Charles Baudelaire also speaks of "idols that have trunks" in the city of voluptuaries:

> Nous avons salué des idoles à trompe;
> Des trônes constellés de joyaux lumineux;
> Des palais ouvragés dont la féerique pompe
> Serait pour vos banquiers un rêve ruineux;

Des costumes qui sont pour les yeux une ivresse;
Des femmes dont les dents et les ongles sont teints,
Et des jongleurs savants que le serpent caresse.

(We have saluted idols that had trunks;
Thrones bedecked with bright jewels;
Finely wrought palaces whose fairy-tale pomp
Would be a ruinous dream for your bankers;

Costumes intoxicating to the eye;
Women with teeth and nails painted,
And wise jugglers caressed by a snake.)[18]

Clearly, in Baudelaire the elephant shares a common semantic context with the snake.

This "new" iconography, marginal to the classical iconographic tradition, includes a further cinematic moment in its history, the film *The Seven Mortal Sins* by George Méliès (1900), which contains an allegorical episode called "The Castle of Pride." The allegory of pride is elaborated in terms of the classical iconography described by Panofsky. Pride is represented by a woman emerging from a peacock's feathers. A peacock has of course classically personified self-pride, but perhaps not only the latter. From Brunetto Latini's thirteenth-century bestiary *Livre du trésor* we learn that the peacock's sinful nature is expressed in the splendid bird's "serpentine head and devilish voice."[19] In any case, we do not need to go back so far in history. The peacock continued to function as a symbol of sin in French culture at the end of the nineteenth century, for example, in Edmond Louys's painting *Jeune fille au paon* (1895) and in Pierre Aman-Jean's poem "La Femme aux paons" (1891), which describes a woman's sexual union with a peacock.[20] The allegorical detail that concerns us here is the representation engraved on the wall of the castle of Pride of an elephant with its trunk raised.

The details we have reconstructed allow us to decode the symbolic meaning of the elephant in Griffith's *Intolerance*. It can be read as a sign of pride or vice, the sins that doom the city of Babylon. But this meaning does not derive purely from traditional iconography: it emerges at the point of intersection of a range of texts belonging to the romantic and symbolist traditions.

This analysis in its turn raises further questions to which there are no simple answers. We cannot say for sure that Griffith was consciously deploying the figure of the elephant in precisely the symbolic context I have outlined. The only solid proof we have is that Griffith knew *Cabiria* and was acquainted with *Belshazzar's Feast*. If we were to conclude that Griffith took the elephants from Pastrone, then we could also assume that the statues in *Intolerance* have no symbolic value and merely reproduce a decorative motif that Griffith saw and liked. Yet this is precisely what we cannot say for sure: they could be a quote from Martin (in whose painting elephants also figure, although not centrally) rather than Pastrone. Nor can we say for sure that Griffith did not also know the engravings of H. C. Selous, Boulanger, or Felicien Roops, the poetry of Hugo and Baudelaire (although the latter is unlikely), or the film of Méliès. Our lack of certainty suggests that this list could be continued. Yet most important, we cannot also reject the possibility that Griffith did not in fact rely on any received tradition, and that he chose to insert the elephants into the set out of caprice, or through an entirely personal and unconscious impulse (e.g., as a phallic image).

The analytical tradition in which we are situated is such that it cannot free us from what the Russian phenomenologist Gustav Shpet once called "genealogical curiosity." When this curiosity sets in, said Shpet, "it creates a species of people who can perform incredible intellectual contortions in order *not* to understand what X says, without knowing who X's parents were, the nature of X's religious upbringing, convictions, etc. The problem is that even after finding all of this out, they are still unable to understand anything, tormented as they are by the doubt that in this case trustworthy Mr. X might be lying and the lying Mr. Y might be telling the truth."[21]

"Genealogical curiosity" is most often methodologically fruitless. In the final analysis we can never establish the authentic source, the motivations underlying the choice, or the precise symbolic meaning of the figure of the elephant in the Griffith decorations. Nonetheless, "genealogical curiosity" is not a trait specific to a singular "species of people" as Shpet describes them: it is a fundamental feature of culture in general. It is connected to the fact that a text always appears to us as emerging from some other text, the Platonic "Idea" of a text, as it were. We cannot conceive of discourse without some metaphysical *origin*. I quote Michel Foucault at length here, since he has best described this common representation of origins:

> All-manifest discourse is secretly based on an "already-said," and . . . this "already-said" is not merely a phrase that has already been spoken, or a text that has already been written, but a "never-said," an incorporeal discourse, a voice as silent as a breath, a writing that is merely the hollow of its own mark. It is supposed therefore that everything that is formulated in discourse was already articulated in that semi-silence that precedes it, which continues to run obstinately beneath it, but which it covers and silences. The manifest discourse, therefore, is really no more than the repressive presence of what it

does not say; and this "not-said" is a hollow that undermines from within all that is said.[22]

This felt need to correlate the text to some silent prior discourse is essentially linked to the fact that discourse, being linear, is perceived by us in time. It is difficult for us to conceive of the possibility that discourse has not been preceded by the flow of time, a "breath" or "voice," and hence something both temporal and unseen, since we cannot see time. The hollow created by the unseen "already-said" is then filled by the material of culture. Meaning is projected onto the text exactly as something "already-said" that functions as a double of manifest discourse. Naturally, all of this applies to the realm of reading, to the phenomenology of our perception of discourse. Iconology reconstructs on a rational basis a precursor discourse, fills it with the concrete material of culture, and renders the "breath of time" visible in the text.

THE ANAGRAM

A far more sophisticated model for linking a manifest discourse to a latent one was elaborated in Ferdinand de Saussure's theory of anagrams, which played a significant role in the creation of a theory of intertextuality. Saussure formulated his theory of the anagram before writing his *Cours de linguistique générale,* but his writings on the anagram gained intellectual currency only after 1964, when they were released along with his other unpublished writings. Saussure's claim was to have discovered in the ancient Indo-European poetic tradition (early Latin, Greek, and Old German) a "general principle for composing verse by 'anagram.' Many poetic texts in this multiple tradition, such as the hymns of the Rig Veda, appear to have been constructed in accordance with the acoustic (phonological) composition of the key word, generally the name (usually never mentioned) of a divinity. The remaining words of a text were chosen in such a way that the sounds (phonemes) of the key word were repeated with a certain regularity."[23]

Saussure accumulated a huge amount of material concerning the place of the anagram in Indo-European poetics, which he was never to publish, for several reasons. First, he was embarrassed by the fact that none of the poets he had studied ever admitted to having consciously employed the anagram as a principle. Second, he was unable to establish definitively that the anagrammatic structures he had found were not the result of chance: "There is no way to resolve the question of chance [in anagrams], as the following illustration will indicate: The most one could say against it is that there is a chance of finding on average in any three lines the means—legitimately or not—to create any anagram whatsoever."[24]

Saussure's doubts have not obscured the broader methodological significance of the anagram as a graphic model of how one text enters another, of how an external element (such as a name) affects the meaning of a text's "internal" elements. Saussure himself, in discussing *Die Niebelungen,* had noted that any change in the character of the name being anagrammatized can alter the entire meaning of the text: "In the arrangement of the narrative, the symbol as material is not simply utilized; it undergoes a modification. For the arrangement is modifiable, and itself becomes an agent of modification. It is enough to *vary the 'external' relations* of the original material in order for its apparently 'intrinsic' characteristics to begin to differ. The identity of the symbol is lost in the diachronic life of the legend."[25]

In this way a certain order of elements (which were traditionally attributed a key role in the generation of meaning) acquires a very different function. It anagrammatizes another text (the precursor text) and thereby produces meaning in the syntagmatic as well as the paradigmatic dimension, in synchrony as well as in diachrony. The order of elements uses anagrams to organize not so much a linear succession as a kind of vertical axis, an exit that leads to other texts, in other words—intertextuality. The anagram permits us to see how another outside text, a hidden quote, can both organize and modify the order of elements in a given text.

Saussure distinguished between several types of anagrams: the *hypogram,* the *logogram,* and the *paragram.* It is the paragram that is of particular significance to a theory of intertextuality: "We use the term paragrammatic network to describe the (nonlinear) *tabular model* for the elaboration" of a text's language. "The term *network* replaces the univocal (linear) principle by incorporating it within itself, and suggests that each ensemble (sequence) is the completion and beginning of a polyvalent relationship." The term *paragram* indicates that each element functions "like a dynamic mark, like a *moving 'gram'* that *makes sense* rather than simply *expressing* it."[26]

The critic Julia Kristeva has devoted some attention to the notion of paragram, as well as to Saussure's general study of the anagram. It was Kristeva, too, who brought the term *intertextuality* into general circulation. Hers was the first attempt at theoretically appraising Saussure's writings on the subject:

> The poetic signified refers back to other discursive signifieds, in such a way that several different discourses are legible within a poetic utterance. Around the poetic signified, then, a multiple textual space is created, whose elements can be inserted into a concrete poetic text. We shall call this space *intertextual.* . . .
>
> In this perspective, it is clear that the poetic signified cannot be seen as dependent upon a single code. It is the point of intersection of several codes (at least two), situated in a relation of negation to one another.
>
> The problem of how several alien discourses are made to intersect (and explode) within poetic language was raised by Ferdinand de Saussure in his work on anagrams.[27]

What is essential here is the fact that the various poetic discourses manifested in the field of a paragram do not simply coexist, jostling together or
impinging on each other; instead, they negate each other to create meaning, just as the paragram itself is a destruction of writing by other writing,
the act of writing's self-destruction.[28] Indeed, if we were to read a poem in
which the name of God is inscribed in coded form, we would perceive either the text of the poem or the name of God. The name, once it enters
the text of the poem, destroys (or at least strongly modifies) its writing.

Some of Kristeva's postulates, particularly concerning the multiplicity of
codes and textual systems existing in a given text, as well as their conflictual and mutually destructive nature, have been taken up and applied to
the field of cinema by Christian Metz—without, however, using the term
paragram.[29] This is hardly surprising, since by its very nature the paragram
occurs in a verbal text, which allows for its division into acoustic segments.
Since the primary means of expression in film is visual representation,
which can be divided into articulate segments only through montage, paragrammatic constructions are hardly possible in cinema.

The most natural way of introducing anagrams into a film would therefore involve its linguistic elements. Here is one example. The title of Jean
Vigo's film *À propos de Nice* (1929) strikes us still for its unusualness. The
construct "à propos de" is rare in the titles of works of art; it seems to belong more to the genre of the scholarly article or essay. Vigo's choice of
title can indeed be read as a variation on the title of Guy de Maupassant's
short essay "À propos de rien" (1886), which deals precisely with Nice. Significantly, both *Nice* and *rien* are paragrams (i.e., incomplete anagrams) of
each other. The paragram thus allows us to reconsider the significance of
Nice in this film: it establishes the equation Nice = nothing, emptiness,
pure negation. But that is not all. The anagrammatic relation between the
titles of the two texts allows us to bring them both together and project
each onto the other, producing some curious results.

Maupassant's essay begins with a description of the flower festival and
carnival in Nice (both figure centrally in Vigo's film also). A pretty and
diminutive blonde throws flowers from the stand at those participating in
the procession. Tired, she freezes for a moment, and then becomes as-
tounded at what she had not noticed before: " 'Dear God! How ugly these
people are!' For the first time, she noticed, in the midst of this festival,
amidst these flowers, this joy, this intoxication, that of all the animals, the
human animal was the ugliest of all."[30] Maupassant then gives a vivid account of all the human deformities that his heroine observes, before
reaching his conclusion:

> Certainly people are just as ugly every day and smell just as bad all the
> time, but our eyes, accustomed to seeing them, and our nose, accustomed

to smelling them, are able to distinguish their hideousness and their stench only when they are made aware of them by a sudden and violent contrast.

Human beings are terrible! In order to put together a gallery of grotesques capable of making even a corpse laugh it would suffice to take the first ten passers-by to come along, line them up, and photograph them, with their varying stature, their legs too long or too short, their bodies too fat or too thin, their faces red or pale, bearded or beardless, their demeanour smiling or serious.[31]

Further on Maupassant enumerates the various other reasons for our human blindness, among which he includes all forms of social prejudice—religion, morality, habit, essentially every manifestation of standardized human behavior. At the end of the essay, Maupassant once more turns to his heroine: "She spoke no more! What was she thinking of? . . . No doubt, about nothing!"[32] This final sentence gives the essay a circular quality, returning us to the title, "À propos de rien."

The Maupassant essay concerns the opposition between vision and consciousness. Vision is here seen as a mechanical and unconscious registering of reality (the photographing of chance passersby), while blindness is equated with consciousness in all its forms, including the verbal. It is in this context that Maupassant's final reference to the heroine, who is no longer thinking about anything and hence is *seeing* for the first time, acquires its full meaning. Maupassant's paradox resides in the fact that what the heroine has seen cannot be related by the writer ("She spoke no more!"), since language would destroy her vision. Consciousness must be (of) "nothing" (*rien*) in order for us to see.

If we suppose that Vigo's film and Maupassant's essay are correlated through the paragram established by their titles, then Maupassant's text can be understood as an explication of, or running commentary on, the film, with its gallery of grotesque monsters and aging men and women. The film becomes a repository of the pure, wordless vision that arises out of the "nothing" of clichéd consciousness, which is equated with the city of Nice itself. As an embodiment of "nothing," Nice allows us to see people as they really are. For both Vigo and Maupassant, Nice becomes the ideal locus of vision (and the visionary).

An anagram based on titles can widen to embrace texts as a whole, correlating both texts in order to shed light on the semantic strategy underlying one of them (in this case Vigo's film). The Vigo-Maupassant nexus is also uniquely intertextual in that it involves a literary text that posits the absence of language as the condition of sight, and a cinematic text that effectively realizes this wordless vision. Yet the very absence of language in Vigo's film finds its motivation verbally, in Maupassant's text, which appears to free *À propos de Nice* from any need to have recourse to language.

Vigo's film thus negates Maupassant's essay but acquires its additional meaning precisely from this negated text.

My second example, which is more complex, deals with the film *La Coquille et le Clergyman* (1927) by Antonin Artaud and Germaine Dulac. The film was the only one of Artaud's screenplays to be actually shot; nevertheless, Artaud remained dissatisfied with Dulac's work, disavowed any part in it, and even tried to obstruct the film's screening at the premiere, which took place at the Studio des Ursulines. We still do not know the reason Artaud rejected the film, although critics and witnesses have offered a multitude of conjectures. Georges Sadoul, who participated in the scandal that took place at Les Ursulines, sums up Artaud's possible reasons: "He had expected to play the principal role in *La Coquille et le Clergyman*, and though in fact it was given to someone else, simply because he [Artaud] had been ill, he was convinced that there had been treachery afoot, and created a disturbance at the première with a rowdy Surrealist demonstration."[33] Another eyewitness, Jacques Brunius, writes that Dulac "had damaged the film with Alex Allin's mediocre acting and by drowning it in an orgy of technical tricks, with only a scattered handful of powerful images surviving."[34]

These hypotheses concerning Artaud's motives for rejecting the film have gained wide acceptance. A range of scholars has tried to provide Artaud's actions with a biographical and psychological basis. Naomi Greene, for example, views the collision between Artaud and Allin as an expression of Artaud's fear of his double; Richard Abel sees Artaud's script itself as reflecting his relations with Gênica Athanasiou, as well as with his mother and father.[35] Nonetheless, Artaud's rejection of the film can be understood in a wider sense, as an expression of Artaud's general desire to create a kind of "absolute text," which fundamentally cannot be realized in material form.

Artaud had seen in theater the possibility of overcoming language, transcending the actual play in favor of a new concrete language of signs, which he equated with Egyptian hieroglyphs: "I mean to say," he declared, "that I will not stage any play based on writing and language."[36] Jacques Derrida has shown that for Artaud the word once uttered, particularly the word of the Other, is something stolen from the body.[37] Hence Artaud's interest in language that is "directly communicative," in the "effacement of words by gestures."[38] Hence the idea of a theater without rehearsals, a theater of pure immediacy, a theater without text—in other words, a utopian, unrealizable spectacle. Linda Williams has suggested—and she is surely right—that the cinema represented for Artaud a means of realizing the utopia of a language that did not have to "steal" its words from the body, a language that "seemed to appeal directly to the imagination without the separation between sound and sense so endemic to language."[39] The search for a language that does not sever meaning from sound points on the one hand to the cinema, in which signifier and signified are fused. On the other hand, it seems akin to the function of the anagram, which in its own way also abolishes the difference between meaning and sound. It will be my thesis that the screenplay Artaud wrote for *La Coquille et le Clergyman*, while oriented toward the cinema, also contains complex anagrams that cannot by nature be translated into visual forms of representation.

Beyond the cinema and the anagram, Artaud's screenplay also displays a third orientation. The text clearly contains a range of alchemical subtexts, which have already been the object of critical attention.[40] In 1932, Artaud wrote the article "Alchemical Theatre," in which he attempted to elaborate an analogy between alchemy and theater. For Artaud both alchemy and the theater are marked by an inner ambiguity, for they both look for gold by simultaneously reworking matter and creating symbolic abstractions. Both are thus involved in a search to link matter to meaning, and in this they reproduce the basic dilemma of language. Artaud, moreover, believed that both alchemy and the theater arose from the collapse of some primordial unity, generating the conflict on which the theater thrives and the division of the world into the spirit and matter that necessitated alchemy. The task of both alchemy and the theater, said Artaud, was "to resolve or even annihilate all the conflicts produced by the antagonism between matter and spirit, idea and form, the concrete and the abstract, and to fuse all appearances into a unique expression resembling spiritualized gold."[41]

Alchemy for Artaud was above all the sundering of a primordial unity into a certain duality, which could once more be overcome thanks to the re-creation of the prior oneness in "gold." This same capacity Artaud attributed to phonetic articulation (whose duality was one of the principal themes of his reflections). In 1934, he published one of his most enigmatic and philosophical works, *Héliogobale ou l'Antichriste couronné*, which reveals the primary source of his linguistic utopias, *L'Histoire philosophique du genre humain* by Fabre d'Olivet, a well-known occultist who wrote at the beginning of the nineteenth century. In *Héliogobale*, Artaud hails d'Olivet's great revelation that the One, the Ineffable, becomes manifest in sound. Sound by nature is dual, bipolar, based on the collision of two principles, the feminine and the masculine: "It is sound, acoustic vibration, that transmits taste, light, and the surge of the sublimest passions. If the origin of sounds is double, then everything is double. And this is where the madness begins—the anarchy that precipitates war, the massacre of partisans. And if there are two principles, one is male, the other female."[42] The history of Héliogobale (a hermaphrodite) is the history of the genesis of the world, which falls apart into a male and a female principle.

Artaud's alchemy thus acquires a markedly acoustic character that is programmatically realized in the form of anagrams. Anagrams, in fusing several meanings into one sound, are capable of restoring a prior oneness. They become a metaphoric means of finding a "spiritual gold." One example is the title of Artaud's well-known collection *Ombilic des Limbes,* which is based on a complex wordplay. The word *limbes* (limbo) is anagrammatically contained in the word *ombilic* (navel), whose three syllables also punningly divide into *homme-bile-liq(uide)* (man-bile-liquid). The word *ombilic* is also a paragram of *alambic* (alembic), an apparatus for alchemical distillation. Most important, the word also contains the utterance *OM* (or *AUM*), the primordial sound in the Hindu tradition, which Artaud believed had a mystical significance. *OM* is at once God, the word, the source of all things, and the vehicle of a trinitarian principle (insofar as its written symbol has three components in Sanskrit). In the Mandukya Upanishad we read that *AUM* is "a symbol for what was, what is / And what shall be. *AUM* represents also / What lies beyond past, present, and future." This unity of all being is projected with particular clarity onto the duality of speech and breath which the Chandogya Upanishad reads as simultaneously masculine and feminine: "Speech and breath, Sama and Rig, are / couples, and in the imperishable *OM* they / come together to fulfill each other's desire."[43]

Also significant is the fact that the Hindu tradition links the utterance *OM* to what is also the film's central motif, the shell. In Hindu mythology the shell produced the first sound to resonate throughout the world, the mystical *OM*. The oyster shell is associated with the ear, and the pearl it contains is the word. In other myths the shell itself becomes sound (the primordial sound contained within it) and language. In the Upanishads the shell is an attribute of Vishnu, and it contains the primary elements of the world, its germ, that is also *OM*.[44]

If *OM* is anagrammatically present in the word *ombilic*, then it is also worth enumerating some of the "hidden meanings" attributed to the same syllable by the Hermetic tradition. Each of its two constitutive letters has its own meaning. *M* is a hieroglyph meaning water, but it can also be a symbol for mother or woman. *O* (the French *eau*) also means water. Thus *OM* contains hidden within itself a symbolic unity *O* = *M* (water = water). When arranged vertically, the same letters acquire another hieroglyphic value:

O—is the sun, the eye of God hovering over
M—water, the first element in the Genesis of the world.[45]

It is worth noting that Artaud's screenplay repeatedly and from the very first line identifies the clergyman as *homme,* the man. Paradoxically, the word *OM/ homme* has been viewed by the Hermetic tradition as a feminine and aqueous symbol. Man (*OM*) functions as an alchemical androgyne.

The shell, which is also the symbolic embodiment of *OM,* serves as man's double, the second principle that is the basis of the world's manifestation in sound. The film as a whole can be read as a mystical parable about the creation of the world from two single yet divided principles.

Since these anagrammatic forms are realized exclusively on the script's verbal level, we need to examine Artaud's own use of language more closely. The film's hero is identified by one of two words, *homme* and *clergyman* (the latter word also appears in the title). The English word *clergyman,* rather foreign to the French ear, refers only to Anglican pastors. One might suppose that Artaud's choice of even this rather obscure word might have been dictated by a phonetic anagram. When pronounced with a French accent, *clergyman* can be distinctly heard to contain the two words *l'air* (air) and *hymen* (hymen), which signifies both marriage and the virginal membrane (a clergyman can demonstrate his modesty by pulling his coattails over his thighs). Artaud's decision to designate the same character with two names might then be equivalent to introducing two elements—air and water—combined into one. Hymen would then refer not only to the feminine nature of the clergyman but also to the idea of an alchemical marriage.

Just as the script's plot involves the encoding of several alchemical processes, so the anagrammatic nature of Artaud's writing serves to encode an alchemical transformation of sounds—the metamorphosis of *OM* into *OR* (gold). Let us recall the last scene in the screenplay:

> In order to clean the house they have to move the glass ball that is nothing other than a kind of vase filled with water. . . . Among [the young people] we rediscover the woman and the clergyman. They appear to be about to get married. But at this moment the corners of the screen begin to project the visions that had passed through the brain of the clergyman while he slept. The screen is cut into two by the apparition of an enormous ship. The ship disappears, but the clergyman, headless, his hand carrying a packet wrapped in paper, is seen climbing down a staircase which seems to recede into the sky. Entering the room where everyone is gathered, he unwraps the paper and reveals the glass ball. The attention of the public is taut to the point of breaking. Then he bends toward the ground and breaks the glass ball: from it there emerges a head, none other than his own.
>
> The head grimaces hideously.
>
> He holds it in his hand like a hat. The head rests on an oyster shell. As he raises the shell to his lips the head dissolves and is transformed into a kind of blackish liquid which he swallows with his eyes closed.[46]

I will not delve too deeply into the clearly alchemical symbolism in this episode, which has already been investigated by Grazyne Szymczyk-Kluszczynska. Suffice it to note the connection between the glass ball, the shell, and the alembic (the alchemical still); the motif of the alchemical marriage; and the staircase receding into heaven—surely Jacob's ladder, a motif that enjoyed some currency in alchemical iconography (and often situated on a seashore).[47] What concerns us lies somewhat to the side of these motifs. The entire final episode (including its somewhat obscure imagery) can be decoded as part of the alchemical production of gold, designated here by the French *OR*. *OR* is a mystical root meaning "light." In the Hermetic tradition it was often written in three letters, as *AUR* (the Latin *aurum*), and was hence linked to a trinitarian principle, like *AUM*. Mystics rediscovered *OR* in the name of the highest Zoroastrian divinity, Ahuramazda (Ormuzd), meaning "the active word." In the more recent European tradition of Kabbalistic thinking, *OR* finds another meaning. Fabre d'Olivet, in his *La Langue hebraïque restituée*, notes that the letter *R* was hieroglyphically a head, while *O* signified water. Thus the combination $O + R$ (the creation of gold from various elements, the overcoming of duality) is in one way or another connected to the process of drinking. Jean Richer has uncovered the play of these hieroglyphs in Arthur Rimbaud's poem "Larme," which ends with the following couplet: "Or! tel qu'un pêcheur d'or ou de coquillages / Dire que je n'ai pas eu souci de boire!" (Gold! Like a fossicker of gold or shells / I no longer cared to drink!)[48] The symbolism of these lines concerns us only in their linking of gold, shells, and the act of drinking (it is possible, incidentally, that Rimbaud had in mind the liquid gold of alchemists). The point is that Artaud's bringing together of the head, the shell, and the act of drinking in one episode functions like a rebus, disguising the creation of gold like a hieroglyph made up of the letters *OM* (shell).

My hypothesis is readily confirmed by the phonetic patterns of the script's last paragraph, which Artaud, always sensitive to the mystical resonance of sounds, certainly would have taken seriously. Let us reread it in the French: "Il la tient dans sa main cOMme un chapeau. La tête repose sur une coquille d'huitre. COMme il approche la coquille de ses lèvres la tête se fond et se transfORMe en une sORte de liquide noirátre qu'il absORbe en fermant les yeux." I have capitalized the syllables through which the "alchemical transmutation" of *OM* into *OR* takes place. The phonetic structure is here sustained with the utmost symmetry. First the syllable *OM* is repeated twice, then the syllable *OR*. In the center are the pivotal words *se transforme*, the moment of transition, in which *OM* and *OR* are fused into *ORM*.

The "blackish liquid" that appears in the last sentence can be further interpreted in the light of a mystical tract well known in France, *L'Oeuf de Kneph: Histoire secrète du Zéro*, published in Bucharest in 1864 by one Ange Pechmeja. The book contains an illustration of the universal egg, which conjoins all the letters of the alphabet. Here the letter *O* is interpreted as the source of all vowels, and *R* as the source of all consonants (cf. the dual nature of sounds in d'Olivet and Artaud). The symbol for the letter *O,* moreover, is the white Jehovah, and for *R,* the black Jehovah (another double that Artaud would have appreciated). In this way the transmutation of the phonetic principle *OM* into *OR* might be described by invoking the symbolically black letter *R.*[49]

There is, incidentally, a curious moment in *L'Oeuf de Kneph,* where the semantic—or rather the symbolic—range of the word *or* (gold) is established etymologically. Among the words listed here (the author even includes anagrams such as *RO*), we find most of the motifs that appear in Artaud's film: *ORtus* ("birth" in Latin), *qOURoun* ("crown" in Arabic), *ÖRaba* ("carriage" in Breton), *gORod* ("city" in Slavic), *gORa* ("hill" in Polish), or the Greek *amphORa.*[50] In this way, the acoustic element of a word can serve as the kernel from which a whole cluster of motifs can evolve on the basis of an anagrammatic connection.

Enough has been said to propose one last hypothesis concerning Artaud's dissatisfaction with Dulac's version of the film. Artaud's script simply could not be filmed, since its logic was to a considerable extent rooted in the phonetic and hieroglyphic layer of Artaud's writing. Clearly this layer could not be translated into the visual idiom of a film. Artaud's script was fated to remain an experimental hypothesis.

But the questions raised by *La Coquille et le Clergyman* go well beyond the factual details of Artaud's encounter with Dulac. The point, rather, is why Artaud, in writing his script, came to choose a paragrammatic model of meaning. It has already been pointed out that the anagram in its own way abolishes the dualism of meaning and sound and finds in this an affinity with the cinema, which is also based on a unique consonance of signifier and signified. Linda Williams has written, "For Artaud, precisely this absence of the cinematic signifier seemed to offer a possible protection against the robbery of his speech by the Other."[51]

The anagrammatic nature of Artaud's writing is clearly oriented toward overcoming the phonetic level of language through the hieroglyphic. In this context *OM* can be equated with *shell* and contain the hieroglyph meaning *water,* while *OR* can become the hieroglyphic combination of *head* and *water.* The anagram is thus the most direct means of transforming the phonetic into the visual: it carries within itself the mechanism of screen adaptation, if by the latter we mean the translation of language into visual terms. Yet this alchemical "transmutation" of the "acoustic" into the "pictorial" also resists any actual attempt at cinematic visualization. Screen adaptation is in fact already inscribed, anagrammatically, in the written text, which finally excludes the actual translation from text to screen.

WHAT IS A QUOTE?

The hieroglyph in cinema is a problem that deserves separate attention, and I shall be returning to it in part 2, which deals with intertextuality in the films of D. W. Griffith. Artaud himself spoke unequivocally in favor of replacing phonetic speech in the theater with hieroglyphics. In the first manifesto of the Theatre of Cruelty he wrote:

> For the remainder, it is necessary to find new means of recording this [phonetic] language, either in ways that resemble musical notation or through some kind of coded language.
>
> Now as far as ordinary objects are concerned, or even the human body, when both are elevated to the status of signs, it is evident that hieroglyphic characters could serve as an inspiration, not only for the purpose of recording these signs in a way that is legible and which permits their reproduction at will, but also for the construction onstage of symbols that are precise and easily read.[52]

Jacques Derrida has shown convincingly that the concept of the hieroglyph in Artaud is closely related to a fundamental change in the idea of representation. The representation of the word has been replaced, says Derrida, by "the unfolding of a volume, a multidimensional milieu, an experience which produces its own space." Derrida signals this displacement as the "closure of classical representation" or as "the reconstitution of a closed space of original representation" ("original" here refers to the preverbal and gestural). Derrida further defines postclassical representation as "the autopresentation of pure visibility and pure sensibility."[53]

Now the closure of classical representation into volume, space, pure visuality, and sensuousness gives the hieroglyph a corporeal quality. The hieroglyph as body acquires an autonomy that undermines its status as sign. The sign ceases to be a transparent medium translating meaning from signifier to signified. This process takes place wherever writing, particularly in its pictorial form, acquires the traits of an object. For Ezra Pound, who considered Chinese hieroglyphics a model for poetic imagery, the image was "a form of super-position, that is to say it is one idea set on top of another."[54] This conception of the image was to become the basis of Poundian "vorticism," which he contrasted to "impressionism," whose greatest expression, for Pound, was the cinema. Sergei Eisenstein was to formulate an idea quite analogous to Pound's, although somewhat later. He dismissed the natural (impressionistic) notion of mimesis underlying premontage cinema in favor of montage, which he saw as a unique way of realizing the very same idea of the hieroglyph-pictogram. Eisenstein had this to say about the constitutive elements of the hieroglyph, which he saw as identical to the elements of montage in cinema: "Each, separately, corresponds to an *object,* to a fact, but their combination corresponds to a *con-*

cept. From separate hieroglyphs has been fused—the ideogram. By the combination of two 'depictables' [*izobrazimykh*] is achieved the representation of something that is graphically undepictable."[55]

If we ponder the essence of this "piling" of one thing onto another, which constitutes the basis of the hieroglyph for Pound, Eisenstein, and Artaud, we easily rediscover both a variation on the anagrammatic principle of combination and the clearly expressed intent to destroy the semiotic transparency of the constitutive elements of the hieroglyph.

When Eisenstein says that in hieroglyphics "the picture for water and the picture of an eye signifies 'to weep,' " then he is also suggesting that in order to achieve the concept "to cry" we have to destroy the simpler, more obvious iconic meaning of the images of water and the eye.[56] The escalation, already noted, of pure spatial and corporeal elements in the hieroglyph thus works in tandem with the destruction of a prior iconic value, of what we might call the *mimetic* level of discourse. For Pound and Eisenstein, the destruction of the meaning of the individual elements of the hieroglyph is readily compensated for by the creation of a general meaning, established on the ruins, as it were, of mimesis. Yet such a conclusion is by no means obvious. The superimposition of "water" and "eye" might constitute the concept "to cry," but it might just as easily not do so. The meaning of a hieroglyph is always far less self-evident than meaning produced mimetically, and in the vast majority of cases is in fact not realized in perception. The breakthrough toward a new meaning thus might end up destroying meaning entirely, leading finally to an escalation of nothing more than pure "corporeality," the self-presentation of the sensuous.

Critics using contemporary theory to analyze the hieroglyphic model of writing (including Eisenstein's) as it applies to the cinema have concluded that the hieroglyph "shatters the sign" by increasing the text's heterogeneity.[57] The shattering of the sign above all involves the destruction of linearity as the basic temporal model of discourse. Linearity is then displaced by a constellation of diverse components. Jacques Derrida describes the pictogram as follows:

> The signifier is broken or constellated into a system: it refers at once, and at least, to a thing and to a sound. The thing is itself a collection of things or a chain of differences "in space"; the sound, which is also inscribed within a chain, may be a word; the inscription is the ideogrammatical or synthetic; it cannot be decomposed; but the sound may also be an atomic element itself entering into the composition.[58]

For Derrida even a sound, linear by nature, acquires the qualities of an "atom" inserted into a constellation. This constellation, founded on differences, acquires, simply by virtue of losing its linearity, the features of a "body," one that is no longer "mimetic," and hence quite unique: a "body-as-sign."

At first glance, the pictogram appears to restore the motivatedness (and hence the mimeticism) of the sign, its connection with the objects of the external world. In fact the opposite is the case: by superimposing its constitutive elements, it in fact undermines the mimetic nature of the text. Marie-Claire Ropars-Wuilleumier provides a clear diagnosis of what is at stake: "It is always a question of going back to Cratylus, motivating the sign and bringing it closer to the thing, thus of making the letter or word a figure for the real. One could then say that inversely the search for the hieroglyph in cinema seems to be based on the possibility of demotivating the image with respect to the object it represents—thus of dissociating figuration and signification."[59]

Our discussion of the hieroglyph, flowing directly from the very nature of the paragram, has an immediate bearing on a theory of intertextuality. Intertextuality, too, superimposes text on text, meaning upon meaning, thereby essentially transforming writing into a hieroglyph. The essential question arising from this can be formulated as follows: Does intertextuality open up new signifying perspectives (meanings), or, rather, does it generate such a complex superimposition of meanings as to finally annihilate the possibility of a final meaning? Is the sign made finally into a hieroglyph, thereby "closing" the moment of classical representation and inaugurating the "autopresentation of the sensuous"?

To proceed further we need to ask the following questions: What is a quote? To what extent is a quote characterized by the qualities we have noted as typical of the anagram and the hieroglyph? To explore this question, let us take the exemplary case of a textual genre made up entirely of quotes. In late antiquity there existed a poetic genre whose texts were effectively a mosaic of quotes from classical authors. This genre was called a *cento* (literally, a patchwork quilt). Mikhail Gasparov and E. G. Ruzina, who have studied centos based on the poetry of Virgil, conclude that the genre is proof not so much of literary continuity as of "a profound historico-cultural rupture between the material at hand and its reworking in the cento."[60] The cento is thus founded on a break with tradition, presenting itself as an internally disorganic text, a patchwork.

In our century Walter Benjamin could be considered a true creator of centos. Benjamin had dreamed of writing a text that would be a "collection of quotes." Quotation for Benjamin replaced a more immediate relationship with the past. The transmission of the past to the present was replaced by the principle of quotability. The act of quoting, however, was by no means a conservative one, a preservation of the past. At stake was a desire to destroy the present, the temporal medium of classical representation that was spoken of earlier.[61]

We know that Benjamin's interest in quotation evolved under the influence of Karl Krauss, who had himself elaborated a "method of quoting without commentary." Krauss, said Benjamin, "has discovered in quotation the power not to preserve but to purify, to tear from the context, to destroy; the only power in which hope still resides that something might survive this age—because it was wrenched from it."[62] Significantly, Krauss insisted on calling quotation a form of "written acting."[63] This irruption of theater into writing reflects a rupture in the text's homogeneity, the introduction of a scene or painting, a heterogeneous and somewhat self-enclosed fragment that we know as the quote.

In the cinema this metaphoric transformation of the quote into something resembling a pictorial canvas or theatrical scene is in a sense confirmed by the specific features of film.[64] Raymond Bellour has pointed out that a cinematic text cannot be quoted by the critic, insofar as the latter works with written words. The fact that a film cannot be quoted in a written text even impels Bellour to suggest that the very idea that a film is a text can be accepted only metaphorically. He concludes that the only way of quoting a film in writing is by reproducing photograms from it:

> A written text cannot reproduce what only the camera can do—create the illusion of movement on which the film's sense of reality is based. This is why the reproduction of even a large number of photograms proves little beyond the critic's inability to capture a film's textuality. Nevertheless, these photograms are of immense importance. They really do function as the reader's equivalent of the freeze-frames which arrive at the editor's table and which have the contradictory role of exposing a film's textuality at the very moment that they seek to interrupt its unfolding. [65]

Bellour's observation is valuable for the way it stresses the fragmentary, static nature of film quotes: in becoming photograms, they violate the "natural" logic of the film's development. But the fact that the photogram as quote is inorganic in its painterliness or theatricality is not the whole story. More important is the fact that the photogram "exposes a film's textuality"; that is, it allows us to touch the hidden processes by which a film creates its own meanings. Paradoxically, then, the meaning or textuality of a film flashes into view precisely where the film's natural life is interrupted.

Roland Barthes once analyzed this phenomenon quite convincingly, showing how the so-called third meaning (*troisième sens:* vague, inarticulate meaning; meaning still in the process of becoming) is best read out of the photogram, which isolates and immobilizes the shot:

> Which is why to a certain extent (the extent of our theoretical fumblings) the filmic, very paradoxically, cannot be grasped in the film "in situation," "in movement," "in its natural state," but only in that major artefact, the photogram. For a long time, I have been intrigued by the phenomenon of being drawn, even fascinated by frames taken from a film (outside a cinema, in the pages of *Cahiers du Cinema*) and of then losing everything in those photos

(not just what I got from them but even the memory of the image) when once inside the viewing room—a change which can even result in a complete reversal of values.[66]

If we are to follow Bellour in seeing the photogram as the model of film quotation, then we are impelled to the conclusion that meaning is manifested only in quotes. Meaning emerges in textual "anomalies," such as the photogram.

The quote stops the linear unfolding of the text. As Laurent Jenny observes:

> What is proper to intertextuality is the introduction of a new mode of reading that explodes the linearity of the text. Each intertextual reference is the site of an alternative: either one keeps reading, seeing the reference as nothing more than one fragment among others, an integral part of the text's syntagmatics; or one returns to the original text, resorting to a kind of intellectual anamnesis whereby the intertextual reference appears as a "displaced" paradigmatic element issuing from a syntagmatic axis that has been forgotten.[67]

This alternative, however, is not always possible to realize. The anomalies that emerge in a text, blocking its development, impel us toward an intertextual reading. This is because every "normative" narrative text possesses a certain internal logic. This logic motivates the presence of the various fragments of which the text is made. If a fragment cannot find a weighty enough motivation for its existence from the logic of the text, it becomes an anomaly, forcing the reader to seek its motivation in some other logic or explanatory cause outside the text. The search is then conducted in the realm of intertextuality. Jenny's alternative is available only when the anomalous fragment can be convincingly integrated into the text in one of two ways—through the text's internal logic or by referring to another text. Michael Riffaterre formulates this dilemma in the following way: "Semantic anomalies in linearity force [the reader] to seek a solution in nonlinearity."[68] Unable to find a motivation contextually, the reader looks outside the text.

Riffaterre also suggests posing the dilemma in terms of an opposition between mimesis and semiosis. One could say that the textual anomaly (a fragment that the reader or viewer is unable to integrate into the text in a convincing manner) violates the calm of mimesis, the transparent and porous character of the sign. But precisely where mimesis is violated, we begin to see vigorous traces of semiosis. In other words, we witness the birth of meaning, which is normally transparent wherever mimesis remains untroubled, dissolving into the effortless movement from signifier to signified. This is because the quote violates the link between sign and objective reality (the mimetic link), orienting the sign toward another text rather than a thing. Riffaterre observes: "This passage from mimesis to semiosis arises either from the superimposition of one code onto another, or from the superimposition of one code onto a structure that is different from what is properly its own."[69] Where the reader expends the effort required to draw on other texts and other codes, the quote acquires its motivation, thereby not only imbuing the text with additional meanings but also restoring the mimesis it had violated. Intertextuality can thus be seen to enrich meaning and to salvage the very linearity of narrative that it had compromised.

In light of the foregoing, I would venture the following definition: *The quote is a fragment of the text that violates its linear development and derives the motivation that integrates it into the text from outside the text itself.* From this point of view, what is traditionally considered a quote may end up not being one, while what is not traditionally seen as a quote may well be one. Let me clarify this point with a few examples. Jean-Luc Godard is well known as one of the most intertextually oriented of film directors. Several of his films are practically collages of quotes. Godard revealed his passion for quotation in his very first film, *Breathless (A bout de souffle)*. Godard himself was to explain:

> My first films were purely the work of a film buff. One could even make use of what one had seen before in the cinema for the sake of making explicit references. . . . Some of the shots I took were connected to others that I had seen before, in Preminger, Cukor, etc. . . . You have to put the blame on my taste for quoting, a taste I have always kept. But why blame me for it? In life people quote the things they like. We have the right to quote whatever we like. So I show people who are always quoting; the only thing is that I arrange it so that whatever they quote also happens be to something that I like.[70]

Breathless is riddled with all sorts of quotes, which Godard was more than happy to point out. The source of the widest layer of quotes in the film was the American film noir. Godard himself was to acknowledge that during the shooting he believed he was making a film in the same genre.[71] In one episode the film's heroine, Patricia, tries to hang a poster, a reproduction of a Renoir painting, in the hero's room. She tries hanging it on one wall and then another, and then finally rolls it into a tube and looks through it at Michel. Then Patricia and Michel kiss, and Patricia goes into the bathroom, where she affixes the poster to the wall. There is nothing in this episode that might seem to violate the linear unfolding of the story line. Yet Godard was the first to admit that the episode contained a hidden quote. When Patricia looks through the tube of the rolled-up poster, the film is quoting a scene from Samuel Fuller's *Forty Guns*, in which one of the heroes looks at his enemy through the sights of the rifle.[72] Fuller's film throws further light on the relationship between Patricia and Michel, a relationship in which Michel appears as the victim or target. The episode anticipates the hero's tragic death after he is betrayed by Patricia.

At the same time, this episode is so organically embedded into the film's narrative, so transparent a part of the film's mimetic structure, that we need Godard's own commentary to recognize the Fuller reference in the heroine's spontaneous behavior. Without Godard's help this quote would remain indiscernible—it would simply melt into the linear flow of the plot. A quote that Godard intended and believed obvious thus remains opaque to the viewer. This is a telling example of a buried quote, one that dissolves in mimesis. Indeed, I would dare to suggest that, prior to Godard's commentary, this episode, paradoxically enough, *was not a quote.*

Let me turn now to another example, taken from Carl Theodor Dreyer's *Vampyr* (1932). The film begins with its hero, David Gray, on the bank of a river, where he finds a strange hotel. The film's second shot shows us this hotel's unusual signpost, a winged angel, holding a bough in one hand and a wreath in the other. Gray books into the hotel and settles down to sleep. Later, just as the hero begins to dream, we once again see the hotel's signpost in close-up; immediately afterward, the owner of a nearby castle, whose inhabitants have all fallen victim to the vampire, enters the room where Gray lies sleeping. I shall not dwell in greater detail on the film's plot (I refer the reader to David Bordwell's very fine analysis of *Vampyr,* which he reads as a parable in which a death experience initiates the hero into a secret knowledge).[73]

What interests us here is the signpost. Had it appeared in a shot along with a frontal view of the building, it might escape the viewer's attention. In fact it is always shown in an isolated close-up shot, never as part of the hotel facade. The obtrusive insertion of the signpost into the story seems particularly forced the second time it appears. We see Gray go to his room after inspecting the hotel, locking the door behind him. There follows a caption, which tells us that the moonlight shed an unnatural light on things, filling the hero with a terror that would haunt him even in his sleep. Then we once more have a shot of the signpost, followed by another of Gray asleep in his bed, lying on his back. The key to his door now turns, and the owner of the castle enters the room. Clearly there is something anomalous about this unexpected outdoor shot of the signpost appearing in the foregoing sequence. For this very reason, it is a quote.

The bough in the angel's hand gives us an early clue to the signpost's meaning. It reminds us naturally of Aeneas's golden bough in Virgil's epic. Aeneas, we recall, required the golden bough in order to cross the River Styx into the underworld and return alive. The reference to Virgil immediately gives Gray's experiences in the film a special significance: his adventure is equated metaphorically with Aeneas's descent into the underworld. The film also makes other references to the *Aeneid.* For example, a conversation is seen to take place between the doctor (the vampire's servant) and Gray about the apparent sound of barking and a baby screaming (neither is audible in the sound track). These are precisely the first two sounds Aeneas hears in the underworld: "Huge Cerberus, monstrously couched in a cave confronting them, made the whole region echo with his three-coated barking. . . . Aeneas, passing its entrance, the watch-dog neutralised, strode rapidly from the bank of that river of no return. At once were voices heard, a sound of mewling and wailing, ghosts of infants sobbing there at the threshold."[74]

The anomaly of the signpost's unexpected appearance in the montage sequence is thus resolved once we recognize the reference to the *Aeneid*. The connection is convincing enough for us to integrate the signpost into the film's context—yet difficulties remain. The angel that holds the bough and the wreath obviously has nothing to do with Virgil. Nor is it entirely clear why the angel's image should function as a signpost to a hotel that in fact plays a minor role in the film. The hotel is merely the place where Gray goes to sleep and where, in what is part dream and part reality, he is visited by the owner of the castle, who gives him a book about vampires. After this moment Gray leaves the hotel, never to return. From the point of view of narrative economy, then, Gray might have more usefully stumbled onto the castle rather than the hotel and asked to stay there.

An intertextual reading allows us to resolve this problem also. I would suggest that the signpost is itself a "quote" from Baudelaire's sonnet "La Mort des pauvres," in which the image of the hotel of death appears:

C'est l'auberge fameuse inscrite sur le livre
Où l'on pourra manger, et dormir, et s'asseoir;

C'est un Ange qui tient dans ses doigts magnétiques
Le sommeil et le don des rêves extatiques . . .

(It is the famous hotel written in the book,
Where one can eat, sleep and sit down;
It is the Angel who carries in his magnetic hands
Sleep and the gift of ecstatic dreams . . .)[75]

The book mentioned in the first quoted verse might explain the mystical book that appears in the hotel. Baudelaire describes death both as a hotel and as an angel bearing the "gift of dreams." The appearance of the angel on the hotel signpost just as the hero drifts into sleep thus finds its motivation. (There actually may be yet another literary subtext here, Balzac's "L'Auberge rouge," which, like *Vampyr,* is also marked by images of death and blood.)

Michael Riffaterre has shown that the Baudelaire sonnet is intertextually linked to a 1922 poem by Jean Cocteau, "L'Endroit et l'envers." The poem also elaborates the image of death as a hotel and contains the image of the mystical book, central to Dreyer's film:

> Nous lisons un côté de la page du livre;
> L'autre nous est caché. Nous ne pouvons plus suivre,
> Savoir ce qui se passe après.

> (We read one side of the book's page
> The other side is hidden from us. We can no longer keep reading
> To know what happens afterward.)

The most intriguing moment in the poem is an extraordinarily dense passage in which Cocteau discusses the signpost on the hotel of death:

> Car votre auberge, ô mort, ne porte aucune enseigne.
> J'y voudrais voir, de loin, un beau cygne qui saigne
> Et chante, cependant que lui tordez le cou.

> Ainsi je connaîtrais ce dont je ne me doute:
> L'endroit où le sommeil interrompra ma route,
> Et s'il me faut marcher beaucoup.

> (For your hotel, o death, does not carry any signpost [*enseigne*].
> And I should like to see, from far off, a beautiful swan bleeding [*qui saigne*]
> And singing, while you wring his neck.
> Thus would I learn what I still do not know:
> The place where sleep will interrupt my path,
> And whether I still have a lot more walking to do.)[76]

The signpost, like the book, here foretells the future. Michael Riffaterre has shown that it is not the swan itself that prophesies but its punning connotations, as well as other paragrams hidden in the text. *Signpost* (*enseigne*) is a paragram of the verb "to bleed" (*saigner*), and *swan* (*cygne*) is a homonym of the word *sign* (*signe*). A "bleeding sign" is thus what teaches us (*enseigne*) the future.[77]

If the prophetic function of the signpost on the "hotel of death" is marked by a bloody sign, then we can better understand its link to vampirism, as well as to books about vampires that act as portents of encounters with death. Unlike the Godard quote, the signpost in *Vampyr* is inserted in such a way as to stand out as anomalous in any sequence of shots. It is never shown as part of the hotel facade: it is thus cut off from the diegetic level and exists in isolation from the space of the narrative. Neither can the angel on the signpost be understood in its relation to the general plot without referring to evidence from outside the film. Indeed, the *Aeneid* is by no means necessarily the end of the story. This apparently "illogical" moment can be recuperated only to the extent that we can recover all the layers of intertextuality in which it lies embedded. *An anomalous moment can reenter the text organically only if it is recognized as a quote.*

What I have said so far might give rise to objections. It could be argued that we have no hard evidence that Dreyer knew Baudelaire, Cocteau, and so forth. I would respond that this question has no relevance to our inquiry. Even if Dreyer had something else in mind, Baudelaire and Cocteau allow us to inscribe the signpost into the film, creating an intertextual link that exists irrespective of the director's intentions.

"CONSTRUCTION EN ABÎME" AND THE PRINCIPLE OF THE "THIRD TEXT"

The signpost motif is of interest from another point of view as well. We have seen that the integration of an anomalous textual moment into its context cannot always rely on just one outside source (such as the *Aeneid*). It may require two, three, or even more texts, making it a case of hyperquotation. This case is far from being rare; indeed, it may well be characteristic of intertextuality as a phenomenon. *A quote becomes a hyperquote whenever one source is insufficient for its integration into the fabric of a text.*

The case of hyperquotation raises several further questions. The hyperquote does not just open a text up to other texts, thereby simply broadening its horizon of meaning. It places a number of texts and significations one on top of the other. The hyperquote essentially becomes a kind of semantic funnel, drawing in all the competing meanings and texts, even if the latter contradict each other and are not readily reconciled into one unitary and dominant meaning. True, the *Aeneid* and the poems by Baudelaire and Cocteau allowed us to integrate the signpost in *Vampyr* into the remainder of the film, but only at the cost of invoking a range of diverse intertexts. In the final analysis, the integration of a quote in a film is won only at a cost: a hyperquote can bring order to a text only by erecting a new Tower of Babel, a babble of meanings.

The dilemma of the hyperquote can be resolved in one of two ways. On the one hand, intertextuality can be seen as an arbitrary accumulation of associations, quotes, and voices, in the spirit of Godard's claim that people quote "whatever they like": "In my notes, where I put down everything that I might need for my film, I might even put down a phrase from Dostoevskii if I like it. Why make a fuss? If you want to say something, there's only one solution: to say it."[78] Godard's notes, a vast repository of everything that struck his fancy along the way, are one model of intertextuality. Roland Barthes came to similar conclusions, which he formulated in the following way: "I savor the sway of formulas, the reversal of origins, the ease which brings the anterior text out of the subsequent one."[79] Barthes values the very randomness of this accumulation of meanings for the way it reflects the unpredictable and mobile character of life.

Nonetheless, the majority of scholars have taken a different position. In Laurent Jenny's words, "Intertextuality does not imply a confused and mysterious accumulation of influences, but the work of transformation and assimilation of several texts performed by a centering text which retains its position of leadership in meaning. . . . I propose to use the term 'intertextuality' only when one is able to recover elements in a text that were structured prior to the text itself."[80] Jenny is here echoed by Riffaterre, who also rejects Barthes's position: "All intertextual comparisons are imposed and controlled not by lexical coincidences but by a structural identity, the text and its intertext being variants of the same structure."[81]

Truly, only if we can detect a structural isomorphism existing between texts or parts of texts is it possible for us to unify meaning within the centering framework of a "leading text." Essentially, what is at stake is the repetition of the same in both text and intertext, although this repetition is naturally subject to a semantic reworking.

Structural isomorphism is particularly evident in paragrams, where two messages are superimposed and thereby inserted into a single textual structure. It is no coincidence that Julia Kristeva sees paragrams as performing a "centering within the framework of a unitary meaning."[82] Yet she herself has reduced the possibility of intertextual relations to a three-fold schema: (1) complete negation (complete inversion of meaning); (2) symmetrical negation (the logic of meaning is retained, while crucial nuances are removed); and (3) partial negation (the negation of part of a text).[83] Clearly, all these patterns become possible only if isomorphic structures are at work, in a dynamic of reciprocal influence. How else could one conceive of "symmetrical" or "partial" negation?

The necessity of a structuring principle within intertextual relations also forces us to confront the question of the "text within the text," which the French have called *la construction en abîme* (literally, construction in the form of an abyss). The term has been borrowed from the culture of heraldic insignias, where it referred originally to a coat of arms that contained a copy of itself reproduced in a smaller size. It was André Gide who first made this heraldic term current as a constructive principle, whose use he illustrated in pointing to paintings that contain a mirror, the rat-catching scene in *Hamlet,* or the puppet-theater in *Wilhelm Meister.* He was referring, in the case of the plays, to the characters theatrically enacting the situation in which they actually found themselves.[84]

Construction en abîme is marked by a heightened level of structural likeness between the framing text and the text it incorporates. Lucien Dällenbach has noted the similarity between *construction en abîme* and a phenomenon Claude Lévi-Strauss named the "small-scale model [*le modèle reduit*]."[85]

What Lévi-Strauss had in mind was the reproduction of an existing object on a smaller scale, as, for example, in a painting. This change in proportion has semantic consequences: it gives the copy the qualities of a handmade object and grants the maker the experience of mastering an object, compensating "for the renunciation of its sensory dimensions by allowing for the acquisition of its intelligible dimensions."[86] At stake is the translation of an object into some other qualitative condition: I would call the "small-scale model" a case of transition from objecthood to representation.

In his analysis of that classic case of *construction en abîme*, the Velázquez painting *Las meninas*, with its complex specular construction of space, Michel Foucault came to a similar conclusion: "And representation . . . can offer itself as representation in its pure form."[87] A text that functions on the basis of a duplication juxtaposes fragments that have been encoded in different ways but carry similar messages, thereby making their encodedness, that is, the fact of representation, all the more palpable. Iurii Lotman has defined this phenomenon as follows: "Duplication is the simplest way of making the code a part of a text's acknowledged structure."[88]

Ultimately, *construction en abîme* creates little more than an illusory play of references, constantly emphasizing one and the same thing—the play of codes, the palpability of representation, structural isomorphism, and, behind all of this, the flickering gleam of shifting meanings. To be sure, no reflection is fully accurate, always involving a variation, a transformation that is stressed by the repetition itself. The concrete production of meaning, however, is often the result of a play of reflections and is quickly submerged in this play. We appear to witness the very birth of meaning, and this is an illusion that always somehow accompanies the phenomenon of "pure representation." Existing analyses of cinematic versions of *construction en abîme* confirm my conclusions: the work of Viacheslav Ivanov or Christian Metz on the subject is entirely devoted to the study of systems of mirroring.[89]

A typical case of *construction en abîme* involving quotes (Dällenbach calls this an instance of *autotextuality* or *self-quotation* rather than intertextuality) arises when a film displays painterly or graphic forms of representation. These can be seen as a kind of "small-scale model." Sharply differentiated from the texture of the film thanks to the way they are encoded, they seem to flaunt the fact that they are representations.

Let us look at some examples of how this form of quotation generates meaning. In the episode from Godard's *Breathless* discussed earlier, we are actually shown several paintings: apart from the Renoir poster there are two reproductions from Picasso. One, showing an idyllic young couple, appears at the moment Patricia says, offscreen, "I would like for us to be Romeo and Juliet." The second Picasso appears a little later: it shows a youth with the mask of an old man's face in his hands. As we see it, Michel says, again offscreen, "It's just like telling the truth when you're playing poker. People think that you're bluffing, and you win."

Both these instances involve a duplication of meaning bordering on tautology. To show a painting of a young couple while someone is speaking of Romeo and Juliet, or the youth with the mask while someone is speaking of deception, adds nothing of substance to what is being said by the actors. And yet by virtue of being juxtaposed alongside quotations from Picasso, these passing comments do seem to gain a certain visibility and weight, acquiring something of the representational character of Picasso's works. In the given instance, meaning is not so much revealed as introduced into a context marked by heightened representativity, where it becomes all the more palpable and unitary for having been repeated. The quotes here function much like a teacher's comments in red ink.

Perhaps to avoid the relative didacticism of mere duplication, the *construction en abîme* gravitates toward triplication, or reproduction in even greater numbers. In Dreyer's *Gertrud* (1964), the heroine is tormented by a persistent dream. She dreams that she is naked and being pursued by a pack of dogs. In the same film we see a large Gobelin tapestry showing the naked Diana being torn apart by Acteon's dogs. The dream is thus duplicated by the tapestry. The same motif is also clearly projected onto Gertrude's life. The dream's meaning, as Pascal Bonitzer puts it, is "as transparent as it is lapidary: the dogs are the men to whose desires, as crude simulacra of the love she seeks, she abandons herself and by whom she is torn apart."[90] The very obviousness of the situation hardly seems to call for duplication, or what Dällenbach calls autotextuality. In fact we are dealing not with a doubling but with a tripling of the same collision in different signifying systems: the words of the heroine and the tapestry. The multiplication of representation becomes analogous to the nagging persistence of dreams. Repetition here imitates the repetition compulsion generated by a trauma that has been repressed into the unconscious. These repetitions do not just reproduce a certain meaning: they point to the presence of a certain repressed semantic kernel whose significance is consistently expressed as *other, different, mysterious*. Repetition thus simultaneously asserts and denies that meaning is univocal.

Variations in repetition can thus lead simultaneously to a centering and a decentering of meaning. This can happen in more than one way. Let us look at one more example, from *The Most Dangerous Game* (1932), by Ernest B. Shoedsack and Irving Pichel. This somber Gothic film relates the adventures of two young people, Rainsford and Eva, who are shipwrecked off the shore of an island belonging to the sinister maniac Count Zaroff. The count agrees to release his two unwilling guests if they survive a hunt against them that he himself will lead. Working for the count is a terrifying bearded servant named Ivan. The film begins with a depiction of the door to Zaroff's castle. A close-up shot shows us the strange knocker to the castle door in the shape of a centaur pierced by an arrow with a young woman, no longer able to resist, in his hands. Then from off-camera we see Rainsford's arm appear, lift the knocker, and knock thrice on the door. The centaur holding the woman in his arms appears again on the Gobelin tapestry that adorns the castle's staircase. This time we clearly notice the similarity between the centaur's face and the servant Ivan's sinister visage. Belaboring the point further, the directors at one point deliberately place Ivan against the tapestry, making him stand immobile until the similarity becomes unavoidable. Not only does the representation of the centaur holding the woman appear twice in the film (on the knocker and on the tapestry); it also establishes a link with one of the film's characters.

The *construction en abîme* once again becomes triple in character, although it is the tapestry that develops the plot in greatest detail: in the overgrowth we also see the young man who shoots the centaur with an arrow—Rainsford, of course, who will soon emerge victorious in the struggle to save Eva and himself. The triple character of these autotextual relations creates a more complex space of references and reciprocal mirroring, and with it the illusion of semantic depth, here particularly effective thanks to the specific variations in the distribution of motifs.

In a powerful psychoanalytic reading of the film, T. Kuntzel writes: "What is articulated in the very *body* of the centaur are man and beast, and this mixture, in all its varied forms (savage/civilized, nature/culture, game/hunter), constitutes the film's problematic, the field of its operations."[91] In this context an autotextual repetition acts to center the film, emphasizing its principal theme without adding anything new. Yet the very image of the centaur, and the mythic layer related to it, allows us to widen the range of the film's references considerably. The figure of the predatory centaur belongs to classical Greek mythology. Centaurs abducted the wives of the Lapithae, the centaur Eurytion tried to abduct the bride of Pirithous, and Nestor attacked Hercules' wife Deianira. Dante placed the centaurs Nessus, Chiron, and Pholus in hell, where they were compelled to pursue sinners in an endless hunt:

> Dintorno al fosso vanno a mille a mille
> saettando qual anima si svelle
> del sangue piú che sua colpa sortille.

> (And many thousands wheel around the moat,
> their arrows aimed at any soul that thrusts
> above the blood more than its guilt allots.)[92]

The Dante quote alone is enough to give the film an added metaphoric meaning that allows us to reconsider the shipwreck, the menacing swamps on the island, and the very meaning of the hunt.

Yet this is not all. More significant is the fact that this multiplication of representations strips the characters of reality, dissolving them into reflections and symbols. Marc Vernet, in his analysis of the motif of the mystery portrait in film, has concluded that the pictorial duplication of the hero "derives its substance from the real," or, as Lévi-Strauss might have put it, gives it an "intelligible" form. Reality becomes the bearer of a meaning that cannot always itself be formulated. Pascal Bonitzer has rightly observed: "The shot of a painting always provokes a doubling of vision and gives a sense of mystery to the image, a mystery that can be understood in religious terms, or like a detective mystery that has to be solved."[93] Indeed, what is at stake here is the creation of mystery as such, the affirmation that meaning, as it emerges, is an enigma. Hence the necessity to create doubles and accumulate more and more references. Nor is it a coincidence that the film *The Most Dangerous Game* effectively combines a criminal case with some kind of religious mystery (if we take into account the reference to Dante).

We discover another kind of *construction en abîme* in D. W. Griffith's *A Drunkard's Reformation* (1909), a film we shall have occasion to return to in chapter 2. The film was conceived against the backdrop of a campaign launched toward the end of 1908 by New York's Mayor George McClellan for the moral regeneration of the cinema industry.[94] It was a true didactic film, intended to show the horrors of alcoholism. In the first scene, we see the head of the family returning home drunk and terrorizing his wife and eight-year-old daughter. He is invited by his daughter to the theater, where he effectively sees the first scene in the film reenacted onstage: a degenerate alcoholic organizes a drunken orgy and then terrorizes his wife and daughter. What he has seen onstage awakens the father's conscience: he goes back home, gives up his drinking habit, and is seen in the film's final episode in an idyllic family reunion by the hearth.

The *construction en abîme* deployed in the film—the duplication of the plot onstage—was noted at the time of the film's making in a publicity statement released by Biograph studios: "The whole construction of the picture is most novel, showing, as it does, a play within a play."[95] The specular nature of the "text-within-text" construction is particularly emphasized by the alternating character of the montage, which shifts from the stage to the audience, where the father, in his daughter's embrace, reacts vigorously to the play, pointing his finger at the stage and then at himself, as if to underline the fact that the play and his life are one and the same. This duplication of the plot in a theatrical performance is a classical trope; the repetition gives the film a didactic flavor, whereby the plot is viewed in the mirror of theatrical representation.

The publicity release put out by Biograph contains one highly significant detail. The play-within-the-play seen in the film is said to be an adaptation of Zola's *L'Assommoir*. Of course the general theme of alcoholism is common to the play and Zola's novel. Yet it is hard to believe that the film's viewers would have necessarily identified *L'Assommoir* as the text behind the play. The film does not acknowledge the novel in its credits, and the plot of the play has little in common with the novel, which has less to do with the decline of the male drunkard (in Zola's novel he is called Coupeau) than with the fall of a woman, Gervaise, herself a heavy drinker as well as a streetwalker who cheats on Coupeau with another man. There is none of this in *A Drunkard's Reformation,* and the analogue to Gervaise in the play, like the heroine of the film itself, is a pure, innocent, and all-suffering woman fallen victim to a husband in decline.

We might even dismiss the reference to Zola in Biograph's publicity as a simple error were it not for the fact that the whole structure of *A Drunkard's Reformation* reproduces an entirely analogous *construction en abîme* in another Zola novel, *La Curée*. In this novel there is a description of a performance of *Phèdre*, attended by the story's heroine, Renée, and Maxime, her stepson by her husband's prior marriage, for whom she is consumed by an incestuous passion. The relationship between Renée and Maxime is mirrored by those enacted onstage between Phaedra and Hyppolitus. Moreover this performance, like Griffith's play-within-the-play, imposes an absolute identification between its own protagonists and the heroes of the novel who constitute its audience, leaving Renée deeply shaken. As Théramène is about to begin his monologue onstage, Renée hysterically equates Racine's play with her own life's drama:

> The monologue continued interminably. She was in the greenhouse, under the ardent foliage, and she dreamed that her husband was walking in and catching her in the arms of her son. She suffered horribly, losing consciousness, when the last death rattle of Phaedra, repentant and dying in the throes of poison, made her open her eyes once more. The curtain was falling. Would she have the strength to take poison one day? How petty and shameful her drama was, when compared to the ancient epic![96]

Griffith's film, we recall, reproduces not only the general structure of the *construction en abîme* but also the specific nature of the protagonists' reaction to what they see. In *La Curée* this device is used twice, although with variations. The novel also describes the performance of a series of *tableaux vivants* based on the amorous exploits of Narcissus and the nymph Echo. This time, however, the actors are Renée and Maxime themselves, who effectively enact their own relationship before a public. The system of mirrors is here reversed. For Zola it was essential that the theatrical performance depict a situation of falsehood, since it was his conviction that the theater, at least in its classical form, was a place of falsehood, in opposition to the naturalist novel: "Here one always has to lie," he observed.[97] Yet theatrical representation is not only the repository of falsehood in Zola's novel: it can also expose falsehood and hence assert the truth. A difference in the way the text is coded is thus projected onto the novel's own drama of deception. As will become clearer from my argument in chapter 2, the director Griffith also came to view the theater as a place of falsehood, deceit, and vice. These views, however, would become explicit somewhat later: at this point they appear in a muted way, through the intertextual links we have reconstructed between *A Drunkard's Reformation* and Zola's *La Curée*.

With the preceding example, we have seen how the *construction en abîme* functions. On the one hand, it duplicates the text and thereby emphasizes its message as unambiguously didactic. Meaning is unified and thereby "narrowed." Yet the introduction of a *third* text (in this case the Zola reference and the parallel *construction en abîme* in *La Curée*, which may have given Griffith the idea of inserting a "text-within-a-text" in his own film) acts to undermine the one-dimensionality of the text's didactic content. Meaning is opened up, made more enigmatic, ambiguous, even to the point of being reversed. There is, at the same time, a dissolution of unitary meaning in a form that acquires increasing complexity.

The third text, by layering form on form, helps to overcome the univocal nature of content. For this reason, the third text works in a manner that is diametrically opposed to the second text. Such threefold (and even more complex) *constructions en abîme* thus simultaneously widen and narrow the range of meaning, creating different potential perspectives in reading. The accumulation of textual doubles impedes the freezing of meaning in specific representational systems, such as theater and painting, even as these very systems are absorbed into the fabric of the film.

The theory of the sign elaborated by Charles Sanders Peirce sheds some light on the work of the "third text." Peirce, we know, asserted that a third element, the interpretant, needs to be added to the traditional dichotomy of sign and object. The third element, for Peirce, was essential to the emergence of meaning as such. This element inserts a difference into the tautology, a difference that allows for the creation of meaning: "Three things east, west and up are required to define the difference between right and left."[98] In Peirce, the interpretant is a secondary sign created by the *representamen* in the human mind. It is precisely this secondary sign, when it is joined to the relation between the representamen and the object, that allows for the manipulation of signs, and hence meaning, via the arrangement of signs into chains. Peirce referred the interpretant to the sphere of "pure rhetoric," whose task was to "ascertain the laws by which in every scientific intelligence one sign gives birth to another, and especially one thought brings forth another."[99]

Paul de Man, departing from Peirce's triadic model, has pointed out that rhetoric considers the "third element" responsible for the creation of figural meaning, which, when superimposed onto the literal meaning, enters into complex relations with it. This creates a situation in which "it is impossible to decide by grammatical or other linguistic devices which of the two meanings (that can be entirely compatible) prevails. Rhetoric radically suspends logic and opens up vertiginous possibilities of referential aberration."[100]

This triadic principle has been applied to the problem of intertextuality by Michael Riffaterre, who has suggested that the third text be given the Peircean name of *interpretant* (in the following quote, T = text, T' = intertext, and I = interpretant): "Intertextuality does not function, and consequently a text is not a text, unless the reading passes from T to T' through I, and the interpretation of the text in the light of the intertext is a function of the interpretant."[101]

The interpretant is important to us for several reasons. First, it allows us to overcome the notion of the link between text and intertext as the link between the source and its text-successor; the related notions of "borrowing" and "influence" can also be abandoned. Second, it allows us to account far more convincingly for the work that goes into the creation of meaning, with all its displacements and transformations. Third, the interpretant, as the third text in an intertextual triangle, is responsible for the appearance of what Mikhail Bakhtin called "semantic hybrids," which practically all artistic works are to some extent.[102] Finally, the interpretant allows us to understand how parody works, since the third text usually turns out to be the "distorting mirror" that parodically critiques the structure of the intertext within a text. The interpretant is responsible for the parodic status of a text to the extent that I and $T(pr)$ are unable to affect each other without conflict or contradiction. The residual traces of these contradictions in a text can be seen as parody.

To conclude this chapter, I should like to look at one more film that shows how structural isomorphism between intertextually connected texts can create meaning as an enigma or mystery, and how the interpretant is involved in the creation of this enigma. I am thinking of Orson Welles's *Citizen Kane* (1941). Let us recall the basic plot: the film begins with the hero, Charles Foster Kane, dying in his castle, Xanadu. His last word before dying is "Rosebud." As Kane dies, a glass ball containing a miniaturized winter landscape drops free of his hand and breaks. The newspaper and newsreel magnate Rawlston orders the journalist Thompson to investigate the meaning of Kane's last word, which he believes to be the key to the dead man's life and personality. The film is a kind of mosaic—and puzzle—made up of the visualized stories about Kane that Thompson hears during the course of his investigation but that finally do not help him get any closer to the secret of Rosebud. The viewer, however, is given the answer. As the film ends, the workers who are burning the accumulated rubbish from Xanadu throw the sled Kane had as a child into the incinerator. A picture of a rosebud, with a caption provided, adorns the sled.

The film repeatedly insists on the link between the word *Rosebud* and the glass ball, a children's toy that has apparently hypnotized Kane. The ball is a kind of mirror that duplicates the world and draws the viewer into a *construction en abîme*. The ball-as-mirror refers us to a visionary space, like the crystal balls used in spiritist seánces or the Salvator Mundi genre of painting, in which a glass ball is meant to provide a vision of the world.[103] The film itself, however, does make one more explicit reference, to a literary text linked to the motif of vision. Kane's Xanadu naturally recalls Coleridge's poetic fragment "Kubla Khan: Or, a Vision in a Dream," whose first verses are quoted in the film. Kane's very name seems to recall "Khan," and the film is filled with motifs taken from the Coleridge poem. The River Alph (cf. alphabet) becomes the stream of newspapers owned by the press magnate Kane; the singing Abyssinian maid is parodied in the figure of Kane's second wife, a singer by the name of Susan Alexander who performs an "oriental opera" in the film; the construction of the palace out of song and music is reflected in the building of the opera house for Susan; and the paradisial garden surrounding Xanadu is echoed by Kane's gigantic zoo, "the largest private zoo since Noah."

Yet these individual motifs are overshadowed by a more important fact. Coleridge had maintained that the vision of Kubla Khan had appeared to him in a dream induced by opium. Waking, the author had begun to write down his vision, only to be interrupted by a visitor: "And on his return to his room, [he] found, to his no small surprise and mortification, that though he still retained some vague and dim recollection of the general purport of the vision, yet, with the exception of some eight or ten scattered lines and images, all the rest had passed away like the images on the surface of a stream into which a stone has been cast, but, alas! without the after restoration of the latter!"[104] "Kubla Khan" thus appears as an enigma, a mysterious visionary fragment with a conclusion that has been lost forever. In this sense it is typologically similar in form to *Citizen Kane*, which is also constructed around an enigmatic vision.

In fact *Citizen Kane* points to yet another work of literature, in a way that is evident if less persistent. Several times during the course of the film, the hypothesis is advanced that *Rosebud* refers to a woman's name. Rosebud is in fact the name of the heroine of the Dickens novel *The Mystery of Edwin Drood*. Since the significance of the name remains a mystery to the very end of the film, the viewer is compelled to seek some basis for including Dickens among the various subtexts of *Citizen Kane*.

The Dickens novel bears a significant resemblance to both "Kubla Khan" and *Citizen Kane*. *The Mystery of Edwin Drood*, like Coleridge's poem, was never completed by its author, and the keys to its investigative mystery have been lost. The novel also betrays several immediate parallels to the film. Like *Citizen Kane,* the novel involves an attempt to decipher the hero's last words: there is a scene in which futile attempts are made to unravel the words uttered by an opium smoker during his trance. These opium-induced hallucinations of the hero, Jasper, like Coleridge's visions in his poem, take up a considerable portion of the novel. The novel begins with Jasper taking up the hermeneutic challenge of deciphering an "opium-text": "When any distinct word has been flung into the air, it has had no sense or sequence. Wherefore 'unintelligible!' is again the comment of the watcher."[105] The enigma of the novel as a whole is mirrored in this passage.

Significantly, the story of the "Abyssinian maid," Susan, is also echoed by Dickens's novel. Kane makes a dogged effort to make a singer out of her. One of these lessons ends with Susan getting hysterical and refusing to sing. Dickens also has Jasper mercilessly hounding Rosebud to sing: "As Jasper watched the pretty lips, and over and again hinted the one note, as though it were a low whisper from himself, the voice became less steady, until all at once a singer broke into a burst of tears, and shrieked out, with her hands over her eyes: 'I can't bear this! I am frightened! Take me away!' "[106] Clearly, this scene closely parallels the analogous episode in the film.

Interestingly, the entire subplot involving the talentless Susan's compulsory singing lessons also has another literary source—George du Maurier's novel *Trilby,* in which the hypnotist Svengali lulls the tone-deaf Trilby into a trance and induces her to sing wondrously. One of the novel's crucial scenes involves the wounded Svengali in a theater box, inducing Trilby to sing under hypnosis. When Svengali suddenly loses consciousness, Trilby comes out of her trance and is unable to continue singing. What follows is a complete disaster: "Indeed she had tried to sing 'Ben Bolt,' but had sung it in her old way—as she used to sing it in the quartier latin—the most lamentably grotesque performance ever heard out of a human throat!"[107]

Kane is also a kind of parodic Svengali—he is convinced that if he succeeds in hypnotizing Susan, then he could also hypnotize others. There is a moment in the film when Kane is in the opera box, casting demonic glances at the unhappy Susan, who emits some grotesque notes: this scene alone allows us to view *Trilby* as another subtext to *Citizen Kane,* all the more so since the du Maurier novel also evolves as an enigma that is solved only *after* Svengali's death. *Trilby,* then, readily serves as an interpretant, transposing the serious Welles/Coleridge parallel onto a parodic register. Interestingly, *Trilby* had already been used by Joyce in *Ulysses* for a similar parodic reversal: in chapter 15, Bloom appears as a fake hypnotist— "Bloom (In Svengali's fur overcoat, with folded arms and Napoleon's forelock frowns in ventriloquial exorcism with piercing eagle glance towards the door").[108]

In fact any of the texts mentioned here can function as an interpretant, since all of them serve to distort the relations between *Citizen Kane* and the texts that form its intertextual environment. This distortion is complemented on each occasion by the marked introduction of some element of mystery, a missing key or fragment. Each intertext consistently reproduces the basic enigma of the film as a whole. N. Carroll has observed that "throughout the film, the heterogeneity of Kane's collections continues as an objective correlative of Kane's personhood."[109] Kane does collect everything, from the sleds he had as a child to Greek and Egyptian statuary. The sheer motleyness of his collection reflects the irreducibility of his personality to any unifying center. As Borges once said, Kane is a "chaos of appearances," a "labyrinth with no center" and hence offering no way out.[110] Intertexts also enter the composition of *Citizen Kane* as things from Kane's private collection. Without providing any real resolutions, they intensify the sense of mystery and deepen the film's meaning: this is the real significance of their distorting function as interpretants.

It is also important to note that the labyrinthine nature of intertextuality imbues the structure of the film itself with a paradoxical quality. Kane, that is, a protagonist who exists within the film's diegesis, is responsible for the creation of his own enigma. Yet this enigma quickly leads us to a range of texts that are to varying degrees formally identical to the film itself (and its discourse). All these texts appear to "describe" the fragmentary and unfinished nature of *Citizen Kane* itself. In other words, Kane as a protagonist of the film is aware not only of his own biography but also of the form that his own biography will take *posthumously*. Kane knows something of Welles's own discourse. It is for this reason that a character in the film poses a quandary that cannot be resolved from within his own life story. This quandary must be solved by someone who is aware of the posthumous treatment of his biography, someone like the viewer of the film rather than the investigative reporter Thompson. At the end of the film, Thompson nevertheless has the perspicacity to observe that it would not be possible to unlock the "meaning" of Kane just by deciphering the word *Rosebud*. This statement is immediately followed by a shot of the sled, which solves the puzzle for the viewer.

This solution, revealed only to the viewer, is doubtless partly fictitious. This becomes all the more evident when we consider the tautological, metadescriptive nature of the choice of all three intertexts: all three are "quoted" because they also involve puzzles. The real status of Kane cannot be established if only for the reason that Kane functions here as a *character* and as an *author* who knows something about the formal properties of the text that describes him. The discourse about him becomes his own discourse.

Kane's mystery, then, has no solution. The enigmatic literary subtexts serve another purpose. They destroy the clarity of the narrative *mode* and create a structure that allows for a slippage from the diegetic level (the level of narrative) to the discursive level (the level of the formal organization of the story). (Curiously, Borges was to deploy the poem "Kubla Khan" in an analogous way in his essay "Coleridge's Dream.")[111] The link between these two levels of the text is established by the literary subtext, or rather by the puzzle involved in intertextual relations that is first posed by the author using Kane's persona and then confirmed by the hermeneutical contest between the viewer and the film's characters (Thompson, Rawlston). In this struggle for meaning, it would appear as if the viewer wins: after all, it is the viewer who sees the sled in the final scene. Nonetheless, the real victory belongs to the characters in the film, since they are the ones who know that there is in fact no real solution.

We have seen that the structure of intertextual relations is largely responsible for the labyrinthine movement of meanings in *Citizen Kane,* meanings that are never distilled into the text's one final meaning. As these meanings sabotage each other, a bottomless semantic funnel is created, which is typical of all *constructions en abîme.* The final meaning is displaced in the process of searching for it. The intertext constitutes meaning as the work involved in seeking it. The very dynamic of slippage from the diegetic to the discursive level, as seen in *Citizen Kane,* plays an important role in this work. When David Gray in *Vampyr* hears the cry of a baby that is not a part of the sound track, he is in fact hearing a cry that resounds not in *Vampyr* but out of Virgil's epic. While still situated within his own story, Gray—like Kane—unexpectedly penetrates the intertext in which the film that tells his story has been inserted. In this sense Gray hears (and knows) something that only the director Dreyer could have had access to. The character takes the place of the author.

This shift cannot be simply understood or assimilated: it necessarily creates a puzzle that resists solution. Intertextuality, then, while resolving certain contradictions within the text, at the same time creates others that are in fact irresolvable. The intertext functions as the resolution of some (resolvable) contradictions even as it creates others that are irresolvable. Understanding is thus accompanied by the appearance of a mystery. From this perspective meaning itself can be seen as an act of understanding that is shrouded in mystery.

PART II

Narrative's Way
D. W. Griffith

CHAPTER TWO

Repressing the Source
D. W. Griffith and Browning

In the preceding chapter it was suggested that the quotation as a specific textual fragment is not essentially linked to authorial intent; rather, it is constituted in the process of reading. The reader or viewer, not the author, is in this sense responsible for creating the quotation as a textual layer. Of course this situation obtains only when the author refrains from naming the source of the quotation directly, so that the quote exists in the text without quotation marks, as it were. When identified as such by the author, quotations can even perform a normalizing role within the text, as indeed can those that are discovered by the reader. And yet this layer of authorial quotation can also fulfill an entirely different function, one that is often diametrically opposed to that just mentioned. Not only can the authorial quotation fail to "normalize" a text, but, on the contrary, it can serve to introduce further anomalies, thereby making the text harder rather than easier to read.

Any kind of quotation that brings further anomalies into the text can be called misquoting. In cinema, misquoting can be most readily found wherever a literary source is indicated as the basis of a film. The tradition of basing a film on a literary source (the "adaptation") itself has the effect of turning the film as a whole into a huge quote, creating a kind of "global" intertextual link between the film and the literary work. Critical readings of such adaptations are numerous and quite revealing in their shared assumptions: they place the film alongside its literary source and locate much of the film's semantic potential in its fidelity to or divergence from its literary origins.

Yet films have been made to misquote their literary source. We see a source misquoted most clearly in films such as Carl Theodor Dreyer's *Leaves from Satan's Book* (1919). Dreyer declared his film to be the screen version of Marie Corelli's *Sorrows of Satan,* a book to which the film in fact bears no relation. *The Passion of Joan of Arc* (1928) was said to derive from the novel *Jeanne d'Arc* by Joseph Delteil, with which the film has nothing in common. *Vampyr* (1932) was proposed as the screen version of Joseph Sheridan Le Fanu's *In a Glass Darkly,* a book that in fact provides the film with only a few minor details.

Something similar, although in a different form, can be found in the vast cinematic corpus of D. W. Griffith. To take one example, Griffith made three attempts at a screen version of the Tennyson poem *Enoch Arden.* The first version, *After Many Years* (1908), acknowledges its literary source but alters the title of the poem and the names of the main characters. For instance, a John Davis takes the place of Enoch Arden in the film. The second version, *The Unchanging Sea* (1910), is falsely traced by Griffith to a poem by Charles Kingsley, "The Three Fishers," that is in fact related to another film by Griffith called *The Sands of Dee,* made two years later. In this version the characters remain nameless. The third version finally makes an open acknowledgment of its connection to Tennyson and is in fact called *Enoch Arden* (1911).

Clearly, this technique of misquoting the source can hardly be said to facilitate the task of understanding. On the contrary, it smuggles a puzzle into the text that is nigh impossible to solve. Siegbert Salomon Prawer, for example, has expended a great deal of effort to discover at least some traces of Le Fanu's book in Dreyer's *Vampyr.* Prawer's conclusions have not proved very convincing, but his effort is itself an indication of the felt need to find some basis for the reference to a misquoted source, in order to remove the anomaly created by the reference itself.[1]

But finding the basis for a misquotation within the framework of intertextuality has turned out in essence to be an impossible task, and understandably so. Intertextuality functions as a logic-generating mechanism only when a similarity between texts can be discovered; wherever there is no such similarity, intertextuality cannot function effectively. A misquotation itself creates a quite specific phenomenon. It generates an anomaly that cannot be solved by linking a given text to any other; it blocks through its own misleading nature (its negativity) the very mechanism of intertextuality.

In this extraordinary situation the reader-interpreter has essentially only one way out: he or she is forced to invoke the figure of the author that can be easily ignored in cases where intertextuality is working normally. The logic behind invoking the author in the context of a misquotation is clear at least to the extent that the author is made answerable for the misquote. Thus the search for an explanation moves into the realm of authorial psychology. This is how Dreyer's biographer Maurice Drouzy explains the misquoted sources that occur in Dreyer's films:

Why does he not dare to admit to having made up the whole story himself? For me the answer is simple: it is because he is frightened of betraying himself, of leading the viewer on to a secret that he cannot and will not reveal to anyone. It is for the same reason that he ordinarily does not dare to write his own screenplays: he fears that his unconscious might play tricks on him, that the drama of his origins which he strives to repress in some way or other might suddenly appear in the stories he could come up with. This is why he prefers to hide behind a writer who is more or less well known, hiding the problem that haunts him behind the work of another.[2]

Drouzy has established that Dreyer, who had been adopted as a child, had always concealed the story of his parents and why they had given him up. The heroes of the film *Vampyr* appear to Drouzy as disguised figures from Dreyer's childhood drama. For Drouzy, the vampire Marguerite Chopin is Dreyer's "false mother," whose name was Marie (the similarity lies in the root shared by the names Marie and Marguerite). Dreyer had identified the servant on his estate as Joseph, but in the screenplay he figures as Bernard. Dreyer's real mother had been called Josephine-Bernhardine, and so on and so forth.[3] A psychological motivation thus gives Drouzy a way to establish his own intertext for the film *Vampyr*—the biography of the director—which thereby explains (normalizes) the misquote.

Yet the logic behind Drouzy's interpretation of Dreyer's intentions can hardly be considered convincing or irreproachable. Formulations of the kind "he is scared that his subconscious will betray him" cannot be verified to a high degree of probability. We can never know what psychological motivations made Dreyer refer his readers to the book by Le Fanu. Any other author might just as successfully have produced another psychological conflict in the director's conscious mind or subconscious. But it seems hardly possible in this case to avoid some recourse to an authorial psychology. Where misquotes occur, intertextuality is almost inevitably reconstituted by means of psychologizing fantasies. However, we must fully realize that this psychologizing is no more than one of the many strategies of reading needed to unblock the mechanism of intertextuality. In this sense any recourse to the author's psychology in fact sheds no real light on this psychology and is rather entirely part of the reader's interpretation of the text. It is true that any emphasis on psychological motivation highlights the figure of the author, which thereby becomes a guarantor of the text's meaningfulness, acquiring the semblance of an active presence in the text. The pseudofigure of the author somehow unites with the semantic anomaly that becomes its condition of representation. The misquotation thus becomes an effective way of transforming the authorial figure into a meaningful element of the text.

A significant if controversial contribution to the theory of intertextuality, particularly in its positing a role for the authorial figure in the workings of the intertext, has been made by the critic Harold Bloom.[4] Working primarily with texts from the Anglo-American poetic tradition, Bloom sees any poem as an author's "act of reading" the poems of his or her precursors. This has the effect of transferring the burden of intertextuality away from the reader as addressee onto the author as reader. This act of creative reading is realized by the poet as a complex system of substitutions that undermines existing "representations" in favor of still newer ones. Within Bloom's model of poetic creation the figure of the precursor thus acquires an extraordinary importance.

The creative act (reading or, in Bloom's terminology, misreading) passes through six stages. The first stage—the choice—establishes the figure of the precursor. The second stage—the signing of the contract—involves establishing an accord between the poetic vision of the precursor and that of his or her successor. The third stage—the choice of a competing source of inspiration necessary for the displacement of the first source (thus Wordsworth, who is oriented toward Milton)—posits a second axis of orientation, nature itself as the origin of the text. Then follow the stages of misreading, which revise the texts of the precursors, and the positing of a poetic Self through a system of substitutions.[5] In the creative process the precursor emerges as the poet's second Self, with whom complex relations of opposition and identification are established. Bloom views poetic creation as "a solitary struggle against the precursor-principle, but struggling in the visionary world of the precursor."[6] It is precisely in this struggle that the mechanism of repression begins to take effect. The masking of one's relation to one's predecessor becomes one of the primary conditions by which the poetic Self can be asserted. All true poets conceal both from themselves and from their readers the influences they undergo, and seek thereby to create the illusion of an unmediated relation to reality, the "truth," or, speaking more metaphorically, the Muse. "We can define a strong poet," writes Bloom, "as one who will not tolerate words that intervene between him and the Word or precursors standing between him and the muse."[7]

Bloom's work reviews the mechanisms by which a literary source can be defensively repressed and the modalities by which its repression is realized. According to Bloom, the traces of repression, misreading, and revision are imprinted as poetic figures or tropes that become signs, as it were, of the creative process.

Bloom's position invites many possible objections. Above all it collapses the entire process of literary evolution into a psychology of creation and reduces it to the artist's aspiration to be original at any price. Laurent Jenny has rightly noted that Bloom's concept is founded on a "true Oedipus complex of the creator" in which the role of the father is played by the precursor.[8]

It seems to me that Bloom's theory is best understood not as a genuine theory of artistic creation but as a specific reading strategy that allows us to resolve a range of contradictions as they emerge in the text. Bloom shows us how the strong author can be textually constituted as a figure by revealing the mechanism of repression on which he rests.

Bloom's theory also allows us to rethink the patterns of literary history. In an essay called "Kafka's Precursors," Jorge Luis Borges once wrote about a range of writers whom he saw as having anticipated Franz Kafka. He pointed to the obvious moments of similarity between Kafka's work and that of Zeno, the ninth-century Chinese prose writer Han Yu, Kierkegaard, Leon Bloy, Lord Dunsany, and Robert Browning. Borges observed that Kafka's precursors in themselves had nothing in common; their commonality was rather brought out by Kafka's own work. "The fact is that each writer creates his precursors," observed Borges, thereby radically inverting our traditional ideas about literary history.[9] For Borges evolution is constituted by each new artistic phenomenon, moving not from past to present but from the present to the past. Borges's paradox finds a possible echo in Bloom's theory to the extent that Bloom also believes it is a writer's task to establish his or her precursors and then mask their existence. But insofar as the process of uncovering the concealed precursor is a result of the reader's effort to "intertextualize" the text, so art history can also be understood as a product of intertextual reading. Borges's own essay is a perfect example of this: while Borges asserts that Kafka alone can make his precursors, in fact it is Borges as reader who does it for him, by showing Han Yu or Kierkegaard to be his precursors. The notion of intertextuality thus emerges not only as a potential theory of understanding but also as a theory of art history.

In the pages to come I propose to examine the mechanism by which literary sources are repressed by looking at D. W. Griffith's film adaptations of Robert Browning's play *Pippa Passes*. Griffith's first version of 1909, in an explicit reference to Browning, is called *Pippa Passes*. The second version, *Home, Sweet Home* (1914), is derived from the title of a popular song by John Howard Payne, who is himself made to appear in the film as one of its protagonists. The film is declared an adaptation of Payne's biography, with which it has little in common.

Griffith thus plays a kind of hide-and-seek with his own source, now revealing it and now hiding its identity. This game serves to turn the spotlight on the author, making him the main guarantor of the film's meaning: Griffith becomes a "strong author," something he had certainly striven to be. Griffith's own statements are constantly marked by a prophetic tone: the director had understood his work as a kind of mission aimed at creating an unprecedented universal language that would be capable of resolving the most acute social contradictions. The representational image was a universal symbol, and the moving image a universal language. Griffith declared that cinema, in the opinion of many, "might have saved the situation when the Tower of Babel was built."[10] Elsewhere Griffith's universal language would be expanded to the proportions of a social utopia: "With the use of the universal language of moving pictures the true meaning of the brotherhood of man will have been established throughout the earth."[11]

As Griffith's prophetic sensibility intensified (particularly from the second half of the 1910s), so too did his tendency to privilege modern art for its harking back to the origins of language, to a pre-Babelic world. This led to a negative contrast between modern and older forms of art and allowed for an extraordinarily powerful repression of the most essential sources of his own art. This may be why references to the theater, to which Griffith devoted a full twelve years of his life, were systematically eliminated from his work.

Griffith in fact continued to borrow significantly from the theater throughout his creative life. His early film versions of classical epic poems and novels, made for the Biograph Company, were based primarily on their theatrical adaptations, popularly performed as one-act plays.[12] A large number of Griffith's most celebrated cinematic effects, particularly in his later films, were borrowed directly from the theater. Russell Merritt lists a series of such hidden quotations: the baptism of the dead infant in *Way Down East* (1920) was taken from an adaptation for the stage of *Tess of the D'Urbervilles;* the sequence in *Orphans of the Storm* (1922), where Jacques-Forget-Not counts off the enemies he has avenged on his fingers, repeats the equivalent episodes from the theatrical adaptation of *The Count of Monte Cristo,* and so on.[13] John Fell and Rick Altman have found innumerable instances in which Griffith borrowed from the theater of melodrama.[14] Interestingly, Altman shows how critics of Griffith's day were content to ignore the theatrical origins of Griffith's films: "They identify the dramatic version from which the film author directly borrowed, but assume that little is to be gained by comparing the film to an ephemeral and undistinguished stage adaptation. More often, critics blithely postulate a direct connection between film and the novel from which it is ostensibly drawn, when even minimal research clearly identifies a dramatic adaptation as an important direct source for the film."[15] The blindness shown by critics worked in direct accord with Griffith's own aspirations. Russell Merritt notes with astonishment that the more extensively Griffith took from the theater, the more aggressively he would deny any connection to it: "But perhaps the most singular feature of Griffith's debt to the theater was his fixed refusal to acknowledge its existence. The elaborate pains he took to cover his tracks went far beyond the usual requirements of artistic camouflage."[16] It is perhaps revealing that Merritt himself seeks to explain Griffith's negative attitude to the theater on the basis of a psychosexual trauma the director suffered while working with a theater company, thus retreating to the same psychological model of motivation we saw operating in Drouzy's account of Dreyer.

Once we abandon the notion of psychological motivation, we are immediately in a better position to grasp the specific strategy of textual organization that regulates the intertextual links in a film. Griffith himself would stubbornly deny any continuity between theater and cinema. In the June 1914 issue of the journal *Theatre* he declared, "Moving pictures can get nothing from the so-called legitimate stage because American directors and playwrights have nothing to offer." In the same year, in a response to Robert Graw, Griffith again denied that theater could have any productive influence on cinema: "The stage is a development of centuries, based on certain fixed conditions and within prescribed limits. . . . The motion picture, although a growth of only a few years, is boundless in its scope and endless in its possibilities."[17] And further on Griffith mused on what might become of the cinema when it had completely exhausted the repertoire of world theater. For Griffith it was this posttheatrical future that would inaugurate the golden age of cinema. In this sense cinema, according to Griffith, develops in a situation where intertextuality has been exhausted and total creativity unleashed. "Unlimited possibility" is equated with the overcoming of theater as a legacy. Griffith consistently emphasizes that the cinematic language he is in the process of creating is, in its each and every element, a negation of the language of theater. The history of cinema becomes the history of its emancipation from older forms of art (this view is still doing the rounds in film criticism).

Griffith came simultaneously to the obsessively held conviction that theater was the embodiment of a strange and blasphemous state of sin, a Babylon, Sodom, and Gomorrah combined. In his later autobiographical writings Griffith would exaggerate the feeling of shame he had felt on entering the stage, a motif that would also appear in his Browning cycle: "Even now, I can feel the humiliation of that moment. . . . I was ashamed to cloud my father's reputation by letting his friends know I was his son. . . . I was ashamed to go home and ashamed to be seen on the streets."[18]

Clearly, then, Griffith chose to disavow with a marked ferocity his nearest and most systematically utilized source. At the same time, he began to seek a "competing source of inspiration." Initially poetry or literary language was proclaimed to be this source. This turn to literature was able to mask the theatrical sources of Griffith's cinema through the introduction of a third text into the system of intertextual relations. We have already called this the *interpretant,* a term to be understood very broadly to mean a whole field of artistic creation, a kind of "superarchitext."

The revelation of Griffith's theatrical sources in essence does little to enrich the semantic possibilities of his films: the play and its film adaptation are too similar for any juxtaposition of the two not to result in a tautology. The third text, the *hyperinterpretant*, does not simply rescue the film from a blandly secondary status: it provides the depth of meaning the film needs to be a fully fledged work of art. In this context Griffith's declarative strategy and the blindness of critics work together to facilitate the viewer's search for a third text that might enrich the film's meaning. To conceal one's debt to history thus appears to be a means of organizing strategies of reading. This moment is particularly significant for us because it allows us to bring together the level of textual reading and the mechanisms by which cinema has evolved.

This moment is also important because it gives us a way out of the interpretive dead end generated by misquotations. In this context a misquote can be understood as indicating the presence of a true quote that it is masking or concealing. The misquote spurs us on to seek out another quote, an intertext that might resolve a given anomaly. In most cases a misquote acts as an effective spur to the intertextual process, all the more significant for its evidently and irreducibly aberrant nature.

Let us now turn to Griffith's screen adaptations of Browning. October 4, 1909, saw the release of *Pippa Passes,* a film that played an enormous role in changing the attitude of American society to cinema. On October 10, the *New York Times,* in its first article on a motion picture, published a review of *Pippa Passes.* From being a form of fairground entertainment, the cinema had become a respectable art. The basis for Griffith's movie, Browning's poetic drama, is rightly considered one of the most complex pieces of dramatic art in nineteenth-century literature. So dazzling was Griffith's success that the reviewer in the *New York Times* was moved to prognosticate somewhat extravagantly that "there seems to be no reason why one may not expect to see soon the intellectual aristocracy of the nickelodeon demanding Kant's Prolegomena to Metaphysics with the 'Kritik of Pure Reason' for a curtain raiser."[19] Griffith's wife, Linda Arvidson, recalls the effect produced by both the film and its review: "Suddenly everything was changed. Now we could begin to lift up our heads, and perhaps invite our lit'ry friends to our movies!"[20]

Griffith remained proud of *Pippa Passes* to the end of his life. In his final interview, he was to choose his film of 1909 over *Birth of a Nation* and *Intolerance* as the greatest achievement of cinema: " 'There has been no improvement in movies since the old days. . . . We did Browning and Keats then, *Pippa Passes.* Today you don't dare do those things. Imagine anyone doing Browning today. They have not improved in stories. I don't know that they've improved in anything.' "[21]

Throughout his life, then, Griffith came back to dwell on *Pippa Passes,* but he never mentioned that the immediate stimulus for the film was a production of the Browning play staged in 1906 by the Henry Miller troupe. E. Giuliano and R. C. Keenan, in an article devoted to the Griffith adaptation, have argued convincingly that Griffith knew the Miller production. The play had its Broadway premiere on November 12, 1906; three days later, also on Broadway, Griffith made his debut performance at the Astor Theatre in *Salomé.* On November 24, the *New York Dramatic Mirror* reviewed both *Salomé* and *Pippa Passes.* Griffith also could have come to know of the Miller production from his own actor Henry Walthall, who had worked with Miller in 1906, playing Gottlieb in the Browning play. James Kirkwood, who acted the part of Jules in the film, had also worked with Miller in 1906.[22] Yet perhaps the clearest evidence of Miller's production influencing Griffith is the fact that both Miller and Griffith chose to eliminate the episode with Luigi (although this is not the only alteration Griffith was to make to the Browning play).[23]

It would be useful at this point to rehearse the play's basic plot. The play is set in the Italian town of Asolo. The prologue introduces us to Pippa, a young girl who works in a silk-weaving factory. She joyfully greets the sunrise to which she dedicates a song. It is New Year's Day, the factory workers' only day of rest. Pippa walks out onto the streets of Asolo and wanders merrily through the town. The remainder of the film is structured into four episodes connected only through the song Pippa sings as she walks through the streets.

In the first episode—morning—we see two lovers, Sebald and Ottima, who have just killed Ottima's aging husband, Luca. Pippa's song induces in Sebald a sense of horror at his actions and a feeling of guilt and revulsion toward Ottima. In the second episode—midday—we see a group of friends play a trick on the artist Jules. They have penned a series of rarefied letters to him in the name of an illiterate and rather ignorant woman called Phene, moving him to declare his love for her. When the deception is revealed, Jules is enraged, but Pippa's song suddenly awakens in him a sense of compassion and even love for Phene. In the third episode—evening—we see Luigi, a member of the Carbonari, taking leave of his mother. About to depart for Austria on a mission assigned to him by the secret society of which he is a member, for a moment Luigi falters. Then Pippa's song hardens Luigi's resolve to sacrifice himself for his country's freedom. The fourth episode—night—depicts an encounter between a monsignor who has come to Asolo and Ugo, the superintendent who had managed the properties of the bishop's deceased brother. It turns out that fourteen years earlier Ugo had killed the elder of the two brothers and kidnapped his young daughter Pippa, holding her in the factory owned by the prelate's younger brother, from whom he hoped to extract a ransom. Ugo had suggested that they send Pippa, who stands to inherit the estate, to a brothel in Rome, where she would be unlikely to survive for long. The monsignor now hopes to redeem the past sins of his two brothers. The bishop appears to waver in his resolve, but once more Pippa's song puts an end to his doubts, and Ugo is arrested. The play ends with an epilogue: Pippa returns home and, entirely unaware of the good deeds she has performed, falls into an innocent slumber.

Apart from the scene with Luigi, which is dramatically the weakest, Griffith also removed the crucial nighttime episode that is effectively the play's culmination. He replaces it with the morning episode, which undergoes a further melodramatic change: Sebald and Ottima do not actually kill Luigi; instead, Pippa's song stops them dead in their tracks. Yet perhaps the strangest aspect of these changes and shifts is the insertion of a new episode that is entirely Griffith's own. This episode takes place in a tavern, where a drunk hears Pippa's singing and, feeling instant remorse, returns to his family.

This episode, thoroughly inappropriate to Browning's play, does not appear in the film by chance. It is essentially a variation on a theme developed in Griffith's earlier film *A Drunkard's Reformation,* released on April 1, 1909, and discussed in chapter 1. The different treatment of the same theme in these two films is itself suggestive. In the earlier film the drunkard is taken by his daughter to see a performance of Zola's *L'Assommoir.* The play's edifying message about the evils of alcoholism has the appropriate effect, and the drunkard instantly reforms. In *Pippa Passes,* the drunkard's moral reformation is brought about by a song. In this second film, Griffith seems to be correcting the older version of an identical theme, while leaving the formal structure of the episode unchanged. Both variants are given in a crosscutting that, according to Tom Gunning, functions symbolically: in the earlier film, shots of father and daughter alternate with the shots of the stage; in the later film, shots of the drunk in the tavern alternate with a vision of Pippa singing. Both episodes include an innocent child (in the first film the child appears in Zola's play). It seems reasonable to say that Griffith's revision of the theme of the drunkard is the result of the privilege accorded in the first film to theater as the locus of moral values, in direct contrast to the director's increasingly systematic attack on theatrical motifs in his own work. *A Drunkard's Reformation,* moreover, establishes theater as a locus of influence. In the words of the *Biograph Bulletins,* we feel the play's message "sinking deeper and deeper into his [the drunkard's] heart, until at the final curtain he is a changed man."[24] This self-quotation reads ambivalently: however unintentionally or subconsciously, it points back to the theater as the film's true origin.

The forced introduction of this third episode to some extent exposes the strategy underlying Griffith's adaptations of Browning. Browning's poetry serves to conceal what is in fact a shift in the axis of influence away from theater toward literature; it serves also as a pretext for rewriting a narrative that had pointed too openly to Griffith's true sources. At the same time, we witness an escalation of the "heraldic construction": *Pippa Passes* enters an existing cluster of texts, including *L'Assommoir, La Curée,* and *A Drunkard's Reformation. Pippa Passes,* in fact, complicates still further Griffith's relationship to the theater, which had been ambiguous enough even in the intertextual context of his earlier film. More than any other film, it is *Pippa* that allows Griffith to establish himself as a "strong author." He can borrow from Miller's stage production and then hide behind the name of Browning, planting a somewhat masked but easily revealed quotation in the movie's plot. This quote acts like a curtain, both revealing and concealing the theatrical stage behind it.

Pippa Passes undermines theater by song, displacing one source with another—in this the film follows Browning's own example. This reorientation, first toward song and then generalized to language as such, carries too great a significance for Griffith's work as a whole to be neglected.

The motif of singing had in fact been important to Browning, corresponding to a particular intertextual strategy the poet himself was to deploy. Harold Bloom has observed that Browning's main precursor was Shelley. The masking of this influence is one of Browning's most important motifs, as is particularly evident in the dramatic monologue "Cleon," which Bloom himself quotes:

I have not chanted verse like Homer, no—
Nor swept strings like Terpander, no—
Nor carved and painted men like Phidias and his friend;
I am not great as they are, point by point.
But I have entered into sympathy
With these four, running these into one soul,
Who, separate, ignored each other's art.[25]

Although it is possible that the real prototype for Cleon was Matthew Arnold, Browning himself saw the monologue as a means to overcome the anxiety of influence by shifting from one aesthetic form to another. The shift from word to music or painting absolves him of the sin of succession. The same motifs are further elaborated in Browning's long poem "One Word More."

Among all the forms working intersemiotically to recode and thereby mask the burden of influence, music emerges as the most important. In fact, music is seen as not subject to influence, and it appears therefore as the supreme art in a cycle of poems Browning devoted to the subject: "A Toccata of Galuppi's," "Abbot Vogler," and "Master Hugues of Saxe-Gotha."[26] Particularly suggestive in this context is one of Abbot Vogler's monologues, spoken after an improvised organ recital:

> All through music and me! For think, had I painted the whole,
> Why there it stood, to see, nor the process so wonder-worth:
> Had I written the same, made verse—still effect proceeds from the cause,
> Ye know why the forms are fair, ye hear how the tale is told;
> It is all triumphant art, but art in obedience to laws,
> Painter and poet are proud in the artist-list enrolled.[27]

We are struck here by the opposition between music as an art that can rise to the divine and painting and poetry as "mediated" forms.

Browning's views are based on the romantic tradition. Romanticism, as James Anderson Winn has pointed out, formulated the myth of music as the direct language of the passions, free of syntactical and other formal constraints. The materials of music "can acquire their meaning entirely from musical context, while poetic materials, though greatly affected by poetic context, bring their dictionary meanings with them into the poem."[28]

The cult of music as a form of immediacy impelled the romantics to idealize the "untutored" or "primitive" forms of folk music, which they perceived as being the closest analogy to the language of nature. The German philosopher and critic Joseph Görres spoke of music as an echo of external nature, to which our inner nature then responds.[29] In the Anglophone tradition, it was Walter Pater who formulated the most authoritative view on the subject. For Pater, all forms of art save music address the reasoning mind; music alone appeals to the essence itself, to "pure perception," and overcomes the rupture between form and content. For this reason, all forms of art aspire to music as their ideal. "Yet the arts may be represented as continually struggling after the law or principle of music, to a condition which music alone completely realises."[30] Singled out for attention within this tradition was the folk music of Italy, hailed by romantics from Achim von Arnim to Pater himself as the ideal of immediacy.[31]

Browning took great care in elaborating the same myth—first in the poem *Sordello*, which ends with the poetry of the meditative hero being transformed into an anonymous quasi folk song sung by a "child barefoot and rosy" as he runs up the hill:

> Up and up goes he, singing all the while
> Some unintelligible words to beat
> The lark, God's poet, swooning at his feet.[32]

In these final lines of *Sordello* poetry attains its highest point as the incomprehensible words to a child's song. To approach the essence, then, is to transcend language in music. It is worth noting that *Sordello*, like *Pippa*, is set in the Italian city of Asolo.

The "child barefoot and rosy" introduces yet one more shared motif—the sun. The poet as author is displaced by nature and the elements; poetry begins to emanate like sunlight. In Browning's *Pippa Passes* the solar symbolism underlying the girl's passage through Asolo is quite obvious. It is made explicit in the first lines of her monologue within a prologue that is essentially a hymn to the sun. Later on, in the evening episode, Pippa sings a song about the Sun King, and at the end of the nighttime episode the motif of song as sunlight reappears. Here the song itself is equated with the voices of the birds and beasts:

> My childhood had not learned to know:
> For, what are the voices of birds
> —Ay, and of beasts—but words, our words,
> Only so much more sweet?[33]

Here the child is the sign of a proximity to nature, a symbol of remote beginnings.

Alongside the myth of music and song as a kind of magical protolanguage, Browning elaborates another myth concerning the instantaneous and incantatory effect that music can exert on consciousness. The instantaneousness of music's influence (we recall the rather artificial deus ex machina that was Pippa's singing) can be explained by the fact that the effect of music on the human psyche is unmediated, readily connecting the mind to the sphere of universal harmony.

Wordsworth had already called music "but a stream that flow'd into a kindred stream, a gale."[34] Walt Whitman's "A Singer in the Prison," a poem that in many ways recalls Browning's *Pippa*, is set in a prison containing hardened criminals and murderers. Suddenly there appears a "lady . . . holding a little innocent child by either hand." She starts strumming an instrument and singing a "quaint old hymn" that has an instantaneous and irresistible moral impact on the prisoners:

> A hush and pause fell down a wondrous minute,
> With deep half-stifled sobs and sound of bad men bow'd and moved to weeping,
> And youth's convulsive breathings, memories of home,
> The mother's voice in lullaby, the sister's care, the happy childhood,
> The long-pent spirit roused to reminiscence.[35]

Song is the poetry of origins, and as such it brings consciousness back to a primordial human innocence. Here the lullaby becomes a symbol of this return.

An astonishingly original reworking of this situation can be found in Matthew Arnold's poetic drama *Empedocles on Etna*. In the first act,

Empedocles' friend Callicles asks Pausanias, a young musician and a pupil
of the philosopher, to assuage Empedocles' pain by singing to him from
afar: "But thou must keep unseen; follow us on, / But at a distance! in
these solitudes, / In this clear mountain-air, a voice will rise, / Though
from afar, distinctly; it may soothe him."[36] The remainder of the play is
structured as the alternating sequence of Callicles' invisible voice and
Empedocles' monologues. The singing, however, produces an unexpected
result. It strengthens Empedocles' view that human beings have moved too
far from their foundations, the four elements, and it finally moves him to
return to the element of fire by throwing himself into a crater. So, paradoxically, song and fire (sun) are once more joined.

The status of music as the metalanguage of nature grants it a unique
role in the dynamic of source repression. Any word is connected to its past
usage and possesses it own cultural memory. Its repression as an anterior
source can thus be realized through its substitution either by an inarticulate *Ursprache* or by music and song. The figure of the Other as precursor is
displaced by a god figure or by the symbol of the sun as the originary
source. The distance between poet and muse is thus drastically reduced.

This recourse to song, music, or solar imagery at the same time provides
an illusory solution to the problems raised by quotation, since neither
music nor light can be invoked citationally in a verbal text. They signify differently and thereby seem to escape the confines of intertextuality, although their external status is an artistic convention: after all, music and
light cannot exist in poetry in any immediate way except as linguistic motifs. Yet on the level of plot they generate within the text the motif of an intersemiotic recoding, a translation of language into the nonlinguistic,
which, however illusory, remains crucial to any reading. This motif is
clearly evident in Browning's own play, which effects a complex chain of
displacements: from language to visual representation (sculpture, painting) to music (song).

The morning episode already contains a critique of verbal expression,
which is said to lose its meaning through repetition or constant usage:

Ottima: Best never speak of it.
Sebald: Best speak again and yet again of it,
till words cease to be more than words.
"His blood"
For instance—let these two words mean,
"His blood"
and nothing more. Notice, I'll say them
now,
"His blood."[37]

In the episode with Luigi, the critique of language takes on another
form. Here the issue is Luigi's inability to translate his knowledge into

words. In both cases Pippa's song eliminates the semiotic blockage. Pippa seems to push Sebald to take a step beyond verbal repetition toward a truth or essence, just as she helps Luigi to overcome his verbal break.

Yet Pippa's musical power is exerted most curiously on the character Jules. To start with, the midday episode itself derives from a series of literary sources. We know that Browning took some details from Hugo's *Ruy Blas* and others from Diderot's *Jacques le fataliste*. Yet the most immediate source for Browning's *Pippa* was a play by his friend Baron Edward Bulwer-Lytton, *The Lady of Lyons: Or, Love and Pride*.[38] Browning had been envious of Bulwer-Lytton's theatrical success: although *Pippa Passes* carefully conceals any overt reference to *The Lady of Lyons* (in fact symmetrically inverting its plot), it nonetheless betrays clear traces of Bulwer-Lytton's work.

Browning's Jules is a sculptor, while Melnotte, the analogous character in *The Lady of Lyons,* is a painter. The wealthy Beausant, who initiates the play's intrigue, is hoping that the heroine Pauline will marry a wandering actor. Pauline, on the other hand, dreams of marrying a rich singer capable of celebrating her beauty in song. The plot's intrigue thus embraces several forms of art. Melnotte has difficulties with his medium: "I shall never be a painter. I can paint no likeness but one, and that is above all art."[39] Melnotte's artistic weakness lies in his inability to move beyond his sole theme, which he takes from nature. Endless repetition condemns him to artistic mediocrity. Browning's Jules is a sculptor equally incapable of grasping the essence of things. Pippa's song does more than awaken his love for Phene; it opens up a new artistic vision: "I do but break these paltry models up to begin Art afresh."[40]

This scenario appears to have held such significance for Browning that he came back to it in the nighttime episode, when the bishop somewhat anachronistically mentions a sculptor, Jules, who had once lived in Asolo (as if the two episodes take place years apart instead of a few hours). I quote the bishop's words:

> He never had a clearly conceived Ideal within his brain till to-day. Yet since his hand could manage a chisel, he has practised expressing other men's Ideals; and, in the very perfection he has attained to, he foresees an ultimate failure: his unconscious hand will pursue its prescribed course of old years, and will reproduce with a fatal expertness the ancient types, lest the novel one appear never so palpably to his spirit. There is but one method of escape: confiding the virgin type to as chaste a hand, he will turn painter instead of sculptor, and paint, not carve, its characteristics. . . . but if there should arise a new painter, will it not be in some such way, by a poet, now, or a musician (spirits who have conceived and perfected an Ideal through some other channel), transferring it to this, and escaping our conventional roads by pure ignorance of them.[41]

This monologue throws a great deal of light on the figure of Pippa—pure, unknowing, yet capable of effecting changes in all who hear her, especially Jules. The same passage also clarifies another crucial motif: the source that gets repressed as the text is itself translated into another expressive medium. Music, then, is not simply an ideal language that masks a source; it is also what provokes the intersemiotic shifts that repress the source. In order to repress evidence of his intertextual dialogue with Bulwer-Lytton, Browning does more than reverse the dramatic scenario of *The Lady of Lyons:* he also effects a further shift of plot within the hero's profession. Melnotte, who keeps drawing the same portrait, finds a clear parallel in Jules, who keeps reworking the ideals of his precursors. Browning's repression of his source provokes a change in Jules's method of working. In changing his expressive medium, he stops repeating the work of his precursors, finally breaking through to what is essential and at the same time regaining his artistic innocence.

A few years after the appearance of Browning's *Pippa,* Bulwer-Lytton published the novel *Zanoni,* in which the dilemma of Browning's hero Jules was elaborated even further. The principal characters in *Zanoni* are a mute violinist by the name of Gaetano Pisani, who is compelled to express himself through his music, and his daughter Viola, an outstanding opera singer. The novel is also based on the demonization of theater, which it depicts as a Sodom posing a threat to Viola's innocence. Viola is in love with Glyndon, an artist who is unable to realize his ideals. Glyndon is finally granted a vision of the essence under the influence of Viola and her music, as well as the enigmatic Rosicrucian Zanoni, a walking repository of higher truth who knows all languages, even the prehistorical. It is worth noting that Zanoni is endowed with solar attributes: his name is derived from the Chaldean root *zan,* meaning "sun."

In Bulwer-Lytton the linked elements of source repression and intersemiotic recoding grow into a veritable aesthetic myth in which each hero personifies a specific artistic idea. *Zanoni* was written in 1845, which itself indicates the extent to which, by the middle of the nineteenth century, the intertextual dilemma here described was an acknowledged and productive part of Western culture.

Let us now, after this lengthy digression, return to Griffith. The appearance of cinema had pointed to the realization of the long-cherished dream of creating a radical rupture in art. This rupture was expected to renew our relation to the world and overcome the automatism of verbal repetition. An art form had appeared that effectively lacked precursors. In the cultural context of the new century, cinema began to aspire to the function that had been accorded to music. The myth of music was projected directly onto film: the latter was repeatedly described as a young baby (hence its innocence) and hailed as a universal and natural language, a status enjoyed previously by music. The notion that music could reconcile all contradictions by bringing us into contact with a universal harmony is repeated almost word for word by Griffith himself: "I believe one hundred years from now the pictures will have had time to educate the masses away from discord and unharmony."[42]

It is hardly fortuitous that Griffith called his adaptation of the Browning play *The Song of Conscience*. The term most likely refers to the movie as a whole and not just to Pippa's song. Nor does it appear coincidental that in 1910 Griffith made another film called *A Plain Song*, which, despite its title, does not thematize music in any way. The film is about the manager of a theater company who tries to seduce the hapless daughter of an aging couple. Just as she is about to yield, the voice of her soul speaks to her as follows: "'Remember thy father and thy mother.' And she does remember, seeing them most vividly in her mind's eye. This thought so impels that she at last realizes that she is playing with fire, and turning on her heel, runs back home."[43] The musical title is simply a reference to the same sudden illumination of consciousness that had also been central to *Pippa Passes*. In this film, the already familiar opposition of theater as sin and music as the sphere of moral awakening now borders on a cliché: once more the external vision of theater is contrasted with the inner vision of music.

Between 1909 and 1910, Griffith made several films that were effectively plot variations on the same Browning scenario. In *The Voice of the Violin* (1909), a music teacher with anarchist convictions is assigned by a terrorist organization to blow up the house in which his favorite pupil is living. The teacher, von Schmidt, approaches the house, "while there the melody of his own violin composition floats out on the night air, and ascending the stoop he peers through the window and beholds Helen playing the violin. The realization of what is about to happen for the moment rivets him to the spot."[44] Von Schmidt suddenly experiences a revelation and turns to attack his erstwhile terrorist colleagues, saving the young woman. This is practically an inversion of the Luigi episode in Browning's play, which Griffith had eliminated from his film version. Another film, *To Save Her Soul* (1909), deals with a young woman who is heard singing in her village church choir by the manager of a vaudeville troupe. She is taken to the city, where she falls prey to sin, but as she is about to fall she is rescued by a young priest named Paul Redmond.

In 1909, Griffith was to make one more film with a "musical" theme, adapted from François Coppée's poetic drama *Le Luthier de Crémone*. Essentially, the drama concerns two violin makers from Cremona, the hunchback Filippo and the handsome Sandro, both rivals for the hand of the young girl Giannina. Coppée's melodrama is founded on the contrast between Filippo's repellent external appearance and his inward purity as it is manifested in his divinely gifted violin playing. In Sandro's monologue Filippo is compared to Philomela, the daughter of the Thracian king Pandeon, who was transformed into a nightingale. The classical motif of metamorphosis in this case serves as a kind of metadescription of the plot device that allows for the transformation of phenomenal reality into essence. Furthermore, the motif essentially recapitulates the myth of the repressed source. It is worth noting that Bulwer-Lytton's *Zanoni* also contains a reference to Cremona ("As Shakespeare among poets, is the Cremona among instruments"),[45] which occurs precisely at a point of transition from poetry to music, as well as a detailed exposition of the myth of Philomela, which is the basic plot of Gaetano Pisano's last opera.

Griffith's *Pippa Passes,* then, emerges as one of a series of variations on the same theme. Together these works elaborate a symbolic lexicon through which they repress their own theatrical origins. In the nineteenth century this lexicon enjoyed a near-universal currency, as the coincidence of motifs between Coppée's French drama and Bulwer-Lytton's English novel indicates. *Pippa Passes* occupies a central place in this series, above all through its direct reference to the primary or "strong" source—Browning's play and the tradition on which the play rested. Browning's discourse appeared as an alternative to Griffith's theatrical sources. But this discourse was marked by its own displacements and repressions: it posited music as an alternative source for what it in turn took from other texts.

Along with music came its visual equivalent, sunlight. In the prologue and epilogue to the film, Griffith applied a special system of additional lighting to create the illusion of sunrise and sunset. Tom Gunning has linked these lighting effects to a then prevalent tendency to end a film with an aesthetically charged image. But at the same time he himself acknowledges that special lighting "carries clear thematic meanings. Most frequently the use of a directional light illuminating figures in an otherwise darkened area carries the association of spiritual devotion."[46] J. Pruitt, in an article devoted specifically to the use of lighting in films made for Biograph, has also pointed to the role of light in conveying "a mystical feeling of hope and reconciliation" in films such as *Fisher Folks* (1909) and *A Cricket on the Hearth* (1909).[47] Pruitt attributes particular significance to the "scenes by the window," where a man stands bathed in sunshine, yearning for a better life. The abrupt nature of his illumination, like the sudden effect of music, is visually realized through the instantaneous use of lighting (e.g., a brightened room), as in *Edgar Allan Poe* (1909).

It is worth recalling that Griffith's *A Drunkard's Reformation* ends with a vision of a happy family sitting by the hearth and framed by a marked use of lighting. In their use of lighting, both *A Drunkard's Reformation* and *Pippa Passes* are "revelatory" films, in the sense that they make language (Zola's theatrical language and Browning's literary language) yield to the nonverbal—that which cannot be quoted but can be embodied in light. Even where a (literary) source is repressed through the very positing of influence, as in the case of Griffith's relation to Browning, there is an increased emphasis on what lies beyond quotation, on what appears, however illusorily, to escape the web of intertextuality.

Even beyond the Browning play, Griffith's work betrays a steady escalation of influences, which appear like the perpetual regress of a mirror reflected within a mirror. Each one of his films represses its own source. Griffith's thematic variations become truly meaningful only within this infinite specular perspective. The existence of these variants suggests that, even in 1909 and 1910, Griffith had begun to conceal his relation to Browning—every plot variation being an attempt to disconnect the very same motif from its source. This means that language is posited as the primary competing source of inspiration and yet also initiates the mechanism of its own repression as the basis of intertextual reference. This mechanism, moreover, is present in Browning himself, whose text is objectively oriented toward the displacement of language by music and light.

At a later stage in his career, Griffith would overcome the very dependence on literature that he had earlier affirmed, repressing, through a series of masks, any reference to literary language. This process went hand in hand with the director's growing ambitions as an artist, as evidenced in his elevation of film into a universal language.

In 1913, Griffith again turned to a Browning text for inspiration. The film *The Escape*, released on May 3, 1913, has been described in the most recent critical literature on Griffith's career as a remake of *Pippa*.[48] Tom Gunning describes its plot as follows (I have been unable to view the film myself): "In this later film a wandering flute player (Henry Walthall) has a beneficent influence on a number of characters through the pure tones of his music as he passes by. He reconciles lovers, prevents a peevish young girl from throwing away a crucifix, and, in the clearest parallel to *Pippa Passes*, stops a pair of adulterous lovers from murdering the woman's husband."[49] As should be clear from this description, in Griffith's second remake of *Pippa*, song is replaced by wordless music, pure melody. This musical element, in opposition to language, becomes even stronger in *The Escape*.

In the following year, Griffith returned once more to the Browning play, this time concealing the source quite thoroughly. In 1914, he made the film *Home, Sweet Home* for the Reliance Majestic and Mutual production companies. In the existing critical literature, *Home, Sweet Home* is taken to be a free adaptation of a biography of John Howard Payne, although the actual biography has never been identified.[50] R. Schickel, in what is the most authoritative biography of Griffith to date, has defined the film as "a highly colored version of the life of John Howard Payne, author of the song from which the title of the movie was borrowed."[51] Schickel's conclusion not only betrays an ignorance of Payne's actual biography but also ignores so authoritative a witness as Griffith's own cameraman Karl Brown, who has indicated the film's source directly: "*Home, Sweet Home* was virtually a remake of *Pippa Passes,* only instead of having the voice of a gay young girl bring cheer and faith to a despairing mankind, the music of *Home, Sweet Home* changed the lives of a set of different characters, a sort of multiple story dominated by a single thematic idea."[52]

The plot of *Home, Sweet Home* is, briefly, as follows. In the first of four episodes, the film's hero, Payne, leaves his mother and his sweetheart to go to the city, where he hopes to become an actor. Once in the theater, he lapses into a life of sin. He is seduced by a woman from the city, falls into debt, and dies abandoned by his friends. As he lies dying, he composes the song "Home, Sweet Home." In his hometown the sweetheart he had abandoned also dies. In the second episode, a country girl called Apple Pie Mary falls in love with a boy from the East. The boy, however, meets a dazzling woman from the city. Just as he is about to forget Mary, he hears Payne's melody. At once realizing the full horror of the betrayal he is contemplating, he returns to the country girl. In the third episode we see a mother who has raised two sons who have hated each other since childhood. In a fight over money the brothers kill each other. In despair at her loss, their mother contemplates suicide but hears the melody, which restores her faith in life. In the fourth episode a philanderer tempts a married woman to infidelity. At the brink of what would seem to be her inevitable fall, the woman hears the strains of a violin playing "Home, Sweet Home." She leaves the philanderer and stays with her husband. The film ends with an epilogue showing Payne in purgatory. He tries to clamber up a rocky slope but is pulled back by various personifications of sin. The figure of his beloved then appears in the sky, and their souls are united in an embrace.

We can see that the structure of *Pippa Passes* is almost fully reproduced in *Home, Sweet Home.* Even the number of episodes—four—is the same. Griffith used the same actors who had worked on *Pippa,* and of the three actors who worked on both films, two—Walthall and Kirkwood—had acted in Miller's theatrical production of the play in 1906.

One might ask of this later and freer adaptation why Griffith chose the figure of Payne as a means of repressing the Browning play as its true source. Payne's real biography is quite remote from the screen version. In 1813, at the age of twenty-one, Payne left New York to make his reputation on the English stage. Even at this stage Payne could hardly be considered the hero of a provincial rural idyll. He had acted since childhood and as a young boy had published a free translation of August von Kotzebue's *Lovers' Vows, or, the Child of Love.* At fourteen he was owner and editor of

the theatrical paper the *Thespian Mirror.* In London Payne entered the sa-
lons of the artistic elite, meeting Coleridge and Southy. After a brilliant
debut in Drury Lane, he enjoyed great success from 1813 to 1818. The fi-
nancial difficulties that beset him in 1819 were not due to any dissolute
lifestyle on his part but were the result of a failed enterprise called Sadler's
Wells Theater. In the 1820s Payne lived in Paris, from where he would
send his adaptations of French melodramas, which ran in Drury Lane and
Covent Garden. He also coauthored several plays with his friend Washington Irving. The most celebrated object of Payne's passion was Mary Shelley, whom he wooed assiduously, only to discover that she was in love with
Irving. In 1832 Payne returned to America to a rapturous welcome. He
died in 1852 in Tunisia, where he had been appointed American consul.

Clearly, Payne's real-life story diverges sharply from its purported film
version even at those moments where both evidently coincide. In Griffith's
film, for example, Payne's death in a generic Arab country is seen to signify his utter ruin: nowhere are we told of his legitimate reasons for being
in Tunisia.

In reworking Payne's biography, Griffith in fact sought to bring it closer
to his own. He was fascinated by the figure of the vagrant actor who becomes drawn into a kind of theatrical Sodom (which was precisely how he
would describe his own theatrical career in a later autobiographical account), only to be saved from the abyss by a song he himself composes
(Griffith's song would, of course, be cinema itself).[53] Griffith also sought
to bring out those motifs in Payne's life that were close to Browning's: his
career in England and his theatrical failures. It is worth noting parantheti-
cally that Payne's famous song had been intended for Sir Henry R.
Bishop's operetta *Clari; or the Maid of Milan,* whose Italian heroine could
be readily associated with Pippa from Asolo.

The figure of Payne once more fulfills the complex task of both masking and revealing the film's true source. On the one hand, it is a concealed reference to Browning; on the other, it subconsciously projects
Griffith as its author, who is clearly identified with Payne himself. Here we
have a particularly eloquent case of what Bloom has called a relationship
of "opposition-identification" with one's precursor. One further aspect of
Payne's life is relevant here. Insofar as Payne reworked the plays of other
writers, he was repeatedly accused of plagiarism. In 1818, at the end of his
English stage career, his play *Brutus, or the Fall of Tarquin* met with considerable success on Drury Lane. Nonetheless, critics were to attack him mercilessly for plagiarism.[54] In Bloom's terms, then, Payne suggests the figure
of a weak writer, the successor who follows tradition. His moral decline
and final death can be understood as punishment for his lifelong commitment to the theater and the epigonal status to which theater had relegated him.

The entire first episode of *Home, Sweet Home,* devoted as it is specifically to Payne's life, can be seen as a vigorous repression of theatrical sources, onto which the further repression of a literary source, Browning, is then superimposed. Let us see how this gets worked out in the text. Payne's mother and sweetheart both receive letters from him informing them that he has become an actor. At this point the film has already depicted Payne's entry into the theatrical world in a scene in which his acting is shown to be fake and affected.

Both women decide to save the sinner Payne. They go back to his empty room, where their discovery of a copy of the Bible provokes a scene of tenderness. They then pass into the adjacent room, where they can hear the voices of some actors speaking through a partition. The mother remarks that their speech is "disgusting"; Payne's sweetheart responds that they're "just rehearsing." When Payne's actress friends appear, his moral decline becomes evident. It is essential to note that all the evidence of sin is produced in the very room where the Bible had been found. But now the Bible is gone. When Payne awakes the next morning slouched over a table, the Bible is once more lying beside him. Now Payne begins to compose his song. He stares emptily a little to the right of the camera (always the sign of a vision in Griffith). His mother and abandoned sweetheart emerge from the shadows. Payne returns to the song he was composing; as he writes, the lyrics appear as captions.

This entire episode is constructed out of the opposition between texts of different kinds and their sources. Vulgar language is equated with the theater; a life of sin is seen as a play. The theater is denied the privilege of a literary source. A song is a different matter. Its sources are directly related to the Word, indeed to the sacred Word, the supreme book that is the Bible. Analogous to song, serving in fact as its second source, is vision. External sight—the theater—is thus opposed to inner sight, a cinematic vision that harks back to the revelations of the Holy Writ.

In the lyrics to the song that appear in the caption we read the following words:

> An exile from home, splendour dazzles in vain!
> Oh, give me my lowly thatch'd cottage again!
> The birds singing gaily that came at my call
> Give me them!—and the peace of mind dearer than all!
>
> (p. 53)

The song is once more seen as analogous to the singing of birds, rising heavenward toward God and bearing a message of peace and harmony.

Interestingly, what this cluster of oppositions excludes is the normal book (such as Browning's text). From this point Griffith will refuse to confront any literary source, preferring to replace it with the Book of all be-

ginnings, the sacred Word as opposed to the profane discourse of literature. This is a kind of secondary repression, which finally denies literature
any place whatsoever.

In a customary paradox, however, the repression of theater in turn
amounts to its unexpected return, and in the most hypertrophied form,
as an epilogue filled with allegorical representations of sin and of souls reuniting. Karl Brown is right to note the highly quotational nature of this
final scene, invoking as it does an entire theatrical tradition from Greek
tragedy to the pre-Elizabethan moralities.[55] What is most curious, however, is that the epilogue also contains a reference to a play by Payne himself, *Mount Savage,* a plagiarized translation of a work of the same title by
Pixérécourt. Just as Payne is seen to languish on the cliffs of purgatory, so
we discover the hero of the play, the Solitary, on some cloud-covered
mountains: "A shade appears to come out of the earth. With one hand it
points to the background and in the other bears a lamp." We then see allegorical representations of sin, war, and the angel of death: "Seized with
frightful convulsions, the Solitary repels these horrible images. . . . he lifts
toward the sky his supplicating hands. At his prayer the picture changes
color. Sweet chords are heard. All which bore the marks of sadness and of
mourning vanishes." A procession can be discerned moving toward the
Solitary—old men, women, and children to whom he had once given assistance. Among the children is a baby he had rescued, now in his
mother's embrace. Finally the entire crowd raises its arms, pointing into
the distance at "the figure of a young female who resembles Elodie," the
Solitary's beloved, from whom he had been separated on account of his
sins.[56]

Herein lies the paradox of theater as a theme serving so obviously as a
framing device for the entire film: Griffith presents his visions as arising
without a source, as texts revealed rather than written, while at the same
time relying on the existing tradition of theatrical visions. The resources
deployed in repressing the source are derived from the very medium that
is being repressed. By putting Payne in the place of Browning, Griffith replaces a strong primary source with a weak near-anonymous figure mired
in rewriting and plagiarism. Eternal repetition becomes the paradoxical
equivalent of an endless beginning. It is natural that the failure to establish
a true origin must be masked by the hunt for a word as anonymous and
repetitive as a dictionary.

The film *Home, Sweet Home* betrays a marked tendency to repress the
profane written word. This tendency is seen most clearly in the film's unusual recourse to letters. In early cinema, letters served as an effective way
of communicating information within a film's diegetic structure. Any
number of letters and notes made their appearance in cinema before captions became established along with the incorporation into film of the

"external narrator." *Home, Sweet Home* contains a flood of correspondence, but, with one exception, these letters are never materialized on the screen as written text. Their content is conveyed either in a caption spoken, as it were, "by the filmmaker" or as the voice of the person reading the letter. Griffith's treatment of letters differs markedly from the narrative strategies common to his day. This anomaly can perhaps be understood as part of the elimination of the written word from the film's diegetic structure.

Griffith's manipulation of the letter partly recalls the use of the letter as a motif in sixteenth- and seventeenth-century Dutch painting. The period is surprisingly rich in representations of women reading letters; these representations are all the more intriguing for their refusal to show us the content of the letters they depict, allowing it to remain an enigma for the viewer. As A. Maier-Meintshel has shown, the original text available for reading was the Bible, whose reader was the Virgin Mary. As the motif of reading became secularized, the content of writing came to be conveyed more indirectly, through persistent iconographic representations, such as a view of a ship at sea placed within an interior, or musical instruments symbolizing love, or even coarse eroticism.[57] The iconographic shift turns out to have produced another shift away from the Supreme Book (whose content does not need to be specially explained) to the profane text (the letter).

Interestingly, *Home, Sweet Home* betrays the traces of such an iconographic shift, albeit in a rudimentary form. In the film's second episode Mary marks her impending separation from her beloved by giving him a Christmas card, explaining that, while she lacks an image of herself, this picture resembles her. Mary identifies with the Virgin (that they share the same name is hardly fortuitous). Thanks to this symbolic gift, the whole story begins to acquire biblical resonances. The young man from the East returns the gesture with a gift that is no less surprising: he gives Mary his own glasses—another sign of visual displacement, the exchange of sight.

The repression of language in *Home, Sweet Home* is also evident in the gradual transformation of Payne's song into a pure melody devoid of words. In the second and third episodes, the melody is played by a street musician; in the fourth, by a violinist. Music definitively represses language.

The last and most significant variation on Browning's theme is the film *Intolerance* (1916). This assertion may come as a surprise, insofar as the film's plot would seem to be quite remote from *Pippa Passes*. Yet the two films are undoubtedly linked, although their commonalities have been painstakingly masked.

Griffith himself betrayed something of this work of concealment in an article of 1916, which he wrote immediately after completing the film (*Intolerance* was released on September 5, and the article was published in the *Independent* on December 11). Here Griffith returned to the subject that

had become his obsession—the relationship of theater to cinema—to de-
nounce the theater once more for its limitations: "Within the confines of
the old theatre it was not possible to relate more than two stories in order
to illustrate a particular phase of the action; actually, even two stories
would have been difficult to stage. But in my film *Intolerance*—this is the
first example that comes to mind—I tell four stories."[58]

Griffith forgets here that the Browning play had also contained four
episodes, a magic number that Griffith took pains to reproduce both in
Home, Sweet Home and now in *Intolerance.* This four-part structure is perhaps
the clearest indicator of the film's link to the Browning play. But that is not
all. *Intolerance* almost entirely avoids any allusion to music so particular to
Browning on the level of plot (what remains is the rudimentary figure of
the rhapsode in the Babylonian episode).

Each new stage in Griffith's reworking of the Browning play is thus
based on the repression of a source acknowledged at a prior stage or in
older variations and on its replacement by another source. In the 1909
film, a theatrical source was repressed and Browning's written work inserted in its place. In the 1914 version, Browning's written work was itself
repressed, masked by the "weak" figure of Payne. Two years later, in *Intolerance,* it was music's turn to be repressed. But here as before, a source,
previously acknowledged and now repressed, acquires a special significance for the new text. The film, in fact, eliminates only the external manifestations of what remains of crucial importance.

How is the influence of music still felt in *Intolerance?* Above all formally,
in its typically musical elaboration and transposition of motifs. But that is
not all. All of the four episodes in *Intolerance*—set in Babylon, Palestine,
Paris, and modern America, respectively—are linked by the image of a
woman rocking a cradle (Lillian Gish), to which we shall return in the next
chapter. This image is in fact taken from Walt Whitman's "Out of the Cradle Endlessly Rocking," which compares the swaying cradle to the sea. As
Leo Spitzer has observed, poetic tradition has always linked the music of
the sea to the singing of birds and to a choir of human souls calling to
Jesus Christ. Spitzer has also pointed to the intimate link between the
tragic fate and final metamorphosis of Philomela and the passion and
transformation undergone by Christ.[59] In Whitman the connection between the sea-as-cradle and the singing of birds becomes part of the
poem's declared theme. Furthermore, the counterpoint to the birds' song
and the roar of the sea is meant to reveal a certain unique "word" to the
poem's hero:

A word then, (for I will conquer it,)
The word final, superior to all,
Subtle, sent up,—what is it?—I listen.[60]

It is this word that Griffith's film finally reveals. Seven times the film will link the image of a cradle to that of a book that Griffith will term the "Book of Intolerance." The captions that follow each appearance of the book appear against a background of different systems of writing—hieroglyphs for the Babylonian episode, Hebrew for Palestine. Along with the musical motif of the cradle (and the lullaby), we see a new kind of written word— the hieroglyph, which signifies the Originary Word, impenetrable to mere mortals, the same word that was known to the Rosicrucian Zanoni.

Intolerance in fact radically expands the sphere of references to an Originary Book that had already been noted in *Home, Sweet Home.* Suppressed as a source, music survives in the form of a coded subtext that finally veils the film in a kind of mystical hieroglyphics that is essentially incomprehensible to the modern mind. This is the final gesture of repression: all references to intermediary sources, the long line of precursors, are now eliminated. As Griffith's "strongest" film, *Intolerance* openly acknowledges its proximity to the Primary Source, the Originary Book or Word. Here Griffith shows his reliance on Whitman, who had regarded his own *Leaves of Grass* as a new Holy Writ deriving from the Source of all things.

This drama of repression has yet another ghostly player, Browning's greatest poem, *The Ring and the Book,* which elaborates a very similar conception of the source. Relating how he took the poem's subject from an "old yellow book," Browning unexpectedly traces his poem back to the book of Genesis and insists on the existence of a Supreme Book capable of galvanizing all life-forms.[61] Griffith's *Intolerance* and Browning's poem have a great deal in common. The very title of Browning's poem *The Ring and the Book* seems amply suited to Griffith's film, with its closed ringlike construction and its constant reference to an Originary Book.

Miriam Hansen has shown how the film *Intolerance* is marked by the opposition between "allegory (hieroglyph)" and "the profane written text." Furthermore, the film's principal allegory, a kind of superhieroglyph, represents the figure of the mother (the source of life), and in the episode set in modern America the profane letter is associated with sterile old maids. Hansen convincingly shows how the hieroglyphic layer of the film serves as a constant commentary on the contemporary episode. Thus the three Fates spinning the thread of life in the background to the cradle correspond to the three ladies from Miss Jenkins's milieu who pursue the young mother, as well as the three hangmen carrying razors in the execution scene. Modern history thus constantly discovers allegorical analogies to itself through which it can hark back to the symbolic origins of the text.[62]

But the most significantly innovative aspect of *Intolerance* lies in what might be viewed as the unexpected qualitative leap it makes in transforming the specific procedures of source concealment into the structure of a new cinematic language. What had elsewhere been the suppression of a source on the level of plot here becomes its spatial distancing. We might recall the strange request made by Pausanias in Matthew Arnold's *Empedocles on Etna:* "Yet thou mayst try thy playing, if thou wilt, / But thou must keep unseen; follow us on, / But at a distance."[63] It is important for Griffith that his protagonists are all scattered, separated. In *Home, Sweet Home,* for example, visual contact is constantly replaced by hearing. People hear but cannot see each other.

Structurally speaking, this distancing becomes the motivation and precondition of the mechanism of successive or parallel montage for which Griffith's work is justly famous. In *Intolerance* the source is eliminated entirely from the film's diegesis. Both the allegorical book and the woman with the cradle are located outside the stories being narrated, allowing for their linkage to occur from within an extradiegetic space. It might even be said, in the final analysis, that the marked distancing of the source in *Intolerance* is what allows for the masterful montage of its layers scattered variously in space and time.

This long story of sources repeatedly repressed finally ends with the transformation of these repressed figures into the elements of a new cinematic language. It may well be that the history of art as a whole, based on the endless repression of one's precursors, aspires to this moment as an ideal. At a given moment the chain of repressions ends with a triumphant linguistic mutation, the appearance of new linguistic structures that allow the artist to crown himself with the wreath of the "strong" poet.

Griffith's work provides us with a unique source of material. The sheer quantity of his films and the frequent variations on the same plot, motif, or linguistic structure allow us practically to touch the hidden mechanisms of repeated quotation, as well as their semantic content.

We have come to believe that the repeated quotation of the same intertext does not merely create the "heraldic construction" with all its attendant semantic consequences. Each subsequent quote can serve to mask the preceding one, to conceal the paths taken by the movement of meaning. The repeated rewriting of a source can in some instances become the basis for understanding film history. This intertextual model of film history breaks with traditional conceptions of cinema's historical development in several ways. Traditional conceptions can be reduced to two dominant tendencies. The first can be called the theory of borrowings; the second posits the slow growth and ripening of film's constitutive elements out of a broader cultural soil. According to the first theory, film borrows structures that have evolved in other cultural spheres and adapts them to its own needs. According to the second, culture as a process itself slowly gravitates toward film, creating quasi-cinematic features within itself. This model of maturation in general betrays a teleological bias, since it posits cinema as a kind of prior given toward which culture must aspire. Both evolutionary models are in fact closely related and share common flaws: neither can explain why cinema chooses to address specific cultural phenomena, such as literature.

More specifically, neither model can provide a rationale for Griffith's use of Browning. The play, scarcely performable in its own right, cannot even be said to contain any specifically cinematic traits. Typically, the critics Giuliano and Keenan, while remaining within a traditional frame of analysis, are effectively forced to discover a hidden cinematic quality in the play, a "cinematism," to use Eisenstein's phrase.[64] This kind of approach finally leads to cinematic traits being found in any and all aspects of past culture that have fallen into the cinema's sphere of activity. Practically any detail can be dubbed cinematic (as analogous to large scenes), as can a discontinuous style (as analogous to montage), or its precise opposite, a demonstratively chronological construct (as analogous to the ribbon or a cinematic memory). As this kind of approach expands its sphere of application, the entire realm of culture retrospectively acquires a cinematic character. In the final analysis, the reasons for borrowing this or that stylistic feature become highly nebulous. It is hard to escape the conclusion that the cinema here performs the same role as Kafka in Borges's essay, converting entirely heterogeneous phenomena from previous historical epochs into its own precursors. But in the Borges essay it is Borges himself who takes on the task of seeking out Kafka's precursors, while according to the "maturation" theory this function devolves imperceptibly onto culture as a whole. What remains obscured here is the fact that this theory is itself the product of a subsequent reading of an entire past culture. In eliminating the reader, the theory is able to transform the result of reading into a functional mechanism of culture as a whole.

The other theory, based on the notion of influence, seems equally unproductive. It provides no real answers to the fundamental question of why influences are felt and how they function. Influence is seen as the mechanical transferral of some related elements from one receptacle to another. If we were simply to postulate Browning's influence on Griffith (or Griffith's debt to Browning), we would be circumventing the basic problems involved by opting for a kind of Neoplatonic model of art history. This model suggests a center from which all force emanates, a center that translates and transforms itself into its future. The primary question is thereby made irrelevant: the agency of those who inherit the past, here reduced to the role of its passive recipients. Whether later texts can have a transformative function is a question this theory cannot answer.

Influence theory cannot even be applied to derivative texts or to cases of open plagiarism (Bloom's "weak texts"), since the latter are also products of an authorial choice—a choice directly linked to the text being cited, and hence without any desire to be innovative or original. The same theory

is even less useful in dealing with "strong writers" who avoid openly acknowledging their intellectual debts.

"Strong works," as well as their authors, constituting the real fulcrum of
art historical evolution, establish their intertextual relations in an entirely
specific way. Their quotations are not just anomalies seeking normative
status. Rather, they both reveal and hide an evolutionary attitude to precursor texts. A quotation thus becomes a paradoxical means of asserting
one's originality. An obvious or acknowledged quote can refer to a text
that in fact serves to conceal a given work's real debt to its precursor,
thereby becoming a sign of originality. At the same time this process
"twists" the simple sense of continuity in art history. New and unexpected
"precursors of Kafka" can be created, distorting our reading of cultural history and thus shifting its course.

Intertextuality, then, works not only to establish precursors but also to
deny them, a denial essential for any text to become "strong." For this reason, the initial moment must always involve the positing of at least two precursor texts (cf. the intertext and the interpretant in chapter 1). The text
that impinges more heavily on its successor is repressed, becoming the object of aggression. The other text, less relevant insofar as its connection to
the artist is not profound, is promoted as the repressor of the first precursor text. The connection to the first text is masked by acknowledging the
connection to a second "unthreatening" text. *Pippa Passes* was chosen by
Griffith precisely because it was considered to be a play unsuited for the
stage and because it lacked any traces of what Eisenstein called "cinematism." The absence of "cinematism" here guarantees the absence of any
real link between Griffith and the text whose influence he acknowledged
as paramount.

It is in precisely this way that quite diverse texts, containing little if any
cinematic traits whatsoever, can be drawn into the cinema's sphere of activity. This process alone, by which structurally heterogeneous texts are
drawn into the strong artist's field of vision, constitutes the principal
mechanism for cinema's enrichment. The rapid growth of cinema is due
not to its capacity to assimilate whatever resembles it but to its ability to assimilate things that bear no similarity to it whatsoever.

At a later stage, however, these dissimilarities are retrospectively found
to possess filmlike qualities that were in fact acquired only during this
process of assimilation. In this way the entire culture of the past gradually
becomes "cinematic," producing the illusion that cinema has grown out of
the soil of an entire older culture. This illusion has become the ritual point
of departure for later attempts to explain the specificity of cinema.

In an article characteristically entitled "Visionary Cinema of Romantic
Poetry," Harold Bloom notes that "the burden of Romantic poetry is absolute freedom, including freedom from the tyranny of the bodily eye."

Bloom shows how the poetry of Blake, Wordsworth, and Shelley, predicated on a negation of visuality, began with the advent of cinema to be perceived in visual and even cinematic codes, undergoing a kind of subsequent "cinematization."[65] (For the sake of fairness, it should be noted that this "cinematizing" process began long before the emergence of film: in the nineteenth century, the poems of Milton and Wordsworth served as a constant source of inspiration for painters and artists.)

The assimilation of diverse sources leads to a change in the way misquotation functions at a subsequent stage. Now the intertext, which had served to conceal the initial borrowing, itself becomes a threat to the artist who had assimilated it in order to avoid appearing derivative. Here we have a further twist, involving the repression of this text as well (in our case *Pippa*), and yet another repressor text has to be drawn from a different sphere. So Griffith was to draw on music, an art form that would seem to be somewhat remote from the silent film. Yet this new moment of repression also contains a mechanism for the assimilation of music into the poetics of cinema, however alien it might be to the film medium.

The strongest repressive mechanisms do not operate just on the level of one signifying form but attract different forms of expression that form new layers in the cinematic structures that are newly emerging. The linear repression of a source takes place hand in hand with other intersemiotic shifts and recodings through which a new artistic idiom is forged.

This complex mechanism is generally made explicit as the search for a mythical Originary Source, Primary Language, or Originary Image: to reconnect with them is to eliminate the entire chain of intermediate precursors, granting access to an essential truth or reality. In this search for an Originary Source, the Book occupies a special place (it is hardly a coincidence that among all the repressive strategies deployed in Griffith's *Intolerance,* even those directed against language itself, the Book has pride of place as the supreme symbol of origination). The privileged place accorded to the Book is of course linked to an entire Judeo-Christian tradition, for which the Word is primary, and God the author of the One Book. The transformation of the Book into the "hypertext" of strong cinematic texts is also connected to the fact that the Book in Western culture embodies the "Text" as such with its typically teleological and narrative biases.

In addition, the cinema needs to refer to the Book as its source in order to legitimate its own textual status. A text acquires social authority only if it is produced by an author who enjoys a specific social and cultural credibility. The literary text has a particularly close link to the authorial instance. Unlike literature, a film produces photographic texts whose index of authorship is lower. Its credibility is based on the photographic self-evidence of what it shows. Yet this photographic self-evidence is not enough, within the framework of traditional cultural assumptions (above all in the early stages of film history), to secure cinema its legitimacy. It is precisely this that might explain, at least to some extent, why films generally acknowledge the book and writer that inspired them: both project onto the film the aura of additional legitimacy that written texts have enjoyed in our culture.

Where an author is repressed and replaced by the symbolic Book as such, this book functions as a kind of "impersonal cause" that dictates the film's narrative. This is exactly what happens in Griffith's *Intolerance,* as well as in practically all of Dreyer's films, where the symbolic Book is systematically invoked.[66] The photographic text, lacking any mechanism for producing relations of cause and effect, acquires narrative status by referring to a Book beyond its confines.

Cinema's deeply rooted need for a symbolic origin or source is far more profound than any analogous need felt by literature. After all, literature readily finds an originating source in the figure of the author, whose presence is far more muffled in cinema. Nonetheless, the obsessive presence in films of the theme of a primary source or cause serves to mythologize cinema as a system. The longing for an absolute beginning can be satisfied in culture only by myth, which organically thinks in terms of origination.

One cannot help noticing that this search for origins has been pursued at a time when culture as a whole is oriented toward constant innovation and the search for the unprecedented. As Mikhail Gasparov has observed, if up until the end of the eighteenth century European culture had been characterized by rereading (*perechteniia*), then romanticism and its wake inaugurated a culture of new readings (*pervochteniia*), along with a cult of originality.[67] Significantly, the earliest signs of the culture of new readings during the Renaissance were marked by a refusal to imitate the great masters and a reorientation toward nature as the true source.[68] Basil Willey has noted the unforeseen consequences of the disavowal of authority that took place in the seventeenth century: "In its effort to throw off authority, the seventeenth century discovered, in each sphere of interest, an Ancient still older than the Ancients; in theology, the Ancient of Days; in science, Nature herself; in ethics, and in literary theory, 'nature and reason.' "[69]

The desire for originality, for new readings, and the refusal of precursors and all authority figures universally go hand in hand with the discovery of origins, among which nature and reality figure predominantly. Realism, then, is readily framed by an ideology of novelty. From this flows the characteristic ambivalence attending every search for origins (this ambivalence is also evident in cinema—indeed, cinema may well be its fullest expression). On the one hand, this search pushes cinema into closer and closer contact with reality as the origin of everything, leading it to cultivate an ideology of realism. On the other hand, cinematic realism is constantly asserted on the basis of a myth, the myth of an absolute, the myth of origins. Cinematic realism is inseparable from cinematic mythology.

Equally significant is the fact that this obsessive search for reality, based as it is on the repression of intermediate sources, serves only to increase the number of assimilated and repressed texts, thus widening the gamut of intertextual relations. The essential paradox involved in this process is that while the artist is constantly affirming his desire to overcome the derivative nature of his text and enter into an unmediated contact with existence, this march toward realism must be made along an ever widening path of quotations, an increasingly complex intertextual chain involving the screen adaptation and subsequent mythologization of literary texts. Cinema seeks reality by increasing its textual links to culture. And it seems no other avenue is open to it.

CHAPTER THREE

Intertextuality and the Evolution of Cinematic Language

Griffith and the Poetic Tradition

In the preceding chapter I looked at ways in which certain parameters of film history might be examined in the light of a theory of intertextuality. In this chapter I will seek to throw light on some of the classical figures of cinematic language and their genesis.

The intertextual problematic can be legitimately projected onto the question of cinematic language and its genesis. The fact is that any new figure of cinematic language, from the moment it appears to the moment it becomes mechanical and is finally assimilated, is perceived as a textual anomaly and as such seeks clarification and normative status. It is not surprising, therefore, that the intertext is constantly invoked in order to normalize new figures of cinematic language. Strange as this assertion may sound, I would suggest that every new figure in cinematic language is essentially a quote that asks to be clarified through an intertext.

As proof of this, one could invoke Sergei Eisenstein's well-known essay "Dickens, Griffith and Film Today," which brilliantly demonstrates how Griffith's use of close-ups, as well as certain figures related to montage, can be clarified by referring to the works of Charles Dickens. In this way Eisenstein seems to elevate Griffith's linguistic innovations to the status of Dickens quotations. The Dickens intertext has provided Griffith's formal innovations with normative status. Eisenstein himself had based his search for the Dickens intertext on prior accounts, including a section from the memoirs of Griffith's wife, Linda Arvidson, who recalls a conversation her husband had had with some unknown person. In this conversation Griffith apparently defended his use of "cutbacks" in the film *After Many Years* by referring to Dickens: so fundamental did this acknowledgment seem to Eisenstein that he republished the piece in the Russian Griffith volume that he himself edited.[1] One can surmise that Arvidson's memoir is just a picturesque reworking of a comment made in Griffith's own article "What I Demand of Movie Stars" (1917), of which Eisenstein was probably unaware. Griffith had said, "I borrowed the 'cutback' from Charles Dickens."[2] Griffith was to make this declaration once more in 1922, which was then quoted in the English-language version of Eisenstein's article.[3] Whatever the circumstances surrounding Eisenstein's acquaintance with Griffith's sources, all this points to his obvious concern to ascertain documentary evidence in support of his own intertextual analysis.

Eisenstein's analysis has crucially influenced our own understanding of Griffith, with Dickens being promoted as practically the primary source of Griffith's inspiration. That Griffith was interested in Dickens is beyond question. Yet we have no reason to believe that Dickens occupies a unique place in the plethora of quotes to be found in Griffith's work. This privileging of Dickens, however, can certainly be seen as symptomatic. It is Dickens, who embodies the principles of narrative development in prose, whose adaptation for cinema has been ascribed to Griffith. Among Griffith's cultural precursors, Dickens has been necessarily singled out as the figure who best corresponds to current notions about Griffith's pioneering role in film.

The history of this recourse to Dickens merits our attention for more than one reason. The cutback, a device legitimized through the precedent of Dickens, had first been worked out in the film *After Many Years,* which is in fact an adaptation of the Tennyson poem *Enoch Arden,* to which Griffith would return repeatedly and with an astonishing insistence. The celebrated "cutback" was transposed directly onto the screen from this poem. In accordance with his broader strategy, however, Griffith repressed the immediate source for this montage device, allowing the all too willing Eisenstein to follow Linda's Arvidson's indications and ignore the Tennyson poem. It is possible that Tennyson held less appeal for Eisenstein as a possible precursor of Griffith. Dickens, as a writer central to the classical novelistic tradition, must have seemed more suited to this role.

The case of a quotation taken from one author being ascribed to another is quite indicative. It suggests that the resulting intertextualization has a tendency to gravitate toward the source that best corresponds to subsequent and established notions about how art evolves. The reader-interpreter is more apt to locate the source of a quote in an intertext that closely resembles the film being discussed and that most readily falls into the art historical narrative that is being reconstructed after the fact. In the previous chapter I attempted to show that the most openly declared borrowings are made from sources formally remote from the text being created. I also suggested that these openly declared quotations facilitate the assimilation of foreign texts within cinema as a system. Nevertheless, this subsequent assimilation is far from inevitable. Openly acknowledged borrowings may remain warehoused as part of cinema's unused reserve, only to fall out of subsequent accounts of film history. This reserve might be called "dead stock." Although highly productive at a certain stage, it is nonetheless subsequently ignored by historians as insignificant, ephemeral, to be rejected as not pertinent to our notions about art history. In later studies it is replaced by another intertext that is seen to be historically productive.

As examples of the dead stock of intertextuality in film, one could point to such genres as poetry and song. Although it is well known that many early Russian films were screen adaptations of popular songs, subsequent film history was to deny the song any role in the evolution of the poetics of cinema. The song as intertext was gradually eliminated from consciousness to become a typical case of dead stock.

Something similar happened to poetry. Cinema has evolved along a path dictated by narrative genres, to the point of being popularly perceived as analogous to the novel. As an evolutionary intertext the novel displaced poetry that, in turn, has become, like songs, a form of dead stock. Dickens has taken the place of Tennyson. An intertext's repression can happen, therefore, not only within an individual text but equally within the confines of an entire genre or form of art, within the framework of an architext. This chapter will deal precisely with how a forgotten or repressed "dead" intertext—in this case, poetry—can participate in "inventing" and normalizing new linguistic structures. We will be dealing with certain forms of intertextuality that have had an active role in the genesis of cinematic language.

To begin with, it is worth recalling that in his youth Griffith had dreamed of becoming a poet. His idols had been Browning, Edgar Allan Poe, and Walt Whitman, who inspired him to write a vast quantity of imitative verse.[4] Apparently, Griffith had identified directly with Poe, seeking to imitate him even in external details, and early on had perceived his own fate as a repetition of Poe's literary career. In his memoirs Griffith describes his own participation in a theater group in the following way: "We had one fellow in our company who was poetically inclined. . . . his face resembled that of Edgar Allan Poe. He had been told this latter fact so often that he now dressed the part and recited poetry by the yard. He was forever quoting homemade rhymes that got him nothing but the Bronx cheer from the boys but made quite a hit with the ladies."[5] In 1909, Griffith made the film *Edgar Allan Poe,* an account—with a clearly autobiographical subtext—of the poet's relations with various publishers who refused to print his work.

Griffith himself succeeded in publishing only one of his poems, "The Wild Duck" (in *Leslie's Weekly,* January 10, 1907), and this is practically all we know of his poetic efforts. The publication of this single poem was of immense significance to Griffith, who later would recall, "I scanned the table of contents . . . but the only thing I could see was 'The Wild Duck.' There it was, as big as an elephant and utterly dwarfing everything else in the list of contents. And there, in type, flaming at me in letters of fire, was my name. My very own name—DAVID WARK GRIFFITH." The letters of fire, which refer to Daniel's prophecy and to the Babylonian theme in *Intolerance,* serve as a kind of presentiment of Griffith's future cinematic "poem." The importance that attaches to Griffith's "real name" is connected to the pseudonym Lawrence Griffith, which the director had adopted in the theater and during his earlier years in the film industry. The pseudonym served to deflect the theatrical career of the future director onto someone else's life, reserving his real name for his literary output. On marrying Linda Arvidson, Griffith, then still an actor, characteristically noted "writing" as his occupation in the church registry, thus disavowing his actor's persona as false.[6]

Even after acquiring a solid reputation in film, Griffith never abandoned his hope of returning to literature. After the success of the adaptation of Browning's *Pippa Passes* (1909), a film that had symbolized for its maker the inextricable bond linking his films to poetry, Griffith organized a dinner party in the hope of reviving his literary career, to which he invited several literati, including Sleicher, publisher of "The Wild Duck." Linda Arvidson recalls what Griffith said to Sleicher during the dinner party: "'They [the motion picture studios] can't last. I give them a few years. Where's my play? Since I went into these movies I haven't had a minute to look at a thing I ever wrote. And I went into them because I thought surely I'd get time to write or do something with what I had. . . . Well, anyhow, nobody's going to know I ever did this sort of thing when I'm a famous playwright. Nobody's ever going to know that David W. Griffith, the playwright, was once Lawrence Griffith of the movies.'"[7]

Thus even at the height of his success at Biograph, Griffith saw literature alone as affording prestige and possessing cultural value, a value that in his mind eclipsed not only his theatrical past but also his present work in cinema. In this light his orientation toward literature, and specifically poetry, even in his earliest films, is readily understood. Griffith wanted to effect a kind of illusory metamorphosis, transforming his films into works made in some other artistic medium. One might surmise that Griffith's symbolic renunciation of his pseudonym amounted to a positive reassessment of his work. To some extent, the cinema would indeed become for Griffith the equivalent of poetry. His recourse to the high literary canon would become a significant means of overcoming a deeply held sense of cultural inferiority. Griffith would note with some pride: " 'In succession we made *Macbeth, Don Quixote,* Poe's *The Tell-Tale Heart,* Kingsley's *Sands of*

Dee. We even had poetry in the screen titles. We also produced *Blot on the Escutcheon* and *Pippa Passes* from the difficult Robert Browning.' "[8]

After the release of *Intolerance*, Griffith's period of reevaluation was complete. Nothing now remained of the director's longing to be a playwright. In 1917, he declared cinema to be a new stage in the development of poetry and hence essentially its equivalent: "Already it is admitted that as to poetic beauty the Motion Picture entertainment is far ahead of the stage play. Poetry is apparently a lost art in the regular theater, but it is the very life and essence of the motion playhouse. We have staged most of Browning's stories, many of Tennyson's innumerable Biblical and classical fables. Not only beauty but thought is our goal, for the silent drama is peculiarly the birthplace of ideas."[9] Such a declaration betrays Griffith's deeply held conviction that in film he had succeeded in finding both an aesthetic and an intellectual equivalent to literary language. In the 1921 article "Cinema: Miracle of Modern Photography," he quotes a letter whose views he shares completely: "From now on we shall have to divide History into four great epochs: the Stone Age, the Bronze Age, the Age of the Printing Press, and the Age of Cinema."[10] Griffith thus came to understand the cinema as a new progressive stage in the development of culture. The argument Griffith provides to buttress his position merits our attention:

> A certain scholar tells us that in viewing a film we perform the easiest of all possible actions at least with respect to the intellectual reactions provoked by the presence of the outside world. The cinematic eye is the most primitive eye that exists. One might almost say that the cinema was born from the slime of the earliest oceans. To view a film is to return to a primitive state. . . . Images were the first means deployed by humans to transcribe their thoughts. We find these primitive thoughts engraved in stone, on the walls of grottos or on the sides of high cliffs. It is as easy for a Finn as for a Turk to grasp the image of a horse. An image is a universal symbol, and a moving image is a universal language. Someone has said that cinema "might solve the problem posed by the Tower of Babel."[11]

Such an "ideology" of cinema, linking the "extralinguistic" status of film to the thought processes of prehistoric man, is well known to us from Eisenstein's work of the thirties. Yet in Griffith this ideology comes out of a context quite different from Eisenstein's. In the preceding passage he merely adopts certain romantic ideas that were popular particularly among poets, including the nineteenth-century poets Griffith himself cherished. Griffith thus represses poetry with the help of an ideology derived from poetry itself. It is not a coincidence that Griffith's crucial statement about the cinema and the Tower of Babel (which he ascribes to someone else!) can be readily traced back to Whitman's "Song of the

Universal," a poem filled with similar declarations, which Whitman himself had intended to resonate in opposition "to the mad Babel-din."[12]

Insofar as the idea of film as a universal language has an older history than cinema itself, it may be worth making a brief digression to retrieve its genealogy. In America such notions were projected onto poetry during the first half of the nineteenth century by the so-called transcendentalists—Ralph Waldo Emerson, Amos Bronson Alcott, Theodore Parker, Elizabeth Peabody, and others. The roots of transcendentalism lie in the religious movement of the Unitarians. A definitive influence on the formation of Unitarian doctrine was the figure of John Locke, who had argued in favor of the arbitrariness of the linguistic sign.[13] For Locke, our human knowledge of the world derives from experience, while language, as the product of a social contract, cannot be considered a source of knowledge. Locke's theory of language posed serious problems in the field of biblical exegesis and led, at least within Unitarian thinking, to the loss of belief in the sacred texts as the source of some higher knowledge of the world.[14] Where the Bible as text had once stood, the transcendentalists now posited the existence of a universe or nature which they interpreted as a text written directly by God in the unmediated language of nature's metaphors.

This notion of nature as a kind of primordial book can hardly be thought of as unique to the transcendentalists—it belongs to a venerable tradition going back to Plato's *Cratylus*.[15] According to the transcendentalists, the text of nature could be understood by applying Swedenborg's theory of correspondences. For Swedenborg, between divine or spiritual reality and the material world there exists an intimate connection—a *correspondence*. God created the book of nature—the world of matter—on the basis of pure correspondences that are waiting to be uncovered. The path of knowledge for the transcendentalists involved a search for correspondences between the spiritual and the material, which could reveal the symbolism of nature, its "natural metaphors." In the United States the idea of nature as a language was probably first formulated by the Swedenborgian Sampson Reed in his work *Observations on the Growth of the Mind* (1826):

> There is a language, not of words, but of things. When this language shall have been made apparent, that which is human will have answered its end; and being as it were resolved into its original elements, will lose itself in nature. The use of language is the expression of our feelings and desires—the manifestation of the mind. But every thing which is, whether animal or vegetable, is full of the expression of that use for which it is designed, as of its own existence. If we did but understand its language, what could our words add to its meaning?[16]

Reed had a profound impact on Emerson, who was to deploy the ideas of Swedenborg and Reed in his celebrated essay "Nature" (1836), where the notion of an "Adamic" language of pure poetry is elaborated:

> Because of this radical correspondence between visible things and human thoughts, savages, who have only what is necessary, converse in figures. As we go back in history, language becomes more picturesque, until its infancy, when it is all poetry; or all spiritual facts are represented by natural symbols. The same symbols are found to make the original elements of all languages. It has moreover been observed, that the idioms of all languages approach each other in passages of the greatest eloquence and power. And as this is the first language, so is it the last.[17]

Griffith naturally knew Emerson. At the time he was making *Birth of a Nation,* Griffith once mentioned Emerson as one of the greatest figures in world culture, alongside Shakespeare and Goethe (the importance of Goethe for the transcendentalists, and Emerson in particular, should be noted). Griffith's conception of the evolution of culture, from a protolanguage to the universal language of cinema that is in fact nothing more than the original protolanguage revived, doubtless goes back to Emerson. Yet well before Griffith, Whitman had already made this idea fully his own. The great goal of his *Leaves of Grass* was an Adamic "poem of the world." The Bible itself was outshone by a new "writing of nature," which the poet had re-created not on sheets of paper but on leaves of grass from the Garden of Eden. The poetry of Whitman is a direct reworking of Emerson's theories. For instance, Whitman's endless lists of things can be understood as the Adamic feat of *nominatio rerum.* According to Emerson, "The poet is the Namer or Language-maker, naming things sometimes after their appearance, sometimes after their essence. . . . The etymologist finds the deadest word to have been once a brilliant picture. Language is fossil poetry. . . . This expression or naming is not art, but a second nature, grown out of the first, as a leaf out of a tree."[18] The leaf for Emerson resembles a letter from the primordial alphabet of nature. (Significantly, Emerson borrowed this idea from Goethe's *Die Metamorphose der Pflanzen* [1790]).[19]

For Emerson and Whitman the resurrection of an Adamic language was also the visible coming together of word and thing, so that the whole world became a collection of words that could be seen and touched, a dictionary of symbols: "Bare lists of words are found suggestive to an imaginative and excited mind. . . . We are symbols and inhabit symbols: workmen, work and tools, words and things, birth and death, all are emblems."[20] Griffith fully shared the transcendentalists' view of nature as a huge lexicon of words and symbols. The world was filled with words, he said, recalling his literary efforts: a dictionary alone contained thousands.[21] Elsewhere he wrote, repeating Emerson and Whitman: "In our drama the trees bend in the breeze and blades of grass gleaming with real dew are significant enough to participate in the action. An attentive director, you see, has the world for his studio."[22]

Emerson's wish to "fasten words again to visible things"[23] acquired a particular significance in the context of cinema, which for Griffith became a means of realizing the cherished utopia of the transcendentalists—to create a visual poem of the universe. From this arose a decisive equation of language and visual representation: "I think that everyone would agree that cinema can be seen as a mode of expression that is at least equal to the spoken or written word."[24] It is curious to note that Emerson had equated poetry with a magic lantern show (a comparison that would have arisen naturally in a precinematic era): "The poet turns the world to glass, and shows us all things in their right series and progression."[25]

The transformation of cinema into a metaphor for a poetry of the future also might have found some justification in Emerson's polemic with Swedenborg. Emerson had criticized Swedenborg's compilation of a "dictionary" of strict correspondences, according to which a tree, for example, signified perception and the moon stood for faith: "The slippery Proteus is not so easily caught. In nature, each individual symbol plays innumerable parts, as each particle of matter circulates in turn through every system. The central identity enables any one symbol to express successively all the qualities and shades of real being. In the transmission of the heavenly waters, every hose fits every hydrant. Nature avenges herself speedily on the hard pedantry that would chain her waves."[26] Elsewhere Emerson added: "Here is the difference betwixt the poet and the mystic, that the last nails a symbol to one sense, which was a true sense for a moment, but soon becomes odd and false. For all symbols are fluxional; all language is vehicular and transitive."[27] In opposition to Swedenborg's static, immobile sign Emerson posited the flux of life and the notion of meaning as perpetually "becoming." Hence Emerson's privileging of metaphors involving the movement of water. In Emerson's essay "Art" (1841) the dynamics of life are presented in opposition to the stasis of painting and sculpture precisely in the context of fluid, metamorphosing correspondences. As against the painted canvas, Emerson envisions "the eternal picture which nature paints in the street, with moving men and children, beggars and fine ladies, draped in red and green and blue and gray; long-haired, grizzled, white-faced, black-faced, wrinkled, giant, dwarf, expanded, elfish,— capped and based by heaven, earth, and sea."[28] One year before the publication of Emerson's piece, the image of the living canvas created by passersby made an appearance in Poe's story "The Man of the Crowd," in which the narrator attempts to establish the connection between a fleeting chain of images and the hidden meaning of existence (i.e., he interprets an analogous vision according to the theory of dynamic correspondences): "The wild effects of the light enchained me to an examination of individual faces; and although the rapidity with which the world of light flitted before me prevented me from casting more than a glance upon each visage, still it seemed that, in my then peculiar mental state, I could frequently read, even in that brief interval of a glance, the history of long years."[29]

The invention of film would allow people to reinterpret these statements by Emerson and Poe as prophetic visions of an art to come. The first American efforts to produce a theory of the cinema were clearly allied to these earlier "prophecies." In 1915, Henry MacMahon was among the first to expound the principles of what was a kind of "transcendentalist" poetics of cinema. MacMahon called the cinema a "sign language" that he took to be "iconic," and he asserted, quite in the spirit of the transcendentalists, that film was a "symbolic art": "Every little series of pictures, continuing from four to fifteen seconds, symbolizes a sentiment, a passion, or an emotion." MacMahon also recommended that these symbols be endowed with speed of movement, pointing out that "the position of the motion-picture spectator is that of one who looks out of doors from an open window upon the whole of Life spread as on a panorama, seeing swiftly, understanding swiftly."[30] Characteristically, MacMahon based his theorization on the example of Griffith's films.

Even more indicative in this sense is the American poet Vachel Lindsay's book *The Art of the Moving Picture* (1915), another "transcendentalist" poetics of cinema that was also the first fundamental attempt at a theory of the cinema. Lindsay knew Griffith and based his theories on Griffith's work. One chapter of Lindsay's book is called "The Picture of Crowd Splendor." For Emerson, the moving crowd had been a transposition onto everyday life of the transcendentalist symbol of flowing water, the ever-changing river or sea. Lindsay developed the Emersonian metaphor (which was Whitman's too) as follows: "The shoddiest silent drama may contain noble views of the sea. This part is almost sure to be good. It is a fundamental resource. A special development of this aptitude in the hands of an expert gives the sea of humanity. . . . Only Griffith and his close disciples can do these as well as almost any manager can reproduce the ocean. Yet the sea of humanity is dramatically blood-brother to the Pacific, Atlantic or Mediterranean."[31] We shall have occasion to return to this metaphor and see how it is further elaborated by Griffith himself.

Lindsay's debt to Emerson amounts to an almost word-for-word transposition. Emerson, for example, had introduced the opposition of sculpture and "man in motion": "There is no statue like this living man, with his infinite advantage over all ideal sculpture."[32] Lindsay too wrote a chapter entitled "Sculpture-in-Motion," in which he gave an elaborate characterization of the motion picture through the prism of Emerson's dynamism.

In the same year, 1915, Griffith would take up Emerson's metaphor made current by Lindsay to declare that "the most beautiful statue ever sculpted is no more than a caricature of real life when compared to the shifting shadows of a film."[33] This negative myth of sculpture would in part be worked out in the Babylonian episode of *Intolerance*.

Another major theoretician of early cinema, the Harvard psychologist Hugo Münsterberg, also had close links to Griffith.[34] According to Lindsay, Griffith had devised *Intolerance* to illustrate certain of Münsterberg's theoretical principles.[35] Münsterberg had been invited to Harvard by William James, whose father had been well known for his prominent role in the Swedenborgian church in America. James himself made use of Swedenborg's metaphor of the cyclic movement of water in working out his psychological concept of "stream of thought," which closely resembles Emerson's metaphors of water and the circle.[36]

That Emerson also influenced Münsterberg is beyond question. From Emerson's perspective, the "dynamic symbol" in a work of art undergoes a kind of isolation to which he attributed the greatest importance: "The virtue of art lies in detachment, in sequestering one object from the embarrassing variety. Until one thing comes out from the connection of things, there can be enjoyment, contemplation, but no thought. . . . The infant lies in a pleasing trance, but his individual character and his practical power depend on his daily progress in the separation of things, and dealing with one at a time. Love and all the passions concentrate all existence around a single form."[37] Münsterberg saw in the isolation of a close-up an analogue to the psychological process of isolating objects through concentrated attention. He was to attribute a primary aesthetic significance to this psychological capacity to isolate an object: "The work of art shows us the things and events perfectly complete in themselves, freed from all connections which lead beyond their own limits, that is, in perfect isolation."[38] Moreover, Münsterberg also attached an enormous significance to movement: "The events are seen in continuous movement; and yet the pictures break up the movement into a rapid succession of instantaneous impressions. We do not see the objective reality, but a product of our own mind which binds the picture together."[39] The stream of moving images on the screen mimics the stream of thought in James and Swedenborg. But for the mimicry to succeed, all representations must be preliminarily isolated from any links that bind them to objective reality. In his book on film, Münsterberg consistently elaborates a psychological theory of the symbol. This theory, directly connected to transcendentalist aesthetics, principally stresses the dynamism of the symbol and its correspondences.

It is hardly fortuitous that Lindsay, whose deeply held commitment to Swedenborg had been formed during his years in the Swedenborgian circle in Springfield, held Münsterberg's theory in great esteem and was happy to echo its general position: "I am delighted to have so much common ground with Münsterberg," he wrote to Jane Addams on October 15, 1916.[40] For Lindsay, it was indisputably true that Griffith's films *Judith of Bethulia, The Avenging Conscience,* and *Intolerance* on the one hand served as models of "good Epic poetry" and on the other "confirm[ed] some of the speculations of Münsterberg's *Photoplay: A Psychological Study,* his last book."[41]

. . .

Griffith, of course, was well aware of these early attempts at theoretical synthesis. Lindsay tells us that Griffith had specifically invited him to the premiere of *Intolerance* in addition to buying a hundred copies of Lindsay's book to hand out to his studio employees as a working manual.[42] While making *Intolerance,* Griffith had quite consciously made use of the works of Münsterberg and Lindsay (including Lindsay's theory of the hieroglyph). Nonetheless, Griffith's first efforts at applying the poetics of transcendentalism to film in fact precede the appearance of these works. Indeed, I would suggest that it was precisely these early efforts on Griffith's part that served to draw the attention of theoreticians toward the cinema. The most significant experiments that Griffith was to make in this area involved the screen adaptation of a series of lyric poems on the sea. Among these works, made during Griffith's years at Biograph, are three versions of the Tennyson poem *Enoch Arden: After Many Years* (1908), *The Unchanging Sea* (1910), and *Enoch Arden* (1911). Mention might be made of a fourth version, entitled *Enoch Arden* (1915) but rereleased as *Calamitous Elopement,* and directed by Christy Cabanne under Griffith's supervision.

Enoch Arden provided the vehicle through which Griffith was first able to realize the device of parallel montage. Griffith had already applied the principal element of this montage, the cutback, in 1908, then barely five months into his directing career (in the film *After Many Years*). It was this feature that Griffith would later justify by invoking Dickens.

The Tennyson poem recounts the fate of a shipwrecked sailor. His wife, Annie Lee, awaits her husband for many years by the seashore. Richard Schickel has commented on Griffith's adaptation as follows: "The film lacked a chase, in itself a considerable novelty, and indeed it contained very little action of any sort. Moreover, he risked a pair of parallel shots: Annie Lee at the seaside, visualizing her shipwrecked husband on his desert isle (how she knew he was on an island was never explained); Enoch on that barren strand, visualizing the long-gone comforts of home."[43]

These "risky parallel shots" involve the unexpected sequencing of Annie Lee by the seashore and Enoch Arden stranded on a faraway island. We are dealing here with a conscious linguistic anomaly that brings together camera shots that are spatially at some remove from each other.[44] This anomaly nonetheless finds a convincing motivation in Tennyson himself, whose poem contains the "visionary" scenes that interested Griffith. The Tennyson poem functions as an intertext motivating the linguistic innovations of the film and thereby removing the reasons for Schickel's perplexity. It is important to note that a full explanation of the film's linguistic obscurity is provided by the literary source alone: the film itself fails to do so and remains, at least in this episode, somewhat unclear.

In the Tennyson poem Annie Lee receives a vision while trying to tell her fortune with the aid of the Bible, just as her hand touches the line that reads "under a palm-tree." Thus, in Tennyson, the vision is motivated by a book, the Holy Writ (cf. the scene from Griffith's *Home, Sweet Home,* discussed in chapter 2, in which the Bible stimulates Payne to see a vision). Tearing herself away from the Bible, Annie Lee suddenly sees "her Enoch sitting on a height, / Under a palm-tree, over him the Sun."[45] The vision is then disturbed by the sound of wedding bells that gradually draws her back to reality.

Enoch's vision is given in a more discursive form. On the seashore he hears the constant roar of the waves and the wind rustling in the foliage. Gradually the sea's dazzling gleam induces a kind of hypnotic effect:

> The blaze upon the waters to the east;
> The blaze upon his island overhead;
> The blaze upon the waters to the west;
> Then the great stars that globed themselves in Heaven,
> The hollower-bellowing ocean, and again
> The scarlet shafts of sunrise—but no sail.
> There often as he watched or seemed to watch,
> So still, the golden lizard on him paused,
> A phantom made of many phantoms moved
> Before him haunting him, or he himself
> Moved haunting people, things and places, known
> Far in a darker isle beyond the line;
> The babes, their babble, Annie, the small house,
> ....
> And the low moan of the leaden-coloured seas.
>
> Once likewise, in the ringing of his ears,
> Though faintly, merrily—far and far away—
> He heard the pealing of his parish bells . . . [46]

Tennyson's poem motivates Enoch's vision by making it the physiological effect of a prolonged contemplation of the sea's immobile surface. The sea becomes a mirror revealing visionary sights, a role that corresponds readily to its acknowledged hypnotic effects.[47] Curiously, in all these versions of *Enoch Arden*, Griffith places Annie Lee by the seashore just before her vision, eliminating Tennyson's scene of fortune-telling by the Bible. Her vision is instead shown to be the result of a concentrated contemplation of the sea.

This episode from Tennyson was of particular importance to Griffith, perhaps because the sea is a motif central to the romantic poets whom the Swedenborgians particularly cherished. Still earlier Winckelmann had written of a poet who "lies on the shore of a sea, in which ideas and feelings at times undulate here or there, and at times come to rest upon its mirror surface."[48] In the Anglophone world, the persistent conjunction of the sea with visionary motifs goes back to Coleridge and particularly to Thomas De Quincey, whose *Confessions of an English Opium Eater* became the chief source for an entire mythology of visions, dreams, and reveries assimilated by romanticism.

De Quincey describes the insistent presence of water in his hallucinations: "The waters gradually changed their character—from translucent lakes, shining like mirrors, they became seas and oceans." He then describes how the face of his lost beloved Ann (cf. Annie Lee) appears through a vision of the sea: "Now it was that upon the rocking waters of the ocean the human face began to reveal itself; the sea appeared paved with innumerable faces, upturned to the heavens."[49]

Charles Baudelaire wrote a detailed commentary on De Quincey, at one point pausing specifically to note the hallucinatory power of water: "Water then was the focus of an obsession. We have already remarked, in our study of hashish, the mind's amazing predilection for the liquid element and its mysterious seductions. Have we not reported a unique relationship between the two stimulants, at least in their effects upon the imagination."[50] Baudelaire directly links the effect of narcotic and "aqueous" visions to Swedenborg's theory of correspondences, and points out that visions alone have the power to realize the sought-for fusion of word and thing: "And grammar, even arid grammar, is then endowed with the evocative power of sorcery; words are reborn, clothed in flesh and blood. . . . And music, that other language so cherished by idlers, or by those intellectuals who seek from it a repose amid their varied toil, unfolds the capabilities of your intellect and recites for you the poem of your life; it enters within you, and you mingle with it."[51]

In America the transcendentalist symbol of the sea was elaborated in the poem "The Ocean" by Christopher Pearce Cranch (1813–1892). Cranch describes "Spirits bathing in the sea of Deity" and contemplating the waters as "Symbols of the Infinite."[52] Also present here is the image of the sea as the cradle and grave of humankind, an image later elaborated by Whitman. At the same time as Cranch, the notion of water as the primary locus of correspondences was developed by one of the leading transcendentalists, Henry David Thoreau, who in *Walden* describes water as a mirror that reflects the air: "It is continually receiving new life and motion from above. It is intermediate in its nature between land and sky."[53] Swedenborg's idea of worlds being duplicated, with the sky reflected in the world below, is centered on the motif of water. More than once Thoreau speaks of dissolving in the ocean; he writes of walks on the shore of the "resounding sea, determined to get it into us. We wished to associate with the ocean."[54] For Thoreau, "the seashore is a sort of neutral ground, a most advantageous point from which to contemplate this world."[55] In reflecting the sky, the sea creates an infinite perspective and becomes the ideal place of entry into the transcendental world. It is offered to humans as a "window" to divine visions.[56]

Yet it was Whitman, Griffith's favorite poet, who made the motif of the sea essential to his work. In his recollections Whitman formulated his relation to the sea as follows. "Even as a boy, I had the fancy, the wish, to write a piece, perhaps a poem, about the sea-shore—that suggesting, dividing line, contact, junction, the solid marrying the liquid—that curious, lurking something, (as doubtless every objective form finally becomes to the subjective spirit,) which means far more than its mere first sight, grand as that is—blending the real and ideal, and each made portion of the other."[57] Whitman spoke of his poetic mission as the project of creating "a book expressing this liquid, mystic theme."[58] *Leaves of Grass* was in many ways to be such a book. Roger Asselineau considers *Leaves of Grass* to be an apotheosis of water, where "life is an irresistible current which circulates through all things."[59] The leading scholar of American romanticism, F. O. Matthiessen, rightly points to the fact that the sea became for Whitman a metaphor for poetry, with the rhythm of the waves imitating the cadences of verse: "Its verses are the liquid, billowy waves, . . . hardly any two exactly alike in size or measure (metre), never having the sense of something finished and fixed, always suggesting something beyond."[60]

For our purposes this identification of the sea with poetry is crucial, but perhaps no less significant is the motif, constant in Whitman and among the Swedenborgians, of a heavenly mirror as the site where many images are combined and reflected. Also significant is the idea of the shoreline as the place of "division, contact and unification." In Whitman's poem "On the Beach at Night Alone" we read:

> On the beach at night alone,
> As the old mother sways her to and fro, singing her husky song,
> ....
> A vast SIMILITUDE interlocks all,
> All spheres, grown, ungrown, small, large, suns, moons, planets, comets,
>   asteroids,
> All the substances of the same, and all that is spiritual upon the same,

All distances of place, however wide,
All distances of time—all inanimate forms,
All Souls—all living bodies, though they be ever so different, or in different
    worlds,
All gaseous, watery, vegetable, mineral processes—the fishes, the brutes,
All men and women—me also;
All nations, colors, barbarisms, civilizations, languages;
All identities that have existed, or may exist, on this globe, or any globe;
All lives and deaths—all of the past, present, future;
This vast similitude spans them . . .[61]

In *Suspiria De Profundis* De Quincey recalls a woman who in her child-hood fell into a river and sunk to the riverbed. This immersion in water had a strange effect on her: "Immediately a mighty theater expanded within her brain. In a moment, in the twinkling of an eye, every act, every design of her past life, lived again, arraying themselves not as a succession, but as parts of a coexistence. . . . Her consciousness became omnipresent at one moment to every feature in the infinite review."[62] Contact with water thus provokes a shift from a consecutive chain to a corresponding but si-multaneous picture, that is, it carries latent within itself the elements of a parallel montage.

There exists one other literary text that in its own way elaborates the scenario we have seen in *Enoch Arden,* reflecting equally the ambiguous character of Griffith's montage. This is Villiers de l'Isle-Adam's story "Claire Lenoir" (1887). Here the dying Claire Lenoir dreams of her de-ceased husband on the shore of a tropical island in the middle of the ocean (the experience of separation is thus here pushed to the point of ir-reversibility). "He was standing, alone, among the deserted rocks, looking afar, at the sea, as if expecting someone."[63] After Lenoir's death, the story's hero, Tribulat Bonhomet, studies the retina of her eyes and uncovers the clear contours of a picture (or cinematic?) frame containing the startling image of a solitary man by the seashore. The astonished Bonhomet comes to the following conclusion: "The VISION had *really* to be outside, to some imponderable degree, *in a living fluid perhaps,* in order to be refracted the way it did on your clairvoyant pupils."[64]

In Villiers's story a vision has the power to materialize itself when it is seen by the eyes of a visionary, practically assuming the form of a photo-graphic imprint. The vision has the capacity to bring together spaces that are absolutely heterogeneous. It is worth emphasizing, however, that the shoreline also functions here as an essential border between distinct worlds, becoming a persistent attribute of such visions. The sea as medium of the universal connectedness of things and creator of a universal lan-guage—a motif common enough in romantic poetry and philosophy—creates an intertext that throws adequate light on the meaning of one of

Griffith's montage figures. The shoreline in *Enoch Arden* becomes for Annie Lee the line of contact with and separation from her husband, serving as the junction line connecting two images in a montage.

In Whitman's "Out of the Cradle Endlessly Rocking," the image of the sea is superimposed onto a singing bird, which creates a kind of double register. Whitman exclaims: "Never more shall I escape, never more the reverberations, / Never more the cries of unsatisfied love be absent from me."[65]

Christopher Collins has called Whitman's poetic method one of "resonating correspondence" and derives the production of sound in Whitman's poetry from the effect of a double echo.[66] Curiously, in the Tennyson poems quoted earlier, both visions are accompanied by the chiming of bells, and in one case by the noise of the sea superimposed onto the sound of the bells. The vision in *Enoch Arden* seems to be produced by this "corresponding reverberation." Another writer who attributed a special significance to echoes within a theory of correspondences was Thoreau. In De Quincey the echo unfailingly stimulates visions. It appears to him as the sonorous equivalent to the hallucinations he sees mirrored on the sea's surface, when certain lines and contours emerge through the cluster of reflections, creating a kind of palimpsest, made visible through the limpid mass of water. In the vision of the dead woman expounded in the essay "Vision of Sudden Death" De Quincey elaborates the motif of bells and speaks of "funeral bells from the desert seas" and of "echoes of fugitive laughter, mixing with the ravings and choir-voices of the angry sea" as they descend from the heavens to the rippling surface of the sea.[67] In the chapter "The Palimpsest of the Human Brain" from *Suspiria De Profundis,* De Quincey again writes of "the echoes of fugitive laughter, mixing with the ravings and choir-voices of an angry sea."[68]

The generation of visions from the reverberations of the sea is characteristic of the romantic literature oriented toward Swedenborg even outside Anglo-American culture. In Balzac's work, which had been strongly influenced by Swedenborg, we find the story "L'Enfant maudit" whose hero, Étienne, establishes a unique form of contact with the sea: "The sea and the sky recounted admirable poems to him. . . . He had finally ended by divining in all these movements of the sea his intimate link with the wheels of a heavenly mechanism, and he saw nature in its harmonious entirety."[69] As a result, the contemplation of the ocean makes Étienne privy to a kind of superhuman knowledge, and he is able to see an image of his mother in the clouds above the sea: "He spoke to her, and they truly communicated through heavenly visions; on certain days, he heard her voice, he admired her smile, and there were finally some days when he had not lost her at all!"[70]

Something quite analogous can be found in Griffith. The famous cutback in *After Many Years,* a moment of great importance for Griffith, can be understood as being the first attempt at creating a cinematic analogy to the transcendentalist poetic text. More specifically, it is also the first bold attempt at a visual reconstruction of an Adamic language on the basis of correspondences at sea—the language of superior vision and knowledge, potentially the universal language of all humanity.

From 1910 Griffith began to travel regularly to the Pacific Coast in southern California (the future site of Hollywood), and the sea became a constant feature of his films. In California, adaptations of "maritime poetry" became more common and more fashionable over time. As early as 1912, outside Biograph, there were two film versions of de la Motte Fouquet's *Undine* and one of Sir Walter Scott's *Lady of the Lake;* in 1913, Heine's *Lorelei* was made into a film, and so on right through to the beginning of the 1920s, when Kingsley's *Unchanging Sea* was filmed in 1921, many years after Griffith's own version of the same text. These poetic "seascapes" became the medium of a new film language, and Griffith's films played a special role in its making.

Let us now look at one of the most significant films from Griffith's own series of films set at sea, *The Sands of Dee* (1912), an adaptation of an eponymous poem by Charles Kingsley. Griffith turned to Kingsley twice for inspiration: first in 1910, when he adapted the poem "The Three Fishers" under the title *The Unchanging Sea,* and second in 1912. Both adaptations deploy the theme of the sea in a similar way, with plots that converge around some kind of catastrophe at sea.

The first and last stanzas of "The Sands of Dee" read as follows:

O Mary, go and call the cattle home,
  And call the cattle home,
  And call the cattle home
Across the sands of Dee;
The western wind was wild and dank with foam,
And all alone went she.
. . . .
They rolled her in across the rolling foam,
  The cruel crawling foam,
  The cruel hungry foam,
  To her grave beside the sea:
But still the boatmen hear her call the cattle home
  Across the sands of Dee.[71]

Griffith's film involves sixty-five montage shots and an uncomplicated melodramatic plot. The girl Mary has an admirer named Bobby but is seduced by a visiting artist. After she marries the artist, it is revealed that he has another wife. Expelled from her family home by her father, Mary wanders onto a deserted shore and commits suicide. Bobby discovers her body, buffeted by waves. In the film's last frame, Mary's ghostly silhouette appears on the sea's horizon.

The film's plot displays a considerable autonomy with respect to the poem. Its development is marked by repeated interruptions in the form of intertitles quoting the Kingsley poem, so that the plot intrigue emerges as a kind of narrative link between several key insertions of poetic text. The film begins with an intertitle asking Mary to "go and call the cattle home" across the sands of Dee. In this line we find embedded a loose anagram of the word *echo:* "And *ca*ll th*e ca*ttle h*o*me." Here not only is the word "echo" approximated twice, but the very superimposition of repetitive patterns is itself imitated. The tone of the film is thus set at the very beginning by a "resonant reverberation." It is no coincidence that this sound element, which gets oddly visualized at the end of the film, is connected to the River Dee. During high tide, the River Dee would suddenly turn back on its course and rise up with an infernal roar and terrifying speed. Here is a typical quote from De Quincey's *Confessions of an English Opium Eater,* which compares the narrator's rendezvous with a woman to the growing uproar of the River Dee and the sea clashing downstream: "Her countenance naturally served as a mirror to echo and reverberate my own feelings, consequently my own horror (horror without exaggeration it was), at a sudden uproar of tumultuous sounds rising clamorously ahead."[72]

The film has two close-ups, both of an incoming wave. The first time, the wave appears before an intertitle, which describes how the rising tide slowly approaches Mary on the sand. Then we see her body on the wave. These three shots take us to the film's concluding moment, when Bobby carries Mary out of the water and Mary's weeping parents approach her body. As it hits the shore, the wave symbolizes the finality of separation, as well as the possibility of an imminent unification. At the very outset this motif appears as part of the plot intrigue, but it is then repeated in a way that is in greater consonance with the spirit of transcendentalist poetics. Two fishermen on the shore listen intently, as the intertitle explains that even now men at sea can hear Mary calling the cows home. In the distance we see the blurred figure of Mary, who is shouting something. The wave reaches the sand. We now see that the heroine makes her final appearance as the pure visualization of an echo. We are once more dealing with a vision at sea manifesting itself out of the reverberations of sound, the rhythmic beat of the poetic text and the steady crash of waves.

R. Tommasino, in an analysis of *The Sands of Dee,* has pointed out an obvious anomaly here. At the film's end the fishermen *hear* Mary (this is emphasized by the caption also) but cannot see her. The phantomlike figure of Mary shouting, Tommasino concludes, is visible to us alone as the film's audience, a visual rendering of an invisible echo.[73] From the perspective of contemporary narrative strategy, this episode strikes one as a real anomaly, while the vision that befalls Enoch's wife, Annie Lee, can be read as a classical crosscutting. Yet it is possible that in the second decade of the twentieth century both episodes were linguistically equivalent: both reenact the appearance of the symbol from a corresponding reverberation. In this sense the repetition of the film's ending acquires a certain significance, the film ends first on a narrative level and then on the plane of transcendent meaning. Both endings are separated from the main text by symbolic planes of waves (the film's final plane occupies a place symmetrically related to the first title, which introduces the theme of the echo and is thus structurally its equivalent). The first ending provides a key to reading the second (the separation and reunion) and seems to be linked to what Swedenborg would have called the material world, while the second ending is connected to the corresponding spiritual world.

The Sands of Dee and *Enoch Arden* show us two ways of normalizing linguistic anomalies. In the first instance, the normalization takes place by means of a literary intertext (the Kingsley poem). In the second instance, the alternating montage can be clarified by referring to a large group of texts deriving from the transcendentalist tradition, but this clarification itself becomes superfluous, since the subsequent evolution of film normalized Griffith's device as the classical form of montage. In the latter case, the literary intertext thus performs a different function. It explains the genesis of a specific figure of montage, its earliest meaning, whose origins no longer appear anomalous. This intertextuality can be eliminated by the subsequent tradition, and this itself can be crucial to the history of cinema. To a large extent film history can successfully integrate cases of anomaly or quotation into a linear pattern of cinematic evolution that appears logical. Intertextuality, then, is replaced in later historiographies of film by an analysis of the evolution of cinematic language, which is understood narrowly to mean the responses of a director to the ongoing challenges posed by film narrative.

Yet the film version of the Kingsley poem, in which the visual image is "born" from an auditory reverberation, shows that some figures of cinematic language, particularly those that appear somewhat unorthodox from today's perspective, are not necessarily intended to resolve narrative dilemmas. They can also, for example, be the result of a search for forms of representation that provide equivalents to the poetic voice (the Swedenborgian tradition relevant here generally equates sound and visual representation). Poetic vocalization, the reverberation of sounds, and the anagram all can function as real intertexts for cinematic figures.

A poetico-philosophical intertext can also throw new light on Griffith's narrative strategies, which are far less orthodox than is commonly assumed. In my analysis of *The Sands of Dee,* for example, I suggested that two layers of film are present, a kind of double plot, one of which develops on the level of a melodrama, the other in some "spiritual" dimension. A legitimate question thus arises: How are these two levels of narrative connected?

If we look at the story line of Griffith's films at their simplest level, we uncover certain common features that tend to escape detection and yet reveal the general direction of Griffith's own evolution. As early as 1909, in the film *The Drive for a Life*, Griffith makes use of a special kind of alternating montage, which he will then employ in many films (including *Intolerance*). *The Drive for a Life* is a classic melodrama in which a woman, abandoned by her fiancé, sends poisoned chocolates to his new bride. The film's central episode is structured on two levels of plot: in the first, the fiancé, learning of the woman's intentions, rushes to his bride to prevent a catastrophe; in the second, the bride, suspecting nothing, receives the chocolates, removes their wrapping, and prepares to taste the candy. Griffith's technique of montage works by interrupting the action of each level at the most dramatic moment, irrespective of whether it is completed (this kind of montage is today utterly normal). Tom Gunning has observed that the narrative traditions prevalent in cinema before Griffith's *The Drive for a Life* had tried to re-create the effect of continuous action, as evidenced in films with frequent chase scenes: if the individual being pursued moved out of a frame in the previous scene, then he or she would necessarily appear in the next. Griffith, by contrast, violates this continuity (whose elaboration he is normally credited with) by splitting the action into numerous arbitrary fragments.

In this way the plots of this and other films by Griffith are constituted by two heroes who have moved closer by the end, but whose movement is constantly and artificially violated by montage. The dramatic collision at the heart of many of Griffith's films is rooted in classical melodrama: people are brought together and then moved apart, yet their psychological bond survives spatial separation or the distantiation of montage. The sundering of planes at the film's climax serves to underline the drama inherent in this scenario, which is of immense importance to Griffith's film technique. The very constitution of the narrative through montage reflects the same range of ideological concerns as those treated in *Enoch Arden* and *The Sands of Dee*. Yet in *The Drive for a Life* these concerns are absorbed into the plot. The success of such absorption can be measured by the quality of the montage devices Griffith deploys, all of which seem completely hackneyed today. The transcendental layer of his films can thus be felt only where one senses a linguistically illogical moment or a visual anomaly.

It should be said that Griffith did not invent these visionary scenes: they go back to a tradition popularized in the nineteenth-century culture of spectacle by the magic lantern shows. An early example of a theatrical vision can be found in *The Frozen Deep* (1857) by Charles Dickens and Wilkie Collins, in which a traveler to the North Pole, warming himself by a campfire, suddenly sees the sweetheart he left behind at home.[74] The similarity between this scene and others found later in Griffith is obvious. Visions in the theater were staged through a transparent veil suspended as a backdrop. In the early cinema of Méliès or Porter (*The Life of an American Fireman, Uncle Tom's Cabin*), visions were depicted as if hovering in the clouds, often appearing on the uppermost section of the screen, or isolated in a special circle or frame. This appearance of visions in the form of masking gives them a certain affinity with shots of eavesdropping or spying, which were also depicted in frames (depicting a keyhole or eyeglass, etc.). These shots of eavesdropping, like visions, created an insuperable distance between the hero and the object of his (often sexual) desire.[75] In all cases, visions would be delineated sharply against the broader narrative flow, and their distance from the viewing subject would serve only to provide this process of delineation with an obvious motivation. Sometimes the visions were presented as frozen *tableaux vivants,* in a stark contrast to the mobility of cinematic representation. These frozen images began to appear in Griffith's work as early as 1909 (in *The Corner of Wheat*). Visions furnished the most elementary means of introducing the remote and unreachable—be it as an erotic object or a transcendental one—into a world marked by spatial proximity and material concreteness. In this sense Griffith's use of visions is nothing out of the ordinary. What is unusual is Griffith's deployment of montage in constructing these visions in his films.

The earliest cinematic work in which Griffith was involved, *Old Isaacs, the Pawnbroker* (March 1908), was probably filmed by Wallace McCutcheon, with Griffith, not yet a director, providing the screenplay. The film has one shot that seems astonishing for its time. The plot involves the usual melodrama: a gravely ill woman and her children have been threatened with eviction. The woman's little girl sets out to raise money from various charitable organizations but is able to borrow only from an old Jew, the pawnbroker Isaacs. In consistently following the movements of the little girl, the entire film develops with an unbroken continuity of narration. Yet suddenly, when the girl finds herself in an office and reads a piece of paper given to her, the action is interrupted and we see her mother, gasping in a fit of coughing and then falling exhausted onto her bed. Further on the action continues from the point at which it was interrupted. The shot of the mother cannot be reconciled with the temporal development of the film, but it lacks any of the familiar markers of a vision (there are no veils, frozen movements, masked frames, or other conventional signifiers of a shift in narrative mode). Eileen Bowser, struck by the strangeness of the film's montage, has in fact concluded that we are dealing with a vision, but her conclusion is based primarily on the anomalous nature of the montage used in this episode. Unable to integrate the shot into the story line,

Bowser—who here differs little from the "naïve" viewer—feels compelled to relate the shot to a more abstract level of the narrative, the realm of visions, the idealized sphere of plot construction.

Historians of early cinema have studied these narratively unintegrated shots—the visionary scenes, and those of spying and eavesdropping—to conclude that they are linked to the theatrical tradition, the culture of spectacle in which showtime was not yet story time. The collapse of the show system and the beginnings of a narrative system have been traced back to 1906.[76] André Gaudreault has even felt compelled to introduce the distinction between narrator and demonstrator, as two divergent authorial instances in cinema.[77]

These visions, related more to spectacle than narrative, in fact behave exactly like quotes, isolated within a text by their heightened representational quality (they are presented by a demonstrator rather than by a storyteller). They fall out of the general process of film mimesis, reproducing those phenomena discussed in chapter 1 in connection with Antonin Artaud. When in 1933 Artaud wrote of his disappointment with cinema, he maintained that the new art did not reproduce life but rather showed "stumps of objects, segments of views, unfinished puzzles made up of things that it combined together forever."[78] Artaud here seems to be projecting onto the entire body of cinema the poetics of those frozen visions unincorporated into the filmic text that form such a palpable part of early cinema.

In negating the legacy of theater, Griffith had to find a new strategy for integrating such unresolved puzzles into a film's narrative montage, to replace the theatrical intertext that had served the same function. This is why the unintegrated shots—so characteristic of Griffith, to the point of typifying his artistic ideology—remain so ambiguous. The transcendental plane is not excluded from the story line as before but is inserted into it with all its semantic instability. In this way two layers of the film are separated (as anomalies created by montage) but also brought together. The melodramatic theme of unity and separation is thus further strengthened in the partial division of the film into a transcendental and a "real" level of narration.

Let us now go back and analyze the intertext underlying Griffith's linguistic innovations. The close links between *The Sands of Dee* and *Enoch Arden* are further confirmed by a fact that to this day has remained unexplained. The second version of *Enoch Arden,* entitled *The Unchanging Sea,* was declared by Griffith to be an adaptation of the Kingsley poem "The Three Fishers."[79] Significantly, while "The Three Fishers" has almost nothing in common with the plot of *Enoch Arden,* it does to a considerable degree rehearse the plot of *The Sands of Dee:* three fishermen go to sea, and their wives and children await their return, but in vain. Only when the tide recedes do the sands reveal three dead bodies. That Kingsley's poetry has profound links to Tennyson's *Enoch Arden* is further confirmed by the frequent appearance in Kingsley of the motif of a "corresponding vision," and its privileging as the essential element of a new universal language, a kind of protosymbol of cinema.

Nonetheless, considerable differences in meaning also separate *Enoch Arden* from *The Sands of Dee*. *Enoch Arden* has a happy ending, in which husband and wife are reunited, whereas the heroine of *The Sands of Dee* dies tragically. The poetic tradition connected with the sea treats death in such a way as to allow for a characteristic duality of transcendent and earthly realms (as when someone singing unites with a spirit that inhabits the heavenly spheres). Death thus creates the tension between two realms necessary for the generation of correspondences.

In romantic poetry, especially Poe, the sound of the surf begins to be read systematically as the "words" *no more* or *never more*. These "words," says Poe, emerge on the line dividing sea and shore, which is also the line dividing two metaphysical realms (cf. Whitman's idea of sundering and reuniting). In Poe's sonnet "Silence," which is something of an illustration of the idea of correspondences, we read:

> There are some qualities—some incorporate things—
> That have a double life, which thus is made
> A type of that twin entity which springs
> From matter and light, evinced in solid and shade.
> There is a two-fold *Silence*—sea and shore—
> Body and Soul. . . .

(And further on Poe clarifies: "his name's 'No More.' ")[80]

Poe repeats the same motif in "To One in Paradise," a poem that frequently echoes Griffith's adaptation of *The Sands of Dee* (in it the poet addresses a woman who is dead, possibly drowned).

> "No more—no more—no more—"
> (Such language holds the solemn sea
> To the sands upon the shore).[81]

The same ideas can also be found in "To Zante":

> How many visions of a maiden that is
> No more—no more upon thy verdant slopes!
> No more! alas, that magical sad sound
> Transforming all![82]

The poets Shelley, Tennyson, Cheevers, Lowell, Longfellow, and others had all used the phrase "never more" or "no more" in analogous contexts. But it was Whitman who fixed the interpretation of this "magical sad sound / Transforming all" as the sea's echo, the reverberations of the surf.

In the poem "Out of the Cradle Endlessly Rocking," the "thousand echoes" of the surf whisper to the poet:

> never more shall I cease perpetuating you
> Never more shall I escape, never more the reverberations,
> Never more the cries of cries of unsatisfied love be absent from me . . .[83]

It seems likely that Whitman's poem is somehow connected to *The Sands of Dee*, since both texts involve an appeal to the beloved who is no more: "Loud! Loud! Loud! / Loud I call to you, my love!"[84] But the echo of the surf brings back just one word in reply—"death."

> Whereto answering, the sea,
> Delaying not, hurrying not,
> Whisper'd me through the night, and very plainly before daybreak,
> Lisp'd to me the low and delicious word Death;
> And again Death—ever Death, Death, Death,
> Hissing melodious, neither like the bird, nor like my arous'd child's heart,
> But edging near, as privately for me, rustling at my feet,
> Creeping thence steadily up to my ears, and laving me softly all over,
> Death, Death, Death, Death, Death.[85]

In this way, the shift from the optimism of *Enoch Arden*'s ending to the tragic finale of *The Sands of Dee* can be understood as the assimilation of the romantic poetic topos of the sea. Typically, Griffith would never again return to Tennyson after 1911. The persistent semantic connection between the sea and death allows the sea to widen its range of symbolic reference. It is not just the reverberating source of visions, a semantic cluster linking space, time, the living and the dead; in other words, it is not just the generator of a poetic montage constructed on the principle of correspondence. The sea is the bearer of a natural language, yet its voice can utter only the same few words unceasingly—"Never more" and "Death." The fluid locus of endless transformations gradually becomes a hieroglyph, drawing into its primordial, Adamic nature the semantic, auditory, and iconic properties of the sign, although, unlike language, it never freezes them into a fixed state.

The view of the world as a book written in hieroglyphics was typical of the American romantics. Emerson, Poe, Cranch in his "Correspondences," and others all write about the hieroglyphics of nature.[86] Even in his early films, Griffith had begun to develop a system of symbolic meanings, a sui generis iconological structure. But this attraction to hieroglyphics acquired a real meaning for Griffith and his work only after he became acquainted with Vachel Lindsay's book *The Art of the Moving Picture*.[87] This book expounds a Swedenborgian and hieroglyphic theory of contemporary art, instantiated primarily through references to Griffith's own work, in which Lindsay found the cinematic model he had been seeking.

The visionary dimension was of immense importance to Lindsay's theory of hieroglyphics, insofar as it was a means of realizing the Swedenborgian link between material form and a higher meaning that the artist-prophet glimpses in revelation. The notion that a hieroglyph's meaning could be grasped only through revelation was proposed long before by Emerson: "For the interpretation of hieroglyphs we were asked not to cipher or calculate but simply to depend upon 'Reason' or spontaneous moments of inward revelation when answers come effortlessly and astonishingly clear."[88] Endowing the film director with the role of a "prophet-magician" who is able to see through to the inner meaning of the universe, Lindsay wrote: "People who do not see visions and dream dreams in the good Old Testament sense have no right to leadership in America. I would prefer photoplays filled with such visions and oracles to the state papers written by 'practical men.' "[89] Later Lindsay would return to further elaborate on this theme in a commentary on the work of Swedenborg's greatest adepts: "They were unwilling to see their thoughts as splendid visions in the air. The most ordinary movie magnate goes further into this than Howells and Henry and William James. Swedenborg should be re-written in Hollywood. We want to know the meaning of all those hieroglyphics that they are thrusting upon us, for the present is as unsolved, in many phases, as the hieroglyphic ruins of pre-historic Mexico and South America. The American mind has become an overgrown forest of unorganized pictures."[90]

In 1914, Griffith released one of his most interesting films, *The Avenging Conscience,* an adaptation of two works by Poe, "The Tell-Tale Heart" and "Annabel Lee." Griffith filled the film with a large number of visions, bringing together the experience he had accumulated in *Enoch Arden* and *The Sands of Dee.* Poe's "Annabel Lee" tells Griffith's favorite story of a young woman who dies and is buried by the seashore:

> And so, all the night-tide, I lie down by the side,
> Of my darling—my darling—my life and my bride,
> In the sepulchre there by the sea,
> In her tomb by the sounding sea.[91]

But the opposition of earth and sea is further enriched in Poe's text by a third element—the sky, peopled by "seraphs of heaven." In his film, Griffith introduces a suicide scene absent in Poe, in which Annabel hurls herself off a cliff into the sea. The film's hero (a youth who dreams of becoming a writer, passionately involved in Poe's writing and apparently modeled on Griffith himself) is haunted by visions and hallucinations. The film's key episode is presented as the hero's dream. *The Avenging Conscience* thus seems to illustrate Poe's maxim: "Is *all* that we see or seem / But a dream within a dream?"[92]

Poe's "Dreamland" is situated at the point where sky and water meet:

> Mountains toppling evermore
> Into seas without a shore;
> Seas that restlessly aspire,
> Surging unto skies of fire . . .[93]

The film contains a wide range of celestial visions represented with a naïveté worthy of Swedenborg. Leona Rasmussen Phillips tells us that the cameraman Billy Bitzer "photographed the skies—in order to get many shots of various types of clouds: Big, white, puffy, whipped cream clouds, and then the opposite type: long, thick, dirty, black, menacing clouds. The different skies were used as a background for angels (the white clouds) and demons (the dark clouds)."[94]

Vachel Lindsay was also to describe these visions in rapturous tones. There are three of Annabel Lee: in two "she is shown in a darkened passageway, all in white, looking out of a window upon the moonlit sky," and in another she is "mourning on her knees in her room."[95] Lindsay also describes more somber visions featuring a man murdered by his nephew. He is particularly enthusiastic about the celestial visions at the end of the film, with its animals, angels, and Cupid and Psyche hovering in the clouds.

It is worth noting in passing that Griffith maintains in *The Avenging Conscience* the same dualism of worlds that was already evident in *The Sands of Dee*. The entire symbolic plane of death, with its panoply of Gothic horrors, is relegated to the realm of dreams and visions. The film's mundane plot intrigue is resolved happily enough, yet finds a more tragic visionary analogy that becomes a repository for occult meanings.

For Lindsay such a structure is ideal for creating a cinematic form of hieroglyphics, thanks to its capacity to elaborate metaphor into a bifurcating plot. Lindsay, not coincidentally, discovers real hieroglyphs in the film: a spider devouring a fly, and ants devouring a spider.[96] Lindsay gives examples of several Egyptian hieroglyphs that he believes have passed readily into the cinema. Among them is the hieroglyph of a duck that unexpectedly echoes Griffith's own poem "The Wild Duck," a poem about a duck that, unable to resist the cold wind, perishes at sea. Lindsay's interpretation of the hieroglyph is close to Griffith's (something that might have astonished the latter): "In the motion pictures this bird, a somewhat z-shaped animal, suggests the finality of Arcadian peace."[97]

More important, however, is the fact that scattered in Lindsay's book are several elements that will reappear in one way or another in Griffith's film *Intolerance*. Among these elements, the most significant is the notion, persistent in Lindsay, of the city as hieroglyph. Lindsay's fantasy had transformed his native Springfield into a mystical cipher; San Francisco too become a visionary space. The very appearance of a film industry in California is transformed by Lindsay into a prophetic moment. "The California photo playwright can base his Crowd picture upon the city-worshipping mobs of San Francisco."[98] The cities of America were always for Lindsay signs of yet other cities, hieroglyphs, metaphors of a beyond. "The principal towns of Southern Illinois are Cairo, Karnak, and Thebes, and the swamp-bordered river moves southward past Memphis, Tennessee, named for the town of King Menes, first King of Egypt. There is a parallel between the psychology and history of the Mississippi delta and the famous delta of the old Nile. . . . And I beg all my readers to look into Swedenborg's theory of Egyptian hieroglyphics."[99]

According to Swedenborg, the earthly city corresponds to a heavenly city in the spiritual realm; there the dwelling places of the angels were organized "in the form of a city, with avenues, streets, and public squares exactly like cities on earth."[100] In the United States this idea gained a certain currency: Joseph Hudnut, for example, wrote of an "invisible city": "Beneath the visible city laid out in patterns of streets and houses there lies an invisible city laid out in patterns of idea and behavior."[101] Lindsay was close to this idea: "The signs in the street and the signs in the skies / Shall make a new zodiac."[102] In Arthur Schlesinger's popular book *The Rise of the City* (1910), American cities were directly interpreted as analogues to symbolic cities of the past: "The City had come, and it was clear to all that it had come to stay. Was its mission to be that of a new Jerusalem or ancient Babylon?"[103]

Griffith's Babylon in *Intolerance* was most likely conceived of in this spirit, as a kind of hieroglyphic city (*Intolerance* is also based on the opposition of Babylon and Jerusalem). In 1923, in Memphis, Tennessee—a hieroglyphic city that toponymically combines Egypt and America—Lindsay published a poem entitled "Babylon, Babylon, Babylon the Great," with a picture of the city as a kind of hieroglyphic epigraph.[104] Lindsay's poem is clearly connected to Griffith's film, which it freely reinterprets.

At one point in Lindsay's *Art of the Moving Picture,* we find a screenplay describing a kind of dream that is meant to take place in a phantasmagoric Springfield. The central scene involves the appearance before the people of a huge statue, a female figure made of marble and gold, sent down to the inhabitants of Springfield from the heavens:

> The people come running from everywhere to watch. Here indeed will be a Crowd picture with as many phases as a stormy ocean.
> The important outdoor festivals are given on the edge of her [the statue's] hill. All the roads lead to her footstool. Pilgrims come from the Seven Seas to look upon her face that is carved by Invisible Powers. More-

over, the living messenger that is her actual soul appears in dreams, or visions of the open day, when the days are dark for the city, when her patriots are irresolute, and her children are put to shame. The spirit with the maple branch rallies them, leads them to victories like those that were won of old.[105]

The same vision inaugurates the Babylonian episode in *Intolerance*. First the intertitle tells us that "all the nations of the earth sat at the feet of Babylon"; then we see crowds of people and a vast procession carrying a "gift from Heaven" into the city—a huge marble statue representing a seated female figure, Ishtar, the goddess of love. Her appearance is accompanied by the dance of the vestal virgins. The heroine of the film, the Mountain Girl, is a kind of double of Ishtar herself: she symbolizes love and strives to save the city. Curiously, a young rhapsode who is in love with the Mountain Girl is inserted into this part of the film's plot line. The young poets who appear in Griffith's films are generally doubles of the director himself. We find ready confirmation of this in an episode, already cited, from Griffith's memoirs concerning the love of a young poet not unlike Edgar Allan Poe for a girl Griffith calls the Snow Angel (cf. the Mountain Girl). Griffith was to recall his sweetheart in the following way:

> She brought a vision of ancient pagan temples of passion . . . temples turreted with oriental gargoyles and with naves cut in the phallic symbol. You could almost see men in the dim temple halls, straining forward, all eyes on a great raised dais where ancient priestesses postured and posed in attitudes of seduction—spinning one's head with heavily perfumed incense and soft, seductive music. Then, through the minor devotees to Love, Ishtar herself appears . . . Ishtar, the goddess of Love, gliding out with slow, alluring gestures, swaying rhythmically with the music, . . . slim, perfumed hands loosing the silver veil from her luminous body.[106]

Griffith later reproduced this erotic vision in the "temple of love" scene, in which the half-naked priestesses of Ishtar dance about the altar in a cloud of burning incense. This scene was of great importance to the director, who went to the extent of expelling from the set all the "uninitiated," so that the very act of filming the scene acquired the aspect of a sacred rite.[107]

Lindsay's vision allows us to give a purely symbolic interpretation of the image of Ishtar, but the latter is in fact informed by purely individual, subjective experiences that for Griffith acquired the dimensions of a fairy-tale vision. Ishtar herself is a hieroglyphic symbol that emerges as the massive materialization of a visionary insight. Lindsay himself had called upon his readers to "build from your hearts buildings and films which shall be your individual Hieroglyphics, each according to his own loves and fancies."[108]

There is, however, one "superhieroglyph" in *Intolerance* that is of crucial importance for the film's structure as a whole: the celebrated vision of a woman rocking a cradle. It occurs at the beginning of the film, immediately after the quotation from Whitman's "Out of the Cradle Endlessly Rocking." The vision of the woman with the cradle appears repeatedly at the intersection of different episodes and threads of plot, bringing them together.

Lindsay immediately understood this scene to be a key hieroglyph.[109] Other critics were of the same opinion, although they generally found it to be a failure as a hieroglyph. Terry Ramsaye's reservations are in this sense typical: "To Griffith, the scenes of Lillian Gish rocking a cradle did mean 'a golden thread' denoting the continuity of the human race and binding his fugue of period pictures. But to the movie audience a picture of a cradle is a hieroglyph meaning: 'there is going to be a baby,' 'there is a baby,' or 'there was a baby.' It does not mean the continuity of the race, and it does not suggest intolerance—rather the opposite."[110] Eisenstein, who for obvious reasons rejected the notion of a cinematic symbol not based on montage, wrote that Griffith "made a blunder because of non-montage thinking in the treatment of a recurring 'wave of time' through an unconvincing plastic idea of the rocking cradle."[111] And again: "The Whitman lines on 'out of the cradle endlessly rocking' . . . served Griffith unsuccessfully as a refrain shot for his *Intolerance*."[112]

Today we no longer need to involve ourselves in a purely evaluative debate on the merits of Griffith's symbol. It is more important to grasp its meaning. Harold Dunham recalls how the idea came to Griffith: "It is said that some twelve to fifteen years before, Griffith was walking with Wilfred Lucas, when they were both working in a road show, when Lucas caught sight of a woman rocking a cradle, and reminded Griffith of Walt Whitman's lines from *Leaves of Grass*: 'Out of the cradle endlessly rocking' and 'Endlessly rocks the cradle Uniter of Here and Hereafter.' "[113]

The Whitman quote serves as the subtext of several Griffith films made at Biograph (as I have tried to show earlier). In *Intolerance* it is invoked unabashedly as the key explanatory text to the entire film. Griffith accorded the role of the woman by the cradle to his favorite actress, Lillian Gish, itself an indication of the importance he attributed to this brief but recurrent episode. Whitman continued to function as the essential subtext even during the actual filming of the scene: "We went back to the studio and did some shots of Lillian Gish rocking a cradle, all to the tune of Walt Whitman's poetry, which Griffith recited with great feeling. . . . It must have been one of his good days."[114]

Mention has already been made of the crucial role of echo and sound reverberation in this poem. Griffith was so committed to rendering this aspect of Whitman's text that he sought to visualize the poem's second line: "Out of the cradle endlessly rocking, / Out of the mocking bird's throat, the musical shuttle"[115] Toward the back of the frame, behind Gish, Griffith had placed the symbolic figures of the Three Fates spinning the thread of life (cf. Whitman's "musical shuttle"). During the shooting, on hearing the sound of the spinning wheel and the creak of Atropos's scissors as they cut the thread, Griffith was heard to exclaim: "Gahhhd! If we could only get that *sound!*"[116]

The woman by the cradle harks back above all to Whitman's series of images—the eternally rocking sea, the cradle, and the grave—but it also suggests the cradle of language, the reverberating mirror of visions. She is the sea, but also the generative force behind all visions. For Lindsay, visions are hieroglyphs. In this sense the cradle in the film's insistent refrain can be seen as a kind of supreme hieroglyph, the force that generates a text of other hieroglyphs.

Just as obvious is the role, openly announced in the intertitles, of the sea as cradle in creating correspondences, linking—as it had for the transcendentalists—all worlds and abolishing distinctions of time and space. "Today as yesterday, endlessly rocking, ever bringing the same joys and sorrows," the caption says just as we see Gish on the screen. The linking of "here" and "there" is a transcendentalist way of expressing the principle of a twofold (or even threefold) world.

Significantly, this is precisely the intellectual context in which the same image of the cradle appears in a poem by Victor Hugo entitled "Éclaircie" (1855):

> L'horizon semble un rêve éblouissant où nage
> L'écaille de la mer, la plume du nuage,
> Car l'Océan est hydre et le nuage oiseau.
> Une lueur, rayon vague, part du berceau
> Qu'une femme balance au seuil d'une chaumière,
> Dore les champs, les fleurs, l'onde et devient lumière
> En touchant un tombeau qui dort près du clocher.
> Le jour plonge au plus noir du gouffre, et va chercher
> L'ombre, et la baise au front sous l'eau sombre et hagarde.

> (The horizon seems a dazzling dream where
> The scales of the sea and the feather of the cloud float,
> For the ocean is a hydra and the cloud a bird.
> A gleam, an obscure ray, is emitted from a cradle
> Which a woman rocks on the threshold of a cottage
> And gilds the fields, the flowers, the wave and becomes light
> As it touches a grave that sleeps close to the belfry.
> The day plunges into the darkest part of the abyss and goes seeking
> The shadow, and kisses it on the brow below the sombre and gaunt water.)[117]

Here, too, the rocking cradle is a metaphor for the sea, which can reflect a shimmer of light back into the sky and yet also repress light near the seafloor: it symbolizes birth and death, and functions as a kind of nodal point for all correspondences.

Hugo turned to the image of the cradle many times in his life. To him it came to symbolize a kind of universal connectedness and the generative force guaranteeing the future of humanity. In the poem "Fonction du poète" he writes:

> Comme l'océan sur les grèves
> Répand son râle et ses sanglots,
> L'idée auguste qui t'égaie
> A cette heure encore bégaie;
> Mais de la vie elle a le sceau!
> Ève contient la race humaine,
> Un oeuf l'aiglon, un gland le chêne!
> Une utopie est un berceau!
>
> De ce berceau, quand viendra l'heure,
> Vous verrez sortir, éblouis,
> Une société meilleure . . .
>
> (As the ocean hurls on the shore
> its death-rattle and its sobs,
> The august idea that delights you
> Is still stammering at this point;
> But it possesses the seal of life! Eve contains the human race,
> An egg the eaglet, an acorn the oak!
> A utopia is a cradle!
>
> From this cradle, when the time comes
> you will observe, bedazzled,
> A better society emerge . . .)[118]

The cradle signifies the same primordiality, the same capacity for origination, that characterizes the ocean, whose speech, impenetrable and inarticulate, is the origin of every human language. To return to the ocean is to return to a pre-Babelic stage of human speech. In Hugo's collection *Les Contemplations,* from which "Éclaircie" is taken, we find another poem that encodes the symbols of water and cradle, transforming them into hieroglyphs of a vast mystical book of being:

> L'eau, les prés, sont autant de phrases où le sage
> Voit serpenter des sens qu'il saisit au passage.
>
> (The water, the meadows are also phrases, in which the wise man
> Sees meanings slither which he seizes in passing.)[119]

An individual capable of discerning this vast cipher in the phenomenal world is himself transformed, and gains the "higher purity of the cradle." (It is hardly a coincidence that Leo Spitzer found a clear link between Whitman's poem and Hugo's poetry.)[120]

Long before Griffith, then, the sea-as-cradle serves as the motivating impulse behind visions (hieroglyphs) of different historical epochs in a range of texts from the romantic period. If the sea is the resonating surface that mirrors the sky, and if heavenly visions originate from contemplating the sky in water, then the kingdom of heaven must naturally correspond to an underwater kingdom, its inverted and—for Swedenborg's followers—degraded double.

Intertwining visions of the city and the sea are typically found in De Quincey. *Confessions of an English Opium Eater* contains a vision of Liverpool superimposed onto a vision of the sea. For De Quincey, Liverpool symbolizes the earth, and the sea symbolizes consciousness. At this very juncture, De Quincey adds that opium-induced visions of cities surpass ancient Babylon in their beauty.[121] In his commentary on De Quincey, Baudelaire calls his visions of Liverpool and the sea "a great natural allegory."[122] De Quincey's *Suspiria De Profundis* contains a vision of the city Savannah-la-mar: "God smote Savannah-la-mar, and in one night, by earthquake, removed her, with all her towers standing and population sleeping, from the steadfast foundations of the shore to the coral floors of ocean." The city seems to be asleep under the smooth surface of the sea, "fascinat[ing] the eye with a *Fata-Morgana* revelation, as of human life still subsisting in submarine asylums sacred from the storms that torment our upper air."[123] De Quincey describes his fantastic descent into this underwater city, where he walks among its silent bell towers.

A similar vision appears in Poe's "The City in the Sea," a poem that Griffith knew well:

> Lo! Death has reared himself a throne
> In a strange city lying alone
> Far down within the dim West,
> . . . .
> There shrines and palaces and towers
> (Time-eaten towers that tremble not!)
> Resemble nothing that is ours.
> Around by lifting winds forgot,
> Resignedly beneath the sky
> The melancholy waters lie.
> . . . .
> But light from out the lurid sea
> Streams up the turrets silently—
> Gleams up the pinnacles far and free—
> Up domes—up spires—up kingly halls—
> Up fanes—up Babylon-like walls—
> Up shadowy long-forgotten bowers
> Of sculptured ivy and stone flowers—
> Up many and many a marvellous shrine
> . . . .

But lo, a stir is in the air!
The wave—there is a movement there!
As if the towers had thrust aside,
In slightly sinking, the dull tide—
As if their tops had feebly given
A void within the filmy Heaven.
The waves have now a redder glow—
The hours are breathing faint and low—
And when, amid no earthly moans,
Down, down that town shall settle hence,
Hell, rising from a thousand thrones,
Shall do it reverence.[124]

It is especially curious to see the contours of Babylon emerge from this reflection of the sky on the water's rippling surface. As the light streams from
the "lurid sea," it illuminates the "Babylon-like walls"—hence the readily
understood motif of the towers of Babylon. Tennyson's "Sea Dreams" also
develops the theme of Babylon, whose destruction by flood is foretold by
an angel, the spirit of the Apocalypse.

Another relevant text here develops the motif of the city underwater—
Victor Hugo's *La Légende des siècles,* whose tendency to link different nations and epochs may well have served as an important intertext for Griffith's *Intolerance.* Hugo's work contains one chapter, "La Ville disparue,"
that echoes the Babylonian episode in Griffith. It tells the story of a city
"built entirely of brick":

On y voyait des tours, des bazars, des fabriques,
Des arcs, des palais pleins de luths mélodieux,
Et de monstres d'airain qu'on appelait les dieux.
. . . .
On y chantait des choeurs pleins d'oubli, l'homme étant
L'ombre qui jette un souffle et qui dure un instant;
De claires eaux luisaient au fond des avenues;
Et les reines du roi se baignaient toutes nues
. . . .
Mais un jour l'Océan se mit à remuer
. . . .
La lune le front blanc des monts, les pâles astres,
Virent soudain, maisons, dômes, arceaux, pilastres,
Toute la ville, ainsi qu'un rêve, en un instant,
. . . .
Crouler dans on ne sait quelle ombre épouvantable;
Et pendant qu'à la fois, de la base au sommet,
Ce chaos de palais et de tours s'abîmait,
On entendit monter un murmure farouche,
Et l'on vit brusquement s'ouvrir comme une bouche

Un trou d'où jaillissait un jet d'écume amer,
Gouffre où la ville entrait et d'où sortait la mer,
Et tout s'évanouit; rien ne resta que l'onde.

(One saw towers there, bazaars, mills,
Arches, palaces filled with melodious lutes,
And monsters of bronzes that were called the gods
....
Choirs sang there full of oblivion, Man being
The shadow which gives a sigh and lasts a moment;
Clear waters shone in the recesses of avenues;
And the queens of the king bathed quite naked
....
But one day the Ocean began to move
....
The moon, the white forehead of the mountains, the pale stars,
Suddenly saw houses, domes, arches, pilasters,
The whole city, as if in a dream, in an instant,
Collapsed in I know not what terrible shadow;
And while all at once, from bottom to top,
This chaos of palaces and towers fell down,
One heard a ferocious whisper rise up,
And one saw opening up suddenly like a mouth
A hole from which a jet of bitter foam was thrust up,
An abyss which the city entered and from which the sea came forth,
And everything disappeared; nothing was left save the wave.)[125]

A vision of an underwater city also appears in Balzac's "L'Enfant maudit": "Through a light brilliant like that of the heavens he admired the
immense cities of which his books spoke; he saw, with astonishment but
without desire, the courts, the kings, the battles, the men and the monuments."[126] Gérard de Nerval gives us a similar description: "And I gazed
dreamily into the water's clear mirror, looking deeper and deeper, until I
discerned on the bottom of the sea—initially like a mist at twilight, then in
gradually more distinct colours—cupolas and towers, and then finally, illu-
minated by the sun, an entire ancient Belgian city filled with life and movement."[127]

In Griffith the sea and the city fuse into one (we recall how Lindsay obsessively returns to the analogy between water and the urban populace).
Griffith's hieroglyphs do not carry a stable meaning, although this was precisely what Griffith's detractors saw as their principal flaw. Rather, they resonate meaning, layers of correspondences, which they unify into signification. This is precisely how it generates the protolanguage, the single
language of a united world. Babylon, symbol of linguistic dispersal (the
Tower of Babel), collapses into the ocean, which dissolves all languages
once more, only to create a supreme unity of meaning.

The book *Le Collier de griffes* by the French poet Charles Cros contains a poem entitled "Hiéroglyphe" (1886) that is startlingly close to the transcendentalist conception of the symbol:

J'ai trois fenêtres à ma chambre:
    L'amour, la mer, la mort,
Sang vif, vert calme, violet.

Ô femme, doux et lourd trésor!

Froids vitraux, cloches, odeurs d'ambre.
    La mer, la mort, l'amour . . .

(I have three windows in my room:
    Love, sea, death,
Hot blood, calm green, violet

Oh woman, sweet and heavy treasure!

Cold window-panes, bells, smell of amber
    Sea, death, love . . .)[128]

The constant refrain "l'amour, la mer, la mort" (cf. Poe's "nevermore") reproduces the endless crashing of the waves on the beach. In itself the poem "Hiéroglyphe" lacks a concrete or fixed meaning: it is rather a meeting point of several meanings, much like the room that it describes, with its three windows that let in sights (the glazed panes), sounds (the sea and the tolling bells), and smells (the aroma of amber). Griffith's hieroglyphs are similarly structured: they organize intratextual correspondences.

The hieroglyph unifies the diverse phenomena of the material world into the general denominator of a transcendental vision. The final scene of *Intolerance* is revealing in this sense: four threads of the same plot are transposed into a series of Swedenborgian celestial visions. A host of angels appears in the sky over a vast battlefield. The angels multiply and slowly crowd out the world below, which is displaced by an idyllic vision of the empyrean. The film's ending recalls Emerson's idea of two histories, one of the earth in all its heterogeneity, and one of the spirit, with its singular and timeless meaning: "Time dissipates to shining ether the solid angularity of facts. No anchor, no cable, no fences avail to keep a fact a fact. Babylon, Troy, Tyre, Palestine, and even early Rome are passing already into fiction. The Garden of Eden, the sun standing still in Gideon, is poetry thenceforward to all nations. Who cares what the fact was, when we have made a constellation of it to hang in heaven an immortal sign?"[129]

Intolerance, however, does not actually end with an "immortal sign" hanging in heaven. The Swedenborgian visions are in turn framed by the final scene of the cradle rocking, the symbol of the sea. It is not a coincidence that this ending practically reproduces the closing moment of Balzac's classically Swedenborgian work *Séraphita,* in which an elaborate depiction of the kingdom of heaven suddenly ends with an abrupt return to the sea, the motif with which the novel began: "The vast ocean that gleams out there is an image of that we saw above!"[130]

. . .

My hypothesis concerning the meaning of Griffith's search for a new cinematic language forces us to reconsider the traditional understanding of parallel montage as a purely narrative device. Tom Gunning's careful study of Griffith's cutbacks has already pointed to the conclusion that they play a "double role. . . . they express the thoughts of the characters and serve as a parallel montage of autonomous and separate events."[131] Griffith often does organize his films on two levels. The narrative level is drawn out into a single thread that respects the logic of spatiotemporal connections and the relations of cause and effect. Yet above this narrative level Griffith creates another textual layer (although it is sometimes fragmentary), with which the plot-generating events are linked along a kind of vertical axis. It is precisely these vertical links that constitute meanings as correspondences.

As if anticipating the structure of *Intolerance,* Hugo Münsterberg had written: "We think of events which run parallel in different places. The photoplay can show in intertwined scenes everything which our mind embraces. Events in three or four or five regions of the world can be woven together into one complex action."[132] But to weave together different facts assumes not a linear but a cyclic development of motifs. Cyclic recurrence and repetition in the spirit of Emerson's transcendent circle of meanings are very close to the principle of repetition and stanzaic refrain in poetry. Not so long ago Eileen Bowser, a specialist in early film, discovered to her own surprise this circularity of structure—unexpected from the perspective of classical narrative—in a great number of Griffith's films.[133] These structures, producing repetition and parallelism, serve to layer and concentrate meaning upon meaning, creating what Iurii Lotman has called a "cluster of structural significations."[134]

Bowser has linked the cyclic nature of the films made at Biograph to Griffith's deep immersion in poetry. But what is important for our purposes is not the simple imitation of poetic structures. Harold Bloom has pointed out that romantic poetry, even as it gravitates superficially toward visual sensations, in actual fact negates the capacity of the seeing eye to embrace the world and its essence. Bloom thus contrasts the visible with the visionary. Taking up a poem by Blake, he writes: "With an eye made active by an awareness of cinema, we see what Blake gives us in his passage, a series of shifting views that are not in continuity with one another, and whose juxtapositions suggest an intolerable confusion between an inward world rolling outward and an outward world that stands apart and is objectified as a mockery of our visual powers."[135]

The hieroglyph can be readily understood in Bloom's terms, as belonging to a visionary realm that actually negates the merely visible. It is a layered structure of meanings, significations, and intertextual connections that are often irreducible to a whole. Griffith's hieroglyphs are more specifically layers of intertexts. That is how the symbol of the woman by the cradle is created: it becomes a hieroglyph through its capacity to mobilize the vast intertext of Swedenborgian transcendentalism. The city—Babylon—becomes a hieroglyph in the same way. Intertextuality, when raised to the level of hieroglyphics (the multilayered juxtaposition of intertexts within the same sign) can generate a new language, which is in turn organized as a series of texts placed in a parallel montage. Parallel montage, when seen in this perspective, becomes a way of re-creating on a narrative level the same intertextuality that exists as a "lump" that we have called the cinematic hieroglyph.

This also explains the opposition between hieroglyphic stasis and a relentless narrative march that is typically found in Griffith's films. Meanings seem to come to a halt in hieroglyphic form or get dissipated in the movement of different intersecting threads of plot. The structure of intertextuality acquires from this a pulsating quality. The opposition "rushing crowd/ immobile city" merely expresses this pulsating shift from hieroglyph to narrative. It is not a coincidence, then, that the supreme hieroglyph of *Intolerance,* the woman by the cradle, is isolated from the narrative flow and cloaked, as it were, in the image of a woman. Mary Ann Doane has noted that "the figure of the woman is aligned with spectacle, space, or the image, often in opposition to the linear flow of plot. . . . The transfixing or immobilizing aspects of the spectacle constituted by the woman work against the forward pull of the narrative."[136] In many of Griffith's films, a woman is the passive object of aggression; in the turbulent intersection of crossing images, she is saved by a man. In such a structure the depiction of a woman is particularly apt to become a symbol.

An initial state of idyllic stasis typically begins many of Griffith's films. This stasis, subsequently violated by the irruption of hostile forces, can, broadly speaking, be likened to a hieroglyph. Miriam Hansen has made the perceptive point that the hieroglyphic system of writing, identified with Babylon, represents "by synecdoche, the utopian unity in all spheres of life."[137] Babylon-as-hieroglyph reflects a general plenitude of connections and correspondences that is powerfully intertextual. It embodies that idyllic stasis that is subsequently broken with the irruption of the linear story (writing that is linear, narrative, and alphabetic)—in terms of actual plot, the invasion of Cyrus the Great. Hieroglyph falls victim to aggression, being undermined both by modern life (where older correspondences and connections have been shattered) and by modern linear narrative.

But if the hieroglyph can be seen as static or immobile in its symbolism, it is by no means some ossified allegory. The struggle between different levels of meaning and multiple intertexts make for its inner dynamism. Griffith's cinematic hieroglyphs are not examples of the symbol criticized by Eisenstein. They point to a field of "mutual attractions," a "room with many windows." This explains the tendency for Griffith's stories to fall readily into two worlds, the real and the visionary, in which the city of God is reflected in others, located on earth or underwater. This also explains the occasional layeredness of Griffith's endings, as in *The Avenging Conscience* and *The Sands of Dee.*

In this sense one can speak of Griffith's hieroglyphs as dynamic "signs" as Emerson would have understood them. Just as Griffith was beginning his work at Biograph, the American sinologist Ernest Fenollosa elaborated his own notion of the poetic hieroglyph, the so-called theory of the pictogram, that exerted some influence on the development of the imagist school of American poetry. Fenollosa, like Griffith, saw the world as made up of "actual and entangled lines of force as they pulse through things. Thought deals with no bloodless concepts but watches *things move* under its microscope. . . . Like Nature, the Chinese words are alive and plastic, because *thing* and *action* are not formally separated."[138] Fenollosa and Griffith were men of their time and reflected its poetic thought.

Griffith's universal Adamic language is above all a language of dynamic correspondences; it begins with the symbol but is not completed there. The universality of Griffith's new language lies in its capacity for transcendence, culminating in a single and higher meaning.

The difficulties involved in understanding Griffith's parallel montage are largely due to the fact that it is seldom deployed in such an abstract and pure form as in the more intellectual cinema of Eisenstein. Based on the notion of correspondence, Griffith's montage constantly weaves its threads linking traditional narrative structure, psychological interest, and a search for transcendental meanings. This shuttling up, down, and back up again makes it difficult to define how Griffith's montage signifies, as one might when dealing with a single textual level. Now a symbol comes to the fore, now a vision, now a simple narrative section. It is their alternating presence that conceals the hieroglyphic writing system of a great director, a system that aspired to be universal but often has been perceived as simply eclectic.

Cinema history has privileged the narrative dimension of Griffith's films. A shift in critical emphasis onto the syntagmatic level of narrative has transformed Griffith into the cinematic equivalent of metonymic, linear prose.[139] By restoring the hieroglyphic, intertextual dimension in Griffith's work, we have been able to evaluate his linguistic innovations in a new way. Intertextuality, moreover, emerges as more than an effective means of rereading the history of cinematic forms. It is also cinema's own mechanism for evolving a new language. Crosscutting, parallel montage, shot/reverse shot, and the transcendentalist hieroglyph as it evolves in the *Enoch Arden* cycle and culminates in *Intolerance* have been shown to be substantial effects of complex intertextual processes that take place in the texts themselves. Intertextual reading, the reduction of linguistic anomalies to a normative logic, can be projected onto the history of cinema and seen as one of its generative mechanisms.

PART III

Beyond Narrative
Avant-Garde Cinema

CHAPTER FOUR

Cinematic Language as Quotation
Cendrars and Léger

For several reasons, avant-garde cinema is of special interest in a study of intertextuality. First of all, the avant-garde film, when perceived against the background of classical narrative cinema (and that is precisely how it is usually perceived), presents itself as an openly acknowledged "anomaly" that needs to acquire normative status. In this sense the avant-garde film seems to lend itself readily to an intertextual interpretation. Seeking to crack the code in which a difficult text is written, the reader or viewer as a rule may turn willy-nilly to other texts that might be able to throw some light on the enigma at hand.

Second, the avant-garde text presents itself as something "new," unprecedented, a complete negation of the preceding tradition—a move vital to its operative situation. The discourse of the author is equated with the utterances of a new Adam who speaks as if he had no predecessors. In this way the avant-garde text, which by its very nature orients the reader toward an intertextual reading, at the same time appears consciously to bracket any intertext that would make this reading possible. This bracketing of intertextuality was a programmatic part of the early avant-garde. A vast array of manifestos of every kind, generated to defend the avant-garde's premises, constantly sought to subvert the received tradition; while in the visual arts and the cinema similar manifestos would insist systematically on their independence from language, which they perceived as the principal bearer of tradition and chief guardian of the "warehouse of quotes."

Avant-garde cinema typically rejects such characteristics as traditional plot interest, suspense, and identifiable human characters—everything normally associated with literature. Nevertheless, it cannot be said that a rejection of suspenseful plots and character interest implies a total break with literature. There are cases of avant-garde films compensating for the absence of plot through a large-scale recuperation of literary language. This can happen in a cryptic way, with language encoded in a chain, as in the montage-rebus we find in Dziga Vertov's *Man with a Movie Camera*[1] or, more programmatically, in the form of artistic manifestos and theoretical declarations that verbally explicate the meaning of an otherwise plastic visual experiment and justify its existence.

It is true that this appeal to manifestos, while permitting the decoding of plastic signs, could create bizarre difficulties of its own. In 1915, Kasimir Malevich made the following "clarificatory statement": "The curtain, in depicting the black square, the seed of all possibilities, acquires a terrible force as it keeps growing."[2] Here the viewer is compelled to take the artist's words on faith: after all, there is nothing in the form of the black square that points us to a "seed" or a "terrible force." The manifesto-as-explication creates a *coercive intertext* for the plastic image, an intertext overtly generated by the artist himself that cannot be reconstructed by the reader. We are dealing with a forced concordance established between a specific plastic sign and a certain verbal concept. Jean-François Lyotard has designated this trait of avant-garde poetics as an appeal to the "sublime," that is, the undefined. The sublime "occurs when . . . the imagination fails to represent an object that is, even if only in principle, matched with a concept. We have the Idea of the world (the totality of what is), but we lack the capacity to show an example of it. . . . I would call modern the art that devotes its 'modest techniques,' as Diderot used to say, to representing the unrepresentable."[3] In this representation of the unrepresentable, the intertext of commentary plays a vital role. Forcibly linking a plastic sign to an abstract concept, a word, it creates a kind of *intertextual shock* that allows for the realization of this epistemological utopia.

The artist's declaration of independence from language can thus scarcely be applied with any consistency. The avant-garde depends programmatically on the shock of intertextuality, on the interpretation of a plastic sign through the verbal fabric of another text.

This applies equally to avant-garde cinema as well. Literary intertexts are a fixed, if hidden, presence in avant-garde films, so much so that an avowedly "antiliterary" film-text can become paradoxically saturated with literary references. Moreover, the originality of any avant-garde film is largely defined by its specific way of linking visual representation to a more fundamental literary program, that is, the intertexts that its visual references imply.

The task of this chapter is to provide, however partially, an account of the literary intertext connected to one of the most well-known avant-garde films in cinema history—Fernand Léger's *Ballet mécanique* (1924)—and an analysis of what is intertextually specific to the film's essential form.

Ballet mécanique is of special interest in the context of this chapter. It traditionally has been viewed as one of the most suggestive and consistent examples of nonverbal cinematic art. Devoid of any semblance of plot intrigue, being no more than a montage of short fragments depicting various forms of rhythmic movement performed by all manner of things, all equally and almost entirely desemanticized—objects, body parts, written signs, and so forth—*Ballet mécanique* has never been examined in its relationship to literature. The generally held opinion of the film's poetics is summarized in the title to an article by the French scholar Andrei Nakov: "De la peinture sans référant verbal." Léger's ambition, Nakov suggests, was the creation of a text in which the object would be totally stripped of its "cultural" significance and reduced to a purely thingly, "objective" presence. "All verbal signification is eliminated; only the image remains," says Nakov. "A man who thought through images and pictures and aspired toward a *pure* manipulation of the image as a visual object without a literary referent, Léger found it somewhat difficult to theorize verbally."[4] Léger's psychological and theoretical assumptions, for Nakov, led him to "create image-objects, as against the (theosophical or simply philosophical) image-myths of someone like Piet Mondrian."[5]

Nakov thus absolves the film of its need to "represent the unrepresentable." In his explanatory notes to the film (June 1924), Léger himself indicates: "This film is objective, realist and in no way abstract." But in the same note he clarifies: "From beginning to end the film has been subjected to mathematical constraints that are quite exact, as exact as possible (number, speed, time)."[6] Abstraction must of necessity enter into the construction of the avant-garde text, even if only in the form of rhythmic laws and "mathematical constraints."

In the pages to come, I shall attempt to prove that a "theosophical or simply philosophical myth" also lies within the intertextual field of *Ballet mécanique*. This myth is obscured by the absence of narration, by Léger's own avowed rejection of "cinema based on screenplays." In 1924, while making *Ballet mécanique*, Léger wrote: "The idea of putting a novel on the screen is a fundamental mistake, connected to the fact that the majority of directors have had a literary background and education. . . . They sacrifice that wonderful thing, the 'moving image,' in order to inflict on us a story that would be better suited to a book. We end up with yet another nefarious 'adaptation'—convenient enough, but which impedes the creation of anything new."[7] Yet Léger's invective against screenplays is never generalized into an attack on literature as a whole, or into a call to eliminate entirely the verbal meaning of representation. The negation of screenplays here often coexists alongside some rather nebulous thoughts concerning the possible narration of "stories" without a "novelistic," "sentimental or literary intrigue." Léger adds: "Enough of literature: the public couldn't care less. We don't need perspective; and why have all these clarificatory texts? Are you really incapable of making a story without a text, with just images? But the modest cartoonist does it, on the last page of the newspaper. If we can reach this point, as well as many other things that will become clearer later, then the cinema will be on the right track."[8] Clearly what emerges here is a utopia based on an entirely specific form of *narrative*. We have no reason to believe that Léger aspired to strip the cinema of language entirely, as is clear from this letter written much later to Sergei Eisenstein: "It's annoying. But writers, men of letters and others feel 'negative' about the screen."[9] Nonetheless, by no means all writers in Léger's milieu shared a negative attitude toward the cinema, as is clear from the following extract taken from one of Léger's main texts devoted to *Ballet mécanique:*

> The history of the avant-garde film is very simple. It is a direct reaction to films that rely on screenplays and movie stars.
>
> It is a *fantasy,* a sense of play, in opposition to the commercial order established by others.
>
> That's not all. It is the revenge of the painters and poets. In an art form such as this, in which *the image should be everything* but gets sacrificed to a novelistic anecdote, it was necessary to defend one's ground and prove that the imaginative arts, which had been relegated to the status of accessories, could, on their own, by relying on their own means, construct films without screenplays by viewing the moving image as the chief protagonist.[10]

Léger then goes on to call *Ballet mécanique* "a little theoretical."

Clearly, what is at stake is the elimination of the anecdotal element and its probable *replacement* by certain purely plastic elements. The equation of the moving image with the characters in the film says a great deal here, as does Léger's inclusion of poets in his pantheon of avant-garde filmmakers.

Which poets did Léger have in mind? We can answer this question with some certainty. It is most likely that Léger had in mind the writers he knew personally. There were four such poets: Guillaume Apollinaire, Max Jacob, Blaise Cendrars, and Ivan Goll. Léger had particularly close relations with Cendrars and Goll, whose books he illustrated more than once. Both poets were passionately interested in the cinema, another reason Léger was probably thinking of them.

Goll's influence is most evident in Léger's elaboration of a cubist representation of Charlie Chaplin. The cubist Chaplin first appears in Léger's illustrations to Goll's "cinepoem" *Die Chapliniade* (1920), to then become part of Léger's own cinematic work as the main hero of the never completed animated film *Cubist Charlie.*[11] A small part of this incomplete film, the animated figure of Charlie himself, appears at the beginning and end of *Ballet mécanique.* Nevertheless, we have no reason to believe that Goll's work had any formative impact on the making of Léger's film. His influence was most likely limited to specific thematic elements.

Blaise Cendrars is an entirely different matter. His influence on Léger's cinematic production is beyond question and has indeed been noted by most scholars in the field. Standish Lawder, in a book devoted entirely to *Ballet mécanique,* has dwelled specifically on the issue of Cendrars's influence in a chapter entitled "*La Roue,* Cendrars and Gance."[12] Yet Lawder effectively limits the range of Cendrars's impact (and that of other writers) to his participation in Gance's *La Roue* (1921–1923), a film that did exert a major influence on Léger, who wrote an article specifically on the subject. Léger's involvement as illustrator in Cendrars's screenplay-novel *La Fin du monde filmée par l'Ange N.D.* is also now routinely acknowledged. Yet neither encounter can be said to exhaust the breadth of the relations that developed between the two artists.

Léger became close to Cendrars in 1912. Their friendship was then renewed in 1916, when both artists returned from the front. Cendrars, as one of the first protagonists of the French avant-garde to become a serious film enthusiast, apparently was instrumental in infecting Léger with the same passion.

Whereas the cinema seems to figure prominently in Cendrars's artistic trajectory, in fact few visible traces remain of his much-trumpeted filmmaking activities. In an interview, Cendrars's own account of his work reads as follows: "I wanted to make movies, and had the chance to work in England. I shot several films for an English company which then sent me to Italy because of the favorable exchange rate. I stayed for nearly a year in Rome making movies, at the time of Mussolini's March on Rome and triumphant entry into the city. Before that I had worked with Abel Gance. Even before that I had filmed some documentaries with Pathé, some shorts, and a series called *La Nature chez elle.* I wrote screenplays, synopses (as they call them), dialogues, did some editing, and so on."[13]

Of this considerable list of achievements only the collaboration with Gance and a few unproduced screenplays can be verified without a trace of doubt. The films made in England and the shorts connected with Pathé have never been unearthed. It seems reasonable to suppose that the "documentaries with Pathé" are none other than Cendrars's own texts, known under the titles "Kodak" or "Documentary Footage" (1924). These, we now know, were a complete hoax, consisting of phrases cut out with a pair of scissors from Gustave Le Rouge's *Le Mysterieux Doctor Cornélius.* Among these fragments is a text called "Chasse à l'éléphant," which is the likely literary analogue to the film Cendrars purportedly made about elephants. In any case, the evident link between this typical literary hoax and the cinema points to a broader pattern in Cendrars's biography. Apparently, the widely announced project of a Brazilian film was also not destined to be realized. Cendrars had gone to Rome at the suggestion of Jean Cocteau, who told him that the Italian film studio Rinascimento was looking for a French director. Cendrars set about filming *La Vénus Noire* but was never able to complete the shooting because the studio was abruptly closed and the film destroyed.[14] The only thing to survive from this Italian period is the screenplay to the film *La Perle fiévreuse*. François Vanoye has tried to shed some light on Cendrars's enigmatic and somewhat patchy film career, only to admit his failure.[15] Perhaps the poet himself intended this aspect of his life to remain obscure.

It is important to dwell further on the question of Cendrars's role in the films directed by Gance. As Léger tells it, it was these films that drew him to the cinema: "The cinema turned my head around. In 1923 I had some friends who were in film and I was so captivated by the movies that I had to give up painting. That began when I saw the closeups in *La Roue* of Abel Gance. Then I wanted to make a film at any cost and I made *Ballet mécanique*."[16] Standish Lawder interprets Léger's statement in the following way: "Undoubtedly the 'copains qui étaient dans le cinema' of whom Léger speaks here were Blaise Cendrars and the film director Marcel L'Herbier. Cendrars created those parts of *La Roue* that turned Léger's head. He worked as film editor on this production, and, in this capacity, brought forth, in the beginning of the film in particular, a splendid montage that must have impressed and influenced Léger."[17] We know that Cendrars worked as an assistant on *La Roue* (as well as on another of Gance's films, *J'accuse*), but we have no evidence that he worked on the film's montage. Why does Lawder insist on attributing the montage of the best sections of *La Roue* to Cendrars himself? Lawder refers to the testimony of Louis Parrot, who in fact speaks somewhat more cautiously: "In 1921 he collaborates with Abel Gance in the making of *La Roue:* Cendrars' part in the film can be seen in the montage, particularly in the scenes depicting the moving train."[18] Parrot does not clarify what exactly he means by "Cendrars' part"; on the whole, however, he overestimates Cendrars's cinematic skills, calling him a real "specialist in cinema technique."[19] In fact Cendrars himself tried to create this impression by overloading some of his own texts (*Le Plan de l'aiguille, La Perle fiévreuse*) with technical film terminology. However, this hypertechnical vocabulary reads as a stylization.

The legend of Cendrars's formative role in the making of *La Roue* seems to have emerged just after the film's release, and it is highly probable that Cendrars had a considerable hand in its diffusion. As early as March 1923, in a "Letter from Paris" published in the journal *The Dial,* Ezra Pound was to give Cendrars credit for the film's primary achievements: "Thanks, we presume, to Blaise Cendrars, there are interesting moments, and effects which belong, perhaps, only to the cinema. At least for the sake of argument we can admit that they are essentially cinematographic. . . . The bits of machinery, the varying speeds, the tricks of the reproducing machine are admirably exploited, according to pictorial concepts derived from contemporary abstract painters."[20] Elsewhere Pound simply calls *La Roue* one of "Cendrars' films." Astonishingly, Abel Gance, the film's actual maker, is not mentioned even once in Pound's article.[21] No less curious is Pound's derivation of the film's aesthetic from contemporary painting. Pound, moreover, was no outsider to the culture at stake: enjoying close relations with the artistic bohemia of Paris, he also specifically knew the American cameraman Dudley Murphy, who collaborated with Léger on *Ballet mécanique*. Léger himself was to acknowledge Pound's indirect impact on his film. The very stylistic eclecticism of *La Roue* served to give the legend of Cendrars's role further credibility. George Charansol, certainly an informed witness, had this to say about *La Roue* in 1935: "This is now Fernand Léger, now Debat-Ponsan, sometimes Blaise Cendrars, sometimes François Coppée, and sometimes all of them at once."[22] Once again, the only person left out here is Gance himself. It seems extraordinary that Léger also figures among the film's "authors," even though he did little more than design the film's poster (probably at Cendrars's request), and certainly did not participate directly in its making. Charansol's appraisal here is a purely retroactive one, with several features made famous by Léger's *Ballet mécanique* attributed to the earlier *La Roue*.

Jacques-Henry Lévesque is even more unequivocal: "After seeing this reel, full of merits and flaws, it is easy to recognize the part that should be attributed to Cendrars in making this film, which created a sensation above all for its scenes of a speeding train, made in what is called simultaneous montage." While Lévesque generally takes Cendrars's statements at face value, even more curious here is the invention of something called "simultaneous montage," pointing directly to simultaneism, a movement in which Cendrars did indeed take an active part. Lévesque's invented term here eloquently betrays the "etymology" of the myth concerning Cendrars's contribution to *La Roue*.

Is there some way of verifying the nature and extent of Cendrars's role in *La Roue*? We surely must not neglect the testimony of Gance, who had this to say about Cendrars: "Working on the set in the proper sense of the term put him out of sorts, and I could see, on looking at his eyes which were always a little surprised and fixed on us, that he understood nothing."[23] Elsewhere Gance repeats this claim and further clarifies the nature of Cendrars's role as assistant: "To tell the truth, I cannot claim to have been the one to have initiated him into the cinema: he always remained external to our work which put him out of sorts, and which he was barely able to follow; he mainly functioned as assistant director, organizing mountain-climbing parties, or gathering wagons and locomotives. He liked this work which was more concrete."[24]

One could certainly dismiss these subsequent recollections as coming out of Gance's irritation at seeing his own efforts constantly attributed to his assistant. Yet even if we discount the categorical nature of Gance's assertion, it does seem to ring a little true. Georges Sadoul accepts Gance's version entirely: "The writer nonetheless remained simply an assistant, and was not involved actively either in the screenplay or the shooting."[25] Cendrars himself was to confirm Gance's assertions indirectly, when he described his work with Gance during the shooting of *J'accuse* in the autumn of 1918: "For *J'accuse* I did everything: I did the heavy work, took charge of the props, I was the electrician, the pyrotechnist, the wardrobe keeper, the extras man, the assistant cameraman, the assistant director, the boss's driver, the accountant, the cashier."[26] This situation could hardly have been radically different during the filming of *La Roue;* in any case, we have the confirmation of at least one authoritative document, Jean Epstein's unfinished memoir, which coincides pretty much with Gance's account. Epstein was present during the shooting of *La Roue,* as a guest of Cendrars. It turned out, however, that when Epstein got there Gance and most of the film crew had already left; remaining were a few people to whom Gance had assigned the task of shooting the connecting shots. Among them was Cendrars, although the group was in fact supervised by another assistant, Robert Boudrioz. Epstein recalls: "During the day I saw very little of Cendrars, who was everywhere, in places where one would never think of looking—on the engine of a train by the boiler, at the post office busy sending his own telegrams in Morse code, at the Bossons ice-cream shop with a group of guides, in search of a box of make-up and some props or other which had fallen into a crevice."[27] Both Epstein and Gance concur on two facts: that all the seriously professional work had been assigned to Boudrioz, and that Cendrars was effectively the odd-jobs man (the list of his activities is the same in both). Epstein also confirms that when montage work was being done for *La Roue,* Cendrars was actually in Italy, and that Gance's sole assistant during this time was Albert Dieudonné.[28] A definitive understanding of Cendrars's role in the making of *La Roue* has been provided by Roger Icart, whose textological research has established that there were two versions of the film's montage. Furthermore, the major innovations and changes to the montage were made by Gance after his conversations with D. W. Griffith in 1921 at the Mamaroneck studios. It took the entire year of 1922 to put together this montage, which was completed that December. Icart makes several technical points concerning variations in the montage that allow us to dismiss with some certainty the possibility that a relative dilettante like Cendrars might have had a part in shaping the final outcome.

Yet does this mean that we can reduce Cendrars's role in the making of *La Roue* to the work of a second assistant? Of course not. At stake, it seems, is something else—the highly intriguing phenomenon of a film getting intertextualized through the involvement of a well-known writer. Even if we were to ignore the intellectual influence that he undoubtedly exerted on Gance, the very presence of Cendrars was enough to connect the film to a specific set of ideas that the poet embodied. Cendrars may have been of use to Gance on the film set as someone able to elaborate "myths" and insert their concrete manifestations into an extraordinarily powerful intertextual context. Cendrars, then, may well have served to create a myth, one that served *La Roue* very well. Gance took advantage of the poet's tendency to "read" his own "cinematic practice" into films that had actually been made without any real input from him.

Cendrars's myths could often be highly whimsical. For example, he would assert that Charlie Chaplin was in part inspired to make his film *Shoulder Arms* (made in America while Cendrars was serving on the war front in France) by some of Cendrars's own ideas.[29] He also accused Francis Picabia of having stolen the idea of *Entr'acte* from him.[30] These accusations of plagiarism, however, did not constitute a claim of authorship; rather, they reflected a characteristic ability on Cendrars's part to see other people's work as the embodiment of his own ideas. This tendency was in fact a consequence of Cendrars's own constant desire to project his artistic aspirations outward, subjectively appropriating a vast range of works as examples of his own poetics.

From the very first moment he began working on *La Roue*, Gance was confronted with the dilemma of finding some mythic means of overcoming the awkwardly melodramatic material at the film's core. It fell to Cendrars, with his incomparable mythmaking powers, to fulfill this task. The very tendency that elsewhere led Cendrars to the brink of conflict and misunderstanding was here used by Gance to make the material at hand sound more respectable. Cendrars thus "imposed," as he was wont to do, his "own" film aesthetic on Gance's film, leading to subsequent divergences of opinions concerning the extent of his involvement in the making of *La Roue*.

This legitimation of material principally took the form of giving the symbol of the wheel a far greater prominence. The film had been based on the book *Le Rail* (1912) by Pierre Hamp. The film's working title long remained *La Rose du rail*—a somewhat crude allegory quite in the spirit of Gance's bombastic style. The pithy and symbolically resonant title "The Wheel" was probably an invention of Cendrars, although one that fits all too readily into the context of his past work. What occurred, essentially, was a linking of Gance's film to the existing corpus of Cendrars's writings, allowing it to resonate intertextually at the expense of Gance's own work, in order to unite the concrete details of the film with an abstract concept and thereby "represent the unrepresentable." Here is how Gance defined the film:

"The Wheel involves a movement of four forms, each of which revolves one inside the other," said Jacob Boehme. The Circle, the Wheel, do not just sustain life, but endlessly begin it again and again. The title is symbolic and positive. In my mind it is positive because the leitmotif of the film is the wheel of a locomotive, which is one of the film's main heroes, reminding us of fate as something that can never come off the grid of the railway track. In more precisely symbolic terms, it is the wheel of Fortune which is directed against Oedipus.[31]

Hamp's novel, which recounts the strike of a railway workers' union, could hardly have provided the basis for such an allegorical interpretation. It lacks any real elaboration of the wheel as a symbol. Something like Gance's "wheel of fortune" does, however, make an appearance. Thus one Delecambre, who works for the main railway inspection board, makes the following observation about railway accidents: "The railway, even if it is subject to a billion improvements, will always have some flaws: either in the tracks or in the people. The Company is the baker in a roulette game in which Death plays a game of probabilities. It is necessary for Death to win from time to time; otherwise it would get bored."[32] But even here there is no direct connection made between fate and the wheel. Cendrars may well have played a prominent role in linking Hamp's game of roulette to the symbolism of the wheel. Gance traced the latter to Boehme and then admitted that he owed his acquaintance with Boehme and mysticism as a whole to Cendrars. Mystical doctrines were, of course, a fundamental intertext for many avant-garde artists, providing a store of abstract conceptual equivalents for concrete plastic images.

Before we examine the actual process by which the wheel, the circle, and the disk gained symbolic currency in Cendrars's work (a currency that would then circulate in Léger—particularly in *Ballet mécanique*—as well as among other artists), let us complete our examination of the myth of the wheel in Gance's work. This myth, which originates in Cendrars (this will become even clearer as we continue), was taken up by Gance in several grandiloquent declarations and then circulated by converts to his faith, who created something of a cult around his figure. One apostle of the Gance cult was his close friend Jean (Juan) Arroy, who dedicated a book to him that has all the trappings of a new gospel. Gance is called a saint and is placed among such exalted figures as Plato, Moses, Mohammed, Christ, Nietzsche, Swedenborg, Byron, and Whitman.[33] Arroy repeats Gance's symbolic interpretation of *La Roue:* the film, a paroxysm of fate, is the meeting point of Aeschylean tragedy, the Roman doctrine of *fatum,* and Nietzsche's Eternal Return:

> La Roue is truly the first cinematic symbol, and up until today, the only one. Once set in motion, it revolves eternally, and every evening, when the shadows fall and silence sets in, Sisyphus [the film's hero, with an emphatically symbolic name] once more takes up his cross, climbs onto his Golgotha, endures the passion, experiences his suffering and dies. He is condemned to die in this way a thousand billion times. The wheel revolves in its daily crucifixion. . . . The cinema hinders him from dying. O cruel fate. O infernal torture not to be able to flee oneself. O the pain of immortality.[34]

Clearly Arroy turns the wheel into a symbol of cinema itself, with its capacity to reproduce endlessly one and the same "reality." The same myth also circulates in the writings of Epstein, another of Gance's "apostles":

> This film saw the birth of the first cinematic symbol. The Wheel. The martyrs who denounce our dogmas as cruel lies, wear it on their brows, a crown of steel. . . . The Wheel. It rolls along, as long as a heart still beats, along tracks predestined by chance, luck that can be good but is generally bad. The cycle of life and death has become so jagged that it has had to be retempered lest it break. Hope glows in its center, a prisoner. The Wheel. . . . The rapidly revolving cross takes on the form of a rose. That is why, at the summit of your Calvary, Gance, there is *La Roue.*[35]

Cendrars, of course, did not take any part in the creation of this new cult. It seems he was quite far from any desire to Christianize symbols. The transformation of the wheel into a cross, and of the film's hero Sisyphus into an alter ego of Gance who assumes the martyr's crown, is entirely a creation of the director and his entourage. Cendrars in fact did pay some homage to this mythologization of Gance and his film, but in an entirely different way. His first novel, from the cycle about Dan Yack, *Le Plan de l'aiguille,* is dedicated to Gance. This dedication, moreover, is dated December 1919, that is, the very moment Gance was completing the massive (seven-hundred-page) screenplay to *La Roue.*[36] I would suggest that the novel, which Cendrars worked on from 1917 until 1928, contains several veiled hints concerning the making of *La Roue.* The novel's heroine, Dan Yack's beloved, is called Mireille. This was also the title of Gance's first screenplay written for Léonce Perret in 1907–1908, precisely the time he first met Cendrars.[37] Nor does it appear fortuitous that the story of Mireille largely coincides with the life of Ida Danis, Gance's lover, who fell ill during the film's shooting and died on the day the film's initial montage had been completed.[38] Even the shooting schedule of the film had to be adapted to the dictates of Danis's doctors, with scenes on Mont Blanc being worked into the film so that Ida could benefit from the mountain air.

Something quite similar happens in Cendrars's novel. A film is shot especially for the benefit of Mireille, who dies at the end of the film.[39] If we can assume that *Le Plan de l'aiguille* reflects certain events that occurred during the shooting of *La Roue,* it is possible that the relationship between Dan Yack and Mr. Lefauché, the film director in the novel, to some degree reproduces Cendrars's understanding of his relations with Gance. Dan Yack (who is undoubtedly an alter ego of Cendrars himself) does not take any direct part in shooting the film, but he is a true connoisseur of the art and has a thorough knowledge of its technical aspects. He makes paradoxical aesthetic judgments. Marginal to the film's making, he nonetheless remains its central figure. Lefauché, by contrast, is a master of the old school of melodrama, a professional with a limited artistic vision. Of course, there is no reason to project the relations between the novel's heroes onto their prototypes in real life in any literal sense. Yet even considering the specificity of a work of art and the fictional compensation it might provide for the artist's psychological complexes (Dan Yack's role as the film's financier in the novel versus Cendrars's technical incompetence and subordinate position in real life), it seems reasonable to assume that the cinematic sections of *Le Plan de l'aiguille* constitute Cendrars's response to the emergent cult of Gance. The dedication of the novel to Gance might then be read ironically, especially the "modest" warning it contains to the director not to seek any new ideas in the novel.[40]

Cendrars's *Le Plan de l'aiguille* thus offers a specular reversal of the situation that Gance created in *La Roue.* If Gance made use of Cendrars, inviting him onto the film set to serve as a live "marker" of intertextuality, then Cendrars inserted Gance into his novel as a prototype, thereby also recreating the entire context of *La Roue,* albeit in reverse. This reversal, as well as Cendrars's nonacceptance of the Gance cult, may have yet another motivation. The fetishization of the wheel in Gance's milieu contradicted Cendrars's own desire to create a new and unprecedented symbol, while the religious transcendental reading to which Gance's adepts subjected the wheel stripped it of its novelty and turned it into an allegory. In one of his earliest texts, *Moganni Nameh* (1911), Cendrars had criticized the symbol as a "formalized axiom": "In effect few and unique are those who have shaped art, and . . . elaborated a symbol, . . . a symbol such that a new metaphysical heaven is cast on its shoulders."[41]

Cendrars's strategy was thus diametrically opposed to Gance's. At stake was not a given plastic element, to be taken and immersed in a field of symbolic intertextual interpretations (the wheel = the wheel of fortune, etc.). Rather, Cendrars strove to elaborate a new and powerful cultural myth out of the very "plasma of art," weaving a contradictory thread of intertextual links, frustrating any reduction of the symbol to a "formalized axiom," as had been attempted by Gance and his adepts. (Cendrars's "collaboration" with Léger—and with Delaunay—was in this sense far more productive.) Let us now attempt a more painstaking examination of the genesis of the symbol in Cendrars, one all the more necessary since, in pointing to its role in the elevation of the wheel as primary symbol in Gance, we have yet to find any textual evidence for this (beyond Gance's own references to Jakob Boehme). It is time to verify the hypothesis.

In 1906, Cendrars read Camille Flammarion's *Popular Astronomy* (1880), which touched him profoundly and led him to take up astronomy and then astrology. Subjecting Flammarion's work to a highly poetic reading, Cendrars transformed the poetic topos of the sky into a series of heavenly spheres that resemble a complex mechanism, in which wheel-like planets decided people's fate. Yvette Bozon-Scalzitti has observed that the novel *Moganni Nameh*, yet to overcome the influence of symbolism, already betrays the influence of Cendrars's passion for astrology, as in the following passage: "As far away as the most distant centers, circles slowly began to move. His brain was now nothing more than a harmonious wave, a mathematical sky in which comets circulated among the planets in a complex play regulated by preordained movements."[42] Cendrars's capacity for a complex and reciprocally charged metaphorization of reality allowed him to discover new elements in the symbol of the celestial wheels each time he returned to it. For example, in a text on Marc Chagall from 1912 he wrote: "The wheels of folly whirl in the furrowed sky and besplatter the face of God!"[43] Gradually the idea of a celestial mechanism begins to be linked to the image of a *perpetuum mobile*, in which the wheel gains pride of place. In 1976, a text by Cendrars on the *perpetuum mobile*, conceived of as an appendix to his description of the cosmic voyage *L'Eubage* (1917), was published for the first time. In this text, written in 1917 and hence predating by several years Gance's first efforts at making *La Roue*, we find a complete elaboration of the myth that was later to be used by Gance. I quote a lengthy passage here, which is all the more necessary since it also bears directly on *Ballet mécanique:*

> Without doubt religious motivations and mythological monuments must have played a large role in the question of the *perpetuum mobile*. One need only think of the enormous importance that the symbolism of the ancient religions attached to the wheel, a symbol that incorporates the idea of movement and the idea of eternal return. In the religion of the Vedas, the wheel is the symbol of divinity. The same goes for the ancient Germans and the Celts. Many customs and myths bear witness to the religious origin of the wheel as a symbol, which is compared mostly to the sun, both in its form and its movement. It is as a form of wheel symbolism that Oldenberg explains the presence of a crown nailed to the top of the stake to which sacrificial animals were tied in many ancient religions. . . . One can ascribe religious motives to the theologians of the Middle Ages who attacked with such ferocity the idea

of perpetual movement, claiming movement to be finite and declaring the *perpetuum mobile* to be incompatible with the Science of God. . . .

The human desire for an artificial machine that might work forever goes back to the most ancient times; this desire is perhaps as old as the desire for immortality itself. Outside any technology, the idea of perpetual movement is one of the oldest questions posed by human civilization.[44]

Cendrars here pauses briefly on the question of religious symbolism, in order to discover concealed behind it the primary idea of movement. This idea, which traditionally has been associated with life as such, here acquires some rather unusual features, in that Cendrars connects it with the evolution of a new language. Many movements in early twentieth-century art—most demonstratively futurism—transformed movement into the sign of a new civilization and a new artistic language. Cendrars's approach was nonetheless somewhat unique. His lecture entitled "Poets," presented in Brazil in 1924 and devoted essentially to the problem of language, has survived. The poet departs from the assumption that language has evolved from the "concrete to the abstract, from the mystical to the rational."[45] In the spirit of numerous modern writers, Cendrars appeals for a return to a primordial language that is at once concrete and mystical. In this appeal, however, he goes far beyond the accustomed rhetorical norm. Not only does Cendrars note the parallelism between the development of language and that of industrial technology; he even "instrumentalizes" language in the most literal way, treating it as a physical act, a mechanical movement. Cendrars generously quotes the linguist Joseph Vendryes, especially from his descriptions of speech mechanisms. "'There are thus accelerations, jolts, reductions in speed, moments of rest. In other words, language contains within itself a rhythmic principle with stronger and weaker tempos.'"[46] And again: "'In this play of complex movements that constitutes the phonic system, it can happen that one of the organs exaggerates or reduces its action to an even minimal degree, or that a muscle executes a movement somewhat gently or slowly, or, on the contrary, with greater vigor and rapidity.'"[47]

Speech here acquires all the traits of a mechanical activity and at the same time loses its capacity for semantic transparency. It becomes something physically visible, tangible (Cendrars even speaks of the possibility of a language based on the sensations of taste, touch, or sight),[48] and acquires the hieroglyphic quality that results from the intertextual layering of quotations. For Cendrars, poetic discourse is a physical mechanism, powerfully intertextual, a vertiginous layering of fragments, quotes, borrowings, heterogeneous blocks. Intertextuality thus becomes part of the sheer physicality of the muscular movement involved in speaking.

The wheel emerges here as an essential metaphor for imagining a new language. Reproducing in its very movement the rhythmic and mechanical aspects of the articulatory apparatus, it becomes a metaphor for the speech organs and turns the kaleidoscope of image quotations. Gradually the circle, the wheel, and the disk grow into fetishes for Cendrars, becoming more than just wheels of fortune, wheels bearing the chariot of being, or the cogwheels in a cosmic mechanism. They become the mechanical elements of a new "metalanguage" of the universe and are integrated as such into Cendrars's texts. This is what the wheel signifies in one of Cendrars's main works, *Moravagine* (1926), which Gance in fact read in manuscript form while working on *La Roue*.[49] These may well be the origins of the metadescriptive symbolism that was projected onto the wheel in the film. In one moment in *Moravagine*, wheels serve to introduce a dream sequence:

> The wheels of the train [cf. *La Roue*] turned in my head, with each turn mincing my brain into tiny pieces. Vast expanses of blue sky entered my eyes, but then the wheels would also madly rush in, wreaking complete havoc. They revolved in the depths of the sky, staining it with long, oily marks. . . . The sky was hardening, bursting like a mirror, and the wheels, taking up their charge for the last time, were smashing it to pieces. Thousands of pieces of debris crackled as they revolved, and tons of noise, cries and voices rolled down like avalanches, going off and reverberating in my eardrums. . . . Above and below, images of the city hung in the air, then spun around, right side up, then upside down, up-down, before collapsing into dust.[50]

This pulverization of the world's images into details and fragments—a kind of cubist transformation of the world that we shall soon rediscover in *Ballet mécanique*—is in fact an effect of the wheel itself, which for Cendrars serves as a mechanism for generating a new vision of the world, a new language. Later on in *Moravagine* Cendrars explains:

> A circle is no longer something round but a wheel.
>   And this wheel turns. . . .
>   *It generates a new language* . . . of words and things, disks and runes, Portuguese and Chinese, numerals and factory labels, industrial patents, postage stamps, tickets, records of shipping and handling, signal codes, the radio—language is remade and becomes flesh, language that is the reflection of human consciousness, the poetry that grants access to the image of the mind that conceived it, a lyricism that is a way of being and feeling, the animated and demotic language of the cinema[51] that speaks to the restless crowds of the illiterate, the newspapers that know nothing of grammar and syntax, in order to bedazzle our eyes all the more with typographic displays of advertisements. . . .
>   Everything is artificial and real. The eyes. The hand. The vast fur of numbers on which the bank lies sprawling. The sexual fury of the factories. The wheel that turns. The wing that soars. . . . Rhythm. Life.[52]

"Language is remade and becomes flesh," says Cendrars, and its body is composed of quotes.

The wheel thus acquires a far wider significance in Cendrars's mythology than it had in Gance's film, becoming strongly associated with the idea of a new language, which is also the language of cinema.

Cendrars was always on the lookout for people who would listen to him; he would deafen those around him with a torrent of unusual ideas, images, and fantastic recollections, creating a certain aura around his own persona. The relations established between him and those who were drawn to his aura were seldom less than complex, but few were able to escape the powerful influence of his ideas. He sought constantly to gauge the efficacy of his ideas in other art forms, involving for this purpose other artists who were already in his sphere of influence. Particularly important and fruitful was the encounter between Cendrars and Robert Delaunay, which even had an impact on the work of Léger.

Cendrars met Delaunay in 1912 and settled in his house in the autumn of the same year. It was the year Delaunay elaborated his theory of "simultaneism" in painting. Cendrars took an active part in this epic quest, whose most celebrated outcome was the first "simultaneist" book coauthored by Cendrars and Sonia Delaunay (the painter's wife), entitled *La Prose du Transsibérien* (1913). John Golding explains the basis of simultaneist theory:

> Delaunay conceived of a type of painting in which the colors used to produce a sensation of light would not blend but would retain their separate identities; by their interaction these colors could furthermore be made to produce a sensation of depth and movement. Since movement implies duration, time was also an element of this new art. Using the terminology of Chevreul [Michel-Eugène Chevreul (1786–1889), a chemist who studied the problem of color and published *On the Law of the Simultaneous Contrast of Colours* (1839), a book that influenced Delacroix, Seurat, and Signac], Delaunay called these color contrasts "simultaneous," to distinguish them from those used by the Impressionists and their successors which were "binary" and tended to fuse together when seen at a distance.[53]

Delaunay's celebrations of color was to have a powerful influence on Cendrars, particularly evident in his *Nineteen Elastic Poems*. Delaunay drew Cendrars into a shrill exchange between himself and Henri Barzun, who also claimed to have invented simultaneism.[54] Getting involved in the struggle between rival movements in painting allowed Cendrars to present himself as a credible theoretician. In fact, a great deal of what he would say was taken from Delaunay. One clear example of Delaunay's influence can be seen in the condemnation, unexpected in Cendrars's texts, of geometry as a personification of death: "Death is the consciousness that humanity has gained of itself (geometry)."[55] This can be compared with Delaunay's statement: "They [the futurists] today arrive at their point of death: geometry, the machine, geometrical dance etc."[56]

Cendrars, we know, would later become one of the great enthusiasts of geometry and the machine.

It would be a mistake, however, to think that Delaunay's influence on Cendrars was only one-way. Cendrars was also to influence the painter, as can be seen in Delaunay's clear abandonment of rectilinear forms in favor of circular and disklike shapes that coincided with his first meetings with Cendrars.[57] If the series *Les Fenêtres,* begun in 1912 and marking the beginning of simultaneism, was by and large expressed in rectilinear forms, then on the cusp of 1912–1913 Delaunay turned to circular forms to create a series of paintings with his typical astronomical symbolism, *Soleil, lune, simultané 2* (1912–1913), *Formes circulaires,* (1912–1913), *Disque, première peinture inobjective* (1913), and so forth. The disk, as we know, would soon become one of the primary base elements of Delaunay's art. The "simultaneous disk" was to acquire clearly symbolic traits in Delaunay's worldview.[58] It allowed the artist to overcome the static quality of his early compositions in color and achieve the sensation of movement. Sonia Delaunay was to have an analogous evolution. From 1914–1915 on, the disk was to dominate her painting as well (*Marché au Minho* [1915], *Danseuse* [1923], etc.). Here is what Sonia Delaunay herself had to say about the origin of the circular form in her painting *Prismes électriques* (1914): "It comes out of observing the halo of moving colors that were produced around the electric lightbulbs celebrated by Blaise Cendrars in his 'Dix-neuf poèmes élastiques.'"[59]

Proceeding from simultaneist premises, Cendrars developed certain elements of Delaunay's doctrine in a way that was all his own. For example, he would radically rethink the notion of contrast, which Delaunay had construed in a somewhat technological fashion.[60] For Cendrars, contrast would become the basis for vitality, something like Bergson's *élan vital.* The poem "Contrast" is filled with motifs derived from the programmatic declarations of the simultaneists (the poem would then inspire Sonia Delaunay to paint her "halos of moving color"). Cendrars rendered Delaunay's painterly principles in powerfully mythic terms: "The movement is in depth [*mouvement en profondeur*]. Life is the most immediate expression of this movement and of this depth. Life is the form of this depth (sensuality), the formula of this movement (abstraction). Animism. Nothing is stable. Everything is movement in depth."[61] Clearly, Delaunay's artistic movement became in Cendrars's eyes the embodiment of life itself, while at the same time being closely linked to the idea of an innovation in language. Contrast serves to introduce the apparatus of vocal articulation into the canvas itself. The painting begins to speak. At the same time, the rhythmic nature of movement in depth is associated with eroticism.[62] Cendrars rewrites Delaunay's artistic declarations as if they were mythological, erotic, or esoteric texts.

In close touch with both Delaunay and Cendrars, Léger did in fact adopt some ideas of the former. Delaunay's influence can be seen, for example, in *Paris par la Fenêtre* (1912), which is probably a response to Delaunay's *Les Fenêtres*. Soon, however, a conflict was to drive a wedge between the two artists. The dispute concerned the use of color. In 1933, Delaunay, who still considered Léger's choices to have been mistaken, wrote that "Léger did not understand that color is the only drawing possible. We cannot do what Léger did—a drawing and then put color on top."[63] In a conversation with Cendrars recorded on October 27, 1954, Léger reminisced with Cendrars—himself an active participant in these controversies—about his disagreements with Delaunay, all of which assumed the proportions of a veritable war: "It was the time of the great battle with Delaunay; he wanted to continue doing impressionistic relations, and I wanted to arrive at a sense of local color. So I'd tell him, 'Old chap, if you go on like that, you are going to start doing Signac to scale.' And he'd say, 'You are going to take us back to museum colors.' And then we'd get into a slinging match. What took place between Delaunay and me was the battle of colors."[64]

The circle was to play a decisive role in this battle between Delaunay and Léger. Léger swiftly assimilated the circular form, derived from Delaunay and Cendrars, into his own artwork. Werner Schmalenbach has described the significance of Léger's debt to Delaunay and Cendrars as follows: "Before the war, Delaunay had made a start on his *formes circulaires*. In his eyes the circle was *the* absolute form, the colored circle *the* symbol of light. Léger, though undoubtedly influenced by Delaunay's suns and moons, was quite free of his sort of light symbolism. . . . Not Delaunay's cosmic, 'Orphic' suns but colored machine wheels that revolve around their axes."[65]

The dispute between Delaunay and Léger, emblematically rendered in the opposition of the cosmic star and the mechanical wheel, became the object of a characteristically laconic and witty parody by Marcel Duchamp, who in 1913 presented his first controversial "ready-made object"—the *Bicycle Wheel*. The very absurdity of Duchamp's creation—the front wheel of a bicycle attached to a stool—served as his ironic contribution to the dispute.[66] When Duchamp's wheel began turning, it produced the same effect as that created by Newton's disks; these had fascinated Delaunay, who sketched them during his research into circular rhythms. Duchamp's *Bicycle Wheel* was thus a rendering of Delaunay's experiments with color executed in Léger's style, with "mechanical" imagery: it thus parodically "resolved" the contradictions between the two artists.

Cendrars—who lent the circle its mythic dimension—also found himself at the center of the debate. The understanding of the circle both as a cosmic symbol and as a mechanical wheel belong to him. The myth Cendrars propagated thus split into two forms readily identified with Léger and Delaunay. Later Cendrars would recall that "every writer had his painter. Me, I had Delaunay and Léger."[67] Slowly, however, Léger was to displace Delaunay and grow in importance for Cendrars. To some extent this process is reflected in "Twelve Elastic Poems." The first poems in the cycle by and large "feed off" Delaunay's painting. The second poem ("The Tower") and the third ("Contrasts"), both written in 1913, are directly related to simultaneist aesthetics and its creator. Léger, by contrast, was the inspiration for the final poem in the cycle, "Construction" (February 1919). This work, dedicated to Léger, can be seen as Cendrars's move away from the poetics of simultaneism to a position that can be described more as constructivist. Here is the poem in full:

De la couleur, de la couleur et des couleurs . . .
Voici Léger qui grandit comme le soleil de l'époque tertiaire
Et qui durcit
Et qui fixe
La nature morte
La croûte terrestre
Le liquide
Le brumeux
Tout ce qui se ternit
La géométrie nuageuse
Le fil à plomb qui se résorbe
Ossification.
Locomotion.
Tout grouille
L'esprit s'anime soudain et s'habille à son tour comme
    les animaux et les plantes
Prodigeusement
Et voici
La peinture devient cette chose énorme qui bouge
La roue
La vie
La machine
L'âme humaine
Une culasse de 75
Mon portrait

(Color, color, and colors
Here's Léger who grows like the sun in the tertiary age
And who hardens
and fixes
the still life [*or* dead nature]
The earth's crust
The liquid
The foggy

Everything that darkens
The cloudy geometry
The plumb line that is reabsorbed
Ossification.
Locomotion.
Everything swarms
And the mind suddenly comes to life and in its turn
    dresses like animals and plants
Prodigiously
And now
Painting becomes this huge moving thing
The wheel
Life
The machine
The human soul
A 75-mm breech
My portrait)[68]

Léger's painting is here described as a crystallization, the mechanization of something amorphous, born of color and sky—in other words, the primary elements, to an extent, of Delaunay's canvas.

Evidence of Cendrars's growing friendship with Léger can be found in many places. In 1913–1914, Léger painted a series of works called *Contrastes des formes,* a title that highlights a theme close to Cendrars. In 1918, Léger began the "disk series": *Les Disques* (1918), *Deux disques dans la ville* (1919), *Les Disques dans la ville* (1924), and so forth. The poster that Léger made for Gance's *La Roue* is in fact a variation on the theme of this series, which marks the beginning of a period of intense collaboration between writer and painter. In 1917, Léger illustrated *La Fin du monde;* in 1918, he illustrated *J'ai tué;* and in 1923, both artists collaborated on the ballet *La Création du monde.*

For Léger, Delaunay's work, as well as the polemical relations that existed between them, receded into the past. He succeeded in overcoming Delaunay's poetics by dissociating object, form, and color. The contrasting placement of objects (and indeed any fragments taken from the world or from texts) can, for Léger, generate the sensation of movement in art. Delaunay found this unacceptable. Pierre Francastel summarizes Delaunay's view of the nature of movement: "There is only one way to apprehend movement, which is a fundamental quality of the nature of the universe, and that is color."[69] In the posthumously published fragment "L'Art du mouvement" (1924?), Delaunay touches on the cinema, whose mechanical movement strikes him as "dead" in comparison with the sensation of movement created by the contrast of colors on a canvas: "Until now the art of cinema has involved a play of photos arranged successively and providing the illusion of real life—very sad as subject matter. The photo, even the ideal color photo by Kodak, can never be worth as much as a bath taken at a pleasant impressionist temperature."[70]

Léger's *Ballet mécanique* partly makes use of Delaunay's idea of contrasts, but in a modified form. In his rapid and rhythmic montages, Léger juxtaposes immobile objects, generating a sense of movement at the expense of contrast, and in a way that dispenses with the need for color. Léger's film in black and white acts to confirm Delaunay's intuitions but at the same time broadens their range and finally debunks them.

It is no coincidence, then, that—this despite Delaunay's own hostility toward the cinema—numerous contemporaries of Léger christened the montage based on the juxtaposition of immobile objects "simultaneous" (e.g., George Levesque cited the scenes of the speeding train in *La Roue* as examples of "simultaneous montage"), thus making Delaunay its immediate progenitor. In his 1920 article "Das Kinodram," Ivan Goll mentions simultaneism as one of the precursors of the cinema. The style of Goll's declaration (which Léger probably knew) is derived entirely from the simultaneist manifestos: "The image is freed from the space of the frame and breathes in time [*atmet zeitlich*]: through the rapid succession of various ascending and descending contrasts, the film is created."[71]

From 1916 on, Cendrars would return again and again to the idea of making a film. We know already that the film he dreamed of creating was never made. As was his habit, Cendrars preferred to "impose" his cinematic vision on others. He took great pleasure in describing to his friends an imaginary film that he would make if he had the chance. Philippe Soupault recalls: "I still remember his enthusiasm for the cinema. Charlie Chaplin, of course! (It was in his company that I saw the film *Shoulder Arms*, which he rightly thought was outstanding.) But his vision of the cinema was completely different. Before writing it, he told me about the extraordinary screenplay that he was to publish several years later."[72] The screenplay mentioned here is without a doubt *La Fin du monde*. Epstein recalls Cendrars's dream of making a Rabelaisian film with "astonishing close-ups of people gorging on food."[73] Among those that Cendrars tried to hypnotize with a verbal portrait of his extraordinary film was the prominent French actor and theater director Louis Jouvet. Cendrars apparently thought Jouvet capable of making his imaginary film. We have Jouvet's account of the vision Cendrars shared with him:

> What a funny film we could make, a stream of gags, endless and absurd . . . with a set located in some industrial area, a graveyard of motor cars, broken gasometers, shattered tar barrels piled up in teetering pyramids, floodgates from sluices floating about, trails of ash, a stretch of broken glass from bottles, mounds of buckets ripped to pieces, embankments riddled with mattress springs and other débris that passes by the name of civilization.[74]

For Cendrars the cinema was connected to the idea of a new language, to be born through the destruction of traditional ways of relating objects and the shattering of the world into fragments. These fragments were not intended to enter the linear flow of the narrative: they preserved their character as distinct corpuscles, unintegrated, "anomalous." The cinematic text was to come together out of a vast, unlimited selection of quotes, all of which could openly display their quotational character. The text essentially had to mobilize the limitless field of intertextuality that was the basis of Cendrars's understanding of cinematic language.

Slowly forming in Cendrars's mind was the still amorphous image of a film resembling a chaotic picture made up of the distinct elements that constitute civilization, forming a kind of human trace. The rubbish heap and the graveyard are images betokening this "catastrophic consciousness," which transforms the final cataclysm into the starting point for creating a new language. For Cendrars the destruction of the world was in principle equivalent to the creation of a new world. An organized disintegration is in its own way identical to creation. Cendrars, moreover, was to project this artistic agenda not only onto the cinema but also onto all the artistic genres, above all painting. It is no coincidence that Cendrars's attention was to focus on Léger's painting, which he interpreted consistently according to his notion of the catastrophic genesis of a new language.

Interestingly, Cendrars's article "Fernand Léger" (1919) describes Léger's painting in terms that resemble the language Cendrars had used to describe his own film project to Jouvet: "Lots filled with machines, instruments and implements. The painter's mind grasps all this. Around him new forms arise every day. Huge volumes move with ease, thanks to a series of movements broken down into short tempos. His gaze moves from the bucket to the zeppelin, from the caterpillar to the tiny spring taken from a cigarette lighter. An optical signal. A bulletin board. A poster. . . . Everything is contrast. . . . Now here's the topic: the creation of human activity."[75] Curiously, the association of Léger's painting with a cinema of chaos remained Cendrars's idée fixe for many years. For example, in a much later conversation with Léger, recalling a trip abroad, Cendrars says: "I thought about you a lot when I saw this extraordinary film, whose title I unfortunately don't remember. The film was set entirely in a graveyard for motor cars; there was a kind of mechanical bird in it, sort of like an American crow, that ate motor cars, gorging on tons and tons of steel, thousands of tyres."[76]

Typical of Cendrars, then, is a constant desire to elevate his own poetics into a myth, which circulated in his work in the form of certain plot scenarios. Thus his program for the creation of a new language, dating back roughly to 1917, is mythologized into two plot sequences that are finally fused into one: *La Fin du monde* and *La Création du monde*. From this moment on, the poet's linguistic agenda is described with extraordinary persistence as the destruction and re-creation of the world. Significantly, the cinema is itself inserted into this eschatological myth. This is easily explained: the cinema symbolized a new language born of the shattered material world, and thus was the ideal vehicle for describing the universal cataclysm. This myth is most dramatically expressed in *La Fin du monde filmée par l'Ange N.D.* (1917), with illustrations by Léger.[77] The novel's plot deals with a journey made by God to the planet Mars, where he decides to fulfill certain ancient prophecies. He sends a telegram to Earth to the angel of Notre Dame cathedral in Paris, who carries out the divine command to film the Earth's destruction. This film is then shown on Mars. But the camera projecting the film breaks down, and the entire film, which has just been spooled into place, begins to unwind in the opposite direction. The script primarily deals with describing this film, which documents the world's end.

Several crucial details should be noted here. By speeding up and slowing down the projection, millennial cataclysms are compressed into a few pages. The world's end is rendered as the precipitous decline of civilization and its return to a prehistoric stage, that of the world's creation. Just as the film is shown in reverse at the end of the book, so the history of the world's end becomes the history of its creation. A technical motivation (the camera breakdown) allows for the beginning and end of the world to become one, made identical by the technology of film.

A careful reading of the novel brings out a further detail that until now has escaped the attention of critics. The poem "Construction," quoted earlier and dedicated to Léger, is in fact nothing less than a summary of *La Fin du monde*. This is how the book describes the extinguishing of the sun: "At the trumpet's first sound, the sun's disk grows sharply in size, while its light grows duller."[78] And the poem: "Here's Léger who grows like the sun in the tertiary age," that is, in precisely the era described in the novel. The sun then grows to improbable proportions and then "dissolves. A kind of granular, phosphorescent mist [hangs] over a decomposed sea in which some obscene, gigantic, swollen larvae move ponderously."[79] Then the world begins to harden: "The joints petrify. . . . The movement, becoming more rarefied, gets fixed in a hinge. . . . We begin to see the formation of crystals."[80] (Cf. in the poem: "And who hardens / and fixes / the still life [*or* dead nature] / The earth's crust / The liquid / The foggy / Everything that darkens.") The script then introduces the motif of darkness—"All is black"—before describing the geometric division of the world: "Segments of shadow become detached. Tapering flames are isolated. Cones, cylinders, pyramids."[81] (Cf. in the poem: "Painting becomes this huge moving thing / The wheel / Life / The machine.") The two texts, then, are clearly parallel,

showing the extent to which Cendrars interpreted Léger's painting as his
own film on the apocalypse: it is no wonder that at the end of the poem
Cendrars is able to call Léger's canvas "my portrait."

Cendrars's capacity to appropriate any given text that treats the problem of genesis is also based on his consistent desire to articulate his own
birth within the myth of universal creation. In his poem "La Ventre de ma
mère," for example, Cendrars attempts to describe his condition before
birth. Later he was to declare with pride that "this poem is the sole testimony known to this day of the activity of consciousness in a fetus; it is, at
the very least, an outline of what prenatal consciousness might be."[82] Cendrars sought in his own prehistory to uncover the prehistory of the world,
the night out of which all intelligible forms took shape. This is why the
phrase "all is black" precedes the geometric segmentation of the world.
This is a classical metaphor of birth, translated into cinematic terms as a
beam of light in the darkness.

Roughly at this time, Cendrars wrote and published a striking text
called "De la partition des couleurs" (June 17, 1919). It is dedicated to a
film by the artist Léopold Survage that was destined never to be made. In
1914, Survage conceived of making a film based on the rhythmic transformations through time of color taken individually or grouped in clusters.
An enormous number of outline sketches were made in preparation for
the film, but the outbreak of World War I effectively prevented Survage
from completing the project. Apollinaire organized an exhibition of Survage's sketches and published Survage's explanatory manifesto in his journal *Soirée de Paris* (1914).[83] Cendrars did not respond immediately to these
events; in fact, his article on Survage appeared three years later! It is clear,
moreover, that the project as Survage had conceived it was of little interest
to Cendrars; the film was only the latest pretext for yet another of Cendrars's cinematic fantasies. After a brief preface in which Survage is taken
to task for failing to complete his film, the article seizes the bull, as it were,
by the horns:

> Alas, it is still impossible to film directly in color. I shall attempt to render, in
> words as photogenic as possible, the bold manner by which Mr. Léopold Sur-
> vage has succeeded in re-creating and decomposing the circular movement
> of color. He has more than two hundred drawings. You would think you were
> present at *the actual creation of the world.*
>
> Little by little a red invades the black screen and soon fills the entire visual
> disk. . . . It [the red] is composed of a multitude of small plates placed one
> alongside the other. Each of these plates is crowned by a pimple that trem-
> bles gently and ends up bursting like cooling lava.

Later some blue appears, "spreading its branches in all directions." The
red rotates along with the blue.

Nothing remains on the screen save two huge marks in the shape of beans, one red and the other blue, facing each other. They look like embryos, masculine and feminine. They meet, copulate, separate, and multiply by splitting one or more of their cells.

Later vegetation appears out of these cells:

Boughs, branches, trunks, everything shakes, falls to the ground and rises. . . . Everything turns dizzyingly from center to periphery. A sphere forms, a dazzling sphere, in a gorgeous yellow color. Like a fruit. The yellow explodes.

And finally,

The white stabilizes and hardens. It turns to ice. And all around the void deepens. The disk, the black disk, reappears and obstructs the field of vision.[84]

It is no longer that easy to establish definitive links between Cendrars's essay and Survage's original ideas. Survage's sketches have not survived in full. They lie scattered in different collections, and to this day have never been reproduced in a size or quantity that would permit us to evaluate the original intent behind *Rythmes colorés*. Nonetheless, even the few surviving sketches suffice to establish Cendrars's commentary as yet another myth-making exercise: once more, Cendrars imposes his own cinematic ideas on another artist. The notion of movement as generated by contrasts in color, harking back to Delaunay, is here interpreted unambiguously in the context of the myth of genesis, while the embryo episode eroticizes the cosmogonic myth in a way that is quite typical of Cendrars. The commentary is filled with quotes from *La Fin du monde:* the description of the growth of vegetation, the motif of the revolving and exploding sphere, and the very Cendrarsian identification of the disk with the faculty of sight.

In any case, Cendrars's analysis of Survage's *Rythmes colorés* shows how far he was prepared to go to appropriate, in the ideal Platonic sense, the film, which he saw as embodying the most fundamental principles of creativity. Cendrars's strategy readily conforms to other attempts on his part, which we have already seen, to give a semblance of reality to his own cinematic fantasies. He would take up a concept, long abandoned and clearly destined never to be realized, and intertextualize it retrospectively, immersing it in a sea of quotes from his own work. In this way a text by "someone else" became one vast quote from his own texts that had somehow been "plagiarized" from him by the film itself. Cendrars persistently nursed his own cinematic utopia, while maintaining it suspended in a condition of "virtual reality." His cinematic model in fact served as a mechanism *internal* to literature: a metamodel of his own literary work that Cendrars projected fictitiously onto the cinema.

Of particular significance in this metamodel of creativity was the destructive moment, the tabula rasa. Moreover, the repeated use of the same themes in different semiotic contexts (a repetition motivated by the auto-biographical nature of almost all his works) led Cendrars to rewrite end-lessly the texts he had already "destroyed." The film being shown in reverse in *La Fin du monde* is thus a perfect metaphor for Cendrars's poetics. Not-ing the persistence of autobiographical elements in Cendrars's intertext, Claude Leroy makes the convincing argument that by fictitiously reducing this intertext to a state of chaos and nonbeing, Cendrars was able to gen-erate new texts.[85]

Cendrars's projection of his own literary model onto the cinema was in fact an ambiguous gesture. On the one hand, Cendrars was truly fascinated by the cinema as the source of a new language; on the other, he was clearly seeking to disguise his own literary methods by giving them a cinematic form. The director Gance, who was deeply influenced by Cendrars, formu-lated this problem as follows in his "major" theoretical text: "The process of constructing a film script is the reverse of what is involved in a novel or play. Here everything comes from outside. First everything is misty, then a scenery gets delineated . . . the earth has already formed, but there are not yet any creatures. Kaleidoscopes appear."[86] Gance then goes on to describe the making of "creatures," "human machines," and how they are prepared for work. The entire process of filmmaking is here equated with the cre-ation of the universe (Gance's demiurgic complex is certainly playing its part here), in sharp contrast to literature. Gance's idea seems to have been dictated to him by Cendrars: while always insisting that cinema and litera-ture were diametrically opposed, Cendrars himself always created his liter-ary texts according to a cinematic model.

Quick to forgive artists and film directors for borrowing his ideas, in-deed always ready to propagate his thoughts among them, Cendrars was nonetheless extremely critical of fellow writers for attempting the same. Any case of writer influencing writer was, for Cendrars, an infringement on his priorities. Jean Epstein recalls a prolonged and bitter quarrel that took place between him and Cendrars, who accused him of plagiarism (Epstein was not at that point working in the cinema) and demanded that he halt the publication of his book *Bonjour cinéma* (1921). Epstein was at a loss to understand the reason for his former benefactor's wrath. Cendrars saw Ep-stein's book as duplicating his own *A B C du cinéma:* both were conceived as providing a literary model for the cinema.[87]

Yet perhaps the most rarefied system of relations between the poetics of different art forms was achieved by Cendrars in his ballet *La Création du monde* (1923). This piece is also essential for the light it sheds on *Ballet mé-canique:* it was devised just before the making of the film, and was the prod-uct of the most intense collaboration between Cendrars and Léger to date. Based on a libretto written by Cendrars himself and music by Darius Mil-haud, the ballet was choreographed by Jean Börlin for the Ballets suédois led by Rolf de Maré. Cendrars's libretto was based on an African creation myth that had appeared in his own *Negro Anthology*. The ballet's theme resonated deeply for him, touching on the genesis of the world and of the text.

The show was presented as a spectacle arising out of chaos. "The circle opens," wrote Cendrars in the libretto, "three divinities cast a new spell, and we see the formless mass seethe. Everything is in motion, a monstrous leg appears." From this chaos a couple then emerges, and "while the couple performs the dance of desire and then of mating, the formless beings remaining on the ground slyly emerge and drift into the circle, accelerating its pace frenetically to the point of vertigo."[88] This description largely coincides with related texts by Cendrars, including his commentary on Survage's film, where embryos copulate to create the universe. Léger succeeded in creating a vivid plastic analogue to Cendrars's literary agenda. His contribution to the ballet has been described by Pierre Descargues:

> For *La Création du monde* . . . at first he created a sense of chaos, in order then to generate progressively in the minds of the spectators the notion of order, organization and the creation of an ordered life. When the curtain went up, one's gaze fell upon an extremely cluttered scene in total disarray, where one was unable to distinguish the set from the actors. Then slowly certain decorative elements began to move, pieces of the set started to move apart, clouds rose toward the sky; one could make out the stirring of strange animal-like masses; the rhythm began to accelerate.[89]

Léger's plastic rendering of Cendrars's text was realized on the very borderline of cinema. I have already noted the strongly cinematic overtones of the cosmogonic theme in Cendrars. The ballet allowed for the introduction of a third semiotic system, dance, into the already complex relationship between literature and cinema. Cendrars's "cinematic" texts had already involved ritual dances (and the ballet by Milhaud had been based on the poetics of African ritual dance). In *La Création du monde* the motif of ritual dance appears twice in the second chapter, "Le Barnum des Religions": "Negro, oceanic, Mexican fetishes. Grimacing masks. Ritual dances and songs." And a little later: "the frozen horror of negro masks, the cruelty of the dances."[90]

The connection between the African fetish and the cinema is most clearly visible in the novel *Moravagine*. Within a description of a psychiatric clinic in which the narrator, Raymond la Science, is incarcerated, there is a particularly eloquent moment: "On the white tiled floor of the various rooms, bathtubs, ergometers, pergolators appear as if on a screen, all of the same savage and terrible largeness which objects possess in films, a largeness of intensity, which is of the same scale as negro art, Indian masks and primitive fetishes, and which express the latent activity, the egg, the

formidable sum of permanent energy which each inanimate object contains."[91]

The African fetish becomes a symbolic equivalent of the close-up shot.
The close-up is also linked to the animistic energy of things and to the symbol of the egg as the primordial element from which everything is created.
It is the genetic corpuscle from which the universe is born. The close-up
shot in cinema and the African fetish on a mythic level are interchangeable. This analogy is introduced by Cendrars into his ballet, in which circular forms are made to move (the mythic-erotic equivalent of copulation), and where fetishes and masks generate the energy underlying
creation.

In another cinematic text, the screenplay *La Perle fiévreuse* (also a symbol
of creation), the theme of dance has already been assimilated into the tex-
tures of cinematic language and is further linked to the fragmentation of the
body through close-up shots (fetishes), and to erotic myths. Here the dancer
Rougha performs an Indian dance that has a specific ritual meaning:

507. Close-up. Rougha becomes still, as if inspired.
508. A rush into the dizzying midst of the dance. Rapid swirls (attempt some
upside-down perspectives) by reversing the camera angle.
509. Flashes and various close-ups of the details of the dance: a finger, a
shoulder-plate, the toes spread apart, the stomach taut with effort, the hips
heaving, etc.[92]

In becoming an erotic symbol, dance is now also inserted into Cendrars's myth of creation as yet another artistic "sublanguage." If the cinema can be understood as a mechanism for destroying and creating the
universe, then dance is a mechanism of reproduction. For this reason various forms of movement, especially the circular and the ovoid, are linked,
subtextually, to the fructification of the world and are described in mythic
terms as dance.

This entire cluster of ideas is equally present in Léger's *Ballet mécanique*,
whose title doubtless reflects both Léger's experience in the Ballets své-
dois and Cendrars's legacy of influence. The predominance of circular
forms in the film, in all their variations, is certainly linked (as was said earlier) to Léger's prolonged discussions with Delaunay. But these forms are
also an erotic symbol of birth, as Léger explained in 1924, praising the circle for its "primordial nature": "Any object that has the circle as its initial
form is always sought out as an attractive value."[93] A later text by Léger, "Le
Cirque" (1950), is a veritable apology for the circle, whose attractiveness is
ascribed to its "sensuous" features: "There is a visual and tactile satisfaction
in a round form. It is really evident that the circle is nicer. . . . Water, the
mobility of the human body in water, the play of sensuous enveloping
curves—a round pebble on the beach, you pick it up, you touch it."[94] The

eroticization of the circular form of course does not have any crudely sexual connotations here: it is linked rather to Cendrars's mytheme of the "creative impulse."

Another artist who eroticized the circle at much the same time as Léger and Cendrars was Marcel Duchamp. In 1926, Duchamp made the film *Anemic Cinema* (a punning title in which both words are anagrams of each other). For the film Duchamp shot a series of revolving disks containing texts with spirals inscribed into them. As they revolved, these "rotodisks" would create the feeling of volume (a "rotorelief") that Duchamp interpreted ironically as a female breast. The texts written on the disks were puns with obscene meanings as their subtext.[95] By uniting a completely sterile, indeed castrated, form with crude obscenities buried in anagrammatic puns, Duchamp was able to make fun of the "anemic" geometric eros of the moving disk. Duchamp's linguistic program, however, was quite different. Annette Michelson has shown that Duchamp's artistic impulse, unlike the extroverted creativity of Léger, was oriented toward a kind of autistic consciousness,[96] a language that is directed, as it were, within the subject. This displacement of language onto a centripetal spiral of complex anagrams makes Duchamp's film the exact opposite of Léger's *Ballet mécanique*.

It is important to note some other equally unexpected transformations of the cosmogonic myth that function as intertextual echoes in Léger's film. Cendrars had introduced into the myth two interconnected elements: representing the space of creation as a gigantic kitchen and eroticizing the everyday world of objects. The image of the kitchen, certainly somewhat unexpected here, was motivated above all by the mytheme of the egg, from which the plot of universal creation originated as a kind of culinary experiment. In *Moravagine* this metaphor surfaces explicitly: "The cradle of today's humanity is to be found in Central America. The stores of kitchenware, the shellmounds of the Gulf of California, the shellheaps that follow the entire Atlantic coastline. . . . These enormous accumulations of debris, piles of shells, the remains of fish, the bones of birds and mammals, as high as mountains, prove that significantly large groups of people lived there a long time ago."[97] The link between birth and cooking implements makes Cendrars evolve an oddly erotic relationship to the domestic object, a relationship that becomes more interpretable through one more intertext. I have in mind the work of Remy de Gourmont, for which Cendrars had a passionate admiration. In 1948, Cendrars wrote: "During the past forty years I think I have not published a single book or text which hasn't mentioned his name, where I haven't quoted him in one way or another. This testifies to the extent to which I have been influenced by the master chosen by me at the age of twenty."[98]

In 1900, Gourmont published a collection of essays entitled *La Culture des idées*, which featured an essay called "The Dissociation of Ideas," a text essential to his aesthetics. Ideas, Gourmont believed, do not circulate in a pure form within culture: they are compacted into what might be called associative aggregates. These aggregates need to be shattered and critiqued in order to rediscover the "pure idea," although the latter in turn will almost instantly link itself to yet another associative pair. In Gourmont's own words: "Just like the atoms of Epicurus, ideas cling to each other however they can, by chance encounters, collisions, and accidents."[99] Among the aggregates of ideas that need to be dissociated, Gourmont identified the notions of art and female beauty. Gourmont argued passionately that woman as a physical object is devoid of harmony: "The idea of beauty is not a pure idea; it is intimately connected with the idea of carnal pleasure."[100] Woman has come to be seen as an embodiment of harmony and beauty only because she is associated with sexual fulfillment. Therefore, in order to arrive at a pure idea of art, we have to dissociate the idea of art from sexuality.

Gourmont was to write an entire book devoted precisely to this question. *Physique de l'amour* (1903) attempts to dissociate art from sexuality by adopting two parallel strategies. On the one hand, Gourmont places human beings among fauna and is thus able to treat their sexual functions alongside analogous ones found in any number of other animals. The "paltriness" of human sexuality becomes evident when seen against the boundless array of sexual unions possible in the animal world. On the other hand, Gourmont studies love as a function of a *mechanism* that is located in instinct. Here he returns once more to the problem of female beauty, interpreting it exclusively in geometric and physically concrete terms:

> The superiority of female beauty is real; and it has only one cause—the unity of line. What makes a woman more beautiful is the fact that her genital organs are invisible. . . . The harmony of the female body is thus geometrically speaking still more perfect [than a man's], especially if one considers the male and the female at the very moment of desire, at the moment they display the most intense and natural expression of life. At that point the woman, by interiorizing her movements, or making them visible only through the undulation of her curves, retains her full aesthetic value.[101]

Cendrars knew Gourmont's *Physique de l'amour* very well, reading it aloud to his lover, whom he took to the zoo for practical demonstrations of his mentor's anatomic insights.[102] Gourmont's insistence on dissociating ideas harmonized well with Cendrars's general orientation toward fragmentation, the breaking down and recombining of the world's elements in order to make a new language. Gourmont's ideology proved valuable in this regard by providing a refined metaphorics of eros that dissociated love from female beauty: erotic attention could thus be deflected onto objects that were "geometrically more perfect"—metallic disks, drums, frying pans, and saucepans.

The novel *Moravagine*, the summa of Cendrars's mythology, performs this dissociation programmatically as part of the author's linguistic agenda:

> It was then that I became seized by a violent passion for objects, inanimate things. . . .
>
> Soon an egg, a stovepipe began to excite me sexually. . . . The sewing machine was like the plane, the cross section of a courtesan, a mechanical demonstration of the power of a dancer in a music hall. I would have liked to split, like a pair of lips, the perfumed quartz and drink the last drop of primordial honey that the life of origins has deposited in these glassy molecules, this drop that comes and goes like an eye. . . . The tin can was an annotated synopsis of woman.
>
> The simplest figures—the circle, the square, and their projections in space, the cube and the sphere—moved me, spoke to my senses like crude symbols, red and blue lingams [a phallic symbol and attribute of the Hindu deity Shiva], obscure, barbarous ritual orgies.
>
> Everything became rhythm to me, an unexplored life. . . . I performed Zulu dances.[103]

The hero finally addresses his lover in the following way: "You are as beautiful as a stovepipe, smooth, wound round, cranked up. Your body is like an egg lying on the seashore."[104] This rather extravagant moment in *Moravagine* is also relevant for its broader exposition of practically the entire paradigm of Cendrars's metamyth. Here a vast array of metaphorical substitutes are deployed to establish one and the same plot: how the creative force grows to generate the world. In the episode just quoted, which is motivated by the hero's mental illness, the motifs chosen are diverse but (as I showed earlier) interconnected: the egg, the kitchen implements, the dancer and the mechanical dance, the African dance, the ritual orgy, the eroticized geometric figures, the organic life of an amorphous primordial matter, and sexual desire. This selection of "primary elements" is also an almost complete inventory of the motifs to be found in the febrile movement of Léger's *Ballet mécanique*.

Léger's painting in the early twenties is typified by a conflation of human and object, their interchangeability. Characteristic of Léger, too, is an escalation of motifs from everyday life, particularly kitchen accessories, in such paintings as *Le Petit déjeuner* (1921), *Le Grand déjeuner* (1921), *La Mère et l'enfant* (1922), and *Le Siphon* (1924). These motifs, equated in plastic terms with human beings, are not presented, it is true, as mythological equivalents. For Cendrars only the cinema, as a world of primal creative chaos, can generate an endless series of transformations and substitutions. A film is a universe of general semantic equivalence; it presents the cosmos as pure seriality, infinite and existing prior to language. In *A B C du cinéma* (1921), Cendrars writes: "Animals, plants, minerals are ideas, feelings, numerals" (cf. the moving numerals in *Ballet mécanique*).[105]

Everything is a signifier of everything else. All static linguistic structures are shattered in a film. In "Pompon" (1957), a late text devoted to the cinema, Cendrars answers the question "What is cinema?" as follows: "You, yourself, you, anonymous as you are to yourself, alive, dead, dead-alive, wild-rose, angelic, hermaphroditic, human, too human, animal, mineral, vegetable, chemistry, rare butterfly, a residue in a crucible, the root of a voltaic arc, a second in the depths of an abyss, two swimming costumes, a spout-hole, mechanical and spiritual, full of gear and prayers, aerobe, thermogenous, famous foot, lion, god, automaton, embryo."[106] This list mixes adjectives and nouns, as well as the most diverse phenomena. Such a definition of the cinema seems more like a random choice of words, arranged like a lexicon and completely without syntax. The cinema becomes a dictionary, a paradigm free to embrace the entire world, a supreme intertext (we might recall the traditional comparison of the universe with a dictionary or encyclopedia).

The paradigm presented in "Pompon" is the logical limit to which the equation of the cinema with the universe as "hypertext" can lead. In fact, neither Cendrars nor Léger expands the lexical range of cinematic language to such an extent: they operate largely within the confines of the list of "interchangeable" mythemes enumerated earlier and limit their description of the world to the theme of its genesis (and that of language) and to the motif of space travel, deployed as a metonymic approximation of cosmic expanse.

Closely linked to this plot is the topos of the end of the world. In the screenplay *La Fin du monde,* it appears as the voyage to Mars. It also appears in the novel *Moravagine,* whose hero writes a vast work also called *La Fin du monde,* which he may have put together "based on a cinema program, during his mysterious sojourn on the planet Mars."[107] In order to translate the screenplay from the Martian language, *Moravagine* compiles a lexicon of the two hundred thousand basic meanings of the only word that exists in Martian. The screenplay is finally written in a language that expresses the infinite diversity of the same. Here we have returned to the same lexical phenomenon of universal semantic equivalence discussed earlier. Further on, the novel's hero, Raymond la Science, who translates the screenplay, notes: "It was this dictionary that allowed me to translate, or better still adapt, the Martian screenplay. I have entrusted its publication and possibly its film adaptation to Blaise Cendrars."[108] As we know, Cendrars was in fact to fulfill a part of his own hero's charge.

The theme of space travel is in fact most elaborately treated in another of Cendrars's works, *L'Eubage* (1917). Cendrars wrote *L'Eubage* in response to a request of the well-known art patron Jacques Doucet. The work is dedicated to Doucet and to Conrad Moricand, a friend of Cendrars and an astrologer-mystic who gained some renown between the 1910s and the 1930s. There is some reason to believe that it was Moricand who introduced Cendrars to astral mysticism. His influence is also evident in other works by Cendrars, as well as by many other writers of the time, such as Henry Miller.[109]

The word *eubage* refers to a Gallic priest who practices fortune-telling and astrology. *L'Eubage* recounts a voyage through space that penetrates the constellations described in the horoscope, proceeds through the Milky Way, and so on. This text, saturated with astrological symbolism, is perhaps the intertext closest to Léger's *Ballet mécanique*. Here the metaphoric equation of cosmic creation with the creation of a new language is expressed graphically, and through images that are very close to those deployed by the film. The book's third chapter, "Des instruments de musique" (the reference here is to the music of the cosmic spheres), presents a vision of a primordial chaos before passing on to the "birth of language":

> Some elementary forms become clearer: a square, an oval, a circle. These rise to the surface and burst like bubbles. Now everything wiggles like flippers: the square becomes longer, the oval becomes hollow, the circle becomes a star; mouth, lips, throat; everything hurls itself into the void with a huge cry; everything rushes together from all sides, regroups, forms a mass, stretches out in the form of the senseless tongue of a mastodon. This tongue gives a jump, begins to work, makes an unprecedented effort, stammers, speaks. It is talking.[110]

The sixth chapter of *L'Eubage* is dedicated to a journey into the eye, according to a metaphoric chain linking planet–eye–object–lens. The seventh chapter contains cinematic associations encoded in the chapter's very title, "De la parturition des couleurs," where the French *parturition* ("birthing") recalls the title of Cendrars's article on Survage, "De la partition des couleurs." This chapter often coincides word for word with the article: "My field of vision is submerged by a whirlwind. A brownish red slowly invades my *screen* and fills it. A dark-red . . . , composed of small plates placed one alongside the other. Each of these plates is crowned by a pimple that trembles gently and ends up bursting like cooling lava."[111] Everything is repeated here: the copulation of the embryos and the growth of branches. Here too the yolk bursts and the disk grows. Nonetheless, the cosmogonic epic ends differently in *L'Eubage*: "All around me, everything becomes solid. Domestic forms develop one out of another, familiar and useful."[112]

Yet the strangest part of the book is chapter 8, "De l'Hétéroclite." This is perhaps the text that most directly anticipates the imagery of *Ballet mécanique* in its account of a journey through space:

> Everything flutters, opens and closes like gills. Minuscule mouths. Round bulbous things disappear, come and go, show themselves, then melt into a gleam. Golden balls rise, descend, trace the outlines of figures. A meditation? A game? One can discern arabesques or drawings. . . .
>
> Everything breaks. Transparent craters open up and reveal a dazzling array of cooking implements, all made of the best copper. An Indian and a blue Negro dance around the hearth and juggle large Spanish onions. An ostrich egg rolls down a slope. . . .
>
> Icy plates fly in all directions like tiles. A woman shakes her skirt. The spokes of a windmill turn.
>
> Then everything becomes like glass, murky, without depth, like a photograph that hasn't been toned.[113]

Cendrars had intended for the book to be illustrated with photographs, treating subjects ranging from astronomy to industrial accessories from everyday life. The aim was to create a working tension between the quotidian and the deliberately esoteric nature of the book. Regrettably, Cendrars's intent was never realized. Yet even Léger's film does involve a certain amount of playing on the opposition between the cosmic and the everyday. Léger himself recalled: "I photographed the painted nail of a woman and magnified it a hundredfold. Then I showed it on a screen. The astonished pubic thought it was looking at a photo taken of outer space."[114] The sense that a blown-up photo of a fingernail was a kind of miracle is something common to Léger's painting as well: from 1924 (with the painting *Reading*), Léger started to include nails on the hands of his human figures. W. Schmalenbach attributes this detail, conspicuous enough yet generally ignored, to the influence of cinema.[115] This chain of associations, linking the blowup of the nail to astrology and the cinema, is also typical of Cendrars himself: "That's cinema! . . . your hands, cracked like lunar craters, with an enormous tube under the nail."[116] The poet observes that the cinema has the capacity to uncover the essence hidden under appearances just as astrology reveals one's fate through the movement of stars, or palmistry predestination in the "shape of the fingers."[117] From this chain of logic it suffices to remove the middle to get the odd equation, cinema = astrology = nails.

These somewhat whimsical chains of association are typical of both Léger and Cendrars. Both artists shared a tendency to see the world in mythic terms; both sought to establish a semantic equivalence between different elements in the objective world. The similarities that obtain between these chains of association clearly suggest a level of intertextual interference between the works of the two artists: the chains seem to shift freely from one text to another, creating a kind of mixed or hybrid authorship. The quote about nails was in fact borrowed by Cendrars from Léger, since Léger's text precedes his by several years. Cendrars's whimsical astrology resonates as part of Léger's work, from which it is borrowed as a quoted motif. We are dealing with a complex system of quotations that intersect so readily as to almost lose their original authorship.

To return now to Léger, his *Ballet mécanique,* we can summarize, is largely made up of small fragments—various geometric figures (circles and triangles), everyday objects (boaters, slippers, tongs, balls), cooking utensils (saucepans, bottles, molds for baking pies), body parts (lips, eyes, legs from display mannequins), and so forth. Each of these objects is a piece of the world, a quote from some general lexicon that constitutes a specific paradigm. Each object can be understood as a quote and linked thereby to its related text by Cendrars; for example, the legs echo the leg in *La Création du monde.*

Yet this kind of fragmentary reading tells us little about the film as a whole. *Ballet mécanique* is in fact a *single and unitary hyperquotation,* referring to a closed corpus of texts outside it, all of which belong to Cendrars. Each smaller composite quote fragment can be seen as an index, a "hypoquotation" that is functional only within its own paradigm. In order to compute the Cendrars intertext, a viewer must be able compile the film's full lexicon. The entire vocabulary of *Ballet mécanique,* that is, the *film's language,* is a quote.

For this to be so, language must first of all appear as a text. This is indeed the case in *Ballet mécanique,* which is in effect a syntagmatic elaboration of a linguistic paradigm. Second, the film's language derives its rationale and normative status from an external literary program, which appears in the selection of fragments from various texts by Cendrars. This allows the film to bring together a range of utterances by the poet and give them a unified and programmatic weight. *Ballet mécanique* thus takes on the task of "reconstructing" Cendrars's mythology. Myth and language emerge as intertextually supplementary.

The presence of this literary myth in Léger's film is not palpable through any direct echoes; nor is it the result of any desire on Léger's part to illustrate Cendrars's ideas. The process involved can be better described in the following way: first Cendrars declares the cinema to be the model for generating a new language, thus locating the matrix of his new poetics outside literature (whose renewal is seen as yet another task for the cinema). Cendrars himself will strive to foster this matrix in other art forms, particularly film. These efforts, always ambivalent in character, are in themselves unsuccessful; however, they do result in several literary works containing descriptions of Cendrars's cinematic vision. A myth is thus elaborated, a ramified interpretive apparatus for appraising a nonexisting film.

This apparatus is thus activated within literature itself, for which, in the final analysis, it had always been intended.

Cendrars had always followed Léger's painting closely: his texts described Léger on their own terms, projecting Cendrars's myth onto his work. Well before *Ballet mécanique,* then, Léger's painting was part of Cendrars's intertext, with all its cinematic overtones. The film, when made, thus readily entered the specific intertext of Cendrars's myth about the destruction and creation of the world and the related creation of a new language.

The question then emerges: To what extent does the film logically continue the work of Léger's painting and reproduce its motifs, and to what extent does it rather move beyond the painterly realm and find its intertext in Cendrars? In other words, is an immanent reading of *Ballet mécanique* possible? There can be no simple answer to this question, since even Léger's older paintings had been subjected by Cendrars to a kind of "forced" interpretation: they were already an effective part of his intertext. Not only did Cendrars invest Léger's paintings with new meaning; he in fact stripped Léger of their authorship by drawing them into a context he himself had constructed. The scenario is further complicated by the fact that, even after *Ballet mécanique,* Léger was to make several paintings that reproduce motifs from the film. One example is *Hommage à la danse* (1925), where against a background of concentric circles we see two mechanical legs that clearly recall the mannequin's legs in the film. Another is *Composition aux quatre chapeaux* (1927), where in the center we see a face with a birthmark on one cheek, while the edges of the canvas reveal a boater, spoons, and bottles. The lower edge shows a hand holding a gray bowler hat. Christophe Derouet has called this painting a "carefully made rebus." In the large face he sees Kiki, a model in Léger's film, and identifies the hat as Charlie Chaplin's (or perhaps Léonce Rosenberg's, he adds cautiously).[118] At this point, Léger's film has clearly begun to dictate the terms by which his painting can be interpreted. Cinema thus becomes a "strong" intertext for painting. This is because the cinema possesses a greater number of the features that we associate with texts: it breaks down readily into fragments, it develops in time, it has a finite beginning and end. Only by invoking a film intertext is Derouet able to make his rather arbitrary interpretive claims, as if the bowler hat in his painting could actually be traced to a concrete owner, be it Chaplin or Rosenberg, with whom Léger traveled to Ravenna in 1924.

If *Ballet mécanique* emerges as quite a powerful intertext for some of Léger's own paintings, we have also seen that Cendrars's imaginary cinema was no less powerful in this regard: more than any single text by Léger himself, it engenders the program according to which *Ballet mécanique* was made. It is this breadth that allowed Cendrars as intertext to function within the film (perhaps even while the film was being made). Whatever the case, the Cendrars intertext also freed the film from the imperative of narrative, allowing it to limit itself to the primary elements of language, which could then refer to a wider system and acquire meaning through literary sources outside the film proper.

Put simply, Cendrars invented films in order for them to be parasitized by his literary works, which they provided with a new language. Léger, by contrast, made films that could parasitize Cendrars's literary works. His films embodied a speech whose apparently senseless stammer conveyed the dramatic myth he had found in the books his friend Cendrars had written.

CHAPTER FIVE

Intertext against Intertext
Buñuel and Dali's Un Chien andalou

Cendrars was not the only writer of the avant-garde to adopt the cinema as his literary model. The cinema provided a fictitious escape from literature, while also holding out the possibility of its radical renewal. The films imagined by the writers of the avant-garde were all too frequently never intended for production, retaining their significance precisely as facts of literature. This seems to me the real reason for the clear discrepancy between the number of films the surrealists conceived and those actually produced. A great number of surrealist screenplays have survived. Among the most important are Philippe Soupault's *Poèmes cinématographiques* and *Le Coeur volé; La Coquille et le Clergyman, Les Dix-huit secondes, La Révolte du boucher,* and others by Antonin Artaud; *Minuit à quatorze heures, Les Mystères du métropolitan, Y a des punaises dans le rôti de porc,* and many others by Robert Desnos; *Paupières mûres, barre fixe,* and *mtasipoj* by Benjamin Fondane; Benjamin Péret's *Pulchérie veut un auto;* Georges Ribemont-Dessaignes's *Le Huitième jour de la semaine;* Georges Hugnet's *La Loi d'accomodation chez les borgnes;* and Francis Picabia's *Sursum Corda* and others. Only two of these films were actually produced: *La Coquille et le Clergyman* (directed by Germaine Dulac and repudiated by Artaud himself) and George Hugnet's *La Perle* (1928–1929, directed by H. d'Ursel). The pantheon of surrealist cinema is an extraordinarily limited one. To the preceding list we could also add two films by Luís Buñuel and Salvador Dali, *Un Chien andalou* (1928) and *L'Age d'or* (1930), and perhaps *L'Étoile de mer* (1928) by Man Ray and Robert Desnos as well.

The desire to create a cinema not destined for the screen was expressed with remarkable candor by Benjamin Fondane in 1928: "SO LET US BEGIN THE ERA OF UNFILMABLE SCRIPTS. Something of the astonishing beauty of the fetus will be found there. Let us say right away that these screenplays written *to be read* will be shortly drowned in 'literature' . . . the real screenplay being by nature very awkward to read and impossible to write. So why should I deliberately get attached to this nothing? To what purpose? The fact is that a part of myself, that poetry had repressed, has found in the cinema a general loudspeaker through which to pose the questions that torment it."[1]

The screenplay, a genre considered "awkward to read and impossible to write," was placed in opposition to literature as poetry. The literature-poetry dichotomy was a general feature of surrealist writing. To literature were attributed all the stereotypic features of writing, which poetry was called upon to overcome. Robert Desnos, for one, believed that the cinema was on the front line of "the great struggle which everywhere pits . . . poetry against literature, life against art, love and hate against skepticism, revolution against counterrevolution."[2] Desnos also saw the cinema as a remarkable and purely mechanical weapon in his war on reading, since the darkness of the movie theater "impedes . . . the illusory reading of textbooks and edifying books of all kinds."[3] The surrealists saw the cinema as standing in opposition to high-bourgeois culture, as its violent negation. In his first *Manifesto of Surrealism* of 1924, André Breton wrote: "Henceforth I am strongly inclined to view the reveries of science with indulgence, as unseemly as it finally is in all respects. The wireless? Fine. Syphilis? If you like. Photography? I don't have any objections. The cinema? Hurrah for darkened theaters!"[4]

Cinema, then, was perceived as a means of attacking high culture, one that by no means necessitated a renunciation of language (the output of surrealist screenplays is ample evidence of this). The cinema promised the overcoming, within language, of the literary tradition. A literary text oriented toward the poetics of film was thus obliged to enter into a negative relation with the intertext of the broader literary arena. The cinema drew such a text into a kind of negative intertextuality, one that denied the wider context of culture.

Un Chien andalou, a Buñuel-Dali collaboration and the first film to have been unconditionally hailed by the surrealists, might be reexamined in this light. The film was consciously conceived as a model of surrealist poetry in film. Buñuel himself declared that *Un Chien andalou* would not have been possible without the surrealist movement: "*Un Chien andalou* would not have existed if the movement called surrealist had not existed. For its 'ideology,' its psychic motivation and the systematic use of the poetic image as an arm to overthrow accepted notions correspond to the characteristics of all authentically surrealist work."[5] To some degree, Buñuel's stated goals also could have encouraged the attempt to transfer the structure of the surrealist trope directly from literature to film. The film's celebrated prologue is interesting in this regard, establishing as it does a parallel between an eye severed by a razor blade and a cloud that intersects the disk of the moon. The prologue has mostly given rise to psychoanalytic readings.[6] More recently, however, scholars have also begun to pay more attention to the quasi-literary structure of this parallel. Linda Williams, for example, has examined the moon/eye metaphor as a rare example of a "metaphor within a syntagm" that inverts the relationship between the elements it juxtaposes. Williams rightly notes that traditional metaphors usually bring together some human action within diegesis and an extradiegetic element taken from nature. In the Buñuel film, by contrast, the moon and the cloud correspond to the diegetic level, a fact that is further emphasized by the direction in which the hero of the prologue (Buñuel himself) directs his gaze as he steps out onto the balcony. The human action thus becomes the second element of the comparison. Thus it is not the eye that is compared to an extradiegetic moon, but a moon situated within diegesis that is compared to the eye of a woman who is herself "poorly" integrated within diegesis.[7] Naturally this reversal of the relations between the constitutive elements of this metaphor can be interpreted as purely surrealist, a reading that, in turn, can lead to far-reaching conclusions about the nature of inversion in the film. In fact the matter appears to be somewhat more complex. One's relationship to culture is not so simply overturned by metaphor.

Buñuel himself maintained that the image of the eye being cut by a razor blade had come to him in a dream: "When I arrived to spend a few days at Dali's house in Figueras, I told him about a dream I'd had in which a long tapering cloud sliced the moon in half, like a razor blade slicing through an eye."[8] Georges Bataille gives a different version of the event: "Buñuel himself told me that it was Dali who had thought up the episode, suggested directly by the fact that he actually did see a long, narrow cloud cutting the disk of the moon into two."[9]

This recourse to dreams, highly characteristic of the surrealists, often serves to repress a source, camouflaging the real intertextual links that remain concealed behind tropes. The dream replaces the quoted source, removing it from the realm of culture and placing it within the domain of physiology, eroticism, and the subconscious. Nonetheless, we have every reason to believe that the slit eye as a motif has several sources. Dali made use of it as early as 1927 in "Mon ami et la plage": "My friend loves . . . the tenderness of gentle cuts of the scalpel on the curve of her pupils."[10] J. Francisco Aranda has traced this motif back to a 1919 poem by Juan Larrea.[11] It can also just as easily be interpreted within the broader context of the theme of blindness, quite prominent in the film: the gouged-out eyes of the donkeys, the blind men who are buried in the sand at the end of the film, and so forth.

It is worth pausing over yet another possible source for this motif—the novel *Cinelandia* (Movieland) by Ramón Gómez de la Serna. Buñuel held

Gómez in high esteem, clearly overestimating his role in the development of the cinema, and even hoping to involve him as a scriptwriter in the making of *Un Chien andalou*.[12] Even before this, Buñuel had plans to make a film based on a script by Gómez entitled *Caprichos,* consisting of six novellas.[13]

There is no doubt that Buñuel was aware of Gómez's literary film utopia. In viewing the world through the prism of cinema, the novel *Cinelandia* has much in common with the surrealists. A chapter in the book, entitled "The Stolen Birthmark," recalls the prologue to Buñuel's film. Here a "tragic incident" is recounted: the film star Edna Blake's husband "had bound her and cut out with a bistoury the magnificent beauty spot that enhanced her back. Ernest Word had dug down so deep in tearing it out, that he had opened a blood vessel through which Edna nearly bled to death, as if the beauty spot had been the cork stopping all her blood."[14] Gómez here takes great pains to emphasize the chameleon-like reversibility of Edna Blake's birthmark. It is readily displaced, becoming an eye: "To tear out a palpitating beauty spot is like extricating an eye."[15] The birthmark can also become a diamond—"Not the biggest diamond set in platinum could repay for her beauty spot"—or a beacon: "She has turned her back on herself and thinks that her beauty spot shines more brilliantly than any beacon."[16] The birthmark suddenly finds itself on the moon: "Even the moon of that splendid night had a coquettish beauty spot punctuating the corners of its wide smile."[17] It can also acquire the trappings of an erotic symbol: "If a man were to do that to me, I'd bite off his nose."[18] Clearly, the nose here is a euphemism drawn from the tradition of erotic disguise. In emphasizing the versatility of the birthmark, Gómez generates a long chain of interchangeable motifs, a kind of extended many-tiered metaphor: birthmark/eye/beacon/moon, and later on, the jupiters and reflectors used in the film studio. The blinding light of the beacon/moon/jupiters is linked by Gómez to the motif of blindness, which is crucial to the novel: "One of the most moving spectacles is when, in a holocaust to her public, the star burns her beautiful eyes in a blaze of light. . . . In the movies, modulation of voice, diapason, musical and elegant diction, are all to be found in a pair of eyes. One can say that blind people are 'cinematographically dumb.'"[19]

Such metaphors, extended and metadescriptive in nature, also are typical of the poetics of surrealism, although the interchangeability of motifs in *Cinelandia* still appears somewhat tentative: "To rip out a birthmark is almost the same as ripping out an eye." The substitution of eye for birthmark is here elaborated on the figurative level of discourse, and its impact on the diegetic and referential level of the text thus appears mediated. The equation of moon and eye within the diegetic plane of *Un Chien andalou* leads to a far more radical dislocation of the discursive and referential planes. This becomes clear in the main section of the film.

The metaphor of the prologue has one other important feature. The juxtaposed images here definitively merge, although essentially on the basis of a purely external and formal similarity. The circle of the moon and the eyeball are rendered interchangeable. This emphasis on external form serves to destroy conventional semantic links, which are replaced by alternative modes of interaction on the level of the signifier. The shift of emphasis away from semantics onto the external and formal properties of the images being compared was an essential part of the surrealists' strategy for renewing language. "The conjunctive, serving as a formal substitute for the synonym, metaphorically brings together words that strictly speaking have no semantic connection."[20] In *Un Chien andalou* the conjunctive function is fulfilled by montage effects or dissolves that unite the elements being compared within a fictive common space, and thus "oddly" unite two or more objects in a single and absurd image. Thanks to its "ungrammatical" nature, a film does not need to rely on a grammatical simulation of synonymy by way of conjunctive constructions.

The concatenation of logically incompatible elements, by way of either conjunctive constructions in a written text or montage in films, leads to a paradox. On the one hand, we have veritable clusters of ungrammatical constructs, anomalies that suggest the need for an intertextual reading. These strange associative chains seem literally to flaunt their quotational character. On the other hand, the abolition of semantic links shifts the emphasis onto the purely syntagmatic level. It is as if we were being asked to read a text whose meaning resides only in its immediate elaboration, a text located entirely in the syntagm, with all paradigmatic links refused. In this sense (and this is what remains to be proved), the surrealist text can be seen as the exact opposite of *Ballet mécanique,* with its repetitions and maniacal elaboration of the paradigmatic axis, to the complete exclusion of the syntagmatic.

The surrealists themselves, with their constant references to dreams, to the mediumistic possibilities of *écriture automatique,* and so forth, seemed to invite a psychologizing reading, such as Freud's. The obscurities of the text's code were thus found to be concealed in the depths of the subconscious. Riffaterre has shown how elements of surrealist writing read like hieroglyphs: "We do not understand them as language or even as isolated symbols. They rather represent a language the key to which has been hidden away somewhere."[21] I have already had occasion to discuss the quote as hieroglyph. In the present case, however, the hieroglyph refers not to an intertext but to the text of the subconscious. This, at any rate, was the surrealists' conscious strategy, which insisted on the "automatic" nature of writing and dreaming. The strategy was finally justified, insofar as a great number of surrealist texts have been usefully interpreted in a psychoanalytic vein.

Nonetheless, the evocation of the unconscious was only a palliative. The essential impulse of surrealist strategy lay elsewhere. Riffaterre has quite rightly observed that the *semantic ungrammaticalities* of surrealist texts are consistently compensated for by a *grammaticality on the level of structure.* "The absurd, the nonsensical, simply by impeding decoding, force us to read the structures directly."[22]

What I propose to investigate is precisely the extent to which structure and syntagm are capable of "normalizing" a text that cannot be rendered normative intertextually, via the traditional means of uncovering and interpreting quotations. In this sense the cinema is of course ideally positioned to lighten the semantic level, by distancing itself from the field of associations that might weigh heavily on the verbal elements. It is easier for cinema than for literature to accentuate the external, visual side of an object, stripping it of the semantic content that literature imposes. This is also why many surrealist texts appear to mimic the cinema.

The easiest way to bring two objects together syntagmatically without reference to their symbolism or other meaning is by relying on their external formal similarity. Such a comparison is easiest to establish if the two objects have a common shape. The most elementary form is the circle, and it is no accident that it became so important to surrealist poetry.

The passage of one circular object into another was elaborated with a striking consistency by Robert Desnos in his screenplay *Minuit à quatorze heures* (1925). Here are a few select images from the script:

23. Circles in water.
27. The setting sun, all round.
30. Nighttime. The lamp is shining. The round shape of the light on the ceiling. The round shape cast by the lampshade on the floor.
32. Nighttime. The round moon . . .
33. . . . Round plates. The round shape of the napkins.
36. The round handle of the door turns slowly . . .
37. . . . . wheels
43. Ferris wheel . . .
47. The wafer grows infinitely in the [priest's] hand.
48. A halo emerges behind the priest's head . . .
50. A beggar at the door of the church. [A woman] gives him a coin.
57. Nighttime outside. It is calm. The round moon.[23]

Frame 59 introduces us to the film's main "hero," a sphere, recalling a cricket ball in size. The sphere falls down a staircase and then rolls out the door. People are seated in the garden, while a round ball hovers over them in the sky. The ball then falls onto their table. Later a peasant digs up a cannonball from the ground (frame 74); a woman tries to stroke a cat, which turns into a ball (frames 76–77). Then we have a series of "adventures," each involving objects that are transformed into spheres that balloon out, aggressively enveloping everything in their path. The screen-play ends as follows:

159. Something spherical in the sky.
160. Circles in the water.
161. Something spherical in the sky.[24]

Clearly there is a certain external similarity between Desnos's screen-play and Léger's film, both of which make extensive use of the circular form. Yet the texts are also very different. Léger's circle is a dynamic form and the embodiment of a vital erotic impulse. It is linked to a specific myth. It "shatters" the world into fragments. True, Léger also paid tribute to the idea of juxtaposing objects on the basis of their external form. He would recall, for example, the pains he took to get a parrot's round eye to look exactly like the outline of the lid of a saucepan that had appeared in the previous frame.[25] Taken in the context of the film as a whole, however, this episode seems more like a joke.

Minuit à quatorze heures presents an entirely different picture. There is no metaphysics here, no mythmaking, and no internal dynamism. The cir-cle serves not to segment the world but to gather it into one syntagm. The very plot of Desnos's screenplay describes the development of surrealist poetics away from simple association based on formal attributes (such as a series of circular objects) toward a transformation of these objects, which are made to pass physically through one another. The initial cumulative se-rialization of objects acquires the dynamism of a plot. Similes begin to gen-erate events. A nearly analogous device can be found in the script *Les Paupières mûres* by B. Fondane, involving white billiard balls. People in a café are seen throwing balls at one another's heads. As in Desnos, the balls begin to move, rolling down the street, encountering corpses, and so forth.[26] Billiard balls also appear in Buñuel's *Une girafe,* where they are hid-den inside the giraffe's "fifth spot" that is said to resemble the drawer of a writing desk.[27] These balls are essentially the physical embodiment of the circle as an abstract geometric universal. In *Un Chien andalou* the circle has a somewhat similar function. The serialization of circular forms in the pro-logue grows into a kind of reciprocal interaction that becomes part of the plot. The moon becomes an eye, a cloud becomes a razor.

The surrealist emphasis on concrete form, the unique importance ac-corded to circular objects, served to strengthen the denotative function of the signifier. The surrealists leveled out the semantic differences between objects that bore any formal resemblance to one another. This is most eas-ily seen when the physical or concrete aspect of a traditional poetic image is emphasized. One such "concretized" image is the eye. On the one hand, the eye gains a highly poetic resonance (especially in the poetry of Paul Éluard or Breton, where the eyes are often compared to stars). On the other hand, the surrealists were fond of "eye-play" as a kind of ball game: "Sur les murs pour les jours de fête on accroche / des yeux joujoux des pauvres." (On the walls during holidays they hang / eyes, toys for the poor.) And elsewhere: "The beaches are full of eyes without bodies; they can be found along the dunes and on the far-off meadows red from the blood of blooming herds."[28] And in Breton's *Nadja:* "I managed to notice the balls of her eyes gleam on the edge of my hat."[29] Traditional tropes, then, get desemanticized by the surrealists through a process of reification. Here is another curious example from *Les Champs magnétiques:* "Their good star is the eye of the women they robbed, upturned to such a height";[30] or from Jean Arp's "De 'Perroquet supérieur' ": "De la bordure de la mort s'avançaient les yeux des jeunes étoiles . . . [From the verge of death the eyes of the young stars advanced . . .]."[31] In both cases the traditional metaphor of star-as-eye is externally preserved, only to be subject to a kind of blasphemous reification. The same ambivalence is also the basis of the prologue to *Un Chien andalou.*

The examples quoted here illustrate more than a persistent desemanticization and reification at work in surrealist texts. They also point to another factor that at least initially might seem less likely: the existence of a rich poetic intertext created precisely through such tropes. A poetry constituted within a broader negation of the intertextual quickly begins to generate a new field of intertextual relations that serve to enact the semantic strategy that had been selected. The surrealist intertext, however, does not just "play" with traditional motifs—it is deeply parodic. In each case, playing with an object involves distancing it from its traditional metaphoric associations in a kind of irreverent debunking. Motifs like "eyes" and "stars" clearly call upon an immense reservoir of traditional poetic associations. Buñuel, for example, might well have intended his comparison of a woman's eye with the moon in *Un Chien andalou* to be seen as a parody of his friend Federico García Lorca, whose poetic imagery provides the intertext for the beginning of the film. In 1924, Lorca dedicated to Buñuel the following verses, which he wrote on the back side of a photograph of the two of them: "The large moon glistens and rolls / in the calm clouds above." Significantly, the film provoked a quarrel between Buñuel and Lorca, who perceived it as an attack on him. "I'm the dog," he was reported to have said.[32]

The extreme form of this irreverent strategy of reification is the motif of the dismembered body. Intended to shock the reader, this motif was in fact revived rather than invented by the surrealists, being a topos that already enjoyed a wide literary currency. The specific motif of the gouged or slit eye is mythicized in an entire body of surrealist texts, specifically those of Georges Bataille, many of which were profoundly influenced by *Un Chien andalou.* Bataille would acknowledge the importance of Buñuel's film for his treatment of this theme in *L'Oeil* (1929), a work written immediately after the film's first screening. The inaugural elements of the myth are already present here: Granville's nightmare involving visions of eyes that pursue him as they transform themselves into fish; the story of Crampon, who gives the priest his glass eye as a memento on the eve of his execution; and so on. Bataille would further elaborate this motif in his subsequent essay "La Mutilation sacrificielle et l'oreille coupée de Vincent Van Gogh" (1930). Here Bataille made use of M. Lortillois's book *De l'automutilation: Mutilations et suicides insolites* (1909), which cites eleven cases in which people voluntarily had their eyes cut or gouged out. Bataille frequently compared the eye to planetary objects, more often the sun than the moon, here acting very much in accordance with Christian tradition,[33] and also examined the Oedipus myth in the context of solar sacrifice. This same motif was then further elaborated in his *Histoire de l'oeil*. Typical of Bataille is a chain of mythic substitutions: eye/insect/some other bodily member/sun. The internal mechanisms of surrealist imagery are here preserved.

In *Uccello, un poil*, a text of 1926, Antonin Artaud produced another associative chain that was even closer to Buñuel: eye/egg/moon. The heads of hanged men are compared to eggs created by the "monstrous palm" of an artist, a palm "of the full moon." The egg becomes a moon: "So you can walk right around this egg that hangs among the stones and stars, and which alone possesses the double animation of eyes."[34] Artaud wrote a series of texts as records of physiological sensations felt by his own body. In these texts, body parts enter into complex metaphoric series, while the body as a whole appears fragmented. Artaud's "sensation" was then elevated into a constructive principle by Hans Bellmer, whose puppets' arms, legs, and heads appear dislocated as if by accident.

The head was another motif favored by the surrealists. Its circular shape seems "naturally" to provoke a comparison with the eye. "Ses yeux sont une tête coupée [Her eyes are a severed head]," writes Éluard.[35] No less typical is the metamorphosis of the head into a sea urchin: "My head is difficult to hold because of the quills."[36] The head often appears as an object such as a sphere. For instance, Tristan Tzara writes, "You hold in your hands as if to throw a ball, bright number, your head full of poetry"; Fondane's screenplay *Paupières mûres* has "55—he turns his head toward the mirror. 56—the woman's head is visible in it, although lying placed on the table."[37] Soupault has "The head which rolls without a leaf and the fruit of the day ripe and red."[38] And Breton wrote in "Allotropies": "My head rolls upside down."[39]

The motif of severed body parts, which goes back to magic shows and the films of Méliès, is not limited to the eye and head alone. In *Un Chien andalou* we find a severed hand, which also appears in the work of Desnos,

Soupault, and Breton.[40] Thanks to its external similarity to a starfish, the hand is also linked to the eye. This particular correlation became the basis of an entire mythology elaborated in Breton. As Jean Roudaut has it: "In its movement and its form, the hand is wing and leaf, seaweed, cockscomb, a root hugging the ground, mandragora. . . . It is the mediator between the domain of the living and the universe. . . . The eye is always attached to a person. The hand, on the contrary, particularly in *Nadja,* tends to be independent. . . . Through it, man's desire intervenes in the world's order."[41] We see, then, how the poetic intertext underlying Buñuel's film establishes a dialogue between the eye in the prologue and the severed hand that appears in the main section of the film. These chains are established through metaphoric links that were formulated in surrealist poetry. The intertext allows for the crystallization of established chains of equivalences and substitutions, creating syntagmatic links (chains) that are then rendered paradigmatic.

The surrealists created a system of external similitudes. These restored universal connections were then charged with a new symbolic weight. (The sphere or ball is only the most elementary nucleus of this metaphoric process.) It is hardly surprising to read Breton and Soupault declare: "A sphere destroys everything."[42] The destruction through metaphor of the established semantic order privileges the process of metamorphosis, in which the first object must be destroyed in order for it to become the second. Film is very effective in portraying this process, thanks to simple tricks such as the dissolve. René Clair's *Entr'acte* and Artaud and Dulac's *La Coquille et le Clergyman,* two works crucial to the genesis of surrealist cinema, both paid homage to the principle of metamorphosis, which is also the basis of one of the first presurrealist film scripts, Philippe Soupault's *Indifférence.*[43]

Among the surrealists' literary works, metamorphoses are vividly present in the writings of Benjamin Péret.[44] In his novel *Il était une boulangère* (1925), trees turn into snakes, a face turns into a siphon, and a woman turns into a bird. In *Mort aux vaches et au champ d'honneur* (1922), objects exist in a state just prior to mutation, soft or liquefied. Salade the heroine rides in a "soft bus," Monsieur Charbon "suddenly liquefies," the railway tracks are "completely liquefied."[45] The later novel *Histoire naturelle* (1945) is perhaps Péret's most consistent attempt to work out the principle of metamorphosis. Here we read that under the influence of the sun's warm rays oil made of snow turns into a chair, the chair into a poisonous lemur, which in turn becomes a kangaroo.[46]

These chains of absurd metamorphoses seem to parody Darwin's evolutionary theory, which in fact often served as a theoretical model for surrealist transformations, including *Un Chien andalou.* Writing about the film Dali said: "It is not by accident that I have taken some simple examples from natural history, for, as Max Ernst has said, the history of dreams, miracles, surrealist history, is above all and in every sense a natural history."[47] The surrealists strove to replace literature, and culture as a whole, with nature as the intertextual source for their metaphoric eccentricities. Hence the importance, in surrealism, of animal imagery. The surrealists singled out the simplest forms of animal life, species that had no symbolic value for human society, such as insects and marine life. The connection between the sea (and water in general) and the theme of metamorphosis is extraordinarily persistent in surrealist writing. Moreover, all marine animals are essentially interchangeable and enjoy the same (essentially erotic) symbolic value.[48] François de la Breteque, a critic who has studied the surrealist bestiary, notes: "Here, then, is a highly marked mythology of woman: she is a crustacean, a mollusk, an echinoderm; a primitive, opaque, animal living out a visceral existence, yet also connected to the loveliest alchemical transformations of nature: the pearl, the mother-of-pearl, or the gleam of a star."[49] The pearl, singled out for its spherical form, was one of the primary symbols of the surrealist universe. Other motifs included the snail and the shell, with their obvious sexual symbolism. In Péret we even find a description of a film theater that gets inundated by the audience's tears, causing the sudden appearance of snails.[50] Sea imagery is also evident in Artaud's screenplay *La Coquille et le Clergyman*, George Hugnet's *La Perle*, Desnos and Man Ray's *L'Etoile de mer*, and Prévert's *Baladart*.

In *Un Chien andalou*, a wide range of fauna is involved in the theme of metamorphosis. Primarily it is the "death's-head" or atropos moth. Moths and butterflies (French doesn't make a distinction between them, using *papillon* in both cases) in general are an ancient symbol of transformation. They appear most often in Breton's works, where they are identified with the changeable nature of women. The butterfly transports pollen, thus prolonging life and serving as a medium of communication. The butterfly embodies death and rebirth. The atropos appears in Breton's *Au lavoir noir* (1936), as an image of a lady of the night who flies in from some hellish space speaking the language of death. Breton's *Arcane 17* (1944), centered on alchemical transmutations, also features butterfly imagery. Here the butterfly emerges as an esoteric sign (or letter) taken from an alchemical code that guarantees "exchanges" and "dark metamorphoses."[51] The atropos moth also figures in the catalog that appears in the "eleventh spot" of Buñuel's *Une girafe:* "In place of the spot, one finds a large, dark night moth with a death's head between its wings."[52] Clearly, the atropos moth in *Un Chien andalou* has a vast surrealist intertext, one that connects it unambiguously to the theme of metamorphosis.

Other animals to figure in these cinematic metamorphoses are the ant and the sea urchin. In a celebrated passage, the use of dissolves creates a series of linked images: we see ants crawl out of a hole in a human palm, hair in the armpits of a man lying on the beach, a sea urchin on the sand, and a severed hand being played with by an androgyne. Ants and hair play an important role in the film's metamorphoses. Elsewhere hair from the armpits of the heroine appear where the mouth of the hero had been before being erased.

The ant-hair correlation is parodically affirmed in Buñuel's essay "Variations sur le thème des moustaches de Menjou." Here Buñuel derides the Don Juanesque trappings of the actor Adolphe Menjou's mask:

> His immense Menjouesque force irradiates from his moustache.... It is usual to assert that the eyes are the best way to arrive at the depths of a personality.... Under the dark magic of the moustache, the trivial gesture or the ghost of a smile acquires an extraordinary expressiveness; a page of Proust realized on the upper lip; ... Menjou's moustaches, which so much incarnate the cinema and his era, will replace in the showcases of the future that horrible and inexpressive hat of Napoleon's. We have seen them, in a close-up of a kiss, alight like some rare summer insect on lips sensitive as mimosa, and devour them complete, coleopterus of love. We have seen his smile, ambushed in his moustache.[53]

The hair-insects on the face of Pierre Batcheff in *Un Chien andalou* introduce the Don Juan theme in a parodic vein; they are also linked to the presence of Proust, which is notable in this film. We know that it was Salvador Dali who suggested the ants to Buñuel.[54] Dali created an entire mythology around ants, which figure prominently in his painting. They appeared for the first time in *Le Grand fourmilier,* then in *Le Grand masturbateur,* where they replaced the missing mouth. Dali's ant mythology quickly became a prominent feature of his painting. They seem on the one hand to symbolize putrefaction. In *Le Grand masturbateur,* Dali replaced the mouth with a cricket whose rotting stomach is seething with ants. Ants also mark the putrefying body of a donkey in *Guillaume Tell* (1930). On the other hand, ants also function erotically, being associated persistently with pubic hair, as in *Le Jeu lugubre* (1929), in the watercolor study for *Le Grand masturbateur* (1929), and in *Combinaisons* (1931), where ants in the pubic region are linked to an obvious Freudian symbol such as the key. In *Le Rêve* (1931), ants once more occupy the place of the mouth and metaphorically signify erotic fantasies. Their ambivalent status allows them to unify the themes of death and eros, a gesture important for Dali.

The connectedness of eros and death is also confirmed by the intertext of surrealist literary production. Many writers associated ants with blood. Breton writes: "This explorer in a struggle with the red ants of his own blood."[55] In Péret we find: "There are two ways to shorten the nose. The simplest method consists in grating it with a cheese grater, until several dozen ants come out of it."[56] (The latter image has clearly erotic connotations.) The associations of ants with wounds and blood can often involve unexpected twists, as in Breton's "Poisson soluble" (1924): "In the shop window the hull of a superb white steamship, whose stem, gravely damaged, is being attacked by some unknown species of ants."[57] Not long before the making of *Un Chien andalou,* Artaud also made the association between ants and death: "A kind of night fills her teeth. Penetrates the caves of her skull with a roar. She lifts the cover of her grave with a hand whose knuckle-bones seem like ants."[58] The chain skull/death/ants is also found in a truncated form in Breton and Soupault's "Les Modes perpétuelles": "On découvre un cerveau il y a des fourmis rouges" (You discover a brain, there are red ants there).[59]

The external similarity that red ants bear to blood, and black ants to wavy hair, and the fact that ants eat carrion make them reversible signifiers, capable of referring to different signifieds and by that very fact connecting quite heterogeneous points of reference. In Buñuel, as in Breton and Soupault, the ant loses its traditional semantic baggage, becoming an empty signifier, open to different metaphoric meanings and substitutive relationships. We are dealing with a trope in the process of formation rather than in its crystallized and established form.

Throughout *Un Chien andalou,* Buñuel and Dali replace fixed meaning with chance meanings. This is most obvious when they are dealing with objects that have an evolved cultural symbolism, such as Vermeer's painting *The Lacemaker* or the pianos in the film on which dead donkeys are brought into a room. Both the painting and the piano are attributes of European high culture, and the viewer is inclined to view them in this light. In reality, the more obvious the cultural symbolism of an object, the more likely it is to be treated in a manner entirely divorced from the intertext into which it is normally inscribed.

The context of *The Lacemaker*'s appearance in the film is as follows. A cross-dressed cyclist is riding down the street. Then we see a girl who (I quote from the script) "is reading a book attentively. Suddenly she shudders, listens curiously, and throws her book on a nearby sofa. The book stays open. On one of the pages is seen a reproduction of Vermeer's *Lacemaker.* The young girl is convinced that something is going on: she gets up, turns halfway from the camera, and walks rapidly to the window."[60] Later on we see the cyclist crash alongside her house, dying in the collision.

In this scene—a typical case of an anomaly produced by montage—the relations of cause and effect seem to be inverted: the girl is startled and runs to the window; only then does the cyclist ride toward her house and fall, breaking his head against the edge of the pavement. Such a violation of causal relations is in fact not typical for Buñuel. What, then, might be the significance of Vermeer's *Lacemaker,* whose presence was already fore-seen in the script?

Contemporary French interest in Vermeer was aroused by an exhibition of Dutch art at the Musée du Jeu de Paume in May 1921. The exhibition created a huge sensation. Pierre Descargues speaks of "magazines . . . filled with articles on Vermeer. Schematic transfers from his works are being published, and the dazzling tile work of Dutch interiors is being compared to the Mondrians of the day."[61] The impact of Vermeer was vast and at times unexpected. It caused Léger to include everyday themes in his work. Vermeer's painting quickly became a myth, gaining a symbolic significance for Proust, who devoted quite a few pages to the Dutch painter in his *Recherche.* Proust went to the Vermeer show but on the way felt himself sud-denly weaken, a fact he interpreted as a sign of his impending death: "On the staircase he [Proust] felt a terrible dizziness, he staggered and came to a halt, but was then able to continue walking. In the exhibition hall of the Jeu de Paume, Vaudoyer had to take him by the arm and lead him panting to the *View of Delft.*"[62] On returning home, Proust worked his prophetic en-counter with Vermeer into an episode of his book dealing with the death of Bergotte. Just before dying, Bergotte contemplates the *View of Delft,* con-centrating on a yellow piece of the wall lit by the sun: "He fixed his gaze, like a child intent on a yellow butterfly he wishes to capture, on the pre-cious piece of wall." This turns out to be Bergotte's last vision: "Then he fell onto a round sofa. . . . Another stroke seized him, he rolled off the sofa onto the floor, at which point all the visitors and attendants came running. He was dead."[63]

The Proustian intertext is in fact even richer, and more capricious. It contains in turn another writer, now mostly forgotten, Robert de Mon-tesquiou, a celebrated Parisian dandy whom Proust admired and even imi-tated, and whom he depicted in his own cycle of novels under the name Charlus. In his *Diptique de Flandre,* Montesquiou also mentions the *View of Delft,* particularly noting its "yellowish pink color,"[64] to launch then into a sudden digression on Vermeer as the painter of death and pearls. "Waters that roll pearls, always. Only four of them become iridescent in the Ver-meer of the Rijksmuseum; they weep longer on the necks of the heroines of the living Vermeer, they weep along with these young women, for they are sad, these Ophelias. . . . Yes, Ophelias who have known and tasted love, but who bathe it in their tears and their pearls."[65] It was this motif, as we shall shortly see, that was taken up and elaborated by the surrealists, and Dali in particular.

As Proust's parodic double, almost surrealist in spirit, Montesquiou might well have served as a subtext for *Un Chien andalou,* providing a grotesque prototype for the role played by Pierre Batcheff. The behavior of this decadent fin de siècle eccentric anticipated much of what was to become the surrealist ethic. For example, he took great pride in his cruelty, as can be seen from the following aphorism: "The greatest and gravest of crimes is to cause only minor pain to those who love you."[66] Montesquiou gained some notoriety for having beaten a woman with a cane during a famous fire at Paris Fancy Fair in 1897 that he was trying to flee. Very much like the surrealists, he collected strange artwork, such as paintings representing body parts. He owned a drawing of the chin of Countess Greffulhe, another of the legs of his secretary Ituri by Boldini, and a plaster cast of the knee of the Countess de Castiglione.[67] The latter became the object of a veritable cult of Montesquiou's own making: both shared a peculiar passion for photography, the countess being particularly partial to having her legs photographed.[68] Their mutual passion for body parts represented out of any natural "context" clearly anticipated surrealist poetics. Moreover, Montesquiou was also known for his improbable mustache and a set of rotten black teeth that he constantly tried to conceal with his hand. Proust was to adopt the latter gesture, without having any reason to do so.[69] The eroticized cruelty of the hero played by Batcheff, as well as his odd gesture of "erasing" his mouth, could thus easily be a reference to Proust himself—a somewhat unexpected presence in the surrealist context, although mediated by his grotesquely parodic caricature Montesquiou.

Montesquiou's example incited the surrealists to a wholesale parody of the Proustian myth. Buñuel and Dali were equally involved in this game. It seems probable that the virulence of the surrealists' polemical rejection of Proust had something to do with their attitude to memory. The cultural symbolism they aimed to destroy had become lodged in cultural memory, which in turn became the logical object of their aesthetic violence. As Soupault proclaimed: "Memory [*la mémoire*] should be replaced by recollections [*des souvenirs*] of the present." Desnos even advocated the destruction of memory.[70] Éluard appealed for a boycott of reading and writing, since writing embodied the mechanism of memory: "Let us stop before we form letters. As far as possible, let us forget reading, writing, orthography."[71] In having equated memory with the universe, Proust became the logical target of the surrealist derision (hence the Menjou-Proust mustache), just as the skull, a mnemonic symbol embodying the maxim of memento mori, was constantly placed in a sacrilegious context.

The painter Vermeer was also interpreted by the surrealists, particularly Dali, as a Proustian symbol of death. Vermeer haunts a series of Dali's works of the early thirties like a phantom (such as *Enigmatic Elements in a Landscape* [1934], *The Phantom of Vermeer of Delft* [1934], and *The Phantom of Vermeer of Delft That Can Be Used as a Table* [1934]). But the clearest example of the Vermeer myth in Dali's work can be found in one of his manifestos of "paranoia-critique," "Light-Ideas." Dali here elaborates a symbolism of the pearl that is in nearly complete unison with Montesquiou's fantasies: "For the pearl," writes Dali, "is none other than the very ghost of the skull, a skull which, at the end of its seething, aphrodisiacal decay, becomes round, clean and hairless, like the crystallized residue of this entire swampy, nourishing, magnificent, glutinous, obscure and greenish OYSTER OF DEATH." The oyster is then identified with the grave: "The pearl is elevated to the highest position in the loftiest hierarchy of objective myth by Vermeer of Delft. It is an obsessive motif in the indefatigably complex, highly lucid and immemorial thinking of this painter who possessed 'the luminous sense of death.' . . . Vermeer is the authentic painter of ghosts. The woman trying on her pearl necklace before the mirror is the most authentically ghostly canvas to have ever been painted."[72]

This "new myth" of Vermeer was destined to circulate in Dali's work for many years. In his reworking of Vermeer's *Woman Reading a Letter* called *The Image Disappears* (1938), Dali depicted a woman's head that is at the same time the pupil of a man's eye and an oyster shell. Dali also called Vermeer a "weigher of pearls" (hinting at Vermeer's painting *Woman Weighing Pearl*). Later, Dali would return to the theme of the lacemaker. In 1954, he began working on a film in collaboration with Robert Descharnes entitled *The Marvellous Adventures of the Lacemaker and the Rhinoceros*, which contains a scene of Dali himself at the Louvre copying Vermeer's *Lacemaker*. The film's primary theme is metamorphosis. Never shown in public and possibly never completed, the film is described by James Bigwood as being based on "Dali's theory of the spiraling and logarhythmic relation that exists between objects . . . illustrated by the scopic metamorphosis of a rhinoceros horn into Vermeer's *Lacemaker*, then into a sunflower, a cauliflower, a sea urchin, a drop of water, and the skin of a chicken. Two seeds on an ear of barley turn into buttocks, and a pastoral scene becomes the face of Hitler."[73]

The Lacemaker became the means to smuggle in the relatively obscure theme of the pearl and the connected theme of metamorphosis into *Un Chien andalou*. We are now in a better position to understand the logic behind the development of the beginning of the film's main section. The Vermeer painting figures here as a prophecy of death, which is immediately fulfilled by the cyclist's accident. The latter, in turn, parodies Proust's account of the death of Bergotte, who also falls dead immediately after seeing the Vermeer painting. This initial scene is related to an episode at the end to which it symmetrically corresponds. The film's hero dies twice, first by falling off his bicycle, then when he is shot by his double. The second time, he falls dead while gripping the body of a naked woman seated in the forest like a *tableau vivant*. This woman, we should note, is wearing a pearl necklace around her neck (the only overt reference to pearls in the film).

Immediately after the hero's death, the atropos moth appears on a wall (we remember the butterfly motif in Proust's account of Bergotte's death). It is also worth noting the connection, well established in surrealist poetry, between the pearl and the skull. One of the "phrases" (Number 7) of Rrose Sélavy (Robert Desnos, perceived as an oracle by many surrealists), reads: "Oh my skull fading star of pearl." Rosa Buchole has shown that this phrase is constructed as an anagrammatical and pseudomathematical equation, where the word *skull* (*crâne*) is equated with *mother-of-pearl* (*nacre*).[74] Also typical is the motif of the star, one of the many persistent and ambivalent images the surrealists used to link heterogeneous phenomena.

The pearl motif also acts as a link between Vermeer's *Lacemaker* and the figure of the moon that appears in the film's prologue. As Mircea Eliade has shown, the link between the pearl, the moon, death, and eros is one of the constant themes of world mythology.[75]

A wider intertext equates the pearl with the eyes of a drowned man. T. S. Eliot's *Waste Land* (1922) frequently quotes from Ariel's song in Shakespeare's *The Tempest*, "Those are Pearls that were his eyes."[76] Both in Eliot and in Shakespeare, this phrase refers to the transformation of a drowned man. A long and highly subtle chain of associations emerges here, much of which can be found in a condensed form in Robert Desnos's poem "A présent," whose very title stands in a polemical relation to memory: "Each lamp I transfigured into a gouged-out eye, from which I poured wines more precious than mother-of-pearl and the sighs of murdered women."[77] Here the chain of metamorphoses is signaled by the verb "transfigure," repeating the motifs of *Un Chien andalou* almost to the letter: luminous object (lamp, moon)/slit eye/liquid/mother-of-pearl/death (murdered women). As is evident from this example, Buñuel and Dali often used semantic links that were already well established in poetry.

These chains, which become part of the general process of metaphoric transformation, nonetheless do not prevent the objects they include from acquiring a narrow occasional meaning, one that becomes evident only in appearing more than once within a specific body of work. Even here, the stability of cultural significance attaching to these objects (e.g., works of art) often prevents us as viewers from understanding their place in the text. Buñuel and Dali act as if this cultural significance were absent, allowing the Vermeer painting or the atropos butterfly to function as if they belonged to one and the same semantic field. The "normal" field of intertextuality, which contains objects with a heightened cultural symbolism, is here overcome by force. Yet the latter is found to be possible only at the price of actively cultivating a new intertext, which serves to counteract the normative intertext of traditional culture. The destruction of classical cultural associations is in the final analysis found to be the result of the rapid and intense growth of a new intertext. A new culture emerges from the struggle against the old, parading as an anticulture, hiding behind the play of external forms. This struggle between two intertexts is not just a conscious strategy: it is in fact utilized to create a new type of text, a textual puzzle, which respects the laws of semantics even while appearing to dismiss them.

There are three references to classical painting in *Un Chien andalou,* and in each case the cultural symbolism of the work of art is viewed negatively. First there is *The Lacemaker,* then the nude with the pearl, and then the prologue, where the reference remains obscure. Here we see a cloud that intersects the disk of the moon. Buñuel, we know, was particularly fond of the narrow, dense, almost tangibly concrete clouds he had found in the works of Mantegna. In 1924, Buñuel specifically asked Dali to draw similar clouds in his portrait of him.[78] The materiality of Mantegna's clouds may well have given Buñuel the idea of transforming his own cloud into a razor. More important, it is in Mantegna's works that we find clouds that conceal hidden figures. His *St. Sebastian* has a rider on horseback concealed in the clouds; and an enormous face can be discerned in the clouds represented in *The Triumph of Virtue*. Mantegna's clouds, then, serve as the raw material for effecting visual metamorphoses.[79] As an intertext for *Un Chien andalou,* Mantegna makes no claim to a culturally symbolic space: he appeals, rather, to a private, subjective, and occasional meaning, the symbolism of metamorphosis.

The insistence with which Buñuel and Dali introduce cultural associations as a subtext suggests the tremendous importance the classical intertext held for them, an importance eloquently illustrated by the urgency of creating an alternative intertext to oppose it. A negative "hyperacculturation" of the text is typical of the film, as it is of the avant-garde as a whole. It is this that finally allowed the avant-garde to be readily absorbed by European culture as a system.

This ambivalent relation to cultural tradition is further illustrated by one of the film's most enigmatic episodes, involving the rotting corpses of donkeys lying on pianos. Most of the existing scholarly literature seeks to throw light on this episode by invoking all the possible nuances of cultural symbolism attached to donkeys and pianos.[80] Such an approach, however, has not really produced satisfactory results.

This scene, in which Pierre Batcheff, close to exhaustion, is seen dragging the two pianos with donkeys on them into the room, does acquire a marginally normative status thanks to a film intertext, specifically connected to Batcheff's mask. The critic Drummond has shown that this mask is connected both to French melodrama and to the figure of Buster Keaton, one of Buñuel's favorite actors: the Keaton film *One Week* (1920) contains a scene in which the hero tries to drag a piano into his house.[81]

Echoes of Charlie Chaplin are also possible here. This is how Louis Delluc describes Chaplin's 1915 film *Work:* "Is this really a film? No, it's a *piano.* Of course, it is pleasant to look at Charlie, fragile as a weak little *donkey,* dragging a cart up the slope of a hill." Delluc goes on to describe the "vertiginous episode" in which Chaplin "transports the piano and where the *piano coolly transports* Charlie."[82] None of these interpretations, however, provide us with a complete set of keys to this episode, with its complex agglomeration of motifs.

Buñuel and Dali themselves sought to mystify the origins of the motif of the putrefying donkey. In this case a mystical coincidence rather than a dream was said to be involved, as Dali noted in 1929:

> In 1927, without there being any contact between them, three men at some distance from each other imagined a donkey putrefying: at Cadaquès, I was doing a series of paintings in which a kind of donkey, rotting and covered with flies, made an appearance. . . . Almost at the same time, I received two letters: one from Madrid, from Penin Bello, who spoke of a donkey in the process of decaying. . . . Several days later, Luis Buñuel wrote to me about a putrefying donkey in a letter from Paris.[83]

This version is confirmed, although in a slightly different redaction, by Georges Bataille: "The rotting corpses of the donkeys in *Un chien andalou* reproduce a hallucination that both Dali and Buñuel had during their childhood, when both of them, while in the countryside, saw the corpse of a donkey decomposing."[84] Bataille's version, with its insistence on two authors, might well explain the fact that the film involves two donkeys.

After 1927 the motif of the putrefying donkey becomes a constant feature of Dali's painting and written work. It appears in the 1927 text *Mon ami et la plage;*[85] it is depicted twice in the 1927 painting *Le Miel est plus doux que le sang,* and twice again in *Senicitas* (1927). In 1928, Dali paints *Ane en putrefaction;* more rotting donkeys appear in *Vache spectrale* (1928) and in *Guillaume Tell* (1930).

The motif of the rotting donkey in fact has a fairly wide intertext, as Buñuel and Dali themselves imply. In his memoirs of 1982, *Mon dernier soupir,* Buñuel recounts his student years in Madrid. His account is abruptly interrupted by a sentence that appears somewhat divorced from the narrative context: "This was the time in which, thanks to *L'Enchanteur pourrissant* [The decaying magician], I discovered Apollinaire."[86] The discovery of Apollinaire appears to have been of fundamental importance to the director, since he mentions it more than sixty years after the fact.

L'Enchanteur pourrissant, a work of Apollinaire's youth, was written between 1898 and 1904 and definitively completed in 1909, when it was published in an edition of one hundred copies with prints by André Derain.

Republished but once in 1921, the book remained out of print until 1965. A text hailed by Breton as one of Apollinaire's most significant works, *L'Enchanteur pourrissant* remained unknown to the general public, even as it became an essential point of reference for *Un Chien andalou,* and for surrealism as a whole.

Formally speaking, *L'Enchanteur pourrissant* recalls the Walpurgisnacht episode from Goethe's *Faust,* as well as Flaubert's *La Tentation de Saint Antoine.* Thematically, it is a parodic interpretation of the medieval legend involving the magician Merlin, who falls victim to the perfidy of the Lady of the Lake and is buried alive in the forest. Apollinaire's short book in effect recounts the procession of a series of strange mythological beings over the grave of the deceased yet still living magician. The book's main themes are love and death. The plot itself centers on Merlin, doomed to immortality yet slowly decomposing in his grave, around whom various creatures gather and dedicate themselves to love. Among them we find hermaphrodites (an androgyne is also the hero of *Un Chien andalou*). The animals who dedicate themselves to love wait in vain to be transformed, an experience known only to Merlin, whose physical decay is discovered to be linked to an unexpected surge of life: "The magician understood that some enormous work was being accomplished in his corpse. All the latent parasitic beings, which languish in boredom during human life, now quickened, meeting and fecundating one another, for this was the moment of putrefaction. . . . He was even glad, thinking that his corpse would be full of life for a while longer."[87]

Putrefaction becomes, for Apollinaire, the central moment of animal eroticism. Flies and dragonflies perform voluptuous dances and then depart for a feast of decay. At the end of *L'Enchanteur pourrissant,* in a chapter called "Onirocritique" (cf. Dali's idea of "paranoia-critique"), masses of people fall into a kind of wine press where they are liquefied (the final stage of decomposition): "A whole mass of people, squeezed into a press, was singing as it bled. Human beings were born out of the liqueur which poured out of the press."[88] In being connected to eros, decay itself becomes the source of new forms of life.

L'Enchanteur pourrissant contains a number of typically surrealist motifs: a "weeping head made of a single pearl," a magician who dives for pearls, a dance of hands and leaves (a typically surrealist correlation based on shape), a "mollified animal," and so forth. In fact, these motifs are older than Apollinaire, who merely elaborated them further. In some of Victor Hugo's most apocalyptic verse we already find the theme of metamorphosis in decay. In the chapter "Montfaucon" from *La Légende des siècles,* Hugo writes "From cadaver to skeleton one can study / The progress which the dead make in rotting."[89] And in *Les Châtiments* we find a poem describing the slow disappearance of bodily shape in the process of decay, to the point where it is no longer possible to establish whether we are seeing "dead dogs or rotten Caesars."[90]

But perhaps the most eloquent account of formal decomposition culminating in a metaphoric transformation is Charles Baudelaire's "Une Charogne:"

> Rappelez-vous l'objet que nous vîmes, mon âme,
> Ce beau matin d'été si doux:
> Au détour d'un sentier une charogne infâme
> Sur un lit semé de cailloux.
> Le soleil rayonnait sur cette pourriture,
> Comme afin de la cuire à point,
> Et de rendre au centuple à la grande Nature
> Tout ce qu'ensemble elle avait joint;
> Et le ciel regardait la carcasse superbe
> Comme une fleur s'épanouir.
> La puanteur était si forte, que sur l'herbe
> Vous crûtes vous évanouir.
> ....
> Les formes s'effaçaient et n'étaient plus qu'un rêve,
> Une ébauche lente à venir,
> Sur la toile oubliée, et que l'artiste achève
> Seulement par le souvenir.

> (Do you recall the object that we saw, my soul,
> This so gentle summer morning:
> At the detour of a path a vile piece of carrion
> On a bed of scattered pebbles.
> The sunshine poured over this corruption,
> As if to cook it medium rare,
> And to render back to Nature hundredfold
> Everything that she had joined together;
> And the sky saw the superb carcass
> Bloom like a flower.
> The stench was so strong, that you thought
> You would faint on the grass.
> ....
> The forms became effaced and were no more than a dream,
> A sketch slow in coming,
> Forgotten on the canvas, and which the artist completes
> By memory alone.)[91]

The decomposition of a corpse here creates a formless chaos in which everything can be discerned—right up to a vision of divine beauty. Hugo's "rotten Caesars" and Baudelaire's "pieces of skeleton like large flowers" seem oddly to prefigure surrealist verse, above all the poetry of Benjamin Péret, who was particularly fond of the motif of decay.[92]

Péret's related poems were probably known to Buñuel and Dali even before they began work on *Un Chien andalou.* Buñuel recalls: "I started reading them [the surrealists], above all Benjamin Péret, whose poetic sense of humor excited me. Dali and I read him and cracked up laughing. There was something about him, a strange, perverse movement, a delicious sense of humor, of a corrosive kind."[93] Péret consistently connected decay to the figures of God, Christ, and various priests, something that appealed to the anticlerical sentiments of Buñuel and Dali. Péret shared their antipathy to the church. Soupault recalls: "He would get angry (to put it mildly) whenever he saw or met a priest. He became furious and would insult what he would call the 'ecclesiastics.' "[94] It is hardly a surprise to read the pope described by Péret as "a crab-louse among *rotting* Christs."[95] Joan of Arc, appearing before a "pile of cow dung crowned with flies near an old piece of *rotten* wood," realizes that she is standing "before the face of God."[96] Jesuits are said to fill their cups with "eucharistic *rot.*"[97] Alongside Joan of Arc stand forty archbishops with "*rotting* glances"; another poem, "6 février," describes the "*rotten* yellow-green curates."[98] Péret composes a "prayer" on the death of Briand, where he writes, "Lord, bless us with a toilet brush / just as we have blessed with a *rotten* fish."[99] At times the motif of putrefaction is inserted into a lengthy series of metaphors. Hence in the poem "Louis XVI s'en va à la guillotine" we read:

Il pleut du sang de la neige
et toutes sortes de saletés
qui jaillissent de sa vieille carcasse
de chien crevé au fond d'une lessiveuse
au milieu du linge sale
qui a eu le temps de pourrir
comme la fleur de lis des poubelles
que les vaches refusent de brouter
parce qu'elle répand une odeur de dieu
dieu le père des boues

(It rains a rain of bloody snow
and of all kinds of filth
which spring forth from his old carcass
a dead dog at the bottom of a washing trough
among some dirty linen
that has had time to *rot*
like the fleur-de-lis of the rubbish-bins
which the cows refuse to nibble at
since it exudes a smell of god
god the father of slime)[100]

There can be no doubt that the makers of *Un Chien andalou* made good use of these motifs of Péret. (The precedent of Péret may well explain the inclusion of priests in the donkey episode, as well as the rotting bishops who appear in *L'Age d'or*. Let us also not forget the traditional link between the donkey and God in European culture.)[101] The presence of the Péret intertext is confirmed by one of Buñuel's own texts, in which we find motifs that are elaborated later in *Un Chien andalou*. In a fragment called "Le mot de passe commode de Saint Huesca," two curates decide to gamble their lives and crawl into a streetcar filled with beehives: "The bees made a fine racket and the Marists lay down in their coffins, ready to stake everything. One of them said in a low voice: 'Are you sure that the Bologna sausage is made for the blind men as Péret said?' The other replied: 'We are already at the bridge.' Below the bridge, in the middle of the water, half green, half putrid, they could see a tombstone."[102]

In *Un Chien andalou* the priests are kept but are displaced in their graves (the pianos) by donkeys. The donkeys assume the attributes of blindness and putrefaction. During the filming, Dali took care to have their eyes gouged out. Interestingly, the film's epilogue also contains a blind man and woman at a beach, buried in sand up to their chests. And Dali's text *Mon amie et la plage* also places the putrefied body of a donkey on a beach. At stake, then, is a complex contamination and echoing of motifs, with the poetry of Benjamin Péret at its center.

These motifs are brought together by yet another intertext, Georges Bataille's book *L'Expérience intérieure*, which was written after *Un Chien andalou*. In what appears to be a reference to the film's ending, Bataille metaphorically substitutes blind men for the donkeys. In Dali's "Mon amie et la plage" we read: "At that very moment, the printed letters of a newspaper devour a bloated and rotting donkey, clear as mica."[103] The letters here are insects, most likely ants. Bataille elaborates this motif and transforms it in the process: "This sand into which we sink in order not to see is composed of words, and the revolt implied in using them forces us to remember—if I can move from one image to another—the man caught in the sand who struggles but as a result only gets even more stuck." Bataille says later that words have "something of shifting sand" about them; the grains of words are then gathered together by ants.[104]

The donkey scene from *Un Chien andalou* interests us for yet another reason: the absolute lack of any motivation that might justify the linkage of the donkeys with a piano. Péret, in the passage quoted earlier, compares a dead dog to a fleur-de-lis. The simile, however extravagant, is still motivated (linen is white, the lily is a water-plant, and there is an analogy between linen and flower petals, and between the dog's body and a flower's pith), all the more so since the fleur-de-lis is the symbol of the French monarchy, whose importance is readily understood in a poem about the beheading of Louis XVI. In an article by Dali entitled "Les Nouvelles Frontières de la peinture," we find a startlingly similar image, although this time entirely unmotivated: "Flowers are highly poetic, precisely because they resemble rotting donkeys."[105] If a decomposed dog can be compared to God, then the gamut of analogies becomes extremely wide, far beyond the limits set by established similes.

This widening of the range of possible comparisons is also realized through the destruction of cultural symbolism. The flower and the donkey emerge as purely formal analogies. For Buñuel, cinema was a splendid tool for ridding the world of the burden of older meanings:

> The film, in the last analysis, is composed of segments, fragments, attitudes, which, taken thus, separate and arbitrarily, are archi-trivial, deprived of local meaning, of psychology, of literary transcendence. In literature, a lion or an eagle can represent many things, but on the screen they will be only two beasts, and that is all and no more, even though for Abel Gance, they can represent ferocity, valor, and imperialism.[106]

It is no coincidence that Buñuel chooses to instantiate his point with an image taken from the bestiary, one of the most symbolically charged codes. Yet the donkey, being both a "lowly" emblem and an embodiment of God, is even more significant here. The image of the donkey was advanced by Dali at a time when he was beginning to develop his theory of "paranoia-critique," according to which one and the same form could be "read" to be entirely different things, depending on the way it was viewed. Dali proposed the notion of "multiple representation," in which the image of the rotting donkey was to occupy a central place.

One of Dali's manifestos of paranoia-criticism, in fact entitled "L'Âne pourri" (The rotten donkey), declares:

> No one can stop me from recognizing the multiple presence of simulacra in an image with multiple representations, even if one of its states took on the appearance of a rotten donkey, and even if that donkey were really in a state of horrible decomposition, covered with thousands of flies and ants. Yet insofar as it is impossible to presuppose the individual significance of different states of representation outside the notion of time, nothing can convince me that the donkey's furious putrefaction is something other than the hard and dazzling gleam of new precious stones.[107]

Dali here also speaks of three great simulacra—"shit, blood, and putrefaction." These great simulacra can assume any guise insofar as they are without fixed form. As metaphors they can be compared to any phenomenon or object. Rotting leads to the dilution of form; it is said to take us back to the "necrophilic source" that is the common denominator of all dissolving form. This "source" was to resurface in Dali's painting also: in *Naissance de désirs liquides* (1932), where water is seen flowing from a cypress tree (symbol of death, the black candle), or in *Source nécrophilique surgissant d'un piano à queue* (1933), in which a stream is pouring out of a piano that has been pierced by the same cypress tree. So the piano (grave) as a symbol of death becomes the source of all forms and, effectively, the source of all texts in which these forms are embodied.

In a sense, Dali's transformation of death into a principle of textual generation is merely a simplified version of the literary mythology that Artaud had created before him. Artaud had described the sensation of his body liquefying and passing into nothingness and had then elevated this sensation into a kind of "artistic gnoseology." According to Artaud, there is an eternal and infinite *reality*, which gives itself to us as *real*. The real, being "one of the most transient and least discernible aspects of infinite reality," is "equal to matter and decays with it."[108] All perception that strays from structure and clarity is, for Artaud, linked to death. Hence the idea that any sign which violates the organized structure of a text is a sign of death. (The very production of a text is also, at its limit, equated with death.) Artaud introduced death into the sphere of textual production as a formal structuring principle. His collection *L'Art et la mort* contains the text "Héloïse et Abélard" (1925), which begins by saying of Abélard that "entire regions of his brain were rotting," after which Abélard's text, the outcome of this mortal decay, follows. The text ends with Abélard feeling "his life become liquid."[109]

Dali follows in Artaud's wake. His dead donkey, generator of metaphoric analogy, in part reworks Artaud's "necrophilic" generative principle. In Dali, however, the production of text from a putrefying source is far more mechanical, allowing him to continue elaborating a paradigm that in turn keeps escalating. Through metaphor the text strives to become a universe. So in the text "Le Grand masturbateur" (1930), which refers to a painting with the same title, Dali writes: "The short / alley with springs / recalled / the clear / decomposition / of rotting donkeys / rotting horses / rotting cats / rotting mouths / rotting chickens / horrible rotting roosters / rotting grasshoppers / rotting birds / rotting corpses of women / oppressively rotting grasshoppers / rotting horses / rotting donkeys / rotting sea urchins / rotting hermit crabs."[110]

The rotting donkey thus becomes a kind of "hypersign," a symbol of hyperconvertibility. Picasso once noted Dali's fondness for having one animal represent another: "These young artists are astonishing. They know everything. They even know that a horse should be represented through a fishbone."[111] In 1928, Éluard, who may have even influenced the formation of the "donkey myth," had written about the wandering skeletons of donkeys that can insinuate themselves into any form of knowledge: "The skeletons of knowledge the skeletons of donkeys, / Eternally wandering around the brains and the flesh."[112]

The unexpected juxtaposition of donkey and piano, then, was intended to reveal their "paranoia-critical" analogy. The episode was largely shot by Dali, who describes his work on the scene as follows:

> The shooting of the scene of the rotten donkeys and the pianos was a rather fine sight. . . . I furiously cut their mouths open to make the white rows of their teeth show to better advantage, and I added several jaws to each mouth so that it would appear that although the donkeys were already rotting they were still vomiting up a little more of their own death, above those other rows of teeth formed by the keys of the black pianos. The whole effect was as lugubrious as fifty coffins piled into a single room.[113]

Let us note how Dali here equates the bared jaws of the donkey with the piano keys. Later on, he would often compare a piano to a skull, on the basis of their remotely similar shape, and of the analogy between bared teeth and a piano keyboard. One example is the painting *Crâne atmosphérique sodomisant un piano à queue* (1934). Dali's "skull-harp"—a skull used as a musical instrument—belongs to the same kind of comparative play, as in the gravure *Crânes mous et harpe crânienne* (1935), the gouache *Jeune fille au crâne* (1934), and the painting *Bureaucrate atmosphérocéphale moyen en train de traire une harpe crânienne* (1933). This motif, moreover, was also anticipated by Apollinaire, whose *L'Enchanteur pourrissant* describes sounds emerging from teeth as from a piano keyboard.[114] But the analogy between the piano and the donkey does not end here.

The piano is also seen as the donkey's coffin—hence its black color and its shape, which is hardly typical for a coffin. This motif is also not original. In a more muted way it is present in a screenplay, never produced, by Gómez de la Serna called *Stradivarius's Burial,* in which a violin is buried in its case: "The funeral director, with a mask of pain on his face, encloses the broken violin in its case which is then carried away."[115] Here, as always with Gómez de la Serna, the eccentric quality of the image is internally motivated.

In the preceding case we are dealing with a fairly traditional metaphoric scheme. If it is harder to successfully read the same metaphor in *Un Chien andalou,* this is so for several reasons. First, both elements of the metaphor are presented to the viewer as a physical conglomerate, almost too shockingly visible to be abstracted into metaphor. It is also extraordinarily difficult to see the piano as a coffin or a skull because of the irreducible cultural symbolism it carries, and without which it cannot enter the text. No viewer could normally "read" a piano as a purely external form, devoid of any previously given semantics. This is why the scene acquires such an enigmatic feel. The enigma is solved when we bracket the piano's traditional symbolism and accentuate its external nature, its structural role as an analogy or simulacrum. The problem of textual construction is here resolved by ignoring the object's traditional semantic weight, on the basis of external formal traits. In order to read this scene, we have to forget our reading habits, renounce the experience of reading over many centuries, the entire intertext of culture. To learn to read, one has to lose the habit (or memory) of reading.

By privileging the category of the analogy or simulacrum, the surrealist text is confronted with the basic opposition of form and formlessness. We have already pointed to two models of juxtaposing objects based on external form in *Un Chien andalou*. On the one hand, we have the bringing together of realia that have a clear geometricized form (most often tending toward a circle). This formal clarity and precision are of fundamental importance from a geometric point of view. On the other, where objects are brought together that lack geometrically defined contours (such as the donkey), the possibility of formal destruction becomes vital, and a protean formlessness is emphasized. Metamorphosis is possible on the basis of both principles. While serving primarily as principles for constructing texts, both form and formlessness gain the status of a worldview in surrealist poetics (something quite typical for artistic systems that equate the text with the world). In December 1929, Georges Bataille published *L'Informel,* in which the formless is opposed to the artificial and rationalist givenness of form. Bataille's revolt against geometry was expressed in his declaration that the world as an embodiment of the formless is like "a spider or a spit."[116] A little later, in *Rejet de la nature,* he was to celebrate monsters that were "situated on a pole dialectically opposed to geometric regularity."[117]

Monsters, insects, and death: all these motifs function in *Un Chien andalou* as embodiments of the formless. The film's prologue, which still echoes the geometricism of Desnos's *Minuit à quatorze heures,* can in this sense also be read as an attempt to cross out the geometric principle in favor of analogies of formlessness.

The plot of *Un Chien andalou* in part reflects the evolution of surrealist metaphor from the pole of form to that of formlessness, an evolution that reflects characteristic changes in the outlook of the surrealists themselves. On the level of formal devices, this evolution can be described as the succession of several stages: an emphasis on spherical forms (the eye as a symbol of the interchangeability of round objects) and the dismemberment of the body as a means of eliminating a sense of the whole, with an emphasis on body parts and their autonomization. The dismemberment of the body leads, in turn, to the motif of death as a textual generative principle.

Taken in its widest sense, death also implies a rupture with the entire intertext of older culture. Death is a frontier: it marks the beginnings of a new poetics, with established tradition expelled beyond its confines. The death, disintegration, or decomposition of established forms is visible in the general convertibility of the world's elements, in the "necrophilic" dilution of forms, the metamorphic flow of one element into another. At stake here is essentially a metaphoric destruction of established cultural paradigms, and their substitution with a syntagmatic form of thinking, in which the chain, the series of reciprocally replaceable parts, assumes the basic semantic function. This, then, is an attempt at radically renewing the language of film. This chain of semantic and formal shifts—the surrealist metaphor—is the real evolutionary path taken by the poetics and world-view of surrealism, a path presented for us in a condensed way in *Un Chien andalou.*

At the beginning of this chapter I raised the question of whether a syntagm, structure, a chain of elements, can "normalize" a text without recourse to the intertext of culture. My question can now be reformulated thus: Can a syntagm or chain of elements based on a purely external analogy replace, repress, or destroy the intertext of culture? The argument thus far has sought to prove the impossibility of this surrealist procedure: the very principle by which the syntagm is created, its mechanism of external analogy or simulacrum, can be assimilated by the reader only on the basis of an intertext. For the principle of the simulacrum to work, it has to be based on a wide range of texts, the linguistic norm provided by surrealist literature. The syntagmatic principle, I have shown, is established through both an alternative, "negative" intertextuality and an intensive but parodic absorption of the intertext of the very culture that is being destroyed (Vermeer, Proust, etc.). The classical intertext is destroyed through the feverish construction of a competing intertextuality.

This clash of intertexts—classical and "negative"—allows us to reexamine the principle of the "third text" or interpretant, which was discussed in chapter 1. In the case of *Un Chien andalou,* the interpretant (the surrealist negative intertext), while largely retaining its function, no longer serves to rectify a semantic error or to create a stereoscopy of meanings. Its function is more radical. It is like a machine for blocking meanings; it normalizes the text by impeding any release into the paradigm of culture, forcing the text to be read in its linear development, the syntagmatic chain of elements. Thus the very syntagmatization of reading, however paradoxical this may seem, is realized through complex intertextual procedures, operations that take place outside the field of the text.

It would appear that such a strategy would be called upon to destroy the film's symbolic dimension, reducing the task of reading to a decoding of external analogies. In fact, the situation is far more complex. Elements wrenched out of their cultural context are not so much subjected to a symbolic reduction as they are rendered obscure, becoming "hieroglyphs" that provoke an endless field of interpretations. They are subjected to a secondary symbolization, one that in a sense is even stronger than might have been possible through the intertext of traditional culture. An arm belonging to a living organism loses its separate meaning by being absorbed into the human body as a meaningful whole. An arm that is cut off from its body (and metaphorically from the entire intertext of culture) becomes a hieroglyph, giving rise to endless interpretations. In fighting the accretions of symbolic meaning, a new cinematic language has to be sneaky. Buñuel's irony concerning the symbolic meaning of the lion and the eagle, which for Gance represented "ferocity, valor, and imperialism," is also the irony of a victor. At stake is the right to establish the extent of symbolic saturation to which an image can be subject. Clearly, the animals found in Buñuel's own films can be seen as symbols that are far more ambiguous and complex than Gance's, inserted in a text that has been constructed knowingly as an enigma.

When D. W. Griffith constructed his hieroglyphs, he remained content to isolate, say, a woman (e.g., Lillian Gish in *Intolerance*) from the general movement of the body. Buñuel and Dali went much further, dismembering Griffith's hieroglyph into its constituent parts and then recomposing them into a chain of simulacra. Text and body are subject to dismemberment, and their autonomized parts become a cluster of hieroglyphic quotations. The fact that we are prevented from reading these quotes (the necessary intertext having been eliminated) in fact heightens their quotability. The search for an intertext is pursued with even greater intensity, as are all operations that generate meaning.

In the case of *Un Chien andalou*, the "negative" interpretant acquires an extraordinary valence: it allows the film as a whole to be read as a system of references to a general meaning. The viewer is offered a series of metaphors, built on external analogies, all of which address the same kernel of meaning. (These metaphors resemble enigmas: the viewer is continuously forced to intuit the physical similarity on which the metaphoric mutation is based.) We have seen that beyond the chain of analogies there emerges a selection of images, such as the pearl, the skull (linked to the pearl through the established metaphor of pearly teeth), ants, butterflies, and so forth—all of which refer to the general theme of death, eros, and the overarching motif of metamorphosis. In Breton and Soupault's *Les Champs magnétiques,* we find the image of a "butterfly from the sphinx species," which personifies the enigma of metamorphosis.[118] This butterfly can readily serve to signify the poetics of *Un Chien andalou*, since the film's meaning is finally found to reside not in a theme but in the enigma of metamorphosis itself, the enigma of the principle of language that lies at the basis of the text.

PART IV

Theorists Who Practiced

CHAPTER SIX

The Hero as an "Intertextual Body"
Iurii Tynianov's Lieutenant Kizhe

The Russian critic Iurii Tynianov is known as one of the founders of the theory of intertextuality. Tynianov was also an important theorist of film, with the added distinction of having practical experience in the film industry. It is this circumstance that prompts me to turn to his work, in particular to one of his film experiments, *Lieutenant Kizhe*, which he made jointly with the director A. Faintsimmer. To a considerable degree, Tynianov's artistic production was informed by the conceptual apparatus he had developed as a theorist. This fact permits us to analyze *Lieutenant Kizhe* as the realization of a specific set of theoretical premises.

This film is relevant to our project for several reasons. Faintsimmer had no original ideas of his own about the poetics of cinema (unlike the directors of FEKS [*Fabrika èkstsentricheskogo aktëra*, The factory of the eccentric actor] who interpreted Tynianov's scripts in a programmatically eccentric way): Faintsimmer appears in essence to have closely followed Tynianov's instructions. Second, the evolution of the film's plot sheds some light on this chapter's principal theme. This plot was reworked several times and exists in several versions (including the short story "Lieutenant Kizhe," which is widely known in Russia). The somewhat whimsical semantic links between these versions can themselves be understood as intertextual relations.

In general terms, the creative evolution of *Lieutenant Kizhe* has been quite adequately studied.[1] Tynianov wrote his first screen version of *Kizhe* for S. I. Iutkevich in May 1927, but the film was not destined to be produced at that time.[2] In December of the same year, Tynianov completed the literary version of "Lieutenant Kizhe," which was published in January 1928. In the early 1930s, Tynianov returned to the film version of *Kizhe*, writing a new draft of the screenplay, which was then produced by Faintsimmer at the Belgoskino studios and released in March 1934.

Lieutenant Kizhe thus exists in four versions (one being the film itself), whose complex interrelations have remained largely unstudied. Existing scholarship continues to relegate the film version to the periphery of Tynianov's opus. We know that in the 1930s Tynianov spoke of himself as someone who "once worked in the movies."[3] The critic Neia Zorkaia, while avoiding a clear articulation of her views of the matter, tends to dismiss Tynianov's participation in the making of this film as minimal.[4] Yet authoritative accounts from eyewitnesses confirm Tynianov's evident involvement in the shooting of *Kizhe*. Just after the film's release, Grigorii Kozintsev, who had worked on *Lieutenant Kizhe* as a film consultant, wrote: "What was Iurii Nikolaevich [Tynianov's] part in the film? He was not just an author who worked in close collaboration with the director; he also worked with the actors, for which he was amply thanked by the Belgoskino studio."[5] An account given by one of the actors, Èrast Garin, fully coincides with Kozintsev's assertions: "Our work on the film alongside Iu. N. Tynianov was a model of how collaborative creation should ideally take place between a team of actors and a director on the one hand and a writer on the other. From the very first rehearsals to the editing of the film, Iurii Nikolaevich never failed to give us directions about the character types embodied by the people we were playing, and about the era in which they lived."[6] Other tangential indications also suggest that Tynianov's role in the film's making was essentially a coauthorship.[7]

The poetics of several episodes in the film—profoundly linked to Tynianov's literary and theoretical legacy—provides ample evidence to dissipate any remaining doubts about whether Faintsimmer's film version of *Kizhe* was personally authorized by Tynianov. Judging by the three surviving variants, each of Tynianov's reworkings of the *Kizhe* story is linked by a complex chain of shifts and displacements. Most striking of all is the disappearance of entire threads of the plot (e.g., the tale of Lieutenant Siniukhaev, which appears in the short story). Just as remarkable is the extraordinary turnover of characters. The plot of the short story takes place primarily in 1797, whereas the film script shifts the action to the spring of 1800 (the script provides a precise temporal indicator—the expulsion of the English ambassador, an event that is omitted in the film). Between 1797 and 1800, a crucial event took place in the life of the court of Paul I: the "retirement" of the czar's court favorite, Nelidova, which precipitated the more general displacement of one faction by another. This factional struggle is reflected in Tynianov's story, which features the maid-in-waiting Nelidova, as well as the court favorites, Arakcheev and Neledinskii-Meletskii, who belonged to her faction. Yet in the script and in the actual film, Nelidova's function is assumed by Lopukhina-Gagarina, while her banished allies are replaced by Count Pahlen and Kutaisov (who has but a fleeting and nameless presence in the story).

This substitution of one historical personage for another can hardly be said to be motivated by the plot itself: it seems to obey some other authorial impulse. The story in fact contains a motif that explicitly dramatizes this problem of substitution: "The lively Nelidova was retired, *giving place* to the plump Gagarina."[8] This phrase becomes the key to Tynianov's reworking of the story. The same idea is expressed even more clearly elsewhere:

> He [the Emperor Paul] stood in the dark, in his underwear. By the window, he took account of his people. *He shifted them, he crossed Benningsen out of his memory and entered Olsufiev.*
> The list did not tally.
> "My reckoning isn't . . ."
> "Arakcheev is a fool," he said in an undertone.
> ". . . the vague incertitude with which he tries to please. . . ."[9]

We shall have occasion later in this chapter to see how this episode is transformed by the film; for now let us note that the Emperor Paul is caught up in Tynianov's own game of erasing, entering, and substituting names. The temporal gap between the various versions of *Kizhe*, reflected also in the shift in historical setting between the story and the film, is oddly echoed here. In 1797, Kizhe is still a second lieutenant. In the film, which takes place in 1800, he is already a lieutenant. At the end of the story, the First Gentleman of the Chamber Aleksandr L'vovich Naryshkin recalls him as a colonel: "Oh yes, Colonel Kizhe. I remember. He ran after Sandunova."[10] The entire intrigue of the film, as well as one of its central heroines, here figures as a vague memory. Since the name Sandunova is also linked to one of Tynianov's unrealized projects entitled *The Sandunov Baths*, it is clear that one of the story's protagonists is here attempting to recall the plot of a film that has yet to be made and of a story that was never to be written.[11]

Something similar happens to the maid-in-waiting Nelidova: she is mentioned in Tynianov's other story "Young Vitushishnikov" (1933), in which her niece Varen'ka, mistress to Emperor Alexander I, also appears: "Varen'ka Nelidova not only had a stately figure and regular features, but she also, as it were, provided the emperor with the assurance that everything around was developing and moving forward with giant strides. She was the niece of his father's favorite, another Maid-in-Waiting Nelidova. . . . The earlier Nelidova was small, swarthy, homely, and given to contradictions. The present one was of serene, splendid stature, with limbs of marble pallor."[12]

This transition from the earlier Nelidova from *Lieutenant Kizhe* to the younger Nelidova from "Young Vitushishnikov" demonstrates a "development," a movement forward, all the more since the older Nelidova appears as a parody of her niece. This continuity of characters is significant, allowing each text to echo the other. Georgii A. Levinton, in a study of the creative process behind Tynianov's fiction, observes that with respect to historical and documentary sources the writer would constantly effect shifts "not only in chronology but also in relation to the characters, their composition and function."[13] These displacements, Levinton suggests, allowed Tynianov to transform the "source" (a purely genetic phenomenon) into a subtext, which becomes an "essential element of the semantics of the text that quotes it."[14] In other words, the source becomes transformed into a kind of deep intertext.

Equally striking is the fact that Tynianov treats his own works in the same manner as the documentary sources for his novels. From one variant to another, he distorts the documentary and characterological context, distortions that in turn generate properly intertextual links between each redaction. No less than texts written by others, Tynianov's own texts are a source of quotes.

This fact alone shows how crucial intertextuality was for Tynianov's work as a practicing writer. In 1929, he wrote to the formalist critic Viktor Shklovskii: "I look on my own novels as experiments in science fiction, that's all. I think that belles lettres based on historical material will soon pass, and there will be belles lettres based on theory. A theoretical period is beginning in our country."[15] What Tynianov said of literature might be even more appropriately said of the cinema. It was the commonly held view among Leningrad philologists of Tynianov's own milieu that the cinema was junior to literature in the evolutionary scheme of things. This allowed them to regard the cinema with less "deference" and with a greater openness to experimentation.[16] Later in this chapter we shall encounter instances of Tynianov removing constructive elements of an obviously theoretical nature from his prose, while leaving similar theoretical "scaffolding" nakedly exposed in his cinematic work.

We have every reason to believe that the initial conception behind *Lieutenant Kizhe* was itself the outcome of his theoretical studies. In *The Problem of Poetic Language* (1924), Tynianov pays particular and detailed attention to words "'devoid of content' [*bessoderzhatel'nykh*] in the wide sense, words that acquire some semblance of a semantics in a line of verse."[17] Fundamental to the "semanticization" ("semasiologization," in Tynianov's terminology) of words "devoid of content" was what Tynianov called the "density and unity of the poetic series," which intensified the so-called wavering indicators of meaning (*kolebliushchiesia priznaki znacheniia*), creating a "semblance of meaning," an "apparent meaning."[18] Moreover, any series created by the dynamic of a line of verse can contain "semantic *gaps,* which are filled by any word, irrespective of its semantic content." These gaps in a line of verse are "semanticized" through an "orientation toward contiguous words" generated by the density of a series and its rhythm.

In order to acquire meaning, a word must be incomprehensible: it then gains a lexical tone in which the "wavering indicators of meaning" can be foregrounded. Tynianov cites the example of Chekhov's "Peasants," in which the incomprehensible word *dondezhe* (cf. the somewhat similar "Kizhe" in Tynianov) brings tears to the eyes of the heroine.[19] Tynianov is particularly fascinated by the "semanticization" of a word's individual parts: "To emphasize parts of a word is to violate the correlation of objective [*veshchestvennogo*] and formal elements in it. It makes words 'fantastic,' as Maiakovskii once put it (i.e., it corresponds to the emergence in them of 'wavering indicators')."[20]

The transformation of a slip of the pen into a name, and thence into the shifting image of the lieutenant, occurs according to principles that Tynianov had already expounded in his great work on poetics. In 1933, Viktor Shklovskii noticed this connection between *Kizhe* and Tynianov's poetic theory: "*Kizhe* is a stanza that has been finally omitted from an epic poem. The stanza, however, operates according to the laws of epic poetry."[21] In Mirra Ginsburg's English translation of the story, this scene reads as follows (what the Russian creates out of the plural ending of *lieutenant* and the particle *zhe*—[*podporuchi*]*ki zhe* = *Kizhe*—Ginsburg approximates with *lieutenants* = *Lieuten. Nants*):

> He [the clerk] also made the following absurd entry: instead of "and the Second Lieutenants Steven, Rybin and Azancheev are appointed," he wrote "and the Second Lieuten. Nants, Steven, Rybin, and Azancheev are appointed." An officer had come in while he was writing the word "Lieutenants," and he had sprung up to salute him, leaving off at the "n." Then he returned to his work and, in confusion, wrote "Lieuten. Nants."[22]

In the film script the same episode is even more closely related to Tynianov's writings on poetics. Here the scene is rendered with greater complexity. The clerk writes "Lieutenants [*poruchiki zhe*] Zherebtsov and Lokhovskii are subject to further orders" (shot 28). In a parallel montage, the Emperor Paul impatiently awaits the order. "He rips a little medal from his chest, strikes the glass screen with increasing frequency" (shot 130). Then we read:

134. The medal strikes the glass.
135. The little clerk writes the letter *N* [in Russian *K*] and freezes there.
136. The adjutant, repeating the sound, tenses up: *N N N N* . . .
137. A bell rings.
138. The adjutant speaks in a quick, hoarse whisper, while stamping his foot: "hurry up, hurry up, hurry up, you scoundrel, you scoundrel . . ."

All of this leads to the clerk's error. His final text reads: "Lieuten. Nants [*Poruchik Kizhe*], Platonov, Liubavskii are appointed."[23]

Unlike the story, the screenplay has the clerk's error result from a rhythmic beat (the striking of the medal, the stamping of feet, the shamanic repetitions of the adjutant), a beat that serves as the primary poetic agent in condensing the series and generating the semantic transformations that are the outcome of this new density. Tynianov saturates this episode with purely poetic alliterations as well: "poruchiki *zhe Zhe*rebtsov," and the phonetically similar Lokhovskii and Liubavskii (note the typical displacement of names in moving from the story to the screenplay). The film places a particular emphasis on the phonic moment: the clerk repeatedly reads aloud the alliterative repetition contained in his own text. A mistake arising from a quasi-poetic phonic premise is transformed into a name, which is then reestablished in writing with the czar's corrections to the clerk's text: the czar adds the Russian character (Ъ), the hard sign, to the end of the word *poruchik*. It is a letter that is never pronounced, a zero sign existing only as an orthographic convention. Tynianov himself believed that a letter or sound could function as a parodic sign (I shall have more to say about this later).[24]

Writing, lapses of the pen, and the distortion of names all play a significant role in Tynianov's cinematic work. In the Kozintsev-Trauberg adaptation of Gogol's *The Overcoat*, for which Tynianov wrote the script in 1926, the hero Bashmachkin is made to change the name "Peter" to "Prov" in a document. If one compared *The Overcoat* with *Kizhe*, one would be tempted to think the latter film recounts the story of a character created by the hero of the first. Other clues confirm this intuition. Bashmachkin's name and patronymic, Akakii Akakievich, which Boris Eikhenbaum saw as a kind of "trans-sense" or "beyond-sense" language (the *zaum'* of the futurist avant-garde) *avant la lettre*. Eikhenbaum also pointed to an earlier draft of Gogol's story, which reads: "Of course, one could have, in some manner, avoided the frequent proximity of the letter 'k,' but the circumstances were such as to make this quite impossible."[25] The derivation of *Kizhe* from the repetition of the letter *k (poruchik Kizhe)* seems to throw some light on the "circumstances" that Gogol here refuses to disclose. The second parallel between *The Overcoat* and *Kizhe* is even more eloquent. In the first version of the *Kizhe* screenplay (1927), the ill-fated lieutenant is represented in the form of an empty overcoat, which is beaten before the soldiers on parade and then dragged off to Siberia.[26] Tynianov thus deliberately juxtaposes the emergence of nonsensical words with an instance of quotation that serves to intertextualize his texts.

The divergences in Tynianov's accounts of the name Kizhe and its derivation can, it seems to me, be explained. It is widely known that while working on his first screenplay, Tynianov was also elaborating the idea that the cinema was akin to poetry:

The movie frame is a unit just like a photograph and a closed line of verse. A line of verse dictates that all its constituent words be interrelated in a special way, according to a tighter reciprocal interaction; for this reason the meaning of a poetic word is not the same, different not only from all forms of practical speech, but also from prose. Moreover, all bureaucratic or office jargon, the imperceptible and secondary words of our speech acquire an extraordinary visibility and valence in poetry.

So the unity of a movie shot arranges a priori the meaning of all things, and each thing becomes correlated to other things and to the shot as a whole.[27]

For Tynianov, rhythm played the dominant role in generating the density of a "poetic" series in film.[28] All of this sheds some clarifying light on the circumstances, and shifting motivations, by which Kizhe emerges: the rhythmic interpretation of his birth in the script, the "phonic" rendering of the same in the film, and the conscious downgrading of this episode in the story.

The Monkey and the Bell, another screenplay that Tynianov wrote in 1930, also makes extensive use of trans-sense (*zaum'*), even to the point of directly quoting his own theoretical writings on poetry. I have already mentioned Chekhov's use of the word *dondezhe* (meaning "when," "as," or "while" in archaic Old Russian). It was Shklovskii who first drew attention to the trans-sensical word *dondezhe* in his article "On Poetry and Trans-sense Language [*O poèzii i zaumnom iazyke*]."[29] Then it was Tynianov's turn, in *The Problem of Poetic Language.* Here Tynianov quotes Chekhov directly: "'in hearing the word *dondezhe* Ol'ga was unable to restrain herself and burst into tears. Gazing upon her, Mar'ia made a sobbing sound, as then did Ivan Makarych's sister.'"[30] In the screenplay, the same word appears (as "nonsensically" as it does in Chekhov's story) in the scene in which the bell is punished, as it is being flogged:

> The hangmen flay the bell with three whips.
> "Oh, I'll burn it alive!"
> The bell groans, and the old women in the crowd begin to howl.
> The priest recites: "*Dondezhe . . .*"[31]

The howl emitted by the old women is linked to the word *dondezhe* in precisely the same manner as the sobbing of Chekhov's heroines. There is no other motivation provided in the text, unless one counts the rhythmic strokes of the whip that accompany the word. When the same word makes a second appearance in this scene, the phonic inertia it generates brings about the monkey's final condemnation: "Burn him!" (*szhech'*). The nonsensical *zhe* from "donde*zhe*" is transformed into the terrifying "*szhech'.*"

A similar kind of unmotivated phonic play is found in the prologue to *The Monkey and the Bell.* Here some choral singers are heard singing: "*Ane— a—gos—ane—na—podi / Khabe—bo—khavu—zhe— / Gospodi Bozhe! . . . /* Caption. *Khabebuvy, anenaiki.* Caption. The singers are required to fill all elongated syllables with the words *ane-na* and *khabe-bu.* Hence they are called Khabebuvy and Anenaiki."[32] These oddly "philological" intertitles emphasize the presence of trans-sense, allowing us to decode the phrase "O Lord God!" (*Gospodi Bozhe*) in the first two verses sung: *Ane—na—GOS—ane—na—PODI / Khabe—BO—khavu—ZHE.* Here, as in *Lieutenant Kizhe,* the *zhe* is separated from the word God (*Bozhe*) and becomes the mysterious "khavu-zhe."

Tynianov's intensive recourse to trans-sense in his cinematic work can be accounted for in different ways. From the very beginning, OPOIAZ (the Society for the Study of Poetic Language), formed around 1915 and destined to become one of the two centers of Russian formalism, had seen trans-sense as a means for transforming "practical" language into the "poetic." In 1921, Roman Jakobson observed that arbitrary verbal creativity tends "not to have any connection to a given practical language."[33] As early as 1916, A. L. Iakubinskii gave one example of the "baring" of the word in poetry, whereby a desemanticized name can acquire poetic self-sufficiency: "If I pronounce my name loudly and several times in a row, I cease to understand anything: at the end I no longer discern anything but distinct syllables. Then I cease to understand everything, and forget about everything. And as if hypnotized, I continue to pronounce the sounds whose meaning I can no longer understand."[34]

The use of trans-sense language in the cinema might thus be seen as an attempt to instill a bias against practical language and create a properly cinematic idiom that would be self-sufficient. It is no coincidence that Boris Eikhenbaum once defined the photogenic image as a cinematic version of trans-sense language: "The photogenic image is the 'trans-sensical' essence of cinema. We observe it on the screen in a way that is completely disconnected from the plot—in faces, objects and the landscape. We see things afresh and sense them as unfamiliar."[35] This "unfamiliarity" of things is precisely the translation of cinematic language from the practical plane to the poetic.

There is another feature that distinguishes Tynianov's use of trans-sense in the cinema. As a rule, trans-sense appears in the context of a quotation; it is constantly being inserted into intertextual relations. It is no coincidence that the word *dondezhe* refers back to Tynianov's *Problems of Poetic Language,* and beyond that to Chekhov's story. But there is more at stake here. The word appears during the scene in which the bell is being flogged, a scene that itself quite obviously refers back to the flogging of Kizhe. The trans-sensical word emerges at the meeting point of several intertexts that overlap to create a hieroglyph. This is probably related to the fact that any product of irrational verbal creativity (a "glossemic combination [*glossemosochetanie*]," in the words of Iakubinskii) arises from the condensation of a phonic series, its thickening, the interpenetration of sounds under the pressure of the series' density. A sound combination slowly condenses to become a semantically charged word, acquiring a corporeality of sorts through this displacement of phonic layers. This is why the trans-sensical word can be understood as a sui generis metaphor for intertextuality, like an anagram that seems to "go looking for its own meaning."[36]

The trans-sensical word aspires to become a quote for the very reason that it always appears as an anomaly, one that seeks and then acquires normative status through an intertext. That is exactly how the ill-fated *dondezhe* is assimilated into the narrative.

What happens to individual words also befalls the disembodied hero of *Lieutenant Kizhe.* Kizhe emerges as a hieroglyph, an enigmatic paragram searching for a suitable meaning, a phonic cluster aspiring to acquire bodily form. Let us now examine how Tynianov's "blank" hero gains a "face" through an intertext, and how the author confronts the problems that arise along the way. As I have already indicated, some vague "secondary," or "wavering indicators of meaning," must necessarily be stimulated so that an "apparent meaning" or the "semblance of meaning" can be materialized. Given the metadescriptive style of the story, its capacity to employ the principles of its own poetics, these wavering indicators constantly appear in the text as that very ripple or oscillation about which I have already spoken. In the story, Kizhe is not just a void or a *gap;* he is also the materialization of some hesitant overtone. These quotes from the text illustrate my point: "Later, the aide-de-camp's *jerky* [*preryvistykh*] thoughts sketched out a face as well, though it was *flickering* [*brezzhushchee*], as in a dream."[37] Shortly afterward, the flogging of Kizhe is described thus: "The whipping post did not seem altogether vacant. Though no one was on it, it seemed as though someone was there all the same. . . . Then the straps were loosened, and it seemed as though someone's shoulders had been freed."[38] And a little later, as Kizhe is being taken to Siberia: "And the empty space which patiently marched between them changed constantly: now it was wind, now dust, now the weary heat, on its last legs, of late summer."[39]

In other words, the story is pervaded by what the Emperor Paul, in describing the switching of characters that he—and Tynianov—effect, calls a "vague incertitude." We are made to feel that if imperial fiat, authorial will, or the dynamic inertia of poetic rhythm can constantly displace or shift the characters of a series like words in a line, then the "gap" that appears in their series can be suddenly filled by the flickering, wavering image of the fantastic meaning that is Kizhe.

Still, cinema is not poetry, as Tynianov, of course, knew. In the uniquely rhythmic prose to which Tynianov aspired, this condensation of a gap to the point of signification was perhaps most visible in metaphors such as "the weary heat, on its last legs, of late summer."[40] In the cinema, where the *image* dominates, the situation is different. In the screenplay, Tynianov not only preserves the "flickering" face but also materializes it to the level of a concrete although distorted image (apparently a double exposure): "354. Slow shift. The colossal figure of the lieutenant stands in front of Paul with his sword bared." "471. A fade-over. The colossal colonel kneels before Paul, holds his sword as if to protect him." "491. A fade-over. At the table arranged for the wedding feast the colossal colonel and the maid-in-waiting are seated," and so forth.[41] All these shots belong to the emperor's visions and are somewhat monotonously realized through dissolves that seems to highlight the semifictional status of the hero Kizhe. The "colossal" dimensions of the lieutenant and then the colonel serve to signify his unreality (since the simplest way of creating differences in size is double exposure, which is precisely what is used to represent translucent visions). There is also a metaphoric dimension to Kizhe's hallucinatory status in the screenplay. When the exiled Kizhe is recalled from Siberia, he is given a "huge bottle of wine" that is crowned with a three-cornered hat, clearly a substitute for the invisible Kizhe (shot 399). As he approaches Petersburg, the aide-de-camp who has recalled him "lifts the bottle out of his overcoat, and looks at it in the light. It is empty. There is a small amount of wine at the bottom. Through the bottle he can see the parapets of the bridge" (shots 405–406).

In the film version, however, this idea of a hallucinatory vision made manifest is abandoned. The visions of a "colossal" lieutenant disappear, and the scene with the bottle loses its metaphoric dimension. It seems likely that both Tynianov and Faintsimmer decided against this solution because of its crudity. While some visual substitutes for Kizhe do survive in the film version (e.g., the wedding scene involving an armchair with a three-cornered hat squeezed on top, the toy soldier), they are significantly fewer in number than in the script. It seems as if the filmmakers were looking for some specifically cinematic equivalent for the "void" that is Kizhe.

In fact such an equivalent does exist, in the form of the film camera, which occupies a locus in space that is easily established (the point of view in linear perspective), even as it is never seen in the frame. It is, and at the same time it is not. Confronted with a similar problem while shooting *Cobweb Castle* (1957; also known as *The Castle of the Spider's Web* and *The Throne of Blood*), the Japanese director Akira Kurosawa chose precisely this solution, identifying the invisible hero with the point of view of the camera. In the scene in which Washizu (Macbeth) sees the ghost of Yoshiaki Miki (Banquo), the camera angle suddenly shifts, occupying the position of the ghost who is invisible to all save Washizu, then advancing rapidly toward the actor playing Washizu, Toshiro Mifune, who shies away from it in horror. Since the film as a whole excludes any form of point-of-view shots, this sudden change in the film's poetics as dramatized by the camera's movement is remarkably successful in conjuring up the presence of the "blank hero."

Lieutenant Kizhe, however, effectively eschews this option: the poetics of the subjective camera (widely debated and taken up after Murnau's *The Last Laugh* in 1924) do not seem to have interested Tynianov or Faintsimmer. For this reason, the scenes in which the absent Kizhe is made visible as a void between the guards purporting to escort him seem the least interesting. The scene in which Kizhe is brought to a fortress is indicative. Kizhe's three guards come to a halt in a triangular formation at the gates, where they are met by the bemused commander of the fortress. Here is how the script describes this moment: "Shot 298: The two grenadiers stand to attention; there is no one between them. The commander keeps approaching them, staring at the space, then moving away."[42] Faintsimmer devised a complex series of movements for the commander, accompanied by equally complex camera movements, but on the whole the scene does not diverge structurally from the indications provided by the script. The grenadiers stand still, while the commander moves around. The void and the guards who frame it are fixed to the ground. The function of sight is completely attributed to the commander. The immobile grenadiers guard the blank hero against any identification with the subjective camera.

This programmatic refusal of the subjective camera very likely had an important theoretical significance for Tynianov and Faintsimmer. After all, to identify with the camera's point of view is to impose a clear structure on the space within the frame, one that assumes the hierarchy of linear perspective, with its fixed and privileged point of view (hence the tendency to use a wide-angled lens in subjective frames, since the resulting images readily emphasize the vividness of perspective). Most often the emphatic perspective created by subjective representation is able to create a powerful sense of the presence both of the camera and of the blank hero.[43] Clearly, imposing a clear structure on the space that Kizhe purportedly occupies would have meant fundamentally violating Tynianov's idea of a "glimmering," oscillating void, the principle of endlessly shifting identifications that deny Kizhe the possibility of even a chimerical location in some privileged geometric point.

This refusal of spatial clarity as the basis of the subjective camera is clearly palpable in a range of episodes scattered throughout *Lieutenant Kizhe.* One such episode is the wedding banquet that takes place after Sandunova weds Kizhe. The screenplay devotes only one shot to it, while the film devotes three. Since Faintsimmer on the whole sought to shorten the script while making the film, the wedding banquet clearly appears to have gained an added importance. In the screenplay the scene functions merely as a linking episode, with just one curious detail that was destined to generate a complex montage in the film version: "Shot 518: Wedding feast in a circular room."[44] It is hard to say for sure why Tynianov needed a specifically circular room for this scene. Faintsimmer replaced it with a round table, at which he seated a vast array of guests, while the room itself was square, absolutely symmetrical, and filled with a series of columns (serving as immobile spatial axes, precisely the function of the guards who brought Kizhe to the fortress). Behind each guest Faintsimmer placed a servant, each identical to the rest.

The scene begins with a close-up of the aide-de-camp, Kablukov (played by E. Garin), peering into the room through one of its doors. There follows a series of close-ups of the various people seated at the table. We see an old woman carrying a lorgnette, Pahlen (B. Gorin-Gorianov), and Sandunova (S. Magarill), who shifts her uncertain gaze from side to side. How these people are linked remains unclear. The eighth shot in this episode finally gives us a general view of the entire scene, but even here we only see the absolute symmetry of a circle placed within a square. Since the circle, in its spatial homogeneity, is difficult to discern in the montage, the viewer is denied any clear spatial orientation and finds himself caught in a kind of specular infinity. After this point we are not given another general view, so that we are forced to try to connect the people we see only through their axes of vision, an attempt doomed to failure, since their constantly shifting glances never cross.

The old lady with the lorgnette has a special role in this episode. To aim any kind of optical apparatus is to affix a gaze, thereby preparing the way for the introduction of a *subjective* perspective. But nothing like this happens in the film. The old lady with the lorgnette moves her head around in an uncertain way, establishing little more than the shifting nature of her vision. No subjective perspectives as seen through the lorgnette follow, and we continue to get close-up portraits of the people assembled at the table.

This banquet scene is in fact a more sophisticated version of the principle at work in the scene of Kizhe's arrival at the fortress: space itself is rendered immobile (the table, with guests sitting seemingly "glued"to their seats), while a general sense of disorientation (the shifting gaze) imposed over the symmetry prevents us from arriving at a clear understanding of spatial relations, thereby creating a kind of oscillating vacuum.

There may have been another equally substantial reason behind Tynianov's refusal of the principle of the subjective camera. A hero originating in the oscillating space of trans-sense could not have acquired his final status within the operative regime of the subjective camera. After all, the subjective perspective necessarily emphasizes a singular point of view as the spatial locus of the hero's appearance. Yet from the very beginning Kizhe is constituted through several phonic segments each placed one on top of the other. He is brought into being as a quote, as something that does not belong entirely to the space of the text and its narrative. This is why he has to be constituted linguistically, as a formal equivalent to the phenomenon of intertextuality. The subjective perspective could never have served as this equivalent.

We have already seen that the trans-sensical words in Tynianov's writings are always embedded in a citational context, perhaps inevitably so given that Tynianov was also the author of one of the founding theoretical investigations of literary parody. *Kizhe* is constructed not only as an ensemble of "glossemic combinations" but also as a parodic text. The parodic moment is of immense importance for understanding the poetics of *Lieutenant Kizhe* as a whole. Critics have yet to take note of the fact that *Kizhe* is in fact parodically related to the E. T. A. Hoffmann novella "Klein Zaches genannt Zinnober" ("Little Zaches, nicknamed Zinnober"). Such an oversight is partly understandable given the fact that the connection between the two texts is less tangible, indeed hardly significant, in the prose version of *Kizhe*.

The striking resemblance that Zaches bears to the Emperor Paul might explain why Tynianov chose to invoke the Hoffmann novella at all. For example, Zaches conceals his peasant origins, only to have the truth circulate in the form of rumor, leading people to suspect that something is being hidden from them. An analogous motif in *Kizhe* are the persistent rumors calling the emperor's legitimacy into question (he was said to have been the son of a peasant woman exiled by Catherine the Great), rumors to which Tynianov pays homage in calling Czar Paul a "homeless orphan."[45] In the film there is also a letter that reads: "What you are like we cannot say save that you are bald-headed, snub-nosed and wicked, and we don't consider you to be the czar at all. We know that you're fake, and those who don't believe this also say that there isn't a czar alive at all."

Hoffmann's Zaches is misshapen and ugly, as is Paul in the standard image we have of him. Zaches is also repeatedly called "Simia Beelzebub": the monkey was also the standard epithet for the Emperor Paul. Zaches's traits are all readily applicable to the literary image of Paul; for example "His Excellency is of small stature, but has a large store of fury, angers easily, and forgets himself when seized by rage."[46] Or "[Zinnober] shouted, raved, made odd leaps in his fury, threatened to set the guards and police on people, imprison them or lock them up in a fortress."[47] Hoffmann's novella also echoes many popular images from Paul's reign, such as the emperor's ignominious assassination (or death) in his private chamber.

What might have drawn Tynianov still more to Hoffmann's novella is the hero Zaches's capacity to make himself visible to some and not to others. He is the very personification of the chimerical, a simulacrum or substitute. As Candida admits: "The monster could dissemble so well that he came to resemble Balthasar; and when she concentrated quite vigorously on Balthasar, she understood that the monster was not Balthasar, but then in some unfathomable way it would seem to her that she loved the monster, precisely for Balthasar's sake."[48]

Tynianov's screenplay is filled with references to Hoffmann, even in the form of direct quotes from "Klein Zaches": they constitute the otherwise missing parodic key to the film as a whole. The screenplay, for example, mentions a homunculus, a "dwarf": "Shot 255: The horse is standing by the entrance. A homunculus helps Paul mount the horse. Groaning, the homunculus in a huge three-cornered hat tries to mount the enormous horse, but cannot. Two servants then help him mount. Paul laughs. They move off, with Paul in front, and the homunculus behind him."[49] This little episode, hardly justified from the narrative point of view, is in fact a direct reference to the first meeting between Balthasar and his twin, Zaches: "All of his attempts to reach the stirrup or clamber onto the large animal were in vain. Balthasar, still earnest and gentle, approached him and lifted him onto the stirrup. The little one must have taken too powerful a leap, for no sooner had he sat on the saddle then he fell over onto the other side. 'Not so rashly, my dear sir!' cried Fabian, and broke out again into a loud chortle."[50] The same dwarf makes other brief appearances in Tynianov's script (shots 261–262, 274, 282–283, and 308–317), without fulfilling any plot-related function. The dwarf is several things: an exact double of the emperor himself, Paul's reflection in a distorted mirror, but primarily a personified reference to the Hoffmann story.

The script contains a range of other thematic moments that recall Hoffmann's story: the marriage between Sandunova and Kizhe corresponds to the marriage between Candida and Zaches; the motif of the emperor asleep and the grotesque fear prevalent at court of waking the sleeping monarch constitute a reworking of the valet's account in Hoffmann of Zaches sleeping: "I crept back to the bedroom door and listened [cf. the analogous scene in the film with Kablukov]. His Excellency was snoring as he is wont to do when something great is afoot."[51]

The Tynianov script and Hoffmann novella also coincide in a number of details. In Hoffmann, when the royal chamber is stormed by the conspirators plotting against Zaches, "Prince Barsanuph cried in horror: Revolt—Rebellion—Guards! and quickly hid behind the fireplace screen"[52] (cf. the oft-repeated cry in the film, "Guards!"); in Tynianov's script, during the analogous moment when the emperor's private room is invaded by his assassins, "Paul moves with quiet stealth toward the fireplace, and comes to a stand between the glass screen and the fireplace." The emperor's declaration that "the state is in danger" is simply a repetition of Zaches's dying words.[53] At night the emperor is twice found not to be in his chamber, once by Pahlen (shots 390–395), then by the conspirators (shots 653–665), highlighting the sense of void that permeates the film as a whole: "Shot 389: Paul's room. Glass screen. Armchairs. The room is empty. . . . 392: Empty chair." And later: "Shot 653: The aide-de-camp and Pahlen rush to the bed; it is empty." These scenes directly recall the disappearance of Zaches just before his death: "Zinnober, it seemed, had disappeared without a trace or a single sound. . . . He [the valet] went back to the bedchamber, in the hope that the Minister would finally be there. He cast a searching glance around the room, and then perceived some thin little legs protruding out of a handsome, silver vessel with a handle, which had always stood next to the toilet."[54] Compare this with the discovery of Paul by Pahlen: "Shot 665. Pahlen sees a reflection or shadow on the screen (Paul). Then his legs. He bends forward, pulls at the aide-de-camp's arm, and points. 666. Paul's legs." And finally, the image of the murdered emperor: "Shot 679. Paul's legs sticking out of the fireplace."[55] Both the film and the script often refer to aide-de-camp Kablukov's legs protruding out of a bed (shots 539–542): this might be compared to the vessel for passing water in which Zaches is drowned. In shots 567–570, Kablukov's legs, discovered under the bed by the emperor after his inspection of Sandunova's room, appear as a sign of Kizhe's death and an anticipation of the future demise of Paul himself: "Shot 567. The aide-de-camp's legs are seen protruding from under the bed. . . . 570. Paul emits a cry of fury: 'General Kizhe has been killed. Here he is.'"

The list of parallel details can be extended. Hoffmann writes: "The funeral of Minister Zinnober was one of the most splendid ever seen in Kerepes; the prince and all the horsemen of the order of the green-flecked tiger followed the coffin in deep mourning."[56] And Tynianov's story has "General Kizhe's funeral was long remembered by St. Petersburg. . . . The regiment marched with furled flags. Thirty court carriages, empty and filled, swayed behind."[57] Equally striking are the similar reactions of the prince and the emperor to the death of their favorites. Hoffmann reads "What a loss, . . . what an irreplaceable loss for the state!" whereas Tynianov has "My best men are dying."[58] Even the leitmotif dominating the final section of the screenplay, Kizhe's empty coffin, is taken from Hoffmann: "He felt surprise as he looked through Balthasar's lorgnette at the splendid coffin in which Zinnober lay, and he suddenly felt that there had never been a Minister Zinnober."[59]

Zinnober's disappearance from his coffin is immediately explained away by the king's physician in a pseudoscientific monologue (the king's physician enjoys a unique position in Tynianov's screenplay, in the film, and in Hoffmann). We are told that as a consequence of a "disharmony between his ganglionic and cerebral systems," Zaches has undergone a "complete surrendering of his personality": "This condition is what we designate with the word *death!* Yes, gracious Sir, the Minister had already surrendered his personality, and was thus quite dead, when he tumbled into this fateful receptacle. Hence, his death did not have a physical cause, but an immeasurably deeper psychic one."[60] Precisely the traits and motifs that characterize Kizhe—the loss of personality and the chimerical and abstract existence of a literary hero—are here attributed to Zaches. The physician continues: "The physical principle is the condition of a purely vegetative life, while the psychic principle conditions the human organism, which finds the driving-wheel of existence only in the spirit, the power of thought."[61] (Let us recall Tynianov: "The aide-de-camp's *jerky* [*preryvistykh*] thoughts sketched out a face as well.")

It is not necessary to add any further parallels to our comparison of Hoffmann and Tynianov. Let us note, however, that Hoffmann's novella is not just any intertext providing a source for this or that quote. At stake is a kind of "hypotext," related to *Lieutenant Kizhe* as a whole, that breaks through the surface of Tynianov's story at any given point with a range of correspondences. This is why we have the right to call *Kizhe* a parodic text that rewrites and transforms its primary source.

This total correlation between the two texts was probably essential to Tynianov's purpose of creating a "doubling effect" within the plot structure and finally within his blank hero as well. This doubling, created by the parodic subtext, prevents the hero from emerging as a clearly defined and physically tangible figure. He is constantly caught in the interplay between two reflections and seems to rebound from one to the other. It is in fact quite typical for Tynianov to avoid materializing his verbal images in any clearly visible form. In his article "Illustration"(1923), Tynianov condemns the unmediated translation of verbal images into figurative representations. For example, in relation to the illustrations to Pushkin's *Evgenii Onegin* that appeared in the *Nevskii Al'-manakh* he says: "Instead of the *oscillating* emotional line of the hero, instead of the *dynamic concreteness* that emerges as the hero's complex *summation* [*itoge*], Pushkin was confronted with something else, a kind of self-appointed concreteness, instead of a subtle 'authorial persona' a largish backside."[62]

Tynianov's choice of words here is extremely suggestive: "the oscillating line of the hero," and especially the "hero's summation." A character comes together like a final summation (*itog*), a sum derived from a "dynamic concreteness." Now this "sum" is the addition of many layers, including texts. Tynianov explains: "Just as Gogol concretizes purely verbal constructions to the point of a comic vividness ('Nevskii Prospekt'), so in Leskov a pun is often magnified to the extent of becoming the plot itself ('The Mender'). As the pun is destroyed, when we clarify its meaning and translate it into everyday life, so the main pivot of the story in the drawing is also destroyed."[63] Here Tynianov defines the story's "main pivot" as a pun, a "purely verbal construction," a series of displacements and condensations, an accumulation of intertexts. These verbal constructions are required to gain in concreteness until the hero's bodily form emerges, even if it cannot be represented graphically.

Tynianov was to strive for this concretization of the "body" as the "hero's summation" in other films as well. Iurii Lotman and Iurii Tsiv'ian have pointed out that the hero of the film *The Overcoat* is a "character who strictly speaking cannot be found in Gogol's original story." He is in fact the summation "under one 'semantic sign' not just of several characters, but of characters taken out of different texts."[64] Tynianov's screenplay for *The Overcoat* is thus comparable to a palimpsest: made up of several texts, it turns into a "sui generis intertext."[65]

Tynianov summed up his view of the pernicious role of illustrations to a text in a critique that relies on the distinction, essential to Russian formalism, between the linear sequence of events before its formalization in a text, the "story line" in its brute chronology *(fabula)*, and the plot as it is actually formulated *(siuzhet):* "An illustration provides a detail of the story line [*fabul'nuiu detal'*], rather than of the plot [*siuzhetnuiu*]. The detail is in fact removed by the illustration from the dynamic of the plot. It in fact uses the story line to impede the plot [*Ona fabuloi zagromozhdaet siuzhet*]."[66] Tynianov returned to this question in his main theoretical work on film, "The Foundations of Cinema" ("Ob osnovakh kino"). The final part of this article (sections 11–14) is devoted to the connection between story line, plot, and style, a problem fundamental to his poetics. In contrast to the remainder of the article, however, Tynianov here resorts primarily to literary examples, limiting himself to a few general declarations and finally acknowledging the work that remains to be done.[67]

If Tynianov dismisses book illustrations as almost exclusively related to the story line, then, in "The Foundations of Cinema," he admits the possibility of a cinema of pure "style," transcending the story line. Yet this very possibility is exemplified not through any reference to the cinema. Tynianov instead refers to Gogol's story "The Nose" (Gogol also features prominently in the article "Illustration," and "The Nose" is yet another parodic subtext to *Kizhe* alongside the Hoffmann story). Here is what Tynianov says about "The Nose":

> The severed nose is transformed by the semantic system of phrases into something ambiguous: it is "something," it is "thick" (*plotnoe*, in the neuter gender); it is often referred to as "him," a pronoun in which its objective or thingly traits often fade; the phrase "to permit the nose" gives it an animate status, etc. And this semantic atmosphere, perpetuated in each line, stylistically constructs the story line [*fabul'nuiu liniiu*] in such a way that the reader, by now alerted and readily drawn into this semantic atmosphere, feels no surprise in reading such bizarre sentences as, "The *nose* looked at the Major, and its [*or:* his] eyebrows became slightly knitted."
>
> Thus a specific story line becomes an element of the plot [*opredelennaia fabula stanovitsia èlementom siuzheta*]: through the style, which provides the semantic atmosphere of the thing.[68]

Thus Tynianov related the capacity of style to generate plot and thereby overcome the linear narrativity of the illustration to Gogol's dismissal of "objective, thingly traits" in favor of "something ambiguous." In poetry this same effect was achieved by shifting the emphasis onto oscillating indicators of meaning. In illustrations, "the first condition must be lack of definition, the widest limits of concreteness."[69] Tynianov notes elsewhere: "The task of drawings in relation to poetry is negative rather than positive. . . . Only by not illustrating, by not imposing a forced, *objective* [*predmetno*] connection between word and painting, can the drawing become a text's environment."[70] Interestingly, Tynianov cites Hoffmann's drawings as the best example of an author's illustrations.

The same negativity that ideally typifies the drawing's relation to the text is also embodied in Tynianov's hero Kizhe. The hero "becomes the text's environment" through parody, outside the reach of "objective" connections. In his first theoretical article on parody, "Dostoevskii and Gogol (Toward a Theory of Parody)" (1921), Tynianov speaks of parody's "double life": "Beyond the plane of the work there lies another plane, that which is being stylized or parodied. But parody demands the disconnection of both planes, their dislodging." Elsewhere Tynianov writes: "Parody exists to the extent that a work allows a second plane, that which is being parodied, to show through it. The more narrow, defined and limited this second plane, the more the details of the work itself bear a double hue, being perceived through a double angle of vision, and the stronger the parody."[71] It is no coincidence that Tynianov, and the Soviet critic Vinogradov after him, invoked Gogol, a model of ambiguity and of the process of dematerialization, as an example of parody. To parody Gogol, whose style is already stratified and "doubled," meant to intensify the fluid and dual nature of the text and thereby overcome the linearity of the story line. This is why Tynianov consciously buried Hoffmann's story, a profoundly ambivalent, parodic, and fluid text, as well as Gogol's "The Nose," his favorite example of "nonillustrative" prose, in his work as subtexts to *Lieutenant Kizhe*.

Significant, too, is the fact that Tynianov's first version of the screenplay, in which Kizhe is dressed in a overcoat, betrays the strong imprint of Gogol's *The Overcoat*, whereas, with the disappearance of the object itself, "The Nose" becomes the definitive, although largely hidden, Gogolian reference.[72] After the publication of Vinogradov's Gogol essay in 1921, "The Nose" itself became a sign in Russia of a heightened intertextuality. Vinogradov showed that the basis of the story was "a then current anecdote that brought together all the philistine talk and punning about noses disappearing and reappearing, to which the literary and educated classes of the early nineteenth century added their own references from the world of art. Even in the eighteen-fifties, Nikolai Chernyshevskii saw Gogol's novella as a 'retelling of a widely known anecdote.' And the literary atmosphere of the eighteen-twenties and -thirties was saturated with 'nosology.'"[73] "The Nose," then, functioned as a kind of hyperquotation: by generating a layer of heterogeneous subtexts, it could displace the physically more tangible overcoat and itself acquire the status of a body.

The parodic element in the conception of *Kizhe* is multifaceted. We can sense it in the deliberate theatricality of many episodes in the film. For the hero to acquire an actorly presence was, according to Tynianov, one of the primary indicators of parody.[74] The actorly element was an essential component of what Tynianov called the "parodic individual."[75] Many episodes of the Faintsimmer film contain signs of the theater, such as a curtain or a theatrical podium. A many-tiered curtain is the basis for the composition of the scene, pure vaudeville parody, in which Kizhe and Sandunova pass their wedding night. A curtain appears in the scene in which Kizhe arrives at the palace. The theatrical nature of the film as a whole is a parodic reflection of the theatrical subtext strongly present in Hoffmann himself (an example of which are the grotesque doctors, classical protagonists of the farce, whom Tynianov in turn borrowed).

The presence of theater within a film is an essential parodic means for translating the text from one system to another. Nonetheless, it cannot serve as a foundational principle of the cinema. A genuinely cinematic equivalent to parody was found in the mirror and in the specular structure of cinematic space. The mirror (especially the crooked mirror) is a classical metaphor for parody. Let us recall the language of Tynianov's own formulations: "A work allows a second plane, that which is being parodied, to *show through it [prosvechivaet]*"; "the more the details of the work itself bear a *double hue [dvoinoi ottenok]*, being perceived through a *double angle of vision*, the stronger the parody." Let us parenthetically note the metasignificance of metaphors for the poetics of parody. Tynianov noted this also: "The strength of metaphors based on *objects* lies precisely in the lack of connection or similarity between the things compared."[76] Still, the very tangible presence of mirrors in the film version of *Kizhe* suggests a kind of meta-metaphor, one that describes the poetics of the film as a whole.

The astonishingly pervasive presence of mirrors (both real and implied) in the Faintsimmer-Tynianov collaboration returns us once more to the problem of the subjective camera. The fact is that a mirror, when placed frontally before the viewer, emphasizes a linear perspective just like a subjective camera (cf. the wide use of mirrors during the Renaissance, when the uses of linear perspective in painting were first discovered).

On the other hand, a mirror that faces the viewer and the object being reflected at an angle functions in the opposite way, destroying the homogeneous linearity of space (and with it the possibility of the subjective camera) and introducing a second vanishing point, which is the chimerical space of the mirror itself. The poetics of these doubled, "angular" spaces was widely cultivated by the German romantics, who liked to represent figures from the back (*Rückenansicht*), excluding the face entirely or having it reflected at an angle in an appropriately placed mirror. In Friedrich Kersting's *Die Stickerin* (1812), for example, a girl busy with her needlework is sitting with her back to the viewer, but her face is oddly reflected in a mirror, so that we have some difficulty in connecting the girl's figure to the reflected face. Even if we place them side by side in our minds, we are still unable to overcome our sense of their spatial disjointedness.

The critic Valery N. Prokof'ev has found an analogous moment in Degas's use of sloped mirrors: "It is this combination of several viewpoints within one painting that creates the impression, typical in the mature Degas, of an oscillating, seesawing, *optically mutating space,* a space which, even while remaining fixed on the canvas, continues to be mobile and evolving—quite like the space of a film being projected."[77]

In creating their own "oscillating indicators," Tynianov and Faintsimmer gravitated toward those mirror constructions that had already been "tested out" by Tynianov in his prose. In another story by Tynianov, "The Wax Figure" ("Voskovaia persona"; 1930), we see the character Iaguzhinskii "stagger about from mirror to mirror," while "all the mirrors showed the same thing." At this point there is an angular displacement of vision, typical of the mirrors we find in Kersting and Degas: "He drifted toward the mirror by the door; it reflected the right-hand window looking onto the yard."[78]

In the screenplay there are innumerable examples of reflecting surfaces, most of which are connected to the Emperor Paul. I have already quoted the scene in which the emperor "stood in the dark, in his underwear. By the window, he took account of his people." In the screenplay, this nocturnal scene echoes another in which Paul is assassinated, thereby acquiring additional overtones: "Shot 374. Paul sits down slowly on his bed. He sees a ray of moonlight on the pillow. He leaps up and lowers the blinds. Penumbra. Paul throws a cloak over his underwear, and huddles from the cold. 375. He opens the door. 376. The hussars-in-waiting are asleep. 377. Paul swathed in his cloak stands with the *glass* behind him as a backdrop. He fitfully shuts the door."[79] The assassination scene replays all the motifs we have just seen: "648. Paul awakens, looks at the door, quietly jumps out of bed, and creeps like a shadow in the dark to the door onto the staircase. He clenches his hand. . . . 650. Paul quietly creeps to the fireplace, and stands between the *glass* screens and the fireplace. . . . Darkness. Half-shadows. . . . 660. Paul in his underwear behind the screen. . . . 664. Paul's legs in the moonlight. 665. Paul sees a *reflection,* a shadow on the screens."[80]

In all three versions of *Kizhe,* this nocturnal scene presents Paul next to the glass. In the story he is by the window. In the script, in the first instance he is by a glass door, in the second—behind a glass screen, where his reflection betrays him to the conspirators. This reflection on glass (even paler and less truthful than a reflection in the mirror, a parodic distortion in itself) acquires a sinister and ambiguous flavor in the script: "4327: Paul enters the room He goes behind the screen—looks into the glass of the screen. A pale reflection. He says hoarsely: '*Vsë neverno.*'"

The phrase "Vsë neverno," meaning "it's all untrue, false, unfaithful, inaccurate, unreliable," is something of a key to the screenplay as a whole, its reverberations reaching far wider than the emperor's other key phrase, uttered in the prose version, about a "vague incertitude." Tynianov plays on the double meaning of the word *neverno* (just as he puns on the polysemy of the word *karaul* ["guard"] in the story).[81] The idea of a reflection being *neverno*—false, unreliable, unfaithful to the original image—immediately invokes the broader connotation of political infidelity (*nevernost'*) or treason: "338. Paul turns around, follows Pahlen with his eyes. '*Vsë neverno.*'"[82] At the same time, *nevernost'* also signifies the parodic distortions performed by the text and the spatial fluidity that results: "349. Paul walks up and down the room, he is cold, he shivers. The fireplace doesn't warm the room. He opens a cupboard shelf, gets out an ermine cape, wraps himself in it, walks in his cape along the edges of the wall, listening carefully. '*Vsë neverno.*'"[83] In this frame, Paul's fear of treason becomes inseparable from the parodic masquerade that he adopts—the cape flung over his underclothes, suggesting that Paul is himself a parody of Peter the Great. The fear of *nevernost'* is Paul's primary sensation: "340. A desolate corridor. Paul is alone.—'*Vsë neverno.*'"

The word *neverno* is the key to understanding the function of mirrors in Tynianov's work: the images they reflect are fluid and do not correspond to the poetics of geometric space implied by the subjective camera. Paradoxically, Paul is convinced that the fictitious Kizhe is his only faithful or true (*vernyi*) servant.[84] But this "faithful" servant is a void glimpsed in the distortions produced of crooked mirrors.

The complex play of mirrors in the film provokes the extensive use of the *Rückenansicht* we also found in Kersting, which constitutes one of the more eccentric aspects of Faintsimmer's filmmaking. Most often it is the Emperor Paul, most directly associated with Kizhe in Tynianov's mind, who is seen from behind. We find Paul fixed in this same pose in the story as well, but here Tynianov feels obliged to explain it: "In times of wrath the Emperor never turned."[85] A whole mini-episode then ensues, as if to justify the motif, in which the emperor scolds the aide-de-camp while standing with his back to him: "'You don't know your duty, sir,' said Paul Petrovich hoarsely. 'Coming up from behind!'"

The emperor's desire to stand with his back to his interlocutors is all the more paradoxical given his fear of people approaching him while his back is turned. As soon as he hears someone approaching, he rushes behind a screen, where he can occupy his own distorted viewing position:

> Paul Petrovich heard the steps of his aide-de-camp. Like a cat he stole up to the armchair behind the glass screen and sat down as firmly as though he had been sitting all the time.
>
> He knew the steps of his courtiers. Sitting with his back to them, he recognized the easy stride of the confident, the hopping tread of flatterers, and the light, airy steps of the frightened.[86]

The screenplay, on the other hand, offers no real motivation for Paul's "backward" pose. Only once (shots 554–564) is there a suggestion of a "false" identification between the emperor and Kizhe on this basis, when Pahlen and Kutaisov come upon the emperor with his back to them in Kizhe's room and take him for Kizhe himself, suddenly materialized. But the film eliminates this episode: we do not see any face, making any identification between Paul and Kizhe impossible and forcing us to look for a mirror in which we might be able to see the face of the man whose back is turned to the viewer. Even where there is no actual mirror within the frame, this spatial composition assumes a certain specularity, anticipating the existence of a mirror in order to restore the normal framework of perception.

The film in fact does have numerous episodes that reproduce the space of Kersting and Degas in the most direct way possible—for example, the scene in Gagarina's salon where Sandunova prays before a mirror for the safety of Kablukov. There is another analogous episode in which Kutaisov shaves the emperor: here a shift in the angle at which the mirror is positioned determines the spatial composition of the scene. In the entire film, this episode is the closest parody to Gogol's "The Nose," specifically to the scene in which Major Kovalëv is being shaved by Ivan Iakovlevich.[87] In the words of Paul to Kutaisov in the screenplay: "Why do you keep grabbing my nose?"[88] A direct continuation of this scene is a later episode in which Paul asks Pahlen to confirm whether or not he is snub-nosed: "443. . . . he stamped his foot. 'Am I snub-nosed, tell me.' Pahlen speaks calmly and with respect: 'Your nose is even and long, your Majesty.' 444. Paul rushes to the mirror and looks into it. 445. The mirror reflects back Paul's snub nose."[89] This scene is in fact a rereading of Gogol:

> Washing himself, [he] looked again in the mirror—the nose was still there. Wiping himself with the towel, he again looked into the mirror—he still had a nose.
>
> "Ivan, look here, I think I have a little pimple on my nose," he said. . . .
>
> But Ivan said, "No, sir, there's no pimple. Your nose is clear."[90]

Equally significant is the fact that the writings of both Gogol and Hoffmann contain scenes involving shaving and noses. In an episode from Gogol's "Nevskii Prospekt," a certain "Hoffmann" tries to cut off the nose of the tinsmith Schiller, "not the writer Hoffmann, but Hoffmann the shoemaker from Ofitserskaya street."[91] We might note that the multilayered nature of the subtexts here is also emphasized by the "phony" Hoffmann mentioned in the story—not the writer but a shoemaker. Thus Gogol's story "The Nose" functions as the interpretant to the Hoffmann intertext.

It is only natural, then, that the mirror as a metaphor for parody also appears in this most parodic of scenes (as a hidden indicator of the multilayered nature of the text), where it is used specifically to create the principle of duality characteristic of "Kizhe's space." The scene, then, involves Kutaisov shaving the emperor. The first shot in this scene involves Paul sitting in front of the mirror with his back to the viewer, so that we see his face frontally as a reflected image. When Kutaisov is rebuked by the emperor, he hides behind the mirror, in other words, behind the reflected face of the monarch. Thus Paul's reproof is directed via the mirror onto the viewer, who occupies the space before the screen.

In the second frame of the same episode, the emperor is shown turned with his profile to the mirror. The mirror, while still directly facing the viewer, nonetheless shows the reflection of the emperor's face, which is then deflected directly onto the viewer's gaze. The mirror's reflection seems to become independent of the object being reflected. In the far recesses of the room a door opens, and Gagarina enters. She moves toward the camera, then addresses the emperor (and the camera), who then replies to her in the mirror, also looking at the camera. This entire episode develops on the basis of a continued discrepancy between the various axes of vision and the angular spatial correlations that obtain between the various characters.

The specular nature of all structures in the film, then, conveys a sense of the parodic and multilayered organization of the text. In fact, the same specularity can be found in any number of Tynianov's works, even the most disparate. To be effective, this motif does not necessarily require actual mirrors or any other "object-metaphors." It emerges wherever some doubling or reflection is at work as a subtext. Here are some examples. Tynianov's story "The Wax Figure" contains the following lines about the dying Peter the Great: "He turned around, rolling his eyes about in all directions . . . , looked darkly above the little varnished barriers and caught sight of an unfamiliar face. A man was sitting to the left of the bed, . . . his bulging eyes were directed at him, at Peter, and his teeth were chattering and his head shaking."[92] This stranger appears to Peter as if he were his own reflection, although there is no mirror present.

In fact mirrors and their reflections are not the only mediums used by Tynianov to produce a distortion of vision: statues and paintings also serve as distorting prisms, in what often amounts to a rather rarefied flourish of Tynianov's imagination. In "Young Vitushishnikov," Nicholas I orders a statue of Silenus to be removed from the palace as a "drunken Greek," because he is identified on the basis of nationality with the concessionaire Rodokonaki.[93] In Tynianov's "Wax Figure," Legendre, on looking at the face of the architect Rastrelli, "recalled that face, which the face of the master had begun to resemble: it was the face of Silenus on the fountains, works all conceived by Rastrelli himself."[94] The statue of Silenus is thus capable of reflecting the image of several people, thereby creating specular links between them. The mirror, even when hidden, unites a vast array of displacements and substitutions, of which I have already spoken. Symbolic in this sense is the linking of emperor, mirror, and statue (three hypostases of substitution in Tynianov's work) in one particular episode of "Young Vitushishnikov," where the emperor, "crossing the Apollo hall, . . . caught sight of himself for a moment in the mirror, with a copy of Phoebus behind him."[95]

Multiple reflections are typical of Tynianov, and of *Lieutenant Kizhe* in particular, as is the linking of a protagonist with mirrors, paintings, sculpture, and mannequin figures—all hypostases of the same (or perhaps several?) oscillating figure(s). Let us recall a phrase of Dostoevskii that Tynianov quotes in his essay "Dostoevskii and Gogol": "Literature is a picture, that is in a sense a picture and a mirror." Pictures and mirrors as mutual substitutes repeatedly surface in *Lieutenant Kizhe*, sometimes in a highly curious context of some phony substitution, such as the scene of the wedding between Sandunova and an empty space.

In the script the emperor promises the maid-in-waiting that he will be present at her wedding,[96] but, fearing an attempt on his life, he effects a "swap" at the last moment. "493. On the wall there hangs an icon, next to it a picture of the Emperor Paul. 494. Paul looks attentively at the maid-in-waiting. His fear is yet to pass, and in his confusion he picks up his own portrait instead of the icon and blesses her: 'This icon is from me, the priest will bless you with it.'"[97] There is a dual substitution at work in this episode: God (the icon) takes the place of the emperor, but in turn God himself is replaced by the emperor, in the form of his portrait.

The actual nuptial scene contributes the additional element of a void, the empty space of the groom, to this series of substitutions. The priest takes fright, first on finding a gap where the groom should be standing, then on finding a portrait of Paul rather than one of God on the icon.[98] The idea of Paul's portrait as a parodic icon in fact appears still earlier in the script, when Witworth receives a command to leave St. Petersburg. At this point he "walks up to the portrait of Paul on the wall and turns its face to the wall,"[99] a gesture that plays on the problem of the emperor's gaze and parodies his habit of standing with his back to the world.

The system of substitutes around the figure of God is not fortuitous here. It can be seen as an original parody of "negative theology," which asserts that God is given to us only in hypostases and attributes that are inessential to him. This substitutive system is particularly persistent in Tynianov's *The Monkey and the Bell:* here the plot is nothing more than a system of parodic substitutes for God—a monkey, a cat, and a goat, all animals traditionally associated with the devil.

Nevertheless, the icon does have a set of features that can also be projected onto the poetics of cinema. The film itself lacks an effective gag involving the icon and the portrait. The chain of substitutions in the script is finally itself displaced in the film by the specular structure of the space in which the episode takes place. This once more confirms our thesis that mirroring is a sign and an equivalent of a heightened level of intertextuality. This displacement might also be linked to specific qualities inherent in the iconic "image." The image always meets the viewer's eyes, thereby creating a "looking-glass" effect that binds the viewer to the image. In cinema the direct "iconic" gaze into the lens is normally taboo. Roland Barthes even considered the taboo on looking into the camera to be the mark par excellence of the cinema in general.[100] A character in a film must direct his or her gaze away from the central axis of perspective created by the camera's "eye" (this deviation is the basis of many forms of spatial montage in film).

By refusing to make use of the icon-portrait, Faintsimmer and Tynianov seemingly eliminate real specularity (the kind typified by the subjective camera) from this episode. In fact this is not the case: the same specularity is reintroduced, paradoxically allowing for a special "chimerical addition." The church interior is dominated by an enormous Eye of God located in a triangle, which appears just after the golden gates of the altar are opened. This vast eye is made to coincide quite precisely with the camera angle, taking the place of a more typical scene that might have been filmed from behind the characters' backs. A number of shots in this episode are in fact shot from the position of the altar, in which the camera takes the position of the all-seeing Eye of God, thereby underlining the specular structural correlation of the eye and the camera.

It would seem that the specular nature of space in this episode would necessitate a clearly defined central axis orienting the course of action. In fact we find the opposite taking place. The scene is constructed as though the camera and the eye were two magnetic poles, dividing the space and systematically disorienting the protagonists, who move without a clear center of gravity. Throughout the episode, some of the protagonists look at the altar, while others look toward the camera. The characters are constantly turning back and forth, making the viewer aware of the reciprocally directed gaze of the camera and the Eye of God, which seem to be constantly exchanging glances. Their disarray also seems to underline the disorienting nature of the central axis of space. The fluid nature of this scene, which is crafted with extraordinary skill, is further emphasized by the systematic disjointedness of people's glances: their wandering gaze stands in a productive tension with the rigidity of the central axis. A range of minor details also serves to intensify the lack of definition that pervades the scene: the drumbeat (signifying Kizhe) that oddly penetrates the cadences of the church service, the extraordinary saturatedness of the frame as a whole, which prevents us from orienting our sight within it, as well as some unmotivated changes in the decor (initially both sides of the altar are framed only by straight walls; then, during the same scene, baroque sculptures appear there, seemingly out of nowhere). The wedding scene, where a range of devices creates a complex and fluid space, is equally based on a subtly specular structure.

Elsewhere, the mirror structure functions within a portrait, and is even to some extent made possible through the insertion of a painted canvas into the frame. There is a brief episode in which the Emperor Paul wanders nervously through the palace at night. The scene begins with Paul, dressed in a cape thrown over his underwear, entering the elaborately decorated main hall of the palace. He then moves away from the camera, with his back to it, deeper into the frame. He reaches a wall, divided on both sides by symmetrical arches, coming face-to-face with the interval between them; interval, which constitutes the center of the frame, is decorated by an enormous portrait of Peter the Great dressed in full regalia. The penumbra creates the momentary illusion that the portrait is a mirror, which the emperor is slowly approaching. This parodic equation of Peter and Paul is suggested several times in Tynianov's script, particularly through a juxtaposition of Paul and the statue of Peter that stands in front of Mikhailovskii Castle (in the film this idea is suggested only in the introductory sequence).

In the film script, Paul often collides with the equestrian statue of Peter the Great.[101] As a rule Paul rides past the statue accompanied by his dwarf, which adds a further parodic element—a reference to Hoffmann—and creates a specular distortion on several levels: Peter—Paul—the dwarf. This mirroring is stressed in Tynianov's script also: "Paul looks at the monument to Peter, and salutes. He assumes a grandiose pose, copying that of the monument."[102] The film in fact adds an additional parallel between the two sovereigns: when Kizhe arrives in the palace, we see the portrait of Paul in full regalia, which is clearly a parody of the other portrait of Peter.

In addition, the fate of the monument itself (its creation is described in "The Wax Figure") seems to have reminded Tynianov of Kizhe's phantasmagoric existence. In the novel *Kiukhlia,* concerning the Decembrist writer Wilhelm Küchelbecker, Tynianov provides the following historical commentary: "The other monument intended for this square, Rastrelli's Peter, had been rejected as flawed, but [the Emperor] Paul had it brought back, just as he had brought back all those people his mother [Catherine the Great] had sent into exile, but the original site had been taken, so he placed it in front of his own castle, a respectable form of exile."[103]

Let us now return to the earlier episode, involving Paul's nocturnal encounter with the portrait of Peter. After Paul approaches the portrait/mirror, montage is used to introduce the next shot. We see the same decor, shot frontally, in what is almost a mirror image of the preceding shot. The same two symmetrical arches are found to the sides, but instead of the central portrait, we see one more arch, under which a soldier is standing at attention, precisely where the portrait of Peter had been hanging in the preceding shot. The marked symmetry arising between the two shots forces us to consider the guard from the second shot as a reflection of Peter/Paul in the first. Let us also recall that the soldier, or his uniform, is one of the primary substitutes for Kizhe in the film (and soldiers are often seen multiplied in mirrors). Subsequently, in the same second frame, Paul unexpectedly appears under a side arch and begins walking toward the camera. Paul's movements finally shatter the possibility that the decor in both shots constitutes mirror images: since the first image shows Paul moving away from the camera, he could hardly find himself suddenly in a space located behind it. Moreover, the emperor's movement toward the viewer forces us to read the new decor not as a wall of the same room, symmetrically opposite the first wall, but as a *dimension existing beyond the looking glass.* Only in such a dimension could a mirror reflection of someone approaching correspond to the same person moving away from the camera toward the mirror.

The complex symmetry of the decor, extended to the carefully elaborated violation of the direction in which the protagonist moves (with the camera apparently shifting viewpoints), really communicates a sense of Paul's entry into a world beyond the looking glass. As the scene continues, Paul approaches the mirror, and, stooping toward it, abandons himself to his fears and fantasies concerning his "savior" Kizhe. In front of the mirror there stands a tiny mannequin dressed in uniform (a replica of the guard from the previous frame, and hence also of Peter, Paul, and the dwarf). Reflections of the mannequin suddenly begin to multiply in the mirror.

The function of the mirror is here definitively established: it is a sign of a doubling, of a dislodging, of a void, of repetition, of intertextuality and the distorting effect of parody. In other words, the mirror as a stylistic device allows the film to overcome the linear entrapments of the illustration and find a visual equivalent to the fluid and near-poetic qualities of Gogol's prose.

Let us once more recall the significance that Tynianov attributed to the relations between style, plot (*siuzhet*), and story line (*fabula*) in all forms of narrative. Though he insisted on its utmost importance even to the cinema, Tynianov was never able to solve this problem in his theoretical writings. I have already suggested that Tynianov's sudden turn to Gogol was effectively an alternative to a purely cinematic resolution. In my opinion, *Lieutenant Kizhe* can be considered an original response to the theoretical question that Tynianov had posed himself, one that serves as a substitute (yet another one!) for the literary analysis of Gogol's "The Nose" found in section 12 of his article.

This transformation of intertextuality into a stylistic device (today we would say into a figure of cinematic language) is fundamental. As in previous cases, it shows that intertextuality, while starting out as a principle for generating meaning, can end up generating the language of cinema as a whole.

The case of *Lieutenant Kizhe* is in many ways unique. The film poses and solves, in a theoretically pure fashion, the problem of how to generate the body and the image out of several intertextual layers. What occurs is an almost physical genesis of a body from a series of mutual reflections. The mechanism of the film functions as if it is constructing a complex system of mirrors: by itself each mirror reflects only an illusory particularity, but taken together they direct their reflections onto a single focus (the abstract space of intertextuality). Each reflection is projected onto another, thereby gaining in density and finally becoming visible.

Tynianov made a distinction between the syn-function (being related to other elements that belong to one system) and the auto-function (being related to elements that belong to other systems and series). Kizhe's process of embodiment is based simultaneously on both principles. Initially Kizhe arises out of the syn-function: his name is the consolidation and displacement of phonic elements from the same series. Then Kizhe establishes a parodic relationship to characters from other texts, in accordance with the auto-function. The disjointed, parodic, intertextual hypostases of the protagonist then once more come together in the specular mechanism of textual space. The body of Kizhe arises through the constant intersection of both the syn- and the auto-functions. The intertext manifests itself in the punning paragrams of the syntagmatic series and develops in the paradigm of parodic relations, to return once more to the text in the form of the body-as-hieroglyph, a unit of meaning penetrable only in part, that has acquired flesh.

CHAPTER SEVEN

The Invisible Text
as a Universal Equivalent
Sergei Eisenstein

The system described in the last chapter, with its shifts and substitutions, its subtexts and the strategies for their concealment, is the basis of Tynianov's literary prose. In the third part of his biographical novel *Pushkin*, Tynianov describes the poet's secret love for E. A. Karamzina. Contemporaneous with the novel is Tynianov's article "A Nameless Love," in which the artistic intuition of the novelist is given a philological basis.[1] Tynianov's findings did not meet with universal acceptance in the scholarly community. Boris Eikhenbaum tactfully called it the fruitful application of "artistic method" to scholarship.[2]

Nonetheless, Tynianov's hypothesis about Pushkin's secret passion was enthusiastically received by Sergei Eisenstein. After reading part 3 of the novel, Eisenstein conveyed his enthusiasm in a letter that Tynianov was never to receive, since he died before it could even be sent.[3]

Eisenstein's rapturous response seems all the more striking given his persistent refusal to discuss the literary theory of the OPOIAZ group or the film theory emanating from the formalist school. Like Tynianov, Eisenstein was intrigued by the theme of substitution, of a subtext that might be hidden, but from an angle quite remote from Tynianov's own preoccupations. Eisenstein's interest lay not so much in the situation of intertextuality itself (in the widest sense of the term, as when a text acquires its full meaning through some reference to an extratextual reality) as in the existence of some mysterious, hidden *equivalent* that permits the juxtaposition of these various extratextual realities.

In his letter to Tynianov, this question is framed in terms of one drive taking the place of another, as a kind of Freudian "transference"—in other words, in psychological terms. Eisenstein is seeking analogous situations in the realm of culture. As an analogy to the displacement of Pushkin's love interest from Karamzina to Goncharova, Eisenstein discusses the "senti-mental biography" of Charlie Chaplin. What interests Eisenstein here is the possibility of establishing the "indicators" that mark the emergence of a substitute:

> And now I have a question for you, both as a scholar and as a novelist (i.e., as someone who can be freer in advancing hypotheses): if possible, then *how, by what means, according to what indicators* [*priznakam*] could Nathalie [Gon-charova] have come to serve as a substitute or Ersatz?
>
> Since you yourself proposed the idea, now please give me an answer! . . .
>
> Where are the premises for this almost reflexive transference of [Pushkin's] passion from one woman onto another, and seemingly with the illusory conviction that at last the *perfect* Ersatz had truly, definitively been found.[4]

This letter to Tynianov was written in 1943. In 1947, while working on his investigation of color, Eisenstein returned to this problem, in order to propose his own solution to the question he had asked Tynianov. We find this solution formulated in a fragment entitled "The Psychology of Com-position," which concerns the work of Edgar Allan Poe. Here Eisenstein refers directly to Pushkin and Chaplin, promising to return to them in later chapters (which were never to be written).[5]

Eisenstein illustrates his musings on the problem of transference in love with a recollection (whose authenticity seems questionable) of a certain "Berlin company" that he claims to have had dealings with. "The com-pany," he writes, "could, through photographs, find an exact substitute for the girl who was the object of a man's hopeless fantasies. . . . One man would be dreaming about the inaccessible Greta Garbo or Marlene Diet-rich. Another would be thinking of a girlfriend from his youth who had since married someone else. Yet another still yearned, like Poe, for the long deceased object of his adoration. The means for finding a substitute were quite varied. And the company managed to do its job brilliantly!"[6]

Eisenstein here treats love (or at least the possibility of an amorous dal-liance) as the search for a substitute, an ersatz, the replacement of an ide-ally desired body by another, as in a photo that has been doctored. On a metaphoric level, we can call this a sequence of simulacra or analogies. This is how Eisenstein understood the Don Juan phenomenon. Pushkin, interpreted through Tynianov's hypothesis, came to be seen as suffering from a Don Juan complex. Pushkin, like Chaplin and Don Juan himself, behaves not unlike the Berlin company of doubtful repute:

> And in all women they try to find the same one.
> Do they resemble her?
> But they're all different.
> And yet . . .

This one's hair. That one's gait. A third has a dimple on her cheek. A fourth has a pouting lip. A fifth has eyes spaced apart and slightly splayed. That one has full legs. But this one has a strange break in her waist. A voice. A certain way of holding her handkerchief. These are her favorite flowers. That one laughs easily. She has eyes that both get misty with tears when the clavichord strikes the same note. The same dangling lock of hair. Or the similar flash of an earring against the fiery gleam of a crystal candlestick.

The mechanisms of association are difficult to fathom: through them we are able suddenly to substitute one thing for another on the basis of a microscopic shared detail, a passing resemblance between two people, sometimes a barely perceptible trait that allows us to replace one human being with another.[7]

Eisenstein was to project this same set of questions onto the work of Edgar Allan Poe. Following Tynianov's lead, Eisenstein embarked on a search for Poe's "nameless love," clearly seeking a parallel between Poe's biography and Pushkin's as Tynianov had understood it. According to Tynianov, Pushkin's had concealed his love not only because the object of his passion was the wife of the celebrated writer Nikolai Karamzin but also because of the considerable gap in age between the young poet and his beloved. Eisenstein went still further in emphasizing the inaccessibility of Poe's lover: "At the age of fourteen Poe conceived a fiery and romantic passion for the mother of one of his schoolmates Robert Stanard. But this did not last long—Jane Smith Stanard was soon to die."[8]

Eisenstein's conclusions here rehearse the basic conflictual scenario that Tynianov had established. This itself not only reveals Eisenstein's indebtedness to Tynianov's works but also suggests a desire to prolong and widen the chain of substitutes that Tynianov had initiated, and then to ascribe to it some kind of cultural universality. Poe reproduces Pushkin's situation, and Chaplin too undertakes the same search for substitutes. At stake, for Eisenstein, is the possibility of some invariant that, unlike the case uncovered by Tynianov, might have a general theoretical value. Eisenstein by no means seeks to conceal his project. In "The Psychology of Composition," the specific dilemma of hidden passion is transformed into the general question of repetition in art, as it affects all levels of creation.

In the case of Poe, Eisenstein sees this desire to relive (and perhaps outlive) the experience of troubled passion, a passion marked by a taboo of silence, as leading to a fundamental metaphoric shift:

Who could forget the story of Dante Gabriel Rossetti who, many years after his wife's death, had her grave opened and was able to savor the lugubrious sight of her hair, preserved in its cascading golden locks.

Edgar Allan Poe, of course, spurned this direct, primitive, "head-on" course of action in favor of another, more refined and original way of satisfying the same need. Instead of opening an actual tomb, he chose to anatomize a host of images that were dear to him, images that embodied his beloved theme, through an analysis of the creative process. This analysis, itself in many ways a poetic invention, was in fact intended, with the help of the scalpel of analysis, to "dissect like a corpse" the music of his favorite images.[9]

The theme of the substitute or ersatz once more emerges in this context. The real body of the beloved is replaced by the "body" of the text, on which Poe performs an analytical vivisection. The ersatz being sought is found in the schematization of the artistic process.

This metaphoric transference from the physical body onto a speculative structure, some other "textual" skeleton, was of fundamental importance to Eisenstein. One could also perhaps read this in a biographical vein, in which case the director's passion for "postmortem" analyses of his own films gains an added resonance. But this comparison of textual analysis to vivisection reveals something else that is crucial. The body's dissection is performed in search of a universal equivalent, one that permits the substitution of one body for another. Similarly, the "vivisection" of a text is pursued in search of an equivalent that might legitimate the workings of intertextuality, the process by which diverse texts can be brought together. Like bodies, texts do not simply replace one other. For this to be possible, in Eisenstein's view, our consciousness must possess some ideal model, a universal equivalent that serves as a connective mechanism.

In invoking the phenomenon of the Don Juan, or Rossetti's necrophilia, Eisenstein is in fact raising a question that is fundamental to intertextuality as a whole: On what basis can two texts (two substitutes) be linked, and is such a linkage possible at all, without the presence of a third text existing in theory, as their equivalent?

The very notion of transferring a problematic from a body onto a hidden textual structure or the mechanics of creation as a whole is rooted in the general complex of Eisenstein's theoretical ideas. These ideas considerably predate Eisenstein's reading of Tynianov's "A Nameless Love" or the letter he wrote in response.

Traditionally, film theory has always recognized resemblance, photographic or iconic reproduction, as "ontological" features of the cinema. Film is seen to be a mimetic form, imitative of reality. Eisenstein's thought is an exceptionally rare example of a radical negation of cinematic mimesis as it is customarily understood.

In 1929, Eisenstein devoted his speech at the Congress of Independent Cinema in La Sarraz to the problem of imitation, which he called the "key to mastering form." He went on to distinguish two kinds of imitation. One is magical, which he compared to cannibalism and essentially rejected, since "magical imitation copies form." It is embodied most clearly in the mirror. This first type of imitation is contrasted to a second, which imitates a principle. "Whoever understands Aristotle to be imitating the form of things is mistaken,"[10] says Eisenstein; he adds: "The age of form is passing. We are penetrating matter. We are going beyond the phenomenon to the principle behind the phenomenon, and thereby acquiring a mastery over it."[11]

This statement contains two complementary postulates, both fundamental to Eisenstein's aesthetics: that contemporary culture has overcome the "stage of form," seen as the outer appearance of a thing, and hence the initial mode of "specular" mimesis; and that it is necessary now to imitate the principle. This last formulation remains somewhat mysterious. What is this principle (or, as Eisenstein often put it, the "order of things" [*stroi veshchei*])? How is it ascertained? Where does it lie hidden? In the same speech, Eisenstein suggests that it is to be found through analysis: "That which is represented through myth yields its place to that which is analyzed as principle."[12] But what is this analysis, whose results we are invited to imitate?

Eisenstein's talk at La Sarraz coincided with his escalating interest in "protological" forms of thought, whose role in his theoretical reflections had been increasing over time. In pursuing this interest, Eisenstein turned to a group of linguists, psychologists, and ethnographers who, during the first thirty years of the century, had once more posed the hoary problem of the origins of language and thought. Invoking the names of Bühler, Cassirer, Marr, Vygotskii, Levy-Bruhl, Piaget, and others, all names Eisenstein would have known, Walter Benjamin once called their thinking "mimetic in the broad sense of the word,"[13] since most of them believed that language emerged from some primary act that was imitative in nature.

Significantly, this mimetic act, which occurs at an undifferentiated stage of thought, contains not only an external form but also its initial generalization—a "principle," according to Eisenstein's terminology. In his collection of books on the problems of "protologic," Eisenstein would constantly underline those passages dealing with the quasi-intellectual nature of primitive mimesis. He was particularly struck by a passage in which the French sociologist Émile Durkheim analyzes the abstract geometric representations of totems among Australian aborigines: "If the Australian is so strongly inclined to make figural representations of his totem this is not in order to have its portrait before his eyes constantly renewing its sensuous presence. Rather it is simply because he feels the need to *represent* the idea that he makes of it by means of a material sign."[14]

A. Lang, whom Eisenstein also knew, also devoted a great deal of attention to the problem of imitation, concluding that "'savage realism' is the result of a desire to represent an object as it is known to be, and not as it appears."[15] How did archaic forms of representation incorporate an idea or principle? To a considerable extent, it was through the movement of the hand, through drawing itself as an act. Eisenstein was almost transfixed by the passage in Levy-Bruhl's *How Natives Think,* in which the author relates the conclusions of the book *Manual Concepts* by Frank Cushing: "Speaking with the hands is literally thinking with the hands; to a certain extent, therefore, the features of these 'manual concepts' will necessarily be reproduced in the verbal expression of thought."[16] Now if these manual concepts are present in verbal expression, they should surely be all the more evident in visual representation. In Jack Lindsay's *A Short History of Culture*, Eisenstein underlined the following: "out of the harmoniously adapted movements of the body are mental patterns evolved."[17]

The *line* is the graphic unit that fixes the gesture or movement from which the manual concept is generated. In his discussion of Cushing, Eisenstein also touches on the "linear discourse" whose form we must assimilate.[18] The line, for Eisenstein, has a special significance. In drawing a line, or even retracing it with our eyes, we miraculously gain access to the "essence" of things, to their meaning. "To 'think' in a completely de-intellectualized fashion: by tracing the contours of objects with our eyes—an early form entirely connected to the—linear!—drawings found in figurations carved on rocks and caves."[19]

Eisenstein arrives at a kind of pangraphism: the world, for all its diversity, is, under the phenomenal surface of things, governed by the semantically charged line. In music, the line is traced by the melody; in theater, through the movement of the actors; in a plot (*siuzhet*), through the bare chronology of the story line (*fabula*); in rhythm, through an invariant scheme; and so forth: "The line is movement. . . . The melody is a line, chords are the volumes of a sound, pierced and threaded together. The plot and its intrigue are like the contours of things, their reciprocal arrangement."[20] Elsewhere Eisenstein states that "one must know how to seize the movement of a given piece of music, and take its trace, that is, its line or form, as the basis of that plastic composition which is intended to correspond to the given music."[21] This line or scheme Eisenstein calls the "generalizing agent of meaning" (*obobshchaiushchii osmyslitel'*): it represents "relations in the most generalized form. If left in this form, the generalization is so vast that it becomes what we term an abstraction."[22] We can grasp the meaning of even such abstractions as the numerical representations of the ancient Chinese if we "displace" them onto "the sphere of geometric outlines" and "represent them to ourselves graphically."[23]

Eisenstein had no need to invoke the culture of primitive societies as the basis of his pangraphism. In fact, the source of his thinking lies closer at hand, in a tradition of modern European aesthetics inspired by Plato, specifically the Platonic idealization of beauty. This tradition has been carefully traced by Erwin Panofsky. To paraphrase Panofsky, a broadly similar notion of the sketch and the line is present in a range of Renaissance artists and theoreticians: Vasari, Borghini, Baldinucci, Armenini, Zuccari,

Bisagno.[24] A statement from Vasari effectively summarizes the concept of the sketch prevalent in the work of many Renaissance artists:

> The drawing, which is the father of our three arts, produces, from a multiplicity of things, a universal judgment [*giudizio universale*] comparable to a form or an idea that embraces all the things of nature, just as nature in all its proportions, is itself subject to rules. From this it follows that, with respect to everything relating to the bodies of humans and animals, as well as of plants, buildings, paintings and sculptures, the drawing knows the proportions that exist between the whole and its parts, and those uniting the parts to one another and to the whole. Now, this knowledge is the source of a determined judgment, which gives this thing its form in the mind, and whose contours the hand will later trace, and which is called a "drawing." One can thus conclude that the drawing is nothing but the creation of an intuitively clear form corresponding to the concept which the mind carries and represents within itself and of which the idea is in some sense the product.[25]

For Vasari, as Panofsky explains it, the idea, "which the artist produces in his mind and manifests through his drawing, does not derive from him but is taken from nature via the mediation of a 'universal judgment.' From this it clearly follows that it finds itself prefigured in a state of potentiality in objects, although it is only known and realized through the actions of the subject."[26] With the onset of mannerism, however, the idea-as-sketch becomes increasingly severed from nature, where it would of course seem to lie, and is displaced onto the consciousness of the artist-creator. Panofsky shows how the mannerists came to consider the sketch an "animating light," the "inner gaze of the mind."[27] Over the course of time, the idea thus began to be seen as an "inner drawing."[28]

Eisenstein's thinking operates entirely within the framework of these Platonic ideas. The elaboration of a line was for him the elaboration of a concept or idea that had to be derived from natural phenomena (this is the Vasari stage). However, in a range of other texts, he began to treat the sketch precisely as the mind's "inner drawing," to which nature is already superfluous.

It is a characteristic of Eisenstein's thought to unite systematically the graph, the line, and Vasari's idea of proportion as a universal judgment that correlates "all the things of nature," as well as the part and the whole. His article "The Organic and the Image" (Organichnost' i obraznost') begins with an analysis of the "imagery of the pure line," which he defines as "containing a profound meaning."[29] Here Eisenstein again advances his beloved hypothesis that "a curve can serve as the graphic trace of any action"[30] and then passes on to an analysis of the ideal, serpentine spiral curve:

> It has fully earned its merit, for this is the spiral that defines the proportion of the so-called "golden section" of Euclid, the basis of the most remarkable

works of antiquity. Its unique aesthetic effect is due to its being the basic formula, translated into spatial proportions, for the process of organic growth
and development in nature, embracing to an equal degree the Nautilus
shell, the head of a sunflower, and the human skeleton. This proportion is,
therefore, the fullest reflection [*otrazhenie*] in the law for constructing a work
[of art] of the law for constructing all the organic processes of development.
Furthermore, it is the *reflection* [*otobrazhenie*] of a single regularity that is the
foundation of both laws.[31]

The analogies with Vasari are striking. The sketch is the vehicle of the
judgment and the concept precisely because it correlates "all the things of
nature." It knows the laws of proportion, the higher patterns of regularity
hidden in nature. The sketch and the line enjoy the role once accorded to
mystical seers, keepers of the Pythagorean mysteries, to whom the one law
was subordinate.

Eisenstein's obvious recourse to Platonism allowed him to see the line
as containing a knowledge of all proportions. The line was thus transformed into a mechanism capable of generally correlating all things (and
all texts). Through the "spatial proportions of the basic formula for the
process of organic growth," a line allowed one to connect a shell, the head
of a sunflower, and a human skeleton, all without any sense of arbitrariness. Buñuel and Dali, we recall, needed some kind of external analogy or
simulacrum to make the same connection. Eisenstein did not. The head of
a sunflower *looks like* a skeleton and can replace it, or become its equivalent, because their commonality is expressed in a line contemplated by the
artist's consciousness (or mind). Phenomena do not relate to one another
by connecting directly: they are linked by an ideal "third text," invisible to
the profane eye, and rendered explicit only through the work of analysis
or an artistic intuition, a theoretical sketch or a grapheme existing in the
sphere of ideas.

The line or scheme has the ability to combine the abstraction of geometry and mathematics (the sphere of pure ideas) with sensory evidence.
But this work of combination occurs in a Platonic realm. It is no coincidence, then, that Eisenstein so often invokes the Platonic notion of
"image," which lies at the heart of his mature aesthetics. Still more revealing is the fact the image itself is thought of as a graphic scheme, an "internal sketch." In the draft entitled "Three Whales," we are told of the three
elements that form the basis of a visual text: "1. The visual representation
[*izobrazhenie*]. 2. The generalized image [*obraz*]. 3. Repetition. In its pure
form, the first is naturalism, the second a geometric scheme, and the third
an ornament."[32] The image is here directly equated with a geometric
scheme, which forms the basis of Eisenstein's theory of metonymy (the famous "pars pro toto"), since "one contour (N.B. a linear contour [*cherta-
liniia*]!) *here stands for the whole.*"[33]

The linearity of the "image" allowed Eisenstein to elaborate the notion of the universal equivalence of phenomena based on the similarities to be found in their internal schemes. This notion was based on a psychology of synesthesia and was essential to the construction of a theory of montage, whose purpose was to connect not visible things but their internal "graphs."

Eisenstein was to pursue this idea most consistently, and most controversially, in his study of audiovisual, or vertical, montage. In the article "Vertical Montage," Eisenstein recalls the battle scene on ice in *Aleksandr Nevsky* as proof that it is possible for there to be a complete correspondence between the musical movement of a score and the plastic composition of a set of frames. For this purpose he constructs a scheme, in which Prokofiev's music is placed notationally over the compositional structure of the visual sequence. Both elements are then united by the scheme of a movement (or gesture) in the form of a curve.

An earlier attempt to represent melodic movement as a spatial curve was made by J. Combarieu, who traced a curve corresponding to the adagio from Beethoven's Sonata no. 8 ("Pathétique"). Combarieu's stated aim was to test the well-known claims of the German musicologist Hanslick that the movement of music corresponded to the arabesque in plastic terms. The sketch that Combarieu finally drew was, in his own words, the "most displeasing, incoherent and absurd thing imaginable."[34] Étienne Souriau, who rediscovered Combarieu's half-forgotten experiments, has shown convincingly that the very attempt to represent music spatially as a curved line derived from musical notation is no less absurd than Combarieu's specific experiment. Souriau's point is that the project is itself inconceivable without the aid of a system of graphics and a set of complex mathematical calculations indicating pitch, intervals, and so forth.

Adorno and Eisler voiced a similar criticism of Eisenstein: "The similarity which Eisenstein's schematic depiction is meant to assert in fact lies not between the actual musical movement and the sequence of images, but between the musical *notation* and the sequence. But musical notation is itself already the fixing of musical movement proper, the static image of a dynamic one."[35] Thus no direct correspondence is possible even here, between a graph constructed on the basis of musical notes and a visual representation. Music might well "imitate" the plunge of a cliff by "a sequence of three descending notes which, in musical notation, do in fact look like a downward curve. But this 'plunge' is realized in time, while the precipice remains stationary from the first to the last note. Since the reader is not reading the notes but listening to music, he has absolutely no means of associating the notes with the precipice."[36]

Two months before his death, after reading the Adorno-Eisler critique, Eisenstein made the following note: "Eisler believes that there is no commensurability, like a pair of galoshes and a drum (although even here, in plastic terms, it is possible). . . . The image passes into a gesture that underlies both. Then we can construct any kind of counterpoint."[37] The linking of galoshes and a drum, a cliff edge and musical notation, is possible because what is being linked is not their external appearance but their images, the linear traces that organize them as gestures.

In "Vertical Montage," Eisenstein came to the realization that linking musical movement to a static frame might be particularly vulnerable to criticism. Anticipating objections, he pointed out that even a static picture is assimilated by the viewer's perceptive faculties in time: the eyes wander over it and thereby insert a temporal dimension, and a hidden gesture, into the static form.[38] Elsewhere Eisenstein pursues this idea in a more paradoxical vein: "The principle of shifting focus onto different points in an object and then combining their representations in order to provide a whole image ideally reproduced the 'way an ear behaves.' Is sound aware of the same possibility of technically reproducing the conditions in which 'an ear behaves'?"[39] Eisenstein finds in orchestration a means of recreating the dynamics of the ear. But the imagery his own thinking is forced to adopt is here revealing. The ear, he says, must "move" like the eye, in order to sketch out some visual arabesques of its own.

The equivalence between a musical and a visual text is finally established thanks to the analogous "behavior" manifested by the eye and the ear, both of which "sketch" unseen graphic texts that coincide completely with each other. Eisenstein's graphics are visible only in the first dimension: they have a clear tendency to become invisible and dissolve in the elusive flourishes sketched by the eye, ear, and brain. The graphic text is thus merely the first step on the way to the invisible text, the first stage as we move toward the image, which lies in the sphere of pure ideas. It is there that the various texts come together; this is where the *primary text* dwells, like the image of a woman long dead, embodying the principle of universal equivalence.

If the mimesis of form acts to undermines the pan-equivalence of all things, then the mimesis of principle opens up a world of unlimited possibilities. Eisenstein quotes Michel Jean-Marie Guyau: "The image is the repetition of one and the same idea in another form and in another environment."[40] The form changes. Forms change. The idea, the principle, or image remains immutable.

To be sure, Eisenstein himself had doubts about the reduction of the "principle" to a linear outline (an arguable maneuver, to say the least). He acknowledged being "disturbed" by the fact that the highest level of abstraction (the generalized image) was being equated with the most elementary—the line. Eisenstein succeeded in avoiding a regression to the archaic stage of thought thanks to the salutary aid of the dialectic, which permitted him to conclude, for example, that, "in terms of content, these lines are polar opposites, but in appearance or form they are identical."[41]

Elsewhere, Eisenstein invokes Lenin's rendering of the dialectic:

> A contradiction seems to emerge here: the highest [form]—the generalized image—coincides, as if on the basis of a *plastic trait* [*po plasticheskomu priznaku*] with the most primitive type of integral perception. But this contradiction is only apparent. For in essence we are dealing here precisely with that "apparent return to the old," about which Lenin speaks in relation to the dialectics of phenomena. The fact is that a generalization is *really integral* [*deistvitel'no tselostnoe*], that is, at the same time both the complex [*kompleksnoe*] (immediate) and differentiated (mediated) representation of the phenomenon [*predstavlenie iavleniia*] (and a representation about the phenomenon [*predstavlenie ob iavlenii*]).[42]

In these explanations, Eisenstein's dialectic basically involves making the lowest and highest forms simultaneously manifest in the act of generalization.

In the end, phenomenal appearance is condemned yet again for exposing too clearly the fragility of logical thinking. The line is understood to carry proto-concepts; at the same time it is also the highest form of abstraction. This "dialectic" in many ways resembles certain postulates found in Wilhelm Worringer's *Abstraktion und Einfühlung* (1908), a similarity seen both in Worringer's posing of the problem and in his manner of resolving it: "A style perfect in its regularity, a style that is highly abstract and strictly excludes life, is characteristic of nations in their most primitive cultural stage. There must therefore be a causal connection between primitive culture and the highest, purest and most regulated form of art."[43]

Eisenstein was to persist in his attempt to distinguish the protological from higher forms of abstraction present in the line. He analyzed cave paintings in search of what might separate the mechanical practice of copying silhouettes from the sketching of contour as abstraction.[44] He also examined ornament as a synthesis of protologic (repetition) and "intellectualism" (geometry).[45] Yet none of these attempts at distinguishing higher and lower forms appears very convincing. And although the "evincing of the principle" was proclaimed to be the outcome of analysis, in practice it was found through the work of imitation or mimesis. After all, in order to "think by the contour" (*dumat' konturom*), the eye has to *repeat* the movement of the hand that drew it. And in order to grasp the essence of a manual concept, Cushing himself "revived the primitive functions of his own hands, living over again with them their experiences of prehistorical days."[46] *To imitate the principle is indeed to master it.* The work of analysis thus

acquires a unique status. Mastering the principle becomes a kind of sym-
pathetic magic. The artist here inevitably acquires the features of a magician, shaman, or seer, and the "principle" or idea becomes a secret or puzzle that needs to be solved.

These tendencies in Eisenstein's thinking find their fullest elaboration
in his essay "On Detective Fiction":

> What is the nature of the "puzzle" [zagadki] as against the "answer" [otgadki]
> that solves it? The difference is that the answer names the object in a formu-
> lation, while a puzzle represents the same object in the form of an image that
> is woven out of a certain number of its features. . . . Someone who has been
> initiated into great mysteries is, as an initiate, granted the ability to master
> the discourse of concepts and the discourse of representation through im-
> ages [rech'iu obraznykh predstavlenii], the language of logic and the language
> of feelings. The degree to which both are capable of reaching a unity and an
> interpenetration is an indication of the degree to which the "initiate" can en-
> compass perfect dialectical thinking. . . . He who can solve a puzzle . . . knows
> the secret of movement itself and of the coming-into-being [stanoveleniia] of
> natural phenomena. . . . The sage and the priest must at all costs know how
> to "read" this ancient prior discourse of sensuous images, without limiting
> themselves to the younger discourse of logic![47]

The same magic trick is also performed by the detective, who is just another hypostasis of the "initiate": "And the detective novel? Its theme
throughout is the transition from image-based appearance [obraznoi vidi-
mosti] to conceptual essence [poniatiinoi sushchnosti]. The same form that
we found in the simple puzzle is present, in nuce, in the detective novel."[48]
The artist is thus quite similar to the magician or the detective: "The
artist operates in the realm of form in precisely the same way, but resolves
his puzzle in exactly the opposite way. The artist is "given" his answer to the
puzzle as a conceptually formulated thesis, and his task is to transform it
into a puzzle, that is, translate it into the form of imagery."[49] The artist's reversal of the normal process (from schematic thesis to form) is also meant
to shift modern art from the realm of protologic to a more rational sphere.
Elsewhere, while commenting on his work on the film Aleksandr Nevsky, the
director was forced to acknowledge that this reversal was not effective:
"The hardest thing is to 'invent' an image, when the immediate 'demand'
[spros] for it has been strictly, even 'formulaically,' formulated ['do for-
muly,' sformulirovan]. Here is the formula for what we need, make an image
out of it. Organically, and more advantageously, the process takes place
differently."[50] In other words, the "puzzle" always emerges first.

In a "Non-Indifferent Nature" [Neravnodushanaia priroda], Eisenstein
points out yet another hypostasis of the detective: "Experts in graphology
are a particular kind of detective."[51] This latest disguise is logical enough,
since a graphologist tries to solve the riddle of personality by looking at an

individual's graphic traces, that is, his or her handwriting. Eisenstein distinguishes two kinds of graphological detectives. The first is an analyst, personified by Ludwig Klages: "In his analyses Klages takes great pains to elucidate, among other indicators, the precise relationship that obtains in an individual's handwriting between the straight, sharp and angular elements and those that are rounded, smooth and elastically flowing."[52] This work is like the deductive thinking of a detective, who has to start working from a clue, an abstraction. Eisenstein compares Klages to Sherlock Holmes. Then there is the second kind of detective:

> The other kind of detective-graphologist works differently, "physiognomically" (in the broad sense of the word), or, if you will, synthetically.
> In this group of graphologists we find Raphael Scherman. . . .
> Scherman does not analyze the elements of a person's handwriting, but rather tries to extract from this handwriting some general—synthetic— graphic image (mainly from a client's signature, which in many ways is a person's graphic self-portrait, as it were).[53]

Scherman is said to have had the ability to reproduce a person's handwriting just by setting eyes on him, and to re-create an artist's signature just by looking at his painting. Eisenstein explains: "Here we are dealing with *imitation,* or rather with *that degree of imitation* necessary for Scherman to 'grasp' you at first sight and instantaneously *reproduce you.*"[54] In essence, Scherman seized the whole as a line, as a graphic outline. He saw each person as a "graphic self-portrait," discerning in one's body not just a structure or line but precisely that line that is contained in the body's potential for movement. Through the "text" of the body he read the invisible text of its hand movements, which he regarded as no different from the movements of the eye or ear.

Eisenstein identified himself with Scherman. It comes as no surprise that he sought to acquire the trappings of a magician or a detective by claiming a supreme knowledge, the magical ability to discern the scheme, line, or principle through and beyond the realm of the visible. He even wrote of the need to have a special "nocturnal vision," the eyes of a "tracker or the tracker's grand-nephew Sherlock Holmes."[55] "I can see very distinctly in front of me," he declared.[56] But this vision was specifically intellectual in nature, connected with an internal delineation of contour, that is, with the very genesis of conceptual thinking: "Even now, as I write, in essence I am almost 'outlining' with my hand the contours, as it were, of what is passing before me in an incessant stream of visual images and events."[57] Hence the rather unexpected criticism of normal vision, unconnected to the tactile beginnings of the concept, that we find in "The Museums at Night," a chapter of Eisenstein's memoirs: "In general, museums should be visited at night. Only at night . . . is it possible to fuse with what is seen, and not just look things over."[58] "Just let the lamp burn out, and you are entirely in the power of dark, subterranean forces and forms of thought."[59] For all his passion for painting, for all the visual bias inherent in his cinematic profession, Eisenstein finally opted for the blindness of the seer, recalling such poet-prophets of the past as Homer and Milton.

Eisenstein's comparison of the seer with the graphologist reminds one of the surrealists, who also saw *écriture automatique* as a means of plumbing some hidden depths. There are moments in Eisenstein's theoretical writings that bear a remarkable resemblance to André Breton's thoughts in "Le Message automatique" (1933). Like Eisenstein, Breton was fascinated by the idea of nocturnal vision. He writes about James Watt, who is said to have locked himself up in a dark room and seen the outlines of his steam engine. Breton also mentions the artist Fernand Desmoulin, who was accustomed to drawing for certain hours in total darkness, with a sack placed over his head. Like Eisenstein, Breton placed great store in graphic outlines and curved lines. But most astonishing of all is his assertion, with which Eisenstein would have readily agreed, that hearing is more important than sight: "*It always has seemed to me that in poetry verbo-auditive automatism creates for the reader the most exalting visual images. Verbo-visual automatism never has seemed to create for the reader visual images that are from any viewpoint comparable.* It is enough to say that I believe as fully today as I did ten years ago—I believe blindly . . . blindly, with a blindness that potentially covers all visible things—in the triumph *auditorily* of what is unverifiable visually."[60] Breton himself goes on to clarify the logic behind his championing of the auditory faculty. Hearing makes it easier to distinguish an imaginary object from a real one, so that "subjectively, their properties are demonstrably interchangeable." Essentially, at stake here is the very same quest for equivalence, for the complete interchangeability of elements through the establishment of an ideal intertext. It is quite logical, then, for Breton to arrive at the notion of an "eidetic image" (Eisenstein would have just said "image"), one common both to primitive cultures and to children.[61]

The eidetic image as a universal equivalent is revealed only to the blind. In the 1940s, Eisenstein made a series of sketches on the theme of blindness. Most of them, such as *Blind Man, Blind Men, In the Realm of the Blind,* and *Forever without Sight!* were conceived in 1944. In this series two sketches stand out—*Belisarius* (1941) and *Tiresias* (1944). Both depict blind men of antiquity, and both are constructed according to the same iconographic scheme: a venerable blind man holding a staff and being led by a young guide. In the case of the Byzantine military commander Belisarius, Eisenstein's scheme is justified by a long European tradition. A young guide appears alongside Belisarius in paintings by Van Dyck, Salvator Rosa, Gérard, and David (in the latter case, the blind man is shown with his guide collapsed in his arms, dying of a snakebite). No such extensive iconographic tradition exists in the case of Tiresias. Perhaps the only time he appears with a guide is in Sophocles' *Antigone*, where he tells the story of how he once had to predict the future by using fire, which, being blind, he could not see. Sophocles motivates the story in the following way: "I learned from this boy of these abortive prophecies . . . : for he is my guide, as I am other men's."[62]

Eisenstein's *Tiresias* can thus be seen as an illustration to *Antigone*. There is another reason for believing this. In January 1899, a version of *Antigone* was staged by the director Stanislavskii. In this production the part of Tiresias was played by Eisenstein's mentor, Vsevolod Meyerhold. A surviving photograph from the performance confirms that Eisenstein's drawing derives from this particular production (the photo itself may have even served as its iconographic source). The sketch shows a young guide whose clothing and hairstyle are precisely like Meyerhold's.[63] Leonid Kozlov has shown that Eisenstein often looked to his mentor, who is subtextually present in many of Eisenstein's artistic conceptions, particularly *Ivan the Terrible*.[64] We can reasonably assume that Tiresias functions as a substitute for Eisenstein's teacher, the wise genius and seer Meyerhold.

At the same time, the figure is also Eisenstein's projection of Meyerhold onto himself. In blinding Tiresias, the goddess Athena "opened his ears, enabling him to understand all the sounds that birds make, and gave him a staff of cornel wood, with which he could walk as well as those who can see."[65] For Tiresias, hearing and touching take the place of sight: this change is not so much a replacement or compensation, since it grants Tiresias access to secrets which the sighted are denied. Tiresias here functions as Eisenstein's mythic teacher, while Eisenstein himself serves as his guide, leading him by the hand into a hidden world beyond the visible. This is the realm of tactile and speculative representations; here lies the "basic" text of universal connections and equivalences, the long-sought sacred text of the universe, the primary intertext of all his work.

Eisenstein's series of drawings of blind men is preceded by yet another enigmatic graphic cycle. In this earlier series, schematically drawn homunculi are shown gazing into "Nothingness." These sketches, made during the Great Purges of 1937, are most likely grounded in a specific political context, but they also suggest a metaphysical content. Everything seems to suggest that these homunculi are blind. Their eyes are designated by large circles without pupils, which is precisely how blindness is indicated in the later sketches. The blind are assigned the task of looking into Nothingness, Hegel's indeterminate being that is the beginning of all things.

In an unpublished fragment of 1934, Eisenstein touches on the possibility of penetrating beyond the confines of the visible while discussing Swedenborg (yet another seer-magician) and "nocturnal sight." "Imagine," he writes, "a light extinguished for an instant, and how the surrounding reality immediately becomes tangible, a *Tastwelt*."[66] The world divides into the visible, the tangible, and the audible, beyond which emerges "a multiplicity of worlds, the real world [*Handlungswelt*], the world of representation [*Vorstellungswelt*] and the conceptual world [*Begriffswelt*]."[67] In this plethora of worlds, which we can reach by "switching off" our eyes, arises the world of things-in-themselves, which the artist-as-seer grasps through a kind of magical dialectic. In this mystical scenario we once more glimpse the shade of Wilhelm Worringer, who had asserted that "in primitive man the instinct, as it were, for the 'thing-in-itself' is strongest."[68] Eisenstein here attributes a thousand-year history to his own consciousness. He claims to know the world as a man who has lived forever, like Tiresias, who was granted great longevity and a knowledge of the beginning of all things.

The genesis of meaning from gesture, meaning, and tactile sensation gives a text the quality of a body. Reading a text thus becomes a "physiognomic" exercise, as Eisenstein himself often points out: "We shall tirelessly inculcate in ourselves a sharp sense of the physiognomics of the expression of curves [*fiziognomiki vyrazheniia krivykh*]."[69] In other words, in each form we must see a body. Heinrich Wölfflin, whom Eisenstein saw as belonging to the genre of detective-graphologists along with Klages,[70] had already shown the possibilities of such a reading in his analyses of Italian baroque architecture. Wölfflin had sought to understand in what way architecture might embody the spirit of its time. Insofar as the primary model of expressiveness is and has always been the human body, then architecture, too, acquires its expressive capabilities by establishing hidden analogies with the human body, whose movements and postures betray the spirit of the era. Wölfflin's project is a systematic reduction of all forms to the human body: "But the principal meaning of this reduction of stylistic forms to the *human* image lies in the fact that this image gives a direct expression of the spiritual."[71]

This idea is extremely close to Scherman's method that discerns the spirit's presence in the body on the basis of a physiognomic intuition. Each plastic or phonic object can be understood as a covering that conceals a metaphoric human body within itself, in which, in turn, its expressive movement lies hidden (existing in it as a potential for form). According to Eisenstein, the coming together of form is preceded by a principle, a scheme, a line (i.e., the trace of a movement), which gradually acquire a body. Examining the experience of mystical ecstasy, Eisenstein points to the fact that the mystic initially finds himself outside any kind of image or thing (*vneobraznost', vnepredmetnost'*). He then encounters an "entirely abstract image" that "painstakingly acquires objective traits [*staratel'no opredmechivaetsia*]." In this way, "an imageless 'origin' quickly dons the image of a concretely objective 'personified' God."[72] The principle here acquires a kind of flesh, a body that grows out of the schematic concept: "The formulaic concept, gaining in sumptuousness, unfolding on the basis of its material, is transformed into image-as-form."[73]

Characteristically, Eisenstein extended this metaphor to the evolution of organic bodies, whose surface he understood as a static cast taken of a body's movements, an outer casing containing the trace of a moving line.[74] Since the manifestation of the principle, for Eisenstein, was meant to repeat in reverse sequence the process by which form is created, it could be seen essentially as a "decomposition" of the textual body, the removal, from an idea, of its bodily layers. That Eisenstein was interested in the body within the body, the casing within the casing—what he called the "kangaroo principle"—comes as no surprise.[75] He was fascinated by an Indian drawing in which the silhouetted outline of an elephant was found to contain a series of female figures; by the fact that Napoleon's body had been transported inside four coffins, each within the other; and even by the Surikov painting *Men'shikov in Berezovo*, in which he uncovered the same metaphoric structure of repeating coffins.[76]

The body, then, is reached by removing its outer covering; even its essence can be reached if the body is anatomically prepared. In "Psychology of Composition," Eisenstein elaborates in great detail the metaphor of writerly self-analysis (which he himself practiced a great deal) as a kind of autopsy. He also analyzed Poe's *Philosophy of Composition* in this light. Poe and Eisenstein in fact have a great deal in common: both develop the myth of the seer-detective, both cultivate physiognomy as a form of knowledge, and so on. Eisenstein compared Poe to an anatomist-pathologist: "Poe performs his 'autopsy' (dissection) in the form of a literary analysis of images of his own invention; in other cases in the form of analytical deductions of the kind a detective would make."[77] Here Eisenstein also speaks of moving from "the inspection of the 'decomposition' of a body devoid of life . . . to a decomposition 'for the purpose of analyzing' the body of a poem."[78]

The analytical dissection of a textual body supplements the physiognomic reading of it. The ideal being pursued here is the ability to see through the body into its organizing graphic structure. This method can be defined as a kind of *artistic x-ray*, which illuminates the hidden skeleton through the flesh.

This skeletal metaphor is of some importance to Eisenstein's understanding of the principle, and the means we have to know it. To imitate the principle is to negate the body in order to uncover its skeleton. To be sure, this rather macabre metaphor is older than Eisenstein himself. We scarcely need to recall the various medieval and Renaissance allegories of death, in which the skeleton embodies a truth that lies concealed under a body that is fated to decay. More recently, Charles Baudelaire has described the skeleton in a way that is strikingly close to Eisenstein. For Baudelaire also, the skeleton is a structure or scheme that has to be extrapolated from the natural body: "The sculptor understood very quickly how much mysterious and abstract beauty there is to be found in this thin carcass, for which the flesh serves as clothing, and which is like the plan of the poem of humanity. And this caressing, biting, almost scientific grace in turn finds its place, clear and purified of the filth of decay, among the innumerable graces that Art had already extracted from ignorant Nature."[79]

The same notion of the skeleton as a beautiful abstraction to be rescued from the flesh appears in Baudelaire's poem "Danse macabre." Here the poet addresses a beautiful woman:

> Aucuns t'apelleront une caricature
> Qui ne comprennent pas, amants ivres de chair
> L'élégance sans nom de l'humaine armature.
> Tu réponds, grand squelette, à mon goût le plus cher!
>
> (Some will call you a caricature
> Lovers drunk on flesh, who do not understand
> The nameless elegance of the human armature.
> You respond, great skeleton, to my dearest taste!)[80]

This metaphor gained currency in Russia too, among the symbolist writers of the early twentieth century who were close to the theosophical and anthroposophical movements. Like Eisenstein's theory, these new mystical doctrines were oriented toward a rather unique kind of evolutionism. According to Rudolph Steiner, older genetic forms are preserved as astral bodies, visible only to the "initiate." In all seriousness, the theosophists sought to fix invisible geometric sketches of what Annie Besant called "thought-forms," referring specifically to x-ray experiments.[81] The Russian poet and artist Maksimilian Voloshin, who was close to the anthroposophists, wrote an article characteristically entitled "The Skeleton of Art" (Skelet zhivopisi; 1904), in which he urged all artists to "reduce the entire multicolored world to the basic combinations of angles and curves."[82] In other words, by removing the visible layer of the flesh, they would reveal the graphic skeleton that lay below. Voloshin also claimed to discern prehistoric skeletons buried in the painting of K. F. Bogaevskii, which he went on to interpret as a paleontological code.[83]

In his novel *Petersburg*, a book filled with split bodies undertaking astral journeys, the anthroposophist Andrei Belyi describes the movement from formula to embodiment in a way that recalls Eisenstein: "Logic had turned into bones, and syllogisms were wrapped all around like sinews. The contents of logic were now covered with flesh."[84] We might note that this passage appears at the end of an episode that is effectively paraphrased in a scene from Eisenstein's film *October* called "The Gods." In both cases, we move through a series of divine metamorphoses—Confucius, Buddha, Chronos, down to the busts of primitive idols. Moving from sumptuous flesh to the skeleton is like moving through the surface appearance of the most recent divinities back to their more schematic precursors. This pattern of thinking is close to Eisenstein's; indeed, the move from theosophy to higher abstraction was a path common to many artists of the time, from Kandinsky to Mondrian.

Like his predecessors, Eisenstein singled out in painting anything related to the metaphorics of anatomy. He wrote a lengthy piece on Hogarth, an artist who strove to abstract an ideal curve out of the structure of bones.[85] He paused to examine the pedagogical elaborations of Paul Klee, which he interpreted according to the metaphor of graphology.[86] It was Klee, in fact, who was most eager to pursue an "anatomical" approach to the structure of a work of art: "Just like a human being, a painting has a skeleton, muscles and skin. One might speak of the specific anatomy of a painting."[87] Klee also recommended "autopsy" as the best way of understanding the inner structure of things: "A thing splits apart, its inside is exposed in its planes of cleavage. Its character is organized according to how many and what kind of cleavages have been necessary. This is a visible internalization, produced either with the help of a simple knife, or with the help of subtler instruments capable of clearly baring the structure and material functioning of the thing."[88]

In Eisenstein's case, it was drawing that made him interested in skeletons. He acknowledged as much in the following statement: "I have been attracted to bones and skeletons since childhood. An attraction that is something of a illness."[89] The sketches of his student days later repelled him for their orientation toward the fleshly body: "The finished sketch requires volume, shade, half-shade and reflex, while there is a complete 'taboo' on the graphic outline of the skeleton or ribs."[90] For Eisenstein, the place of flesh in painting was suspect, in that it concealed the more essential bones. He copied out the following passage from Chiang-Yee's *The Chinese Eye*, in which the author discusses the work of Chinese painters: "'And then a moment of illumination occurs, they look at the water and the very same rocks and realize that they are face to face with bare "reality," no longer obscured by the Shadow of Life. They must immediately take up their brushes and draw the "bones" as they are in their true form: there is no need to go into detail.'"[91] Eisenstein then comments: "Here we encounter the term 'bones.' This bony outline [*lineinyi kostiak*] is required to embody the 'true form,' the 'generalized essence of the phenomenon.'"[92] Here we see the linear scheme directly linked to the metaphor of the skeleton. Elsewhere, Eisenstein clarifies the comparison: "This 'determining skeleton' [*reshaiushchii kostiak*] can be then clothed in any particular kind

of painterly resolution."[93] Here the skeleton appears to acquire an autonomy from the artistic flesh that clothes it.

For Eisenstein himself, any postulate was proved right if it could be projected successfully onto an evolutionary model. Hence the skeletal
metaphor was also elaborated in this way. Among Eisenstein's notes we
find a fantastic passage taken from *Representative Men,* Emerson's adaptation of Swedenborg's philosophy, in which all of evolutionary history from
the snake and the worm to humankind is depicted as a history of skeletons,
through all their permutations and improvements.[94] In a note dating from
1933, he announces his enthusiastic discovery of a quite fantastic evolutionary law, according to which the skeleton is shown to correspond to a
thought process: "Self-imitation. (Hurrah!!). Surely that was what I was
writing about when I discussed the process by which consciousness developed: the nervous tissue reproduces the skeleton, etc., and thought reproduces action."[95] The nervous system, as the agent of thought, graphically
re-creates a sketch of the skeleton as the agent of action. Each person realizes an internal specular mimesis of the schemes, structures, and principles
that engender consciousness.

Eisenstein often wrote about how the scheme, the line, and the skeleton
can show through the body of a text. This magical x-ray faculty was deeply
rooted in the specific workings of Eisenstein's own psyche. From Frank
Harris's memoirs, *My Life and Loves,* Eisenstein would recall "only one
scene": the one in which a man laughed so much that "from the shaking
his flesh 'began to come off his bones' [!] "[96] Here the bones literally break
through the layer of flesh. In the autobiographical fragment "On Folk-
lore," Eisenstein recalls comparing a certain Comrade E. to a "rose-colored
skeleton dressed in a suit," and then tries to reconstruct the logic by which
he arrived at this "sinister image": "First one formed an image of a skull
protruding out of a head, or the mask of a skull coming through the surface of a face."[97] Later on the director himself acknowledged that the
image of a "skull thrusting its way to the surface of a face" was his metaphor
for expressive movement, a model for the work of mimicry. From this we
can more clearly grasp the place of physiognomy in Eisenstein's work as a
means of reading essences. The science of physiognomy seeks to read the
skeleton through the layer of the flesh. From this point it is also only one
more step to Eisenstein's concept of ecstasy, which involves a kind of bodily release: the skeleton leaves the body, just as the principle is abstracted
from the text, just like a "skull thrusting its way to the surface of a face."[98]

The motif of the skeleton also appears in Eisenstein's films, such as *Aleksandr Nevsky* and especially *¡Que viva México!* In the All Saints' Day sequence in the Mexican film, the "determining skeleton" turns into a highly
elaborate baroque metaphor. Under the death masks used in the carnival
one can see real skulls, a fact that Eisenstein himself saw as crucially im-

portant: "The face is a kind of simulacrum of the skull, and the skull is a kind of face on its own. . . . One living over the other. One hiding under the other. One living an autonomous life through the other. And each showing through the other in turns. The one and the other repeating the physical scheme of the process by manipulating the images of face and skull which keep exchanging masks."[99]

In this constant play of physiognomic readings, meaning shows through the flesh (a mask) in order then to become a mask itself. The interchangeability of mask and face is a metaphor for the play of substitutes, the universal equivalences of meaning.

At the beginning of this chapter, I discussed Iurii Tynianov's hypothesis concerning Pushkin's romantic life, which Eisenstein adapted to his own complex set of long-cherished ideas. The hypothesis revealed an almost imperceptible play of substitutes, which Eisenstein was quick to insert into his own operative context, projecting Pushkin's "nameless love" onto the life of Edgar Allan Poe. This projection was almost slavishly faithful to Pushkin's scenario, albeit with one alteration. Poe's sweetheart Jane Smith Stanard died while he was still a boy. The place of the living Karamzina was taken by the dead Jane, and with this Tynianov's original thesis acquired an added range of macabre motifs, discussed earlier. Metaphorically speaking, the movement toward a universal substitute must pass through the stage of death, and the disintegration of the body. While no single body can replace another, a skeleton readily takes on the function of substitute. To pursue this metaphor to its gruesome conclusion, one could say that Goncharova could replace Karamzina because their skeletons are similar. This, at the limit of its logic, was Eisenstein's own answer to the question he had posed Tynianov.

Earlier in this book, while examining the problem of the simulacrum, or external resemblance, in *Un Chien andalou* (chapter 5), we discovered that the universal equivalence of things is possible only if their external form is "softened" and then transformed. While remaining within the figurative realm of the body, Eisenstein takes the metaphor several steps further. Equivalence, we discover, is possible only when form has disintegrated, and all that remains is its bare scheme, the skeleton. In a 1939 sketch entitled *Life Leaving the Body Forever,* we see life represented paradoxically as a schematic line resembling a skeleton and coming out of the inert material frame that once encased it. If we were to project this idea onto the problematics of a text, then we could say that the life of a text begins when it frees itself of the body, from the external form that clothed it.

Two texts (or fragments thereof) can actively interact with each other if they are connected not formally (as bodies) but structurally. Here Eisenstein is quite in tune with contemporary theories of intertextuality, such as Riffaterre's, for which "text and intertext are invariables of one and the same structure."[100] Only a commonality of structure allows for the correlation of text and intertext.

The fact of correlation between two texts—the basis of intertextuality—also raises the further and urgent question of the *criteria* needed for their correlation. How are we to establish that a given text is a transformation or variant of an intertext? The necessary criterion is resemblance, precisely the point that Eisenstein will adopt as the focus of his analysis.

In the autobiographical fragment "On Bones" (Na kostiakh),[101] Eisenstein mentions Georges Rodenbach's *Bruges-la-morte,* a book devoted almost entirely to the idea of a resemblance between the living and the dead, the real and the imaginary. Interestingly, Rodenbach analyzes the mechanism of resemblance, to observe: "The resemblances are ever only in the figures and in the overall impression. If one strains over details, everything differs."[102]

Rodenbach's observation, that the careful examination of detail inevitably shows up only differences, points to the essential paradox of similarity. As Walter Benjamin had astutely remarked:

> When we say that one face resembles another, we mean that we can discern certain features of the second face in the first, while the latter does not cease to be what it is. But the possibilities of phenomena of this kind are not subject to any criterion, and are thus unlimited. The category of resemblance has only a very limited meaning for waking consciousness, but acquires limitless meaning in the world of hashish. Each thing here has a face, and rightly so; each thing is endowed with such a level of physical presence that we can seek to discern in it, as in a face, the appearance of certain features. . . . the truth becomes something living; and it lives by rhythm alone, in accordance with which a statement is placed over a contrary statement, allowing us by that very fact to think ourselves. [103]

Benjamin's point is that the category of similarity is not useful when consciousness is fully lucid, while highly effective in the ecstatic state of mind that was Eisenstein's desired goal. Without ecstasy, the superimposition of face on face does not "allow itself to be thought" as truth.

It was this solution to the problem of resemblance between bodies, texts, and objects that impelled Eisenstein to suppose the existence of an invisible inner text, a kind of graphic memory. For Eisenstein, text and intertext could not be correlated unless an invisible text could be extrapolated from them, which could then bring their correlation into effect. For Riffaterre we are simply dealing with a structural invariable. For Eisenstein this invariable becomes a "third text," a speculative, almost mystical interpretant, existing in the Platonic sphere of pure ideas, which only the blind Tiresias is able to divine.

This abstract text is profoundly linked to the language, and montage, of Eisenstein's films. The densely "intellectual" juxtaposition of objects in Eisenstein's montage appears anomalous from the point of view of normal narrative logic, something like a quote that interrupts the flow of linear narrative. These montage sequences, each responsible for creating conceptual coherence out of the clash of fragmented images, provoke the mechanism of intertextuality in order to find normative status within the film's semantics. Eisenstein himself often pointed out that the task of bringing together these diverse montage fragments devolved onto a dominant plastic form, such as the abstract line that unites Prokofiev's music and the sheer cliff in *Aleksandr Nevsky*. An invisible and rather enigmatic "third text" thus makes Eisenstein's montage read as a normative text.

Eisenstein saw montage as a stage in the production of meaning, one that would not have been possible without an earlier moment. This initial stage involved imitating the "principle," elucidating the scheme, the intellectual grapheme that fixes an image, the beginnings of meaning. This beginning stage is based on the intuitive, magical physiognomic discovery of something hidden in the body—a thing, a text or line, a "skeleton." These "skeletons" then enter into contact and begin to function reciprocally as substitutes. The artist must reach the more abstractly intellectual stage of montage through a "corporeal" stage of creation: this is described as a decomposition, an x-ray, or an autopsy of the visible flesh. Before the work of combining generalized schemes of imagery can begin, a skeleton visible only to the initiate must make its way through the face of the world. This is the invisible "third text" that finally resolves the dilemma of external resemblances.

Conclusion

We are nearing the end of our investigation. Perhaps unexpectedly, in the last chapter we came across some motifs in Eisenstein that were already known to us from analyzing the films of D. W. Griffith. Both Eisenstein and Griffith cultivated a myth of origins, to which all their films aspired. For Griffith this origin was figured as music, or some originary Book, whereas Eisenstein looked to the beginnings of conceptual thought in "primitive" societies. In fact, the same quest for origins is equally characteristic of the other filmmakers I have examined in this book. Cendrars and Léger adapted a myth of universal creation to the exigencies of creating a new (cinematic) language. Tynianov investigated the genesis of the hero through the genesis of his name, thereby invoking a prerational transsense (*zaum'*) as the originary language. Finally, Buñuel and Dali derived the birth of form from a necrophilic understanding of creative metamorphosis. In each case, we have seen that the theme of mythic origins enters the text along with the process of intertextuality.

In systematically cultivating a myth of origins, a culture also raises the question of *how anything begins,* the point, more specifically, from which a text emerges. Yet this very hankering for origins ultimately reveals that texts finally lack a definitive source. As Rosalind Krauss puts it: "But what if there were no beginning uncorrupted by a prior instance—or what in most of poststructuralist writing is rendered as the 'always already'?"[1] From this conclusion, we are led to reject as meaningless any notion of an origin from which a text is said to derive, along with the notion of author as the "originary source." Literary and other critics have long questioned the authorial function, so that the notion of author as sole generator of the text now appears to stand on shaky ground. The text is seen to be constructed as an endless chain of prior instances, to the point where, as Krauss would have it, the originary appears to us in the form of repetition.

In his study on Winckelmann's aesthetics, Michael Fried has pointed to a kind of vicious circle that arises in Winckelmann's own reasoning. The renewal of art is linked by Winckelmann to a return to origins, realized through the imitation of the great masters of antiquity. Yet as models for emulation he names Raphael, Michelangelo, and Poussin, that is, modern rather than classical artists. Fried points out the contradictory nature of this "gesture," by which these artists become "*at once* ancients and moderns, . . . originals worthy of imitation and successful imitators of antecedent originals."[2] Yet this is apparently only a paradox. In fact, this is the situation of most significant artists and writers: they not only are unable to establish the beginnings of their own texts but also are themselves obliged to submit to a "non-Euclidean" account of history.

At the very beginning of this book, I suggested that a theory of intertextuality allows us to incorporate history into the structure of a text. But during the course of the book "history" began to seem less and less like a chronological sequence of events. By creating a specific intertextual field as its own environment, each text in its own way seeks to organize and regroup its textual precursors. Furthermore, the intertextual field of certain texts can be composed of "sources" that were actually written after them. For example, in my analysis of *Un Chien andalou* I often had occasion to cite statements by Dali and Bataille that were written after the film but constitute part of its intertextual field. In this sense, Borges's opinion, that Kafka was the precursor of those who preceded him, is less paradoxical than it might appear at first glance. In his analysis of the sources of the poet Lautréamont, the French critic Pleynet reaches a similar conclusion that "Lautréamont appears to be no more than the precursor of his own sources."[3] Such a conclusion is not just a concession to faddish trends. It is in fact typical of our experience as readers to find ourselves able to understand a work only after reading a later piece by the same author. Surely this somewhat more familiar scenario proves the same point: that in some way a later text can serve as the source of an earlier text. This reverse chronology is of course only possible from the perspective of reading, which is precisely the basis of an intertextual approach to culture.

In organizing its own intertextual field, each work of art also creates its own history of culture. This involves a restructuring of the entire stock of older culture. For this reason, we can say that a theory of intertextuality is a means of renewing our understanding of history, a history that enters the structure of the text as a dynamic and constantly evolving factor. An intertextual approach encourages us to rethink given notions of artistic evolution, which can be seen to embrace not only immediate artistic precursors but all kinds of diverse cultural phenomena, even those historically quite remote from the text at hand. At stake is the possibility of generating new phenomena from the body of an entire preceding culture, not just from a contemporary sense of cultural relevance. Better yet, what is popularly understood as "contemporary" or "relevant" should be projected onto culture as a whole.

The intertext, then, binds a text to a culture, with culture functioning here as an interpretive, explanatory, and logic-generating mechanism. The role of the intertext in generating a logic has been highlighted more than once in this book. Still, it would be a mistake to reduce intertextuality to pure interpretation, resulting in a kind of textual "hermeneutics." I have tried to show that the semantic role of the intertext is not exhausted by the rationalization of anomalies such as the strange signpost in Dreyer's *Vampyr*. An intertext can inform even radically new cinematic figures, such as the montage figurations in Griffith's *Enoch Arden* or the specular spatial constructions in *Lieutenant Kizhe*. In the latter cases, the intertext no longer functions simply as an interpretive agent. *By inserting the "source" of a cinematic figure into a film as its subtext, the intertext can also function as a generative mechanism.* This also implies a new approach to cinematic language, one distinct from traditional semiotic analysis, which normally limits its reading of a figure to the confines of a given film (or group of films).

Film studies today still largely view cinematic figures from a functional viewpoint. This perspective sees the language of film as serving primarily to construct spatial structures or convey a sense of cinematic time. Naturally enough, narrative cinema has benefited the most from this kind of approach, since narrative problems shed the clearest light on a film's functional dimension, its immediate link to the time-space of a given story.

The theory of intertextuality is particularly effective in addressing narrative leaps, moments in which narrative logic gives way to discursive anomalies. As we have seen from reviewing some of D. W. Griffith's works, cinematic figures are not immediately integrated into the normative framework of a story line: they first appear as anomalous formations (cf. the bewilderment caused by the first close-up shots in early cinema).

The traditional approach to cinematic form as a rule tends to ignore this initially anomalous appearance of new linguistic figures, reducing them to brilliant intuitions whose functional use would be understood later. Such an approach is forced to explain all kinds of cinematic innovation from the perspective of a linguistic norm that generally arises well after the innovations themselves. A theory of intertextuality permits us to analyze these innovations not from the vantage point of a future norm but through the intertextual links characteristic of the film in which these innovations are evident. We are thereby also in a position to avoid unifying or homogenizing these phenomena, an almost inevitable temptation whenever we read any text with normative assumptions. As a result, each linguistic figure within each individual text can be given its own genealogy. Thus the sequence of a close-up of the heroine's face followed by a long shot of the hero in Griffith's "Tennysonian" films must be understood precisely with reference to Tennyson and the surrounding intertext. The linguistic norms of later narrative cinema, in which this sequence is canonized and associated with specific plot situations, are not really germane here.

Any attempt to go beyond narrative in film studies has wide-ranging consequences. The linguistic figures being analyzed no longer appear as purely functional, a role that makes them invisible to the lay viewer by dissolving them into the logic of narrative. It is well known that the normative figures of cinematic language (such as shot-countershot and crosscut editing) are scarcely noticed by most viewers (what is called the "transparency of linguistic form"). Intertextuality, which is particularly active in moments of narrative rupture, where the linear logic of the story breaks down, provides cinematic language with a certain corporeality, which I have often called its hieroglyphic quality. A cinematic hieroglyph does not dissolve into the narrative, remaining opaque to the end. Its meaning seems to be composed of many textual layers, often lying outside the text itself. In this sense an intertextual hieroglyph resembles the interpretation of dreams in Freud. Like dreams, the hieroglyph is also the product of condensations, shifts, and displacements.

As Christian Metz has shown, the processes that typify dream work are akin to those that generate so-called cinematic tropes, above all, metaphor and metonymy. This is not the place to go into the rhetoric of cinema, a vast field in itself. It should be noted, however, that an intertextual hieroglyph does in some ways resemble the cinematic tropes analyzed by Metz. He has shown that a cinematic trope becomes "automatic"—that is, no longer perceptible as figuratively charged—when the semantic processes that generated it become fixed or stalled. Then the "horizon closes, the product overshadows the process of production, condensation and displacement (present in a dead way) are no longer manifested as such, although one can assume their effective presence in some past."[4] It is this phenomenon that heightens the representational nature of a quotation, to the point of isolating it from its context. An increase in what I have called corporeality is precisely the outcome of this "fixing" of a trope.

A theory of intertextuality also allows us to rethink the very nature of cinematic metaphor. For Metz, the classic example of metaphor in film is the juxtaposition through montage of the grotesque old lady and the image of an ostrich in Vigo's *Zéro de conduite*.[5] Others still (e.g., students of the "structural rhetoric" of film) point either to the scene from Resnais's *Hiroshima mon amour,* in which two dead men, both lying in the same position, are linked through montage, or to the metaphoric chains in Eisenstein's *October*.[6] A theory of intertextuality allows us to regard metaphor as the linking of an element present in the text with an element from another text that may not be tangibly or physically present to the viewer. In this book we have seen metaphors generated out of several such juxtapositions: Kane and the Svengali character from *Trilby*, the saucepans from *Ballet mécanique* and Cendrars's "cosmic kitchen," the figure of Kizhe and Hoffmann's Zaches.

To rethink the status of metaphor in film also implies a reconsideration of the function of representation, particularly of the "isolated" figure. The representational function of a quotation is not so much the meaning being "stalled" or even erased as it is a sign of an imprint: the figure at stake contains the mark of a process, which we are asked to reconstruct or revive. The representational nature of a metaphor is thus at the same time the outcome of the crystallization of prior semantic processes and the generator of new meanings. Here we are once again confronted with an inversion of traditional logic (that of chronology). *A metaphor, like a quotation, presents itself to us before we are able to decode its metaphoric meaning, and before we have established the source of the quotation.* The corporeality of intertextual formations points to a mystery that asks to be understood. This corporeality presents itself draped in an aura of mystery. This is contrary to what is traditionally said of metaphors and tropes, that they are the *outcome* of semantic activity.

Still, the field of structural rhetoric can be helpful in allowing us to regard cinematic figures not simply as functional elements that facilitate narrative but as something resembling tropes. From this perspective, a device such as crosscutting is not just a codified figure that unites two spaces, but a metonymic process (depending on what is being brought together by the given figure). A cinematic figure emerges as a complex semantic process, whose complexity escalates the more it ramifies into a wider intertextual field.

These figures and tropes can scarcely be tabulated or described in the form of a "cinematic grammar." They themselves mobilize various semantic strategies. When they appear to resemble one other, this is often because they are yet to be understood. A quote, and the trope alongside which it stands juxtaposed, appear in a text as moments of hermeneutic difficulty, prior to the work of meaning, which begins precisely as a result of their provocation. The linguistic mechanism is thus initiated by the phenomenon of incomprehension, by which a quote appears initially as inert or impenetrable. Language thus makes its appearance as the overcoming of incomprehension rather than as a sign system or code that is already known to the reader.

As soon as the work of understanding takes place, the fundamental diversity of cinematic figures becomes evident. Thus, in the examples examined here, we can find tropes or linguistic figures that appear to be similar: for example, the montage sequences with the dominant spherical motif from *Ballet mécanique,* the prologue to *Un Chien andalou,* in which an eye and the moon are linked on the basis of their circular shape, and finally Eisenstein's invisible sketches linking diverse objects. All of these montage-based comparisons appear analogous at the initial stage of incomprehension, and might even be placed together as figures of the same type. Yet on an intertextual level, they are all quite different. In Léger this kind of metaphor is a reference to Cendrars's circular symbolism, which functions as part of an originary language. In Buñuel and Dali, the circular form highlights the problem of external analogy: this, in turn, can be read, through the Gómez de la Serna intertext, as referring to a system of "simulacra" that it mobilizes. In Eisenstein we are dealing with an initial graph, which constitutes an invisible "third text."

Intertextuality thus allows us to read figures of speech that appear externally homogeneous as operating semantic strategies that are in fact quite divergent. This is why cinematic figures of speech can be brought together only when they are integrated into a narrative, where they are perceived "automatically." This is why we can speak of the shot-countershot as having the same function within dialogue, while we cannot attribute any unity of function to those figures of speech that remain anomalous, that is to say, function as quotations.

Cinematic language can thus be described on the one hand as a set of coded elements with roughly similar functions (the language of narrative), and on the other hand as a set of figures able to organize quite diverse semantic strategies on an intertextual basis. This dichotomy can be somewhat schematically reduced to an opposition between "figures of comprehension"("transparent" linguistic signifiers) and "figures of incomprehension"(the hieroglyphs of intertextuality). This book has sought to move from a condition of initial incomprehension to describe the various languages of cinema, and their diverse semantic strategies.

These analyses have relied on a linguistic field whose very formation was paradoxical, situated between textually visible elements (quotes, anomalies) and an invisible intertext. The latter, after all, exists not on film or on paper but in the memory of the viewer or reader. Meaning is generated between a physically given datum and an image residing in the memory. The paradox inherent in this situation is further emphasized by the fact that a quotation, as the generator of meaning, appears more densely corporeal than other elements of the text, the transparent signifiers that readily dissolve in the narrative. In other words, the less visible the intertext, the more visible the quote that indicates its presence. Meaning is thus situated in this linguistic field between a heightened corporeality and a physically evacuated nonbeing.

The very way I have designated these two contrasting poles itself renders metaphorically the movement of meaning as one from concreteness to abstraction. This movement, it should be said, occurs within coordinates that are profoundly alien to the project of classical semiotics. Even semiotics, to be sure, moves toward abstraction insofar as it rejects the concrete. It calls this abstraction "meaning" or "structure," neither of which is available to the reader as something physically given. Nevertheless, the difference between semiotics and the approach taken in this book is enormous. Semiotics does not work with elements that appear as inert bodies, or with invisible texts that exist outside material agencies. Nor does it view the generation of meaning as a kind of pathway leading from a "monstrous embodiment"(such as the angel on the signpost of Dreyer's *Vampyr* or the donkeys on the piano in *Un Chien andalou*) to an invisible text situated in the memory.

The initial characteristics of the quote—its corporeality, its inability to dissolve into the logic of narrative—disappear to the extent that we are able to construct its intertexts. The quote is then said to be integrated into the text. The movement from the concrete to the abstract is thus seen in reverse in the process by which a quote acquires "normalcy." Since the qualities that characterize an anomaly, its inertness and isolation, disappear when we identify its relationship to the invisible intertexts, we can see this very bodily inertness as the creation of several intertexts heaped one on top of another. In this case we are once again dealing with an inverted logic: precisely what allowed us to overcome the corporeal nature of the intertextual hieroglyph now appears as the cause of this very trait. The final stage in the pathway of meaning now appears to be the cause determining the qualities of the initial stage of its movement.

The work of meaning can be represented schematically through the following scenario. A man closes his eyes, and his memory begins to conjure up certain images and figures. In the darkness of his consciousness (or subconscious), they begin to form layers and gradually become more visible, thickening to the point of becoming palpable: we call this a hyperquotation. This scenario is of course the reverse of the actual process of reading, which *departs* from an existing textual "thickening" in order to disperse it, in the darkness of memory, into intertextual fragments that are then dissolved into the text itself.

This dual process by which meaning is generated through an intertext was once described with some originality by the formalist Viktor Shklovskii, in an account of his own creative method. Shklovskii would immerse himself in various books, in which he marked the quotes he needed. His typist would then retype the passages he had marked onto separate pieces of paper. Shklovskii continues:

I hang these passages on the walls of my room (often in great numbers). Unfortunately, my room is tiny, and I feel cramped.

It is very important to understand a quotation, turn it around, and link it to other quotes.

These passages can hang on the wall for a long time. I put them in groups, where they hang side by side. Then the transitional connections appear, each quite short in length.[7]

Shklovskii's point of departure is a prior intertext, a series of quotations that are not intrinsically linked. He moves among them, seeking out possible connections, trying to regroup them into new logical clusters from which a text might be constructed.

Now, the process of reading has to move in the opposite direction. In reading Shklovskii, for example, we would have to dismantle his text into its constituent quotations and then put them back on the walls of the room of memory that we all, metaphorically speaking, possess—the room containing the universal intertext of culture. In attaching them back onto the walls, we can claim to have definitively assimilated the text, which has been effectively dissolved in the act of reading.

Shklovskii's creative method in part recalls the mnemonic techniques prevalent in antiquity. Even in classical times, there existed a specific form of memorization. A text was collapsed into sections, which would then be associated with certain tangible figures (such as pictures or statues). These figures would then be assigned by the imagination to different places within a well-known edifice (such as a temple or theater). In order to recall the text, one simply had to take an imaginary walk about this edifice, surveying the various figures from memory. Shklovskii's room can be seen as a modern echo of the imaginary temples of classical mnemonics.

Frances Yates, in her well-known study of this tradition, described mnemotechnics as the art of holding "invisible memory-images" within the adept's mind.[8] Even the famous treatises on memory had no illustrations. Any visual representations were meant to reside in the mind, and to bear a physical likeness to the idea or thing requiring memorization. These imaginary "similitudes" were thus transformed into a kind of intertext, on the basis of their resemblance to the various parts of the texts being committed to memory. It is important to note, however, that this likeness was possible only insofar as the mnemonic figures remained invisible. It is the invisibility of the intertext that allows it to create correspondences. In one of his treatises on mnemonics, Giordano Bruno hails the famous Greek artist Zeuxis as a creator of mnemonic images that, by virtue of their ethereality, could be identified with the images of poetry or philosophy.[9] Being invisible, the intertextual image can serve as an intertext for any kind of quotation, be it cinematic, musical, or literary. These mnemonic images generate an endless intertextual field that can link a given text to human culture as a whole. (The invisibility of the mnemonic image might also explain the persistent motif of blindness in certain texts analyzed in this book, such as *Un Chien andalou* or the works of Georges Bataille and Sergei Eisenstein. The memory of the blind man—Tiresias—becomes the sign, as it were, of intertextuality.)

Albertus Magnus, an adept of the mnemonic arts, recommended placing "corporeal similitudes" within a darkened space, where they might be "arranged in a regular order."[10] This darkroom of memory is where the blind man dwells. It is easier for the blind man to bring invisible texts together, arrange them, and note their similarities. Even in the cinema, the intertextual process only *begins* with a visual moment—the images on screen—in order then to retreat into the darkroom of memory that Albertus Magnus had described. Walter Benjamin, who regarded the mystery of resemblance to be of great significance to the formation of civilization, once wrote about the creation of "a universal archive of resemblances that cannot be grasped sensuously."[11] This archive is to be found in the darkroom of memory, the metaphoric space of intertextuality.

During this final discussion, the reader may have noted a palpable increase in the use of metaphors, many of which appear remote from the conceptual apparatus of serious scholarship. I have talked about memory as a "darkroom" and about the "abstract corporeality" of the image. Metaphors are a means of rendering the underlying processes of a reader's or viewer's consciousness—its displacements, condensations, and sedimentations. As such they inevitably enter the sphere of metalanguage. The conceptual apparatus of intertextual theory thus retains a link with the image, as often occurs in the case of new theories. But this layer of imagery has the added use of being derived from the experience of reading, which it then retraces during the work of analysis. It starts out from a moment of incomprehension, one or more textual fragments that cannot be interpreted with the aid of an existing conceptual apparatus.

As a theory of reading (as well as a theory of language and its evolution seen through the prism of reading), the theory of intertextuality does not lay claim to universality. It does not seek to replace other approaches, and even willingly ignores such basic phenomena as narrative. Its task is more modest: to provide, through the act of reading, a new insight into the functionings of a text, in those moments where mimesis, the desire for imitation or likeness, breaks down, giving way to semiosis.

Notes

INTRODUCTION

1. Eliade, *Myth and Reality*.
2. Freidenberg, *Mif i literatura drevnosti*, 353.
3. Eliot, *The Waste Land*, ll. 215–225.
4. Cf. Fabricius, *The Unconscious and Mr. Eliot*, 160.
5. Quoted in McFarlane, "The Mind of Modernism," 90.
6. Ibid.

CHAPTER ONE

1. Aumont, "Crise dans la crise," 199.
2. Lagny, "Histoire et cinéma," 74.
3. Lotman, "Neskol'ko myslei o tipologii kul'tur" (Some thoughts on the typology of cultures), 11.
4. Laplanche and Pontalis, "Fantasme des origines," 1833–1868.
5. Durgnat, *Films and Feelings*, 230; see also 229–235.
6. Cf. Cieutat, "Naissance d'une iconographie," 6–15; and Gubern, "Contribution à une lecture de l'iconographie griffithienne," 117–125.
7. Panofsky, "Style and Medium in Moving Pictures," 25.
8. Panofsky, *Meaning in the Visual Arts*, 31.
9. Hanson, "D. W. Griffith: Some Sources," 500; cf. also Montesanti, "Pastrone e Griffith," 8–17; and Belluccio " 'Cabiria' e 'Intolerance' tra il serio e il faceto," 53–57.
10. Cherchi Usai, *Pastrone*.
11. Brownlow, *The Parade's Gone By*, 53–54.
12. On this tradition, see Heckscher, "Bernini's Elephant and Obelisk," 65–96.
13. Collin de Plancy, *Dictionnaire Infernal*, 231; cf. also Panofsky, *Idea*, 248, on chastity; *Physiologus: Frühchristlicher Tiersymbolik*, 81; Muratova, *Srednevekovyi bestiarii*,

103, on the elephant cub as Christ; *Notebooks of Leonardo da Vinci,* 173; Hibbard, *Bernini,* 213.

14. Hanson, "D. W. Griffith: Some Sources," 504.

15. On Boulanger and Martin, see Geiger, "Louis Boulanger," 11; and Thompson, " 'Le Feu du ciel,' " 255; for Hugo's poem, see Victor Hugo, *Les Orientales,* 20; for Martin and H. C. Selous, see Feaver, *The Art of John Martin,* 110–111.

16. Cf. Collin de Plancy, *Dictionnaire Infernal,* 86.

17. See L. Langlès, *Monuments anciens et modernes de l'Hindoustan,* 2:147–170.

18. Baudelaire, "Le Voyage," 397.

19. Latini, "Livre du Trésor," 210.

20. Delevoy, *Le Symbolisme,* 124.

21. Shpet, *Sochineniia,* 396.

22. Foucault, *Archeology of Knowledge,* 25.

23. Ivanov, *Ocherki po istorii semiotiki v SSSR,* 251.

24. Ferdinand de Saussure, quoted in Starobinski, "La Poursuite de la preuve," in *Les Mots sous les mots,* 128.

25. Starobinski, *Les Mots sous les mots,* 17.

26. Ducrot and Todorov, *Dictionnaire encyclopédique,* 446.

27. Kristeva, *Sémeiotikè,* 255.

28. Ibid., 195.

29. Metz, *Langage et cinéma,* 76–79.

30. Maupassant, *Chroniques,* 234.

31. Ibid., 234–235.

32. Ibid., 237.

33. Sadoul, *French Film,* 38.

34. Brunius, *En marge du cinéma français,* 82.

35. Greene, "Artaud and Film"; and Abel, *French Cinema,* 478.

36. Artaud, *Le Théatre et son double,* 168.

37. Derrida, *L'Écriture et la différence,* 268.

38. Artaud, *Le Théatre et son double,* 162.

39. Williams, *Figures of Desire,* 21.

40. Hedges, *Languages of Revolt;* and Szymczyk-Kluszczynska, *Antonin Artaud.*

41. Artaud, *Le Théatre et son double,* 78.

42. Artaud, *Héliogabàle ou l'anarchiste couronné,* 130.

43. *The Upanishads,* 60, 176.

44. Chevalier and Gheerbrant, *Dictionnaire des symboles,* 277–278.

45. Richer, *L'Alchimie du verbe de Rimbaud,* 36–37.

46. Artaud, *Oeuvres complètes,* 3:24–25.

47. "Nemaia kniga," Illustration 1.

48. Richer, *L'Alchimie du verbe de Rimbaud,* 50–51.

49. Ibid., 81.

50. Ibid., 128–129.

51. Williams, *Figures of Desire,* 22.

52. Artaud, *Le Théatre et son double,* 143.

53. Derrida, *Writing and Difference,* 237–238.

54. Pound, *Ezra Pound: A Critical Anthology,* 53; cf. also Maliavin, "Kitaiskie improvizatsii Paunda."

55. Eisenstein, "The Cinematographic Principle and the Ideogram," in *Film Form*, 30.

56. Eisenstein, *Izbrannye proizvedeniia*, 2:285.

57. Ulmer, *Applied Grammatology*, 271.

58. Derrida, *Of Grammatology*, 90.

59. Ropars-Wuilleumier, *Le Texte divisé*, 71.

60. Gasparov and Ruzina, "Vergilii i vergilianskie tsentony," 210.

61. A quote brings the past closer to us, as it were, but cannot make it part of the present. The present is in fact further distanced from us by quotation. This process can probably be described in spatial categories. Martin Heidegger has directed our attention to the fact that the cinema, while bringing objects close to us, does not make them near. "What is least remote from us in point of distance, by virtue of its picture or film or its sound on the radio, can remain far from us. What is incalculably far from us in point of distance can be near to us. Short distance is not itself nearness. Nor is great distance remoteness" (Heidegger, "The Thing," in *Poetry, Language, Thought*, 165). Heidegger believes that the nearness of a thing to the subject is defined by its "thingliness." In transforming a thing into a sign, the cinema naturally destroys its thingliness, and for this reason also undermines its nearness. A quotation, which is in essence a sign that refers to another text, only heightens the effect of distantiation. This is also why a quote constitutes itself theatrically as a *stage*, that is, something removed from the spectator. Hence the effect of rupturing the present in the system of representation.

62. Benjamin, *Reflections*, 271.

63. Krolop, "Dichtung und Satire," 668–669.

64. The fact is that the semanticization of the visual on screen is realized to a significant degree thanks to a shot's frame, which essentially imitates the function of a frame in painting or the footlights in theater. A film thus acquires meaning as a result of assimilating elements from the poetics of painting and theater. For the semantics of film, the stage that Eisenstein called mise-en-cadre is of fundamental importance (Eisenstein, *Izbrannye proizvedeniia*, 2:334–376). S. Heath has described the process by which a film's initial meaning evolves from the standpoint of semiotics: "What is crucial is the conversion of seen into scene, the absolute holding of signifier on signified: the frame, composed, centered, narrated, is the point of that conversion" (Heath, "Narrative Space," 83). In this process, it is essential to note that the frame does not belong to the diegesis or the narrative aspect of the film. It belongs rather to the space of the viewer and is thus able to translate the narrative onto the plane of the reception, where semiosis occurs. Meyer Schapiro was one of the first to describe this problem in relation to painting: "The frame ... belongs to the space of the viewer rather than to the illusory three-dimensional world of representation that is revealed in it and beyond it. The frame is a mechanism located between the world of the viewer and the representation, whose function is to induce and to focus" (Schapiro, "Nekotorye problemy semiotiki vizual'nogo iskusstva," 141). In this way, the quote, which often acquires the character of painting or the stage, merely introduces into the film in the guise of a material object something that is invisibly present in the film's every shot. This creates a doubling of the semiotic process, which gets stressed and materially manifested. The physical frame of the "quote" heightens its materiality, its exteriority to the actual body of the film (cf. Aumont, *L'Oeil interminable*, 110–115).

65. Bellour, "Le Texte introuvable," 40.

66. Barthes, "The Third Meaning," 65–66.

67. Jenny, "La Stratégie de la forme," 266.

68. Riffaterre, *La Production du texte*, 86.

69. Riffaterre, "Le Tissu du texte," 198.

70. Godard, *Jean-Luc Godard par Jean-Luc Godard*, 216–218.

71. Godard, *Introduction à une véritable histoire du cinéma*, 25.

72. Andrew, "Au Début de Souffle," 18.

73. Bordwell, *The Films of Carl-Theodor Dreyer*, 93–116.

74. Virgil, *The Aeneid*, 129.

75. Baudelaire, "La Mort des pauvres," in *Les Fleurs du mal*, 152.

76. Cocteau, *Poésie 1916–1923*.

77. Riffaterre, *La Production du texte*, 80–81.

78. Godard, *Jean-Luc Godard par Jean-Luc Godard*, 218.

79. Barthes, *The Pleasure of the Text*, 36.

80. Jenny, "La Stratégie de la forme," 262.

81. Riffaterre, "Sémiotique intertextuelle."

82. Kristeva, *Sémiotikè*, 255.

83. Ibid., 256–257.

84. Gide, *Journal 1889–1939*, 41.

85. Dällenbach, "Intertexte et autotexte," 284.

86. Lévi-Strauss, *La Pensée sauvage*, 36.

87. Foucault, *The Order of Things*, 16.

88. Lotman, "Tekst v tekste," 14.

89. Ivanov, "Fil'm v fil'me"; Metz, *Essais sur la signification au cinéma*, 1: 223–228.

90. Bonitzer, *Peinture et cinéma*, 93.

91. Kuntzel, "Le Travail du film, 2," 143.

92. Dante, *Inferno*, Canto XII, v. 73–75. The translation is Allen Mandelbaum's, *Divine Comedy of Dante Alighieri*, 109.

93. Bonitzer, *Peinture et cinéma*, 32.

94. Gunning, "De la fumerie d'opium au thêâtre de la moralité."

95. *Biograph Bulletins, 1908–1912*, 77.

96. Zola, *Les Rougon-Macquart*, 1:509.

97. Zola, *Le Roman expérimental*, 166.

98. Peirce, *Philosophical Writings*, 92.

99. Ibid., 99.

100. de Man, *Allegories of Reading*, 10.

101. Riffaterre, "Sémiotique intertextuelle," 135.

102. Bakhtin, *Voprosy literatury i èstetiki*, 172.

103. Cf. Bialostocki, "Man and Mirror in Painting."

104. Coleridge, *Complete Poetical Works*, 1:295.

105. Dickens, *Mystery of Edwin Drood*, 3–4.

106. Ibid., 65.

107. Du Maurier, *Trilby*, 379.

108. Joyce, *Ulysses*, 526.

109. Carroll, "Interpreting 'Citizen Kane,'" 53.

110. Cozarinsky, *Borges in/and/on Film,* 55–57.
111. Borges, "The Dream of Coleridge," in *Other Inquisitions,* 14–17.

CHAPTER TWO

1. Prawer, *Caligari's Children,* 138–163.
2. Drouzy, *Dreyer né Nilsson,* 256.
3. Ibid., 257–259.
4. Bloom, *The Anxiety of Influence: A Map of Misreading; Poetry and Repression.*
5. Bloom, *Poetry and Repression,* 27.
6. Ibid., 204.
7. Ibid., 10.
8. Jenny, "La Stratégie de la forme," 258.
9. Borges, *Borges: A Reader,* 243.
10. Geduld, *Focus on D. W. Griffith,* 56.
11. Griffith, "The Movies 100 Years from Now," 49–50.
12. Merritt, "Rescued from Perilous Nest," 6.
13. Ibid., 8.
14. Fell, *Film and the Narrative Tradition,* 12–36.
15. Altman, "Dickens, Griffith, and Film Theory Today," 323–324.
16. Merritt, "Rescued from Perilous Nest," 11.
17. Geduld, *Focus on D. W. Griffith,* 32, 33.
18. Merritt, "Rescued from Perilous Nest," 12.
19. Schickel, *D. W. Griffith,* 142.
20. Arvidson, *When Movies Were Young,* 130.
21. Goodman, *Fifty-Year Decline and Fall of Hollywood,* 11.
22. Giuliano and Keenan, "Browning without Words," 145–146.
23. Hogg, "Robert Browning and the Victorian Theatre," 8.
24. *Biograph Bulletins, 1908–1912,* 77.
25. Browning, *Poetical Works,* 359.
26. On this cycle of Browning's poems, see Klimenko, *Tvorchestvo Roberta Brauninga,* 99–116.
27. Browning, *Poetical Works,* 359.
28. Winn, *Unsuspected Eloquence,* 238–239.
29. Görres, "Aforizmy ob iskusstve" (Aphorisms on art), 86.
30. Pater, *The Renaissance,* 145.
31. Cf. Arnim, "O narodnykh pesniakh," 403; and Pater, *The Renaissance,* 150–151.
32. Browning, *Poetical Works,* 127.
33. Ibid., 144.
34. Wordsworth, *The Prelude: Or Growth of a Poet's Mind,* 103.
35. Whitman, *Complete Poems,* 399–400.
36. Arnold, *The Poems of Matthew Arnold,* 337.
37. Browning, *Poetical Works,* 131.
38. For Browning's debt to Hugo, see Hogg, "Robert Browning and the Victorian Theatre," 65; for Diderot, see A. Symons, *Introduction to the Study of Rob-*

ert Browning, 49; Jennings, "A Suggested Source of the Jules-Phene Episode in 'Pippa Passes' "; and for Bulwer-Lytton, see Faverty, "Source of the Jules-Phene Episode."

39. Lytton, *Bulwer's Plays*, 20.

40. Browning, *Poetical Works*, 138.

41. Ibid., 142.

42. Griffith, "The Movies 100 Years from Now," 50.

43. *Biograph Bulletins, 1908–1912*, 251.

44. Ibid., 73.

45. Lytton, *Zanoni*, 118.

46. Gunning, "D. W. Griffith and the Narrator-System," 596.

47. Pruitt, "I Film Biograph 1908–1910," 57.

48. Cf. Graham, Higgins, Mancini, and Vieira, *D. W. Griffith and the Biograph Company*, 179–180.

49. Gunning, "D. W. Griffith and the Narrator-System," 591.

50. Cincotti and Turconi, "I film, i dati, gli argomenti," 241; Brion, "Filmographie de D. W. Griffith," 169.

51. Schickel, *D. W. Griffith*, 209.

52. Brown, *Adventures with D. W. Griffith*, 31.

53. Cf. Hart, *The Man Who Invented Hollywood*.

54. Hislop and Richardson, *Plays by J. H. Payne*, xii.

55. Brown, *Adventures with D. W. Griffith*, 45.

56. Hislop and Richardson, *Plays by J. H. Payne*, 82–83.

57. A. Maier-Meintshel, "Vermeer Del'ftskii i Grigorii Teplov."

58. Griffith, "Le Théâtre et le cinéma," 88.

59. Spitzer, "Explication de texte applied," 17–18.

60. Whitman, *Complete Poems*, 280.

61. Browning, "The Ring and the Book," in *Poetical Works*, 33.

62. Hansen, "Rätsel der Mütterlichkeit."

63. Arnold, *The Poems of Matthew Arnold*, 152.

64. Giuliano and Keenan, "Browning without Words," 149–152.

65. Bloom, "Visionary Cinema of Romantic Poetry," 39.

66. Bordwell, *The Films of Carl-Theodor Dreyer*, 34–36.

67. Gasparov, "Pervochtenie i perechtenie," 19.

68. Panofsky, "Style and Medium in Moving Pictures," 66.

69. Willey, *The Seventeenth Century Background*, 53.

CHAPTER THREE

1. Cf. Arvidson, *When Movies Were Young*, 66; Eisenstein, "Dickens, Griffith and Film Today," in *Film Form*, 195–255; and Eisenstein and Iutkevich, *D. U. Griffit*, 130.

2. Geduld, *Focus on D. W. Griffith*, 52.

3. Eisenstein, "Dickens, Griffith, and Film Today," 205. It is worth noting, however, that neither the published Russian version nor the original manuscript of Eisenstein's article (Sergei Eisenstein Archive, f. 1923, op. 2, ed. khr. 328, RGALI,

Moscow) contains this quote. It was most likely inserted (at Eisenstein's own request?) by the translator Jay Leyda.

4. Ramirez, *El cine de Griffith*, 15.

5. Hart, *The Man Who Invented Hollywood*, 67.

6. Schickel, *D. W. Griffith*, 70. The previous quote is also from Schickel, 41.

7. Arvidson, *When Movies Were Young*, 133.

8. Hart, *The Man Who Invented Hollywood*, 88.

9. Geduld, *Focus on D. W. Griffith*, 53.

10. Griffith, "Cinéma, miracle de la photographie moderne," 18.

11. Ibid., 21.

12. Walt Whitman, "Song of the Universal," *Leaves of Grass*, 286.

13. Locke, *Essay Concerning Human Understanding*, book 3, chapter 2 ("Of the Signification of Words"), 323–326, and chapter 9 ("Of the Imperfection of Words"), 385–397.

14. Gura, *Wisdom of Words*, 19–31.

15. See Kayser, "La Doctrine du langage naturel."

16. Miller, *The Transcendentalists*, 57.

17. Emerson, *Complete Writings*, 8–9.

18. Ibid., 245.

19. Irwin, *American Hieroglyphics*, 17, 20, 33.

20. Emerson, *Complete Writings*, 243–244.

21. Hart, *The Man Who Invented Hollywood*, 68.

22. Griffith, "L'Avenir du film à deux dollars," 23.

23. Emerson, *Complete Writings*, 9.

24. Griffith, "Le Cinéma et les bûchers," 21.

25. Emerson, *Complete Writings*, 244.

26. Emerson, *Works of Ralph Waldo Emerson*, 2:254.

27. Emerson, *Complete Writings*, 249.

28. Ibid., 232.

29. Poe, *Works of Edgar Allan Poe*, vol. 2, *Tales*, 318. J. Hagan, in "Cinema and the Romantic Tradition," 233–235, has pointed to the connections existing between Poe's story and cinema, as well as the theory of correspondences. Well before Hagan, the theme of the urban crowd, including its treatment in Poe's text, was linked to the appearance of cinema by Walter Benjamin in *Charles Baudelaire: Lyic Poet*, 54. Benjamin discovers two specific kinds of attitudes toward urban reality in nineteenth-century European culture that seem to me to be fundamental to cinema as well. The first is typified by Poe himself, when the narrator merges with the crowd and wanders in its midst, becoming a kind of moving eye—the eye of the *flaneur*. Benjamin traces the second attitude back to E. T. A. Hoffmann's "The Cousin's Corner Window," where the mobile universe of the street is studied by the paralyzed hero from his window (ibid., 48–55). Hoffmann's hero observes the world through a pair of binoculars, from an elevated box in his own improvised theater. Benjamin rightly observes that he chooses a position that allows him to elevate reality to the level of art. As the development of early cinema and cinema theory shows (e.g., cf. Macmahon below), this latter mode of "elevating" reality to art was initially dominant; hence the prolonged hegemony enjoyed by the metaphor of the cinema screen as a *window* onto the world.

30. Kauffman and Henstell, *American Film Criticism*, 93.

31. Lindsay, *Art of the Moving Picture*, 67.

32. Emerson, *Complete Writings*, 234. Emerson's critique of sculpture is linked to his sense of the evolution of language: "The art of sculpture is long ago perished to any real effect. It was originally a useful art, a mode of writing. . . . But it is the game of a rude and youthful people, and not the manly labor of a wise and spiritual nation. . . . I cannot hide from myself that there is a certain appearance of paltriness, as of toys and the trumpery of a theatre, in sculpture . . . I do not wonder that Newton, with an attention habitually engaged on the paths of planets and suns, should have wondered what the Earl of Pembroke found to admire in 'stone dolls.'. . . true art is never fixed, but always flowing."

33. Griffith, "Le Cinéma et les bûchers," 20.

34. Cf. Mancini, "La Teoria cinematografica di Hugo Munsterberg."

35. Lindsay, *Letters*, 133.

36. Varilä, "Swedenborgian Background of William James's Philosophy."

37. Emerson, *Complete Writings*, 231.

38. Münsterberg, *The Film*, 64,

39. Ibid., 74.

40. Lindsay, *Letters*, 133.

41. Ibid., 158.

42. Ibid., 137.

43. Schickel, *D. W. Griffith*, 112.

44. Jacques Aumont, in his analysis of this episode in the 1911 film *Enoch Arden* ("Griffith, le cadre, la figure," 58–60), has noted that the diegetic heterogeneity of the spaces occupied by Annie Lee and Enoch Arden is at the same time undermined by their figurative proximity, which can be explained by the fact that both husband and wife were filmed at the same site by the seashore. This similarity in landscape unconsciously heightens the contradictory nature of the spatial codes at work, creating a powerful sense of closeness even where the places at stake are thematically situated thousands of kilometers from each other.

45. Tennyson, "Enoch Arden," in *Poems of Tennyson*, 2:638.

46. Tennyson, *Poems of Tennyson*, 2:641.

47. See Hartlaub, *Zauber des Spiegels*, 22.

48. Quoted in Langen, "Zur Geschichte des Spiegelsymbols," 272.

49. De Quincey, *Confessions of an English Opium-eater*, 273. Cf. the vision of "spring-faced cherubs that did sleep / Like water lilies on that motionless deep," in the fragment by Thomas Hood, "The Sea of Death" (in *Complete Poetical Works*, 184). These visions of "celestial" faces in water in De Quincey and Hood clearly assume the notion of water as a mirror to the heavens. Cf. also the universal identification of the heavenly bodies with mirrors reflecting the eyes of the dead (see Roheim, *Spiegelzauber*, 232–251).

50. Baudelaire, *Artificial Paradises*, 123.

51. Ibid., 63–64.

52. Miller, *The Transcendentalists*, 386–387.

53. Thoreau, *The Portable Thoreau*, 22.

54. Thoreau, *Works of Thoreau*, 588.

55. Ibid., 593.

56. Cf. the notions prevalent in the philosophy of nature concerning water as a universal medium. Johann Wilhelm Ritter (1810), for example, wrote: "Water is the medium of hearing. . . . Water is a bridge linking all things possible in the world to us" (Ritter, *Fragmente aus dem Nachlasse eines jungen Physikers*, 195).

57. Whitman, *Complete Prose Works*, 88.

58. Ibid., 89.

59. Asselineau, *Transcendentalist Constant in American Literature*, 44.

60. Matthiessen, *American Renaissance*, 566–567.

61. Whitman, "On the Beach at Night Alone," in *Leaves of Grass*, 327.

62. De Quincey, *Selected Writings*, 884–885.

63. Villiers de l'Isle-Adam, *Oeuvres Complètes*, 3:193.

64. Ibid., 204.

65. Whitman, "Out of the Cradle Endlessly Rocking," in *Leaves of Grass*, 316.

66. Collins, *The Uses of Observation*, 107.

67. De Quincey, *Collected Writings*, 13:321, 346.

68. Ibid., 883.

69. Balzac, "L'Enfant maudit," in *La Comedie humaine*, 10:913–914.

70. Ibid., 914.

71. Kingsley, *Poems*, 67; Gandolfo, "*The Sands of Dee:* Analisi di un dramma marino di D. W. Griffith," 26–28.

72. De Quincey, *Confessions of an English Opium-eater*, 104.

73. Tommasino, "Griffith: Una catalisi trasgressiva," 175.

74. Fell, *Film and the Narrative Tradition*, 31.

75. Cf. Marie, "La Scène des fantasmes originaires."

76. Abel, "Point-of-view Shots," 75.

77. Gaudreault, *Du littéraire au filmique.*

78. Artaud, *Oeuvres complètes*, 3:82.

79. Strangely enough, Griffith's playful attitude toward the titles of texts has not provoked any surprise among his critics. R. M. Henderson, a Griffith specialist, in *D. W. Griffith: His Life and Work*, writes as if it were something natural: "Griffith had now decided to expand that film, no longer relying on the Charles Kingsley poem as a source, but following the original Tennyson poem and taking the original title *Enoch Arden*" (101).

80. Poe, *Poetical Works*, 99.

81. Ibid., 96.

82. Ibid., 106.

83. Whitman, "Out of the Cradle Endlessly Rocking," in *Leaves of Grass*, 316.

84. Ibid.

85. Ibid., 313.

86. Irwin, *American Hieroglyphics*.

87. The recent publication of Eisenstein's article "Po lichnomu voprosu" (Speaking personally) establishes beyond a doubt that Eisenstein knew Lindsay's book, which he refers to (*Iz tvorcheskogo naslediia S. M. Èizenshteina*, 34). This fact raises the question of the link between Eisenstein's pictographic theory of cinema and Lindsay's hieroglyphic theory of cinema.

88. Yoder, *Emerson and the Orphic Poet*, 40.

89. Lindsay, *Art of the Moving Picture*, 23. The connection between hieroglyphics

and dreams had already been established in the eighteenth century by W. Warburton, who had written: "At that time all the Egyptians saw their gods as creators of a science of hieroglyphics. Nothing could thus be more natural than supposing that these same gods, whom they also believed responsible for creating dreams, employed the same language for dreams as for hieroglyphics" (Warburton, *Essai sur les hiéroglyphes*, 193). Warburton believed that Egyptian oneirocriticism (the interpretation of dreams) was based on the hieroglyphic system of writing.

90. Lindsay, *Collected Poems*, xxii.

91. Poe, *Poetical Works*, 81.

92. Poe, from "A Dream within a Dream," *Poetical Works*, 103.

93. Poe, *Poetical Works*, 104.

94. Phillips, *Griffith: Titan of the Film Art*, 109.

95. Lindsay, *Art of the Moving Picture*, 152.

96. Ibid.

97. Ibid., 202.

98. Ibid., 250.

99. Lindsay, *Collected Poems*, xxiv.

100. Swedenborg, *Heaven and Its Wonders and Hell*, 137.

101. Hudnut, *Architecture and the Spirit of Man*, 352.

102. Lindsay cited in Massa, *Vachel Lindsay: Fieldworker for the American Dream*, 33.

103. Schlesinger, *Rise of the City*, 436.

104. Lindsay, *Letters*, 302.

105. Lindsay, *Art of the Moving Picture*, 176, 177–178. We have already seen elsewhere the image of the crowd as sea, which appears on page 176.

106. Hart, *The Man Who Invented Hollywood*, 67.

107. Brown, *Adventures with D. W. Griffith*, 168, 172,

108. Lindsay, *Art of the Moving Picture*, 19. Later on Lindsay wrote a poem specifically devoted to this episode from *Intolerance* called "Darling Daughter of Babylon." The poem brings in all of Griffith's themes, such as Balthasar as the priest of love, the antagonism between Ishtar and Baal, and so forth.

109. Phillips, *Griffith: Titan of the Film Art*, 197.

110. Ramsaye, *A Million and One Nights*, 758–759. Michael Rogin has written a significant study of the feminine symbols in *Intolerance*. He points out that, to a great extent, the film is based on the opposition between Ishtar as the embodiment of fertility and eroticism, and Lillian Gish who rocks the cradle and whose image is derived from "classical and Christian representations" that "desexualize motherhood" (Rogin, "The Great Mother Domesticated," 524). The notion of maternity without eros is precisely what allows Gish to be hieroglyphically coded as the overarching sign that originates the text. Rogin notes that the cradle is the place in which both films and children are raised (522).

111. Eisenstein, *Izbrannye proivedeniia*, 5:169.

112. Ibid., 159.

113. O'Dell, *Griffith and the Rise of Hollywood*, 42.

114. Brown, *Adventures with D. W. Griffith*, 166.

115. Whitman, "Out of the Cradle Endlessly Rocking," in *Leaves of Grass*, 310.

116. Brown, *Adventures with D. W. Griffith*, 166.

117. Hugo, *Oeuvres complètes*, 2:498.

118. Hugo, "Fonction du poète," in *Oeuvres complètes*, 2:921.

119. Hugo, "Je lisais. Que lisais-je?" in *Oeuvres complètes*, 2:342–343.

120. Spitzer, "Explication de texte applied."

121. De Quincey, *Confessions of an English Opium-eater*, 193.

122. Baudelaire, *Les Paradis artificiels*, 105.

123. De Quincey, *Collected Writings*, 13:360.

124. Poe, *Poetical Works*, 97–99.

125. Hugo, *La légende des siècles*, part 5, "La Ville disparue," 64–66.

126. Balzac, "L'Enfant maudit," in *La Comédie humaine*, 10:915.

127. Nerval, *Oeuvres*, 870. The city as a metaphor for the ocean is a venerable folkloric motif. So, for example, the "City of Bronze" from the *Thousand and One Nights* has been viewed by some as a metaphor for the ocean: "In Arab philosophy there is a current that views the ocean as evil and a mortal threat. The simplest contact with it can kill, it smells of putrefaction, it designates the end of the world, the principle of darkness and the nether world. [Thus] the city on the far west, being on the ocean's [*Tekhoma*] edge, is the city of death: it bears the same traits as the ocean itself. And, like the nether world, it is full of treasures. . . . The story of the City of Bronze is, in essence, a myth of the ocean" (Gerhardt, *Iskusstvo povestvovaniia*, 179–180). On the underwater city in Russian and specifically St. Petersburg eschatalogy, see Iurii M. Lotman, "Simvolika Peterburga i problemy semiotiki goroda," 31–34.

128. Cros and Corbière, *Oeuvres Complètes*, 1:179.

129. Emerson, *Complete Writings*, 127.

130. Balzac, *Seraphita*, 157.

131. Gunning, "Note per una Comprensione dei film di Griffith," 21.

132. Münsterberg, *The Film*, 74.

133. Bowser, "Griffith e la struttura circolare in alcuni film Biograph."

134. Lotman, *Analiz poèticheskogo teksta*, 68.

135. Bloom, *The Anxiety of Influence*, 43.

136. Doane, *The Desire to Desire*, 5.

137. Hansen, "The Hieroglyph and the Whore," 369.

138. Fenollosa, *The Chinese Written Character as a Medium for Poetry*, 12, 17. Fenollosa formulated his theory of the ideogram in 1908, but his book *The Chinese Written Character as a Medium for Poetry* was published by Ezra Pound in 1919. I have consciously not insisted on any possible resemblances between Griffith's films and Pound's poetry, since (as Ronald Bush has pointed out in *The Genesis of Ezra Pound's "Cantos,"* 10–11) Pound's move toward a poetics of the ideogram dates only to 1927; before this date, Pound in fact used the term dismissively (as in his 1921 review of a volume of poetry by Cocteau). In the early thirties, Pound retrospectively claimed to have experimented with ideogrammatic poetry as far back as 1913 (in *ABC of Reading*). It is worth noting, however, that Vachel Lindsay (*Art of the Moving Picture*, 267–269) with characteristic perspicacity pointed to the proximity of imagism to the cinema back in 1915, urging the imagist poets to move consciously toward the cinema as a form.

139. Jakobson, *Essais de linguistique générale*, 63.

CHAPTER FOUR

1. Cf. Tsiv'ian, "K istorii idei intellektual'nogo kino," 1988.
2. Malevich, "Pis'ma k M. V. Matiushinu," 180.
3. Lyotard, *Le Postmoderne expliqué aux enfants*, 26–27.
4. Nakov, "De la peinture sans référant verbal," 50, 48.
5. Ibid., 50.
6. Léger, "Présentation du 'Ballet mécanique,'" 64–65.
7. Léger, *Fonctions de la peinture*, 138–139.
8. Ibid., 140.
9. Léger, "Moskva, Eizenshteinu," 86.
10. Léger, *Fonctions de la peinture*, 165.
11. Cf. Iampolski, "Problema vzaimodeistviia iskusstv i neosushchestvlennyi mul'tfil'm Fernana Lezhe 'Charli-kubist.'"
12. Lawder, *Cubist Cinema*, 79–97.
13. Cendrars, *Oeuvres complètes*, 13:93.
14. Cendrars, *Blaise Cendrars*, 543–546.
15. Vanoye, "Le Cinéma de Cendrars."
16. Lawder, *Cubist Cinema*, 89.
17. Ibid., 89–90.
18. Parrot, *Blaise Cendrars*, 46.
19. Ibid., 46.
20. Pound, *Ezra Pound and the Visual Arts*, 175. This text, the only significant statement Pound ever made about the cinema, is very interesting. Several of its formulations betray points in common with Léger's article "A Critical Essay on the Plastic Significance of Abel Gance's *La Roue*." In any case, Gance's film is interpreted by Pound as a plastic experiment in film.
21. The composer George Antheil has asserted that the idea of *Ballet mécanique* is his, and that it was Pound who got Dudley Murphy involved in the film; Murphy, in turn, joined forces with Léger (see Lawder, *Cubist Cinema*, 117). Léger acknowledged that the multiplication of the object in the prism was suggested to him by Murphy and Pound (Lawder, *Cubist Cinema*, 137; Léger, "Présentation du 'Ballet mécanique,'" 64). This idea, in fact, originated not with Pound but with Alvin Langdon Coburn, the leading theoretician of the movement known as vorticism, whose photos are remarkably similar to certain frames in *Ballet mécanique*.
22. Charansol, *40 ans de cinéma*, 76.
23. Gance, "Blaise Cendrars et le cinéma," 171.
24. Gance, "Témoignage d'Abel Gance," xx.
25. Sadoul, "Fernand Léger ou la cinéplastique," 74.
26. Cendrars, *Oeuvres complètes*, 13:188.
27. Epstein, *Ecrits sur le cinéma*, 1:55.
28. Ibid., 47–48, 55.
29. Cendrars, *Oeuvres complètes*, 13:95–96.
30. In 1950, Cendrars recalled the ballet *Relâche* by Erik Satie: "I wrote the libretto for old Satie. Francis Picabia ripped off my idea for the plot and the cinematic interlude of *Entr'acte*, thanks to which René Clair was able to make his debut as a director. Picabia had taken advantage of my departure for Brazil" (ibid., 148).

31. Quoted in Sadoul, *Histoire générale du cinéma,* 5:146.

32. Hamp, *Le Rail,* 121.

33. I quote a typical section from Arroy's book, which is a unique phenomenon in the history of film criticism: "His face emits a warm glow, the gleaming spirituality and dull transparency of glasswork. In vain I strive to remember all the rosettes I have seen, I cannot remember which rosette emitted such a glow from its center. But I know that I will soon see this devouring flame in the heart of the great rose of that cathedral of light which he is now building, completely alone, in the anguished joy of a superhuman labor of birth. And I know too that the Gothic sun which will transform this *wheel* fitted with crystal rods into laughter and tears of light cannot wound the souls with love more dangerously than they are already being devoured by this dull fever, that singes the face which preserves forever its age of twenty years under its silver hair" (Arroy, *En tournant "Napoléon" avec Abel Gance,* 6; emphasis added). Gance himself liked to play the saint, typically portraying Christ in one of his films, and then handing out photographs of himself dressed for the part with a crown of thorns on his head. One copy was given to Sergei Eisenstein. Gance's favorite theme was the church of the future, a cinematic "church of light."

34. Ibid., 12–13.

35. Epstein, *Ecrits sur le cinéma,* 1:175. Gance transformed the wheel as an instrument of torture (breaking on the wheel) into his personal insignia. He had special letterhead paper made with bloody illustrations of victims being broken as a rather pretentious decorative motif for the margins. Cf. Gance's letters to I. Mozzhukhin in the Russian State Archives for Literature and Art (RGALI), Moscow, F.2632, op.1, ed. khr.170.

36. Icart, "A la découverte de 'La Roue,' " 186.

37. Brownlow, *The Parade's Gone By,* 600.

38. Danis died on April 9, 1921 (see ibid., 623).

39. Cf. Dan Yack's reply: "I created a company for her, the Mireille Film Society. That's a nice April's Fool's Day surprise, don't you think? Think of it, nowadays you can create a company just to please a woman" (Cendrars, *Oeuvres complètes,* 13:173). As an assistant, Cendrars must have constantly been a witness to Gance's arbitrary whims, as the latter arranged the entire shooting schedule and even the conception of the film according to the needs of his lover.

40. I should also like to advance the suggestion that there are reminiscences of *La Roue* in Ivan Goll's poetry. Published in 1951 shortly after Goll's death on March 13, 1950, the cycle "Magic Circles" clearly indicates Goll's immersion in mystical culture, including the Kabbalah. It is also worth noting that Léger was to provide the text's illustrations. The cycle opens with a text that is devoted to the symbol of the circle: "Caught in the circle of my star / Turning with the wheel that spins in my heart / And the millstone of the universe that grinds the seeds of time." There then follows a fragment that can be read as the intertextual contamination of scenes from two films, Gance's *La Roue* and Cocteau's *Orphée* (1949). In the first case, I am thinking of the scene in which Eli perishes by falling into a ravine in the mountains; in the second—the moment where the angel Heurtebise penetrates beyond the looking glass through the mirror-water (this scene, in turn, is a response to an analogous episode from Cocteau's earlier *Sang du poète* (1931). Here are the

lines from Goll: "Who is the personage who runs on the edge of the wheel / Who climbs the mountain while falling to the bottom of his grave? / Neither he nor I expect a reply / The wind of the astral vault severs our memory / I try all the worn-out keys in order to break the circle / I throw the letters of the alphabet like anchors in the oblivion. . . . And if I attempt the angel-like leap into the mirror / A thousand new circles run to the edge of the world" (Goll, *Ivan Goll*, 172–173).

41. Cendrars, *Oeuvres complètes*, 4:96.

42. Ibid., 77. Bozon-Scalzitti's comment can be found in "Blaise Cendrars et le symbolisme," 57.

43. Cendrars, *Oeuvres complètes*, 6:51.

44. Cendrars, "Origine de l'idée de 'Perpetuum mobile,'" 207–208.

45. Cendrars, *Oeuvres complètes*, 4:207.

46. Ibid., 214.

47. Ibid., 218.

48. Ibid., 211.

49. Gance, "Témoignage d'Abel Gance," xxi.

50. Cendrars, *Moravagine*, 196–197.

51. Cendrars also connects cinema with demotic writing in *A B C du cinéma* (1917–1921), where the evolution of the cosmos is metaphorically rendered as the evolution of the different forms of writing (*Oeuvres complètes*, 6:22).

52. Cendrars, *Moravagine*, 231–234.

53. Golding, *Cubism: A History and an Analysis*, 173.

54. See Chefdor, "Blaise Cendrars et le simultanéisme."

55. Cendrars, *Inédits secrets*, 386.

56. Delaunay, *Du cubisme à l'art abstrait*, 115.

57. One exception is the 1905 painting *Landscape with Disc*, in which Michel Hoog sees "the circle as a formal element and a cosmic symbol" (*Delaunay*, 25). I am inclined to think that Hoog is here reading into the painting a meaning that could not have been intended at the time of its making.

58. Jaffé, "Symbolism in the Visual Arts," 247.

59. Damase and Delaunay, *Sonia Delaunay: Rythmes et couleurs*, 83.

60. Jean-Claude Lovey has observed: "Into his notion of simultaneism Cendrars introduces an extremely fecund principle: the principle of contrast as productive of depth" (*Situation de Blaise Cendrars*, 236). I would suggest that Cendrars did not invent this principle—which by and large was of a painterly and technical nature and was probably invented by Delaunay—but can be credited for giving it a mythic currency.

61. Cendrars, *Inédits secrets*, 385.

62. Ibid., 386.

63. Delaunay, *Du cubisme à l'art abstrait*, 76.

64. Cendrars, *Oeuvres complètes*, 14:303.

65. Schmalenbach, *Fernand Léger*, 98.

66. Sarane Alexandrian (*Marcel Duchamp*, 33) has pointed to the connection between Duchamp's *Bicycle Wheel* and Delaunay's Newtonian disks. Duchamp is also probably hinting at another of Delaunay's favorite motifs, the "Big Wheel," an attraction located next to the Eiffel Tower and depicted by Delaunay in his famous painting *L'Équipe de Cardiff* (1912–1913), as well as in other works that are less well

known. The "Big Wheel" was also celebrated many times by French poets of Cendrars's milieu.

67. Cendrars, "Fernand Léger," 215.

68. Cendrars, *Du monde entier,* 104–105.

69. Francastel, *L'Image, la vision et l'imaginaire,* 196.

70. Delaunay, *Du cubisme à l'art abstrait,* 209.

71. Goll, "Das Kinodram," 224.

72. Soupault, "Enfin Cendrars vint . . . ou tel qu'en lui-même enfin," 86.

73. Epstein, *Ecrits sur le cinéma,* 1:35.

74. Quoted in Buhler, *Blaise Cendrars,* 80.

75. Cendrars, *Oeuvres complètes,* 4:191.

76. Ibid., 14:296.

77. Somewhat later this motif would resurface in the screenplay for Gance's film *Les Altantes* (1918), where, judging by the surviving plans for the film, the representation of the apocalypse was to take up a great deal of space (see Cendrars, *Inédits secrets,* 410–412). *Les Altantes* was never made. But much later Gance did make the film *La Fin du monde* (1931), which, although quite remote from Cendrars's ideas, is in fact a variation on themes that originated with the writer Camille Flammarion, who exerted a great influence on both Cendrars's and Gance's myth of the apocalypse.

78. Cendrars, *Oeuvres complètes,* 2:21.

79. Ibid., 28.

80. Ibid., 29.

81. Ibid., 30.

82. Cendrars, *Bourlinguer,* 234.

83. Survage, "Le Rythme coloré."

84. Cendrars, *Oeuvres complètes,* 6:49–51; emphasis added.

85. Leroy, "Cendrars, le futurisme et la fin du monde."

86. Gance, *L'Art cinématographique,* 2:93.

87. Epstein, *Ecrits sur le cinéma,* 1:42, 48–49.

88. *Ballet suédois 1920–1925,* 29.

89. Descargues, *Fernand Léger,* 67–68.

90. Cendrars, *Oeuvres complètes,* 2:14.

91. Cendrars, *Moravagine,* 36.

92. Cendrars, *Oeuvres complètes,* 2:111. A similar erotic description of Rougha's cinematic dance can also be found in the epilogue (sections 829–840), 2:128.

93. Léger, "Moskva, Èizenshteinu," 141.

94. Léger, *Fonctions de la peinture,* 153.

95. See Sitney, "Image and Title in Avant-Garde Cinema," 102–105.

96. Michelson, "'Anemic Cinema': Reflections on an Emblematic Work," 69.

97. Cendrars, *Moravagine,* 225.

98. Cendrars, *Bourlinguer,* 349.

99. Gourmont, "The Dissociation of Ideas," 28.

100. Ibid., 26.

101. Gourmont, *Physique de l'amour,* 69.

102. Cendrars, *Bourlinguer,* 356–358.

103. Cendrars, *Moravagine,* 63–65.

104. Ibid., 66.

105. Cendrars, *A B C du cinéma*, in *Oeuvres complètes*, 6:21. Cendrars's numerology here has a clearly mystical import. The text continues as follows: "A numeral. As in the Middle Ages the rhinoceros is Christ; the bear is the devil, the jasper—liveliness, the chrysoprase—pure humility. 6 and 9." Cendrars's symbolism is clearly fantastic (e.g., the purely personal association of Christ with a rhinoceros). This poetic Pythagoreanism is probably connected to Cendrars's love for astrology. Nonetheless, a numerical or rhythmic yoking together of the stars with all living things through a principle of a cyclic sexual energy was a notion pursued by other artists as well. There is a curiously similar numerological myth of astral eroticism in the writings of Freud's friend Wilhelm Fliess, particularly in his chief work, *The Rhythm of Life* (1906). But there is no evidence that Cendrars knew Fliess's work.

106. Cendrars, "Pompon," in *Oeuvres complètes*, 15:137.

107. Cendrars, *Moravagine*, 351.

108. Ibid., 351-352.

109. Miller's famous works *Tropic of Cancer* and *Tropic of Capricorn* were written under Moricand's influence. Miller also dedicated *A Devil in Paradise* to Moricand, a book that throws some light on Moricand's life. It is curious that in this work Miller named Cendrars's *L'Eubage* as one of the most important books on mysticism that he had studied (*A Devil in Paradise*, 23). It is also possible that Moricand introduced Cendrars to the teachings of Jakob Boehme, who, in turn, would have influenced Gance's rendering of the symbol of the wheel via Cendrars. In any case, Boehme is one of the authors Moricand passed on to Miller (cf. Martin, *Always Merry and Bright*, 318).

110. Cendrars, *Oeuvres complètes*, 2:43.

111. Cendrars, *L'Eubage*, 56; emphasis added.

112. Ibid., 57.

113. Ibid., 59-60.

114. Léger, *Fonctions de la peinture*, 164.

115. Schmalenbach, *Fernand Léger*, 116.

116. Cendrars, *Oeuvres complètes*, 15:136.

117. Ibid., 135.

118. Derouet, "Léger et le cinéma," 132-138.

CHAPTER FIVE

1. Virmaux, *Les Surréalistes et le cinéma*, 73.

2. Desnos, *Cinéma*, 157.

3. Ibid., 165.

4. Breton, *Les Manifestes du surréalisme*, 73.

5. Buñuel, "Notes on the Making of 'Un Chien andalou,'" 29-30.

6. In one case the prologue has been understood as the description of infantile sexuality, whereby the eye is a symbol of the female sexual organ and the razor of the male (see Durgnat, *Luis Buñuel*, 23-24). Elsewhere the prologue has been seen as an embodiment of various castration complexes and phantasms (see Marie, "Le Rasoir et la lune," 196-197). Marie, however, does ground his reading in a surre-

alist intertext by linking the prologue to Georges Bataille's *Histoire de l'oeil,* which was written not long after and not without the influence of Buñuel.

7. Williams, "Prologue to 'Un Chien andalou,'" 30–31.

8. Buñuel, *My Last Sigh,* 103.

9. Bataille, *Oeuvres complètes,* 1:211.

10. Dali, *Catalogue de la rétrospective,* 48.

11. Aranda, *Buñuel: A Critical Biography,* 67.

12. Ibid., 59. Immediately before commencing work on *Un Chien andalou,* Buñuel would claim in *La Gazeta Literaria* that the close-up shot was invented in literature by Ramón Gómez de la Serna long before Griffith, who may well have borrowed it from the latter (Buñuel, "O fotogenichnom plane," 119).

13. Drummond, "Textual Space in 'Un Chien andalou,'" 60.

14. Gómez de la Serna, *Movieland,* 61–62.

15. Ibid., 61.

16. Ibid., 62.

17. Ibid., 63.

18. Ibid., 64.

19. Ibid., 104.

20. Riffaterre, *La Production du texte,* 223.

21. Ibid., 249.

22. Ibid.

23. Desnos, *Cinéma,* 22–24.

24. Ibid., 28.

25. Derouet, "Léger et le cinéma," 142.

26. Virmaux, *Les Surréalistes et le cinéma,* 221–227.

27. Kyrou, *Buñuel: An Introduction,* 135.

28. Breton and Soupault, *Les Champs magnétiques,* 116, 76.

29. Breton, *Nadja,* 61.

30. Breton and Soupault, *Les Champs magnétiques,* 42.

31. Arp, *Jours effeuillés,* 31.

32. Buñuel, "Buñuel par Buñuel," 63–64.

33. Cf. Boczkowska, *Tryumf Luny i Wenus,* 38–39.

34. Artaud, *Oeuvres complètes,* 1:141.

35. Éluard, *Poèmes,* 105.

36. Breton and Soupault, *Les Champs magnétiques,* 71.

37. Tzara, *L'Homme approximatif,* 27; Virmaux, *Les Surréalistes et le cinéma,* 223.

38. Soupault, *Poèmes et poésies,* 140.

39. Breton, *Le Revolver à cheveux blancs,* 111.

40. This motif migrates to other French films as well, although no longer in the form of a visualized trope but rather as an element of the plot (the assimilation of a trope into the plot is characteristic of the period in which the avant-garde disintegrates). In Vigo's *L'Atalante* (1934), a severed hand preserved in spirits is kept as a curiosity by an old eccentric seaman. In Maurice Tourneur's *La Main du Diable* (1943), a severed arm in a casket serves as the Devil's talisman that leads to the death of the hero. Here are further examples from Soupault: "You probably have to cut them [the hands] off in order to stop loving them" (*Poèmes et poésies,* 135). Elsewhere the poet sees "clouds and birds (naturally), stars and arms" (ibid.,

136). Here the subtext actualizes the motif of the starfish, which resembles a hand.

41. Roudaut, "Un geste, un regard," 836–838.

42. Breton and Soupault, *Les Champs magnétiques*, 117.

43. "To my side there abruptly appears a man who changes into a woman, and then into an old man. At that moment there appears another old man, who changes into a baby and then into a woman" (Soupault, *Poèmes et poésies*, 136). Linda Williams has rightly called these primitive metaphors typologically "Mélièsian" (*Figures of Desire*, 5). "Mélièsian" metaphor might be termed one of the founding elements of avant-garde cinema even in its most diverse orientations (cf. Sergei Eisenstein's film *Glumov's Diary* [1923], which is constructed entirely on such devices). The profusion of metamorphoses in *Entr'acte* has allowed Marc Bertran (somewhat baselessly) to collapse the distinction between surrealist cinema and the film by Clair and Picabia. Bertran considers metamorphosis to be the principal feature of surrealist film ("Image cinématographique et image surréaliste").

44. Breton wrote of Péret that at the basis of his works lies a "generalized principle of mutation, metamorphosis" (*Anthologie de l'humour noir*, 385). Cf. also Matthews, *Benjamin Péret*, 87, 113.

45. Péret, *Mort aux vaches et au champ d'honneur*, 40, 76, 56–57.

46. Matthews, *Benjamin Péret*, 47.

47. Dali, *Catalogue de la rétrospective*, 68.

48. The erotic function of marine animals has a subterranean presence throughout surrealist writing. Sometimes it surfaces in a more obvious way: "I then noticed that a jellyfish had lodged between my legs, resulting in a voluptuousness so incommensurable that in a moment there was nothing more that I could desire" (Péret, *Mort aux vaches et au champ d'honneur*, 24).

49. Breteque, "'A l'échelle animale': Notes pour un Bestiaire," 64.

50. Péret, *Mort aux vaches et au champ d'honneur*, 118. The film theater is showing a film on the "different ways to tame snails." The sea also appears extensively in the "scientific" films of Jean Painlevé, which the surrealists held in high esteem: *La Daphnie* (1928), *La Pieuvre* (1928), *Les Oursins* (1928), *Le Bernard-l'Ermite* (1930), *Les Crevettes* (1930), and so forth. Also important in this regard are Eric Satie's *Les Embrions déséchés*, with its fictitious crustaceans, and Breton and Soupault's *Les Champs magnétiques*, sections of which are written as if by a mollusk.

51. Breton, *Arcane 17*, 90. Cf. also Eigeldinger, *Poésie et metamorphose*, 207–208.

52. Kyrou, *Buñuel: An Introduction*, 136.

53. Aranda, *Buñuel: A Critical Biography*, 270.

54. Buñuel, *Mon dernier soupir*, 125.

55. Breton, *Le Revolver à cheveux blancs*, 57.

56. Péret, *Mort aux vaches et au champ d'honneur*, 47–48.

57. Breton, *Poèmes*, 50–51.

58. Artaud, *Héliogabale ou l'anarchiste couronné*, 139.

59. Breton and Soupault, *Les Champs magnétiques*, 106.

60. Kyrou, *Buñuel: An Introduction*, 243.

61. Descargues, *Fernand Léger*, 64.

62. Painter, *Marcel Proust 1904–1922*, 398.

63. Proust, *La Prisonnière*, 222–223.

64. Montesquiou, *Diptyque de Flandre. Triptyque de France*, 13.

65. Ibid., 19.

66. Castelnau, *Belle époque*, 232.

67. Painter, *Marcel Proust 1871–1903*, 179.

68. Solomon-Godeau, "The Legs of the Countess," 296.

69. Painter, *Marcel Proust 1871–1903*, 177.

70. Balakian, *Literary Origins of Surrealism*, 17.

71. Quoted in ibid., 18.

72. Dali, *Catalogue de la rétrospective*, 202.

73. Ibid., 352–353.

74. Buchole, *L'Évolution poétique de Robert Desnos*, 46.

75. Eliade, *Images et symboles*, 164: "Oysters, seashells, snails, pearls, are connected both to cosmologies of the sea and to sexual symbolism. They all effectively partake of the sacred powers that are concentrated in the Waters, in the Moon, in Woman; they are, for various reasons, emblems of the latter forces: there is a resemblance between the seashell and the genital organs of a woman, a relationship that links oysters, water and the moon; there is also a gynecological and embryological symbolism in the pearl that is formed in a shell. The belief in the magical virtues of the oysters and the shell is found the world over, from prehistory to modern times." (For a detailed investigation of the connection between the pearl and rites of burial and death, cf. Eliade, ibid., 178–190.)

76. Eliot, *The Waste Land*, lines 48, 124; pp. 71, 75.

77. Desnos, "A présent," in *Anthologie des poètes de la N.R.F.*, 145.

78. Buñuel, "Buñuel par Buñuel," 65.

79. Cf. Damisch, *Théorie du (nuage)*, 54–55. Of *The Triumph of Virtue* Damisch writes that "after the space of analogies the painting opens up the space of metamorphoses from which art derives its nourishment and origin: the painting has only to profit from an 'invention' by finding inspiration in the constantly changing forms of the clouds" (55). Interestingly, Proust also found Mantegna's clouds to be of particular symbolic importance (cf. Chevrier and Legars, "L'Atelier Elstir," 46–47).

80. For a review of this literature, see Drummond, "Textual Space in 'Un Chien andalou,'" 73–82.

81. Ibid., 78–80.

82. Delluc, *Charlot*, 31; emphasis added.

83. Dali, *Catalogue de la rétrospective*, 56.

84. Bataille, *Oeuvres complètes*, 1:211.

85. Dali, *Catalogue de la rétrospective*, 48.

86. Buñuel, *Mon dernier soupir*, 70.

87. Apollinaire, *Oeuvres complètes*, 1:80.

88. Ibid., 90.

89. Hugo, "Montfaucon," in *La Légende des siècles*, 114.

90. Hugo, *Les Châtiments*, 287.

91. Baudelaire, "Une charogne," in *Les Fleurs du mal*, 34–35.

92. Cf. Matthews, *Benjamin Péret*, 144–146.

93. Buñuel, "Interview by J. de la Colina and T. Perez-Turrent," 12.

94. Soupault, *Vingt mille et un jours*, 70.

95. Matthews, *Benjamin Péret*, 144; emphasis added.

96. Péret, "Jeanne d'Arc," in *Oeuvres complètes*, 1:145; emphasis added.

97. Ibid., 258; emphasis added. Cf. Apollinaire's statement in *L'Enchanteur pourrissant* that "the Pope's shit" should be counted as one of the world's "great rarities" (40).

98. Péret, *Oeuvres complètes*, 1:246, 280; emphasis added.

99. Ibid., 262; emphasis added.

100. Ibid., 238.

101. Cf. Freidenberg: "Jesus on the ass is in fact himself a repetition of the ass, which is already a divinity, although one more ancient than Christ himself" (*Mif i literatura drevnosti*, 502). The two donkeys in *Un Chien andalou* may well also be a biblical reference: "And the disciples went, and did as Jesus commanded them, And brought the ass, and the colt, and put on them their clothes, and they sit him thereon" (Matt. 21:6–7).

102. Aranda, *Buñuel: A Critical Biography*, 258. Many years later, Buñuel recalled Péret's passage about blind men and bologna sausage: "Péret writes: 'Is it really not true that mortadella is made by the blind?' Damn! What extraordinary precision! I know of course that blind people don't make bologna, but THEY DO MAKE IT. You see them making it" (Buñuel, "Interview by J. de la Colina and T. Perez-Turrent," 7).

103. Dali, *Catalogue de la rétrospective*, 48.

104. Bataille, *L'Expérience intérieure*, 31.

105. Dali, *Catalogue de la rétrospective*, 58.

106. Aranda, *Buñuel: A Critical Biography*, 27.

107. Dali, "L'Âne pourri," 11. The notion of simulacrum is highly polyvalent; it can mean representation, phantom, vision, invention, analogy, or semblance. In 1925, the word appeared in the title of a collection of poetry by Michel Leiris. Leiris's *Simulacre* is one of the most obscure surrealist texts; appearing before Dali, it does, however, prefigure some aspects of his theory of "multiple representation." Leiris, for example, writes of the "desert of annihilated comparison" (*Mots sans mémoire*, 15; cf. Dali's privileged field of simile—the desert, the beach). Leiris also speaks of the "monotonous pulp of forms" (ibid., 16) and metamorphoses (ibid., 19). The question of Leiris's possible influence on Dali is yet to be studied.

108. Artaud, *Oeuvres complètes*, 1:126.

109. Ibid., 288.

110. Dali, *Catalogue de la rétrospective*, 145.

111. Quoted in ibid., 52.

112. Éluard, *Poèmes*, 92.

113. Dali, *Secret Life of Salvador Dali*, 213.

114. Apollinaire, *L'Enchanteur pourrissant*, 90. The juxtaposition of piano keys and teeth is self-evident enough for it to appear elsewhere, for example, in the work of the Russian writer Ol'ga Forsch: "The yellowish teeth without saliva were like the keys of a toy piano" ("Sumasshedshii Korabl'," 272).

115. Gómez de la Serna, "L'Enterrement du Stradivarius," 163. The comparison of coffin and piano also appears often in Joyce's *Ulysses*. Typically, Joyce, sensitive as always to formal metamorphoses, also plays with the metaphor of keyboard as teeth.

116. Bataille, *Oeuvres complètes*, 1:217.
117. Ibid., 230.
118. Breton and Soupault, *Les Champs magnétiques*, 32.

CHAPTER SIX

1. Toddes, "Posleslovie"; Sèpman, "Tynianov-stsenarist," 74–76.
2. Iutkevich, *O kinoiskusstve*, 42.
3. Sèpman, "Tynianov-stsenarist," 76.
4. Zorkaia, "Tynianov i kino," 292.
5. Kozintsev, *Sobranie sochinenii*, 2:28.
6. Garin, "Obogashchenie literatury."
7. One such indication is the sorry episode of a public defamation of Tynianov at Belgoskino studios, which apparently led to Tynianov's definitive break with the cinema. The scriptwriter B. L. Brodianskii qualified *Lieutenant Kizhe* as the "rearguard action of formalism's remaining forces." Tynianov, present at the meeting at Belgoskino concerning the issue, protested in strong terms against such provocative declarations: " 'Rearguard actions' no longer represent a threat to your firm, and its scriptwriters have every reason not to be concerned. I will trouble them no longer with my presence. . . .' And [Tynianov] left before the meeting ended" (see A-va, "Skromnitsy iz Belgoskino").
8. Tynianov [Yury Tynyanov], *Lieutenant Kizhe*, from *Lieutenant Kijé*, 43; emphasis added. All quotations from the story *Lieutenant Kizhe* refer to this edition, with the spelling of Russian proper nouns occasionally altered to conform with the transliteration system used throughout this book: this most notably affects the title and name of the hero Kizhe, which Ginsburg styles as Kijé. Wherever the English translation reads "Nants," the name Kizhe has also been restored, except in the central episode in which the name is first coined (see the quote corresponding to note 22) and where the pun involved in the name subsequently needs greater clarity in English (translator's note).
9. Ibid., 47; emphasis added.
10. Ibid., 49.
11. On *The Sandunov Baths*, see Stepanov, "Zamysly i plany," 239.
12. Tynianov, *Lieutenant Kijé*, 331.
13. Levinton, "Istochniki i podteksty romana 'Smert' Vazir-Mukhtara'," 7.
14. Ibid., 6.
15. Shklovskii, "Gorod nashei iunosti," 28.
16. Lotman and Tsiv'ian, "SVD: Zhanr melodramy i istoriia."
17. Tynianov, *Problema stikhotvornogo iazyka*, 80.
18. Ibid.
19. Ibid., 95.
20. Ibid., 116.
21. Shklovskii, *Gamburgskii schet (1914–1933)*, 469.
22. Tynianov, *Lieutenant Kijé*, 9.
23. Tynianov, *Poruchik Kizhe*, shot 139a.
24. Tynianov, *Poètika*, 27, comments on the function of letters such as the now

obsolete *V* (the *izhitsa*) in the epigrams of Pushkin, where it denotes an individual, becoming his "parodic designation." It is possible that the *izhitsa* may be connected as a parodic sign with the phonic value of the name Kizhe. Cf. also Georgii Levinton, "Istochniki i podteksty romana 'Smert' Vazir-Mukhtara'," 14, who points to an explicit thematization of the *izhitsa* in Pushkin.

25. Eikhenbaum, *O proze*, 313.

26. Tynianov, *Podporuchik Kizhe* [1927].

27. Tynianov, *Poètika*, 336.

28. Ibid., 338–339.

29. Shklovskii, "O poèzii i zaumnom iazyke," in *Gamburgskii schet (1914–1933)*, 52.

30. Tynianov, *Problema stikhotvornogo iazyka*, 94.

31. Tynianov, *Kiukhlia*, 143.

32. Ibid., 131.

33. Jakobson, *Raboty po poètike*, 313.

34. Iakubinskii, *Izbrannye raboty*, 169.

35. Eikhenbaum, "Problemy kinostilistiki," 17. Cf. also my article on trans-sense in the film theory of the OPOIAZ critics: Iampolski, " 'Smyslovaia veshch' v kinoteorii OPOIAZa."

36. Jakobson, *Raboty po poètike*, 313.

37. Tynianov, *Lieutenant Kijé*, 24; emphasis added. I have retranslated the two italicized words from the Russian in place of Mirra Ginsburg's version (translator's note).

38. Ibid., 25.

39. Ibid., 33, with one phrase retranslated.

40. On the realization of principles proper to poetry in Tynianov's prose, see Boris Eikhenbaum, *O proze*, 405, who notes the wavering indicators of meaning that are mobilized by Tynianov in his novel *The Death of the Vazir-Mukhtar*.

41. Tynianov, *Poruchik Kizhe*.

42. Ibid., shot 298.

43. Instead of emphasizing perspective for the purpose of creating a subjective camera vision, one can also do the reverse: destroy perspective through the use of masking, out-of-focus images, and so forth. This device was characteristic of early cinema, but it demanded a specific psychological motivation that would have been out of the question in the case of *Kizhe:* for example, a heroine's tears might motivate a blurring of vision, or intoxication might justify a jerky camera movement.

44. Tynianov, *Poruchik Kizhe*.

45. Tynianov, *Lieutenant Kijé*, 35.

46. Hoffmann, "Klein Zaches genannt Zinnober," 1:238.

47. Ibid., 240.

48. Ibid., 235.

49. Tynianov, *Poruchik Kizhe*.

50. Hoffmann, "Klein Zaches genannt Zinnober," 1:168.

51. Ibid., 238.

52. Ibid., 232.

53. Tynianov, *Poruchik Kizhe*, shots 650, 586; Hoffmann, "Klein Zaches gennant Zinnober," 234.

54. Hoffmann, "Klein Zaches genannt Zinnober," 241–242. There is also an analogous moment in Tynianov's novel *Smert' vazir-Mukhtara,* in which Griboedov, lying sick in bed, sees the image of his father: "He began to approach the bed in which Griboedov lay gazing at him, and the small, white, wonderful hand of his father became visible. His father moved the blanket and looked at the sheets. 'Strange, where's Alexander?' he said, and walked away from the bed. And Griboedov began to weep and shout with a thin voice; he knew that he did not exist" (257–258).

55. Tynianov, *Poruchik Kizhe.*

56. Hoffmann, "Klein Zaches genannt Zinnober," 248–249.

57. Tynianov, *Lieutanant Kijé,* 50.

58. Hoffmann, "Klein Zaches genannt Zinnober," 245; Tynianov, *Lieutenant Kijé,* 51.

59. Hoffmann, "Klein Zaches genannt Zinnober," 250.

60. Ibid., 247.

61. Ibid.

62. Tynianov, *Poètika,* 314.

63. Ibid.

64. Lotman and Tsiv'ian, "SVD: Zhanr melodramy i istoriia," 47.

65. Tsiv'ian, " 'Paleogrammy v fil'me 'Shinel,'" 26.

66. Tynianov, *Poètika,* 26.

67. Ibid., 345.

68. Ibid., 343.

69. Ibid., 313.

70. Ibid., 316.

71. Ibid., 212.

72. The film adaptation of *The Overcoat* contains a direct reference to the future film version of *Lieutenant Kizhe.* Bashmachkin is made to leave a note, which ends with the following words: "The Titled Counsellor Akakii Akakievich Bashmachkin subsequent to his death is no longer listed. A. Bashmachkin." This note is clearly an anticipatory declaration concerning what will become the Siniukhaev subplot in the story *Kizhe.* So we can say that Kizhe comes directly out of Tynianov's screenplay for Gogol's *The Overcoat.*

73. Vinogradov, *Izbrannye trudy,* 5.

74. "In theatrical or dramatic parody an *actor* performs in place of the *hero*" (Tynianov, *Poètika,* 302).

75. Ibid., 303–308.

76. Ibid., 206.

77. Prokof'ev, "Prostranstvo v zhivopisi Dega," 116.

78. Tynianov, *Kiukhlia,* 388.

79. Tynianov, *Poruchik Kizhe;* emphasis added.

80. Ibid.; emphasis added.

81. Cf. Toddes, "Posleslovie," 183–186.

82. Tynianov, *Poruchik Kizhe.*

83. Ibid.

84. Ibid., shots 353, 621.

85. Tynianov, *Lieutenant Kijé,* 13.

86. Ibid., 23.

87. The Gogolian subtext is also present in the motif of smells, present both in *Kizhe* and in Gogol's "The Nose": In Tynianov's story (ibid., 20, 47), we find: "Paul Petrovich was in the habit of sniffing people"; " 'If I could crawl into the snuffbox,' thought the Emperor, snuffing the tobacco." In these scenes Paul behaves exactly like the Gogolian nose-become-person: "Lieutenant Sinukhaev . . . distinguished people by smell" (45). The screenplay repeatedly returns to the idea of Pahlen's snuffbox as a threat to the emperor, and Paul is said to have discerned Pahlen's pro-English sentiments by smell, and so on.

88. Tynianov, *Poruchik Kizhe,* shot 202.

89. Tynianov, *Poruchik Kizhe.*

90. Gogol, "The Nose," 188.

91. Gogol, "The Nevsky Prospect," in *Tales from Gogol,* 147.

92. Tynianov, *Kiukhlia,* 334.

93. Tynianov, *Lieutenant Kijé,* 117.

94. Tynianov, *Kiukhlia,* 376.

95. Tynianov, *Lieutenant Kijé,* 63–64.

96. Tynianov, *Poruchik Kizhe,* shot 188.

97. Tynianov, *Poruchik Kizhe.*

98. Ibid., shots 499–508.

99. Ibid., shot 256.

100. Barthes, *L'Obvie et l'obtus,* 282.

101. These scenes may contain parodic subtextual references to Pushkin's celebrated *Bronze Horseman.* The following section, for example, contains a grotesque echo of Pushkin's description of the flood: "316. Paul looks. Suddenly his face assumes a defiant expression, and he quickly rides to the gates of the castle. 317. The dwarf runs after him. A little stream runs down the head of the statue and falls on his collar. He huddles up. Caption: 'Great-grandfather.' The dwarf says: 'Your great-grandfather is crying' " (Tynianov, *Poruchik Kizhe*).

102. Ibid., 258.

103. Tynianov, *Kiukhlia,* 196.

CHAPTER SEVEN

1. See Iu. Tynianov, *Pushkin i ego sovremenniki,* 209. The article "Bezymennaia liubov" was first published in *Literaturnyi sovremennik* 5–6 (1939).

2. Eikhenbaum, *O proze,* 383.

3. Shub, *Zhizn' moia-kinematograf,* 167–168.

4. Eisenstein, "Pis'mo Tynianovu," 179.

5. Eisenstein, "Psikhologiia kompozitsii," 281.

6. Ibid., 280.

7. Eisenstein, *Izbrannye proizvedeniia,* 3:496–497.

8. Eisenstein, "Psikhologiia kompozitsii," 276.

9. Ibid., 278. The phrase "dissect music like a corpse" is Pushkin's, from *Mozart and Salieri* (1830) (translator's note).

10. Eisenstein, "Nachahmung als Beherrschung," 34.

11. Ibid., 36.

12. Ibid.

13. Benjamin, *Essais II: 1935–1940*, 33.

14. Durkheim, *Les Formes elementaires de la vie religieuse*, 179; Eisenstein's emphasis.

15. Lang, *Custom and Myth*, 303.

16. Levy-Bruhl, *How Natives Think*, 140.

17. Lindsay, *Short History of Culture*, 49.

18. Eisenstein, *Izbrannye proizvedeniia*, 1:484.

19. Eisenstein, archival material from RGALI (Moscow), f. 1923, op. 2, ed. khr. 239.

20. Ibid.

21. Eisenstein, *Izbrannye proizvedeniia*, 2:241.

22. Ibid., 351, 342.

23. Eisenstein, "Chet-nechet: Razdvoenie edinogo," 235.

24. Panofsky, *Idea*, 233.

25. Ibid., 80.

26. Ibid., 82.

27. Ibid., 103.

28. Ibid., 107–108.

29. Eisenstein, "Organichnost' i obraznost'," in *Izbrannye proizvedeniia*, 4:652.

30. Ibid., 653.

31. Ibid., 662–663.

32. Eisenstein, RGALI, f. 1923, op. 2, ed. khr. 239.

33. Ibid.

34. Souriau, *La Correspondance des Arts*, 226.

35. Adorno and Eisler, *Komposition für den Film*, 205.

36. Ibid. As authoritative a figure as Pierre Boulez confirms the position of Adorno and Eisler in 1989: "The interest of a melodic line does not lie in permitting a transcription that is visually more or less beautiful. Inversely, an admirable curve translated into musical notes might generate the most banal kind of melodic line. And the eye is incapable of appreciating from a curve the finesse of intervals, the way some of them return, their relations with the harmony, that is to say, everything that gives a melodic line its value. We need other criteria here, and there are dimensions here that cannot be represented visually, to which no sketch can do justice" (*Le Pays fertile*, 53).

37. Quoted in Kleiman and Nesteva, "Vydaiushchiisia khudozhnik-gumanist," 72.

38. Eisenstein, *Izbrannye proizvedeniia*, 2:252–253.

39. Eisenstein, *Iz tvorcheskogo naslediia S. M. Èizenshteina*, 72.

40. Eisenstein, RGALI, f. 1923, op. 1, ed. khr. 1041.

41. Ibid., ed. khr. 239.

42. Eisenstein, *Izbrannye proizvedeniia*, 2:386–387.

43. Worringer, *Abstraktion und Einfühlung*, 22. Eisenstein quotes Worringer in his work "In Search of a Father" ("Poiski ottsa," RGALI, f. 1923, op. 2, ed. khr. 234). Eisenstein's search for abstraction proceeds in a way that closely follows the line of abstract thinking in the aesthetics of Riegel, Hilderbrand, and Wölfflin, through to Klee and Kandinsky.

44. Eisenstein, RGALI, f. 1923, op. 2, ed. khr. 239.

45. Ibid.
46. Levy-Bruhl, *How Natives Think,* 139.
47. Eisenstein, "O detektive," 142–144.
48. Eisenstein, RGALI, f. 1923, op. 2, ed. khr. 239.
49. Eisenstein, "O detektive," 144.
50. Eisenstein, *Izbrannye proizvedeniia,* 1:177.
51. Ibid., 3:374.
52. Ibid..
53. Ibid., 375.
54. Ibid., 376.
55. Ibid., 1:507.
56. Ibid., 509.
57. Ibid.
58. Ibid., 1:433.
59. Ibid., 441.
60. Breton, "The Automatic Message," 108.
61. Ibid., 108–109.
62. Sophocles, *Antigone,* ll. 1001–1015 (p. 105).
63. Cf. Rudnitskii, *Russkoe rezhissërskoe iskusstvo 1898–1907,* 67.
64. Kozlov, "Gipoteza o nevyskazannom posviashchenii."
65. Apollodorus, *Gods and Heroes of the Greeks,* 147.
66. Eisenstein, RGALI, f. 1923, op. 2, ed. khr. 233. Eisenstein acknowledges that Swedenborg, "like all mystics, possesses a certain knowledge" (ibid.). Swedenborg's great error for Eisenstein lies in having too objective (*veshchestvennoe*) an understanding of the image or, to put it more metaphorically, in failing to "switch off" his diurnal vision. In mysticism, Eisenstein feels, "the seedling of *sensation* [*oshchushcheniia*] grows and develops not into cognition (in our sense of the term), but into a metaphysical ideogram: an image of concepts conceived as objects." Thus Eisenstein can guardedly acknowledge his bond with mysticism while claiming to provide the corrective of a higher level of abstraction.
67. Eisenstein, RGALI, f. 1923, op. 2, ed. khr. 233.
68. Worringer, *Abstraktion und Einfühlung,* 23.
69. Eisenstein, *Izbrannye proizvedeniia,* 4:125. Cf. also Eisenstein, "O detektive," 148: "Step by step a shift occurs in the reader toward reading phenomena according to the image of objects and the representations that accompany their form or appearance, rather than according to their content or designation, that is, a reorientation toward so-called 'physiognomic'—purely sensory—perception."
70. Eisenstein, *Izbrannye proizvedeniia,* 3:375.
71. Wölfflin, *Renaissance und Barock,* 86.
72. Eisenstein, *Izbrannye proizvedeniia,* 3:204.
73. Ibid., 2:285.
74. Eisenstein, RGALI, f. 1923, op. 1, ed. khr. 236.
75. Eisenstein, *Izbrannye proizvedeniia,* 3:225–226.
76. Ibid., 2:354, 389, 389–390.
77. Eisenstein, "Psikhologiia kompozitsii," 279.
78. Ibid., 280.

79. Baudelaire, "Salon de 1859," in *Curiosités esthétiques: L'Art romantique,* 391–392.

80. Baudelaire, *Les Fleurs du mal,* 109.

81. Besant, *Thought-Forms.*

82. Voloshin, *Liki tvorchestva,* 211.

83. Cf. ibid., 316: "Under the hills next to these valleys one can discern the contours of bloated ribs; long trunks expose spinal columns concealed below them; flat and predatory-looking skulls rise out of the sea." Voloshin also payed homage to evolutionary theory by dividing art history into three periods (ibid., 216): (1) the arbitrary symbolism of the sign, (2) strict realism, and (3) generalized stylization. This schema in essence coincides with those advanced by Worringer and Eisenstein.

84. Belyi, *Petersburg,* 168.

85. Eisenstein, *Izbrannye proizvedeniia,* 4:660–661.

86. Ibid., 125–126.

87. Klee, *Théorie de l'art moderne,* 11.

88. Ibid., 44–45.

89. Eisenstein, *Izbrannye proizvedeniia,* 1:300.

90. Ibid., 267.

91. Ibid., 2:350.

92. Ibid., 351. In this quote Eisenstein also uses the English word *bones,* which he translates as *"kostiak"* (translator's note).

93. Ibid., 1:506.

94. Eisenstein, RGALI, f.1923. op.2, ed. khr.233.

95. Ibid.

96. Eisenstein, *Izbrannye proizvedeniia,* 1:211.

97. Eisenstein, RGALI, f. 1923, op. 2, ed. khr. 1082.

98. There is a similar account of bodily release in Belyi's *Petersburg:* "As if a bandage had fallen off all sensations . . . as if you were being torn to pieces, pulled in opposite directions, in the front your heart is being ripped out, and your own spine is being ripped out of your back like a stick from a wattle fence. . . . My body was prickling all over, and I could distinctly feel the prickling—at a distance of about seven inches from my body! Just think! I was turned inside out. . . . Beside yourself is completely bodily, physiological" (180–181).

99. Eisenstein, RGALI, f. 1923, op. 2, ed. khr. 1082.

100. Riffaterre, "Sémiotique intertextuelle," 132.

101. Eisenstein, *Izbrannye proizvedeniia,* 1:296.

102. Rodenbach, *Bruges-la-morte,* 46.

103. Benjamin, *Paris, capitale du XIXe siècle,* 436.

CONCLUSION

1. Krauss, "Originality as Repetition," 36.

2. Fried, "Antiquity Now," 92.

3. Pleynet, *Lautrémont par lui-meme,* 90.

4. Metz, *Le Signifiant imaginaire,* 274.

5. Ibid., 337–338.
6. Cf. J. Dubois, F. Edeline, J. M. Klinkenberg, P. Minguet, F. Pire, and H. Trinon, *Rhetorique générale par le groupe μ,* 183.
7. Shklovskii, *Kak my pishem,* 185–186.
8. Yates, *Art of Memory,* 96.
9. Ibid., 249.
10. Ibid., 79.
11. Benjamin, *Allegorien kultureller Erfahrung,* 130.

Works Cited

Abel, Richard. *French Cinema: The First Wave, 1915–1929.* Princeton, N.J.: Princeton University Press, 1984.

———. "The Point-of-View Shots from Spectacle to Story in Several Early Pathé Films." In *Ce que je vois de mon ciné,* edited by André Gudreault, 73–76. Paris: Méridiens, Klincksieck, 1988.

Adorno, Theodor, and Hans Eisler. *Komposition für den Film.* Leipzig: Deutscher Verlag für Musik, 1977.

Alexandrian, Sarane. *Le Surréalisme et le rêve.* Paris: Gallimard, 1974.

———. *Marcel Duchamp.* Paris: Flammarion, 1976.

Altman, Rick. "Dickens, Griffith, and Film Theory Today." *South Atlantic Quarterly Review* 88 (1989): 323–324.

Andrew, Dudley. "Au Début de Souffle: Le culte et la culture d' 'À Bout de Souffle.' " *Revue Belge du Cinéma* 22–23 (1988):11–21.

Anthologie des poètes de la N.R.F. Paris: Gallimard, 1936.

Apollinaire, Guillaume. *Oeuvres complètes de Guillaume Apollinaire.* Vol. 1. Edited by Michel Decaudin. Paris: Gallimard, 1965.

———. *L'Enchanteur pourrissant suivi de Les mamelles de Tirésias et de Couleurs du temps.* Paris: Gallimard, 1972.

Apollodorus. *Gods and Heroes of the Greeks: The Library of Apollodorus.* Translated by Michael Simpson. Amherst: University of Massachusetts Press, 1976.

Aranda, J. Francisco. *Luis Buñuel: A Critical Biography.* London: Secker and Warburg, 1975.

Arendt, Hanna. *Vies politiques.* Paris: Gallimard, 1986.

Arnim, Achim von. "O narodnykh pesniakh." In *Èstetika nemetskikh romantikov,* edited by Aleksandre V. Mikhailov, 376–406. Moscow: Iskusstvo, 1987.

Arnold, Matthew. *The Poems of Matthew Arnold, 1840 to 1866.* London: J. Dent, 1908.

———. *The Poems of Matthew Arnold.* Edited by Kenneth Allott. London: Longmans, Green, 1965.

Arp, Jean. *Jours effeuillés*. Paris: Gallimard, 1966.

Arroy, Jean. *En tournant "Napoléon" avec Abel Gance: Souvenirs et impressions d'un sansculotte*. Paris: La Renaissance de livre, 1927.

Artaud, Antonin. *Le Théatre et son double*. Paris: Gallimard, 1968.

————. *Oeuvres complètes*. Vol. 1. Paris: Gallimard, 1976.

————. *Oeuvres complètes*. Vol. 3. Paris: Gallimard, 1978.

————. *Héliogabale ou l'anarchiste couronné*. Paris: Gallimard, 1979.

Arvidson, Linda [Mrs. D. W. Griffith]. *When Movies Were Young*. 2d ed. New York: Dutton, 1968.

Asselineau, Roger. *The Transcendentalist Constant in American Literature*. New York: New York University Press, 1980.

Aumont, Jacques. "Griffith, le cadre, la figure." In *Le Cinéma americain: Analyses de films*. Vol. 1. Edited by Raymond Bellour, 51–68. Paris: Flammarion, 1980.

————. "Crise dans la crise." *Hors cadre* 7 (1989): 199–203.

————. *L'Oeil interminable: Cinéma et peinture*. Paris: Séguier, 1989.

A-va. "Skromnitsy iz Belgoskino." *Kino*, no. 7 (February 10, 1934).

Bakhtin, Mikhail. *Voprosy literatury i èstetiki*. Moscow: Khudozhestvennaia literatura, 1975.

————. *Èstetika slovesnogo tvorchestva*. Moscow: Iskusstvo, 1979.

Balakian, Anna. *Literary Origins of Surrealism: A New Mysticism in French Poetry*. New York: King's Crown Press, 1947.

Ballets suédois 1920–1925/Catalogue de l'exposition. Paris: Musée de l'Art Moderne, November 3, 1970—January 17, 1971.

Balzac, Honoré de. *Seraphita*. Translated by Clara Bell. New York: Dutton, 1913.

————. "L'Enfant maudit." In *Oeuvres complètes*. Vol. 9. Edited by Guy le Prat. Paris: De Chambéry, 1960.

————. "L'Enfant maudit." In *La Comedie humaine*. Vol. 10. Edited by Pierre-Georges Castex. Paris: Gallimard, 1979.

Barthes, Roland. "The Third Meaning." In *Image, Music, Text*. Translated by Stephen Heath. New York: Macaulay, 1930.

————. *The Pleasure of the Text*. Translated by Richard Miller. New York: Farrar, Straus and Giroux, 1975.

————. *S/Z*. Paris: Seuil, 1976.

————. *L'Obvie et l'obtus: Essais critiques III*. Paris: Seuil, 1982.

————. "Tretii smysl: Issledovatel'skie zametki o neskol'kikh fotogrammakh S. M Èizenshteina." In *Stroenie fil'ma*, 176–188. Moscow: Raduga, 1984.

————. *Izbrannye raboty: Semiotika. Poètika*. Moscow: Progress, 1989.

Bataille, Georges. *L'Expérience intérieure*. Paris: Gallimard, 1967.

————. *Oeuvres complètes*. Vol. 1. Paris: Gallimard, 1970.

Baudelaire, Charles. *Les Fleurs du mal*. Paris: Éditions Garnier Frères, 1959.

————. *Curiosités esthétiques: L'Art romantique et autres oeuvres critiques*. Edited by H. de Lemaitre. Paris: Garnier, 1962.

————. *Les Paradis artificiels*. Paris: Garnier, Flammarion, 1966.

————. *The Flowers of Evil*. Edited by Marthiel Mathews and Jackson Mathews. New York: New Directions, 1989.

————. *Artificial Paradises: Baudelaire's Classic Work on Opium and Wine*. Translated and with an introduction by Stacy Diamond. New York: Citadel Press, 1996.

Bellour, Raymond. "Le Texte introuvable." In *L'Analyse du film*. Paris: Albatros, 1979.

———. "Nedosiagaemyi tekst." In *Stroenie fil'ma*, edited by Kirill Razlogov, 221–230. Moscow: Raduga, 1984.

Belluccio, Adriana. " 'Cabiria' e 'Intolerance' tra il serio e il faceto." *Bianco e nero* 5–8 (1975): 53–57.

Belyi, Andrei. *Petersburg*. Translated by Robert A. Maguire and John E. Malmstad. Bloomington: Indiana University Press, 1978.

———. *Peterburg*. Leningrad: Nauka, 1981.

Benjamin, Walter. *Reflections*. Edited by Peter Demetz. New York: Schocken Books, 1978.

———. *Charles Baudelaire: Lyric Poet in the Era of High Capitalism*. Translated by Harry Zohn. London: Verso Editions, 1983.

———. *Essais II: 1935–1940*. Paris: Denoël, Gonthier, 1983.

———. *Allegorien kultureller Erfahrung*. Leipzig: Reclam, 1984.

———. *Paris, capitale du XIXe siècle: Le Livre des passages*. Paris: Cerf, 1989.

———. "Proizvedenie iskusstva v èpokhu ego tekhnicheskoi vosproizvodimosti." *Kinovedcheskie zapiski /VNIIK* 2 (1989): 151–173.

Bertran, Marc. "Image cinématographique et image surréaliste." *Les Cahiers de la Cinémathèque* 30–31 (1980): 43–47.

Besant, Annie, and C. W. Leadbeater. *Thought-Forms*. Madras: Theosophical Publishing House, 1967.

Bialostocki, Jan. "Man and Mirror in Painting: Reality and Transience." In *Studies in Late Medieval and Renaissance Painting in Honor of Millard Meiss*, edited by Irving Lavin and John Plummer, 61–72. New York: New York University Press, 1978.

Biograph Bulletins, 1908–1912. New York: Octagon Books, 1973.

Bloom, Harold. *The Anxiety of Influence: A Theory of Poetry*. New York: Oxford University Press, 1973.

———. "Visionary Cinema of Romantic Poetry." In *The Ringers in the Tower: Studies in the Romantic Tradition*, 37–52. Chicago: University of Chicago Press, 1973.

———. *A Map of Misreading*. New York: Oxford University Press, 1975.

———. *Poetry and Repression: Revisionism from Blake to Stevens*. New Haven, Conn.: Yale University Press, 1976.

Boczkowska, Anna. *Tryumf Luny i Wenus*. Krakow: Wydownictwo Literackie, 1980.

Bonitzer, Pascal. *Peinture et cinéma: Décadrages*. Paris: Editions de l'Etoile, 1985.

Bordwell, David. *The Films of Carl-Theodor Dreyer*. Berkeley: University of California Press, 1981.

Borges, Jorge Luis. *Other Inquisitions, 1937–1952*. Translated by Ruth L. C. Simms. Introduction by James E. Irby. Austin: University of Texas Press, 1964.

———. *Labyrinths*. Harmondsworth, England: Penguin Books, 1970.

———. *Borges: A Reader*. Edited by E. R. Monegal and Alastair Reid. New York: Dutton, 1981.

Boulez, Pierre. *Le Pays fertile: Paul Klee*. Paris: Gallimard, 1989.

Bowser, Eileen. "Griffith e la struttura circolare in alcuni film Biograph." *Bianco e nero* 5–8 (1975): 46–51.

———. " 'Old Isaacs the Pawnbroker' et le raccordement d'espaces éloignés." In *David Wark Griffith*, edited by J. Mottet, 31–43. Paris: L'Harmattan, 1984.

Bozon-Scalzitti, Yvette. "Blaise Cendrars et le symbolisme." *Archives des lettres modernes* 137 (1972).

Breteque, François de la. " 'A l'échelle animale': Notes pour un Bestiaire dans le cinéma des surréalistes." *Les Cahiers de la Cinémathèque* 30–31 (1980): 58–67.

Breton, André. *Les Manifestes du surréalisme.* Paris: Sagittaire, 1924.

———. *Nadja.* Paris: Gallimard, 1928.

———. *Le Revolver à cheveux blancs.* Paris: Editions des Cahiers libres, 1932.

———. *Poèmes.* Paris: Gallimard, 1948.

———. *Arcane 17.* Paris: J. J. Pauvert, 1965.

———. *Anthologie de l'humour noir.* Paris: J. J. Pauvert, 1968.

———. *Point du jour.* Paris: Gallimard, 1970.

———. *Manifestes du surréalisme.* Paris: Gallimard, 1973.

———. "The Automatic Message." In *What Is Surrealism? Selected Writings,* edited by Franklin Rosemont. New York: Monad Press, 1978.

Breton, André, and Ph. Soupault. *Les Champs magnétiques.* Paris: Gallimard, 1968.

Brion, Patrick. "Filmographie de D. W. Griffith." In *D. W. Griffith,* edited by Patrick Brion, 93–209. Paris: L'Equerre, Centre Georges Pompidou, 1982.

Brown, Karl. *Adventures with D. W. Griffith.* London: Secker and Warburg, 1973.

Browning, Robert. *The Poetical Works of Robert Browning.* Introduction by G. Robert Stange. Boston: Houghton Mifflin, 1974.

Brownlow, Kevin. *The Parade's Gone By.* New York: Bonanza Books, 1968.

Brunius, Jacques-B. *En marge du cinéma français.* Lausanne: L'Age d'homme, 1987.

Buchole, Rosa. *L'Évolution poétique de Robert Desnos.* Brussels: Palais des Académies, 1956.

Buhler, Jean. *Blaise Cendrars, homme libre, poète au coeur du monde.* Bienne: Editions du Panorama, 1960.

Buñuel, Luis. "Notes on the Making of 'Un Chien andalou.' " In *The World of L. Buñuel,* edited by J. Mellen, 151–153. New York: Oxford University Press, 1978.

———. "Interview by J. de la Colina and T. Perez-Turrent." *Positif* 238 (1981): 2–14.

———. "Buñuel par Buñuel." *Le Nouvel Observateur* 904 (1982): 60–66.

———. *My Last Sigh.* Translated by Abigail Israel. New York: Knopf, 1983.

———. *Mon dernier soupir.* Paris: Robert Laffont, 1986.

———. "O fotogenichnom plane." In *Iz istorii frantsuzskoi kinomysli: Nemoe kino, 1911–1933,* edited by Mikhail Iampolski, 115–119. Moscow: Iskusstvo, 1988.

Bush, Ronald. *The Genesis of Ezra Pound's "Cantos."* Princeton, N.J.: Princeton University Press, 1976.

Carroll, Noël. "Interpreting 'Citizen Kane.' " *Persistence of Vision* 7 (1989): 51–62.

Castelnau, Jacques Thomas De. *Belle époque.* Paris: Librairie académique Perrin, 1962.

Cendrars, Blaise. *L'Eubage aux antipodes de l'unité.* Paris: Au Sans Pareil, 1926.

———. *Moravagine.* Paris: Bernard Grasset, 1926.

———. *Du monde entier: Au coeur du monde: Poèmes de Blaise Cendrars.* Paris: Editions Denoël, 1957.

———. *Oeuvres complètes.* Vol. 4. Paris: Denoël, 1962.

———. *Bourlinguer.* Paris: Denoël, 1964.

———. *Inédits secrets.* Paris: Denoël, 1969.

———. *Oeuvres complètes.* Vols. 2, 6. Paris: Le Club français du livre, 1969.

———. *Oeuvres complètes*. Vols. 13–15. Paris: Le Club français du livre, 1971.

———. "Fernand Léger." *Europe* 566 (1976): 214–216.

———. "Origine de l'idée de 'Perpetuum mobile.'" *Europe* 556 (1976): 195–208.

———. *Les Confessions de Dan Yack*. Paris: Denoël, 1983.

———. *Blaise Cendrars*. Paris: Balland, 1984.

———. "Azbuka kino." *Iz istorii frantsuzskoi kinomysli: Nemoe kino 1911–1933*, edited by Mikhail Iampolski, 38–42. Moscow: Iskusstvo, 1988.

Charansol, Georges. *40 ans de cinéma, 1895–1935: Panorama du cinéma muet et parlant*. Paris: Editions du Sagittaire, 1935.

Chefdor, Monique. "Blaise Cendrars et le simultanéisme." *Europe* 566 (1976): 24–29.

Cherchi Usai, Paolo. *Pastrone*. Florence: La Nuova Italia, 1986.

Chevalier, Jean, and Alain Gheerbrant. *Dictionnaire des symboles*. Paris: Laffont, Jupiter, 1982.

Chevrier, Jean-François, and Brigitte Legars. "L'Atelier Elstir." *Cahiers critiques de la littérature* 3–4 (1977): 21–69.

Cieutat, Michel. "Naissance d'une iconographie: Les courts-métrages de D. W. Griffith (1908–1913)." *Positif* 262 (1982): 6–15.

Cincotti, G., and D. Turconi. "I film, i dati, gli argomenti." *Bianco e nero* 5–8 (1975): 77–79.

Cocteau, Jean. *Poésie, 1916–1923*. Paris: Gallimard, 1925.

Coleridge, Samuel T. *Poems*. Vol. 1 of *The Complete Poetical Works of Samuel T. Coleridge*. Edited by Ernest Coleridge. Oxford: Clarendon Press, 1912.

Collin de Plancy, Jacques-Albin-Simon. *Dictionnaire Infernal*. Paris: Plon, 1863.

Collins, Christopher. *The Uses of Observation: A Study of Correspondential Vision in the Writings of Emerson, Thoreau, and Whitman*. The Hague: Mouton, 1971.

Coppée, François. *Le Luthier de Crémone*. Varsovie: Arct, 1909.

Cozarinsky, Edgardo. *Borges in/and/on Film*. Translated by Gloria Waldman and Ronald Christ. New York: Lumen Books, 1981.

Cros, Charles, and T. Corbière. *Oeuvres Complètes*. Vol. 1. Paris: Gallimard, 1970.

Dali, Salvador. "L'âne pourri." *Le Surréalisme au service de la révolution* 1 (1930): 9–12.

———. *The Secret Life of Salvador Dali*. New York: Buton C. Hoffman, Dial Press, 1942.

———. *Catalogue de la rétrospective, 1920–1980: 18 déc. 1979–14 avr. 1980*. Paris: Centre Georges Pompidou, Musée National d'Art Moderne.

Dällenbach, Lucien. "Intertexte et autotexte." *Poétique* 27 (1976): 282–296.

Damase, Jacques, and Sonia Delaunay. *Sonia Delaunay: Rythmes et couleurs*. Paris: Hermann, 1971.

Damisch, Hubert. *Théorie du nuage: Pour une histoire de la peinture*. Paris: Seuil, 1972.

Dante, Alighieri. *The Divine Comedy of Dante Alighieri: Inferno*. Translated by Allen Mandelbaum. New York: Bantam Books, 1980.

Delaunay, Robert. *Du cubisme à l'art abstrait: Documents inédits publié par Pierre Francastel*. Paris: SEVPEN, 1957.

Delevoy, Robert L. *Le Symbolisme*. Geneva: Skira, 1982.

Delluc, Louis. *Charlot*. Paris: M. de Brunoff, 1921.

de Man, Paul. *Allegories of Reading.* New Haven, Conn.: Yale University Press, 1979.

De Quincey, Thomas. *The Collected Writings of Thomas de Quincey.* Edited by David Masson. London: A & C Black, 1897.

———. *Selected Writings of Thomas de Quincey.* New York: Random House, 1937.

———. *Confessions of an English Opium-eater.* London: Oxford University Press, 1949.

———. *Selected Essays of De Quincey.* London: Scott, n.d.

Derouet, Christian. "Léger et le cinéma." In *Peinture—cinéma—peinture,* 120–143. Paris: Hazan, 1989.

Derrida, Jacques. *Of Grammatology.* Baltimore, Md.: Johns Hopkins University Press, 1976.

———. *Writing and Difference.* Translated by Alan Bass. Chicago: University of Chicago Press, 1978.

———. *L'Ecriture et la différence.* Paris: Seuil, 1979.

Descargues, Pierre. *Fernand Léger.* Paris: Cercle d'art, 1955.

Desnos, Robert. *Anthologie des poètes de la N.R.F* . Preface by Paul Valéry. 5th ed. Paris: Gallimard, 1958.

———. *Cinéma.* Paris: Gallimard, 1966.

Dickens, Charles. *The Mystery of Edwin Drood.* Edited by Margaret Cardwell. Oxford: Oxford University Press, 1972.

Doane, Mary Ann. *The Desire to Desire: The Woman's Film of the 1940's.* Bloomington: Indiana University Press, 1987.

Drevneindiiskaia filosofiia: Nachal'nyi period. Moscow: Izdatel'stvo sotsial'no-èkono-micheskoi literatury, 1963.

Drouzy, Maurice, Carl Th. *Dreyer né Nilsson.* Paris: Cerf, 1982.

Drummond, Phillip. "Textual Space in 'Un Chien andalou.' " *Screen* 18, no. 3 (1977): 55–119.

Dubois, J., F. Edeline, J. M. Klinkenberg, P. Minguet, F. Pire, and H. Trinon. *Rhetorique générale par le groupe μ.* Paris: Librairie Larousse, 1970.

———. *Obshchaia ritorika.* Moscow: Progress, 1986.

Ducrot, Oswald, and Tsvetan Todorov. *Dictionnaire encyclopédique des sciences du langage.* Paris: Seuil, 1979.

Du Maurier, George. *Trilby.* New York: Harper, 1895.

Durgnat, Raymond. *Luis Buñuel.* Berkeley: University of California Press, 1967.

———. *Films and Feelings.* Cambridge, Mass.: MIT Press, 1976.

Durkheim, Émile. *Les Formes élémentaires de la vie réligieuse: Le Système totémique en Australie.* Paris: Librairie Félix Alcan, 1912.

Eigeldinger, Marc. *Poésie et métamorphose.* Neuchâtel: La Baconnière, 1973.

Eikhenbaum, B. M. "Problemy kinostilistiki." In *Poètika kino,* 13–52. Leningrad: Kinopechat', 1927.

———. *O proze.* Leningrad: Khudozhestvennaia literatura, 1969.

———. *O literature.* Moscow: Sovetskii pisatel', 1987.

Eisenstein, Sergei M. *Sergei Eisenstein Archive.* Fond 1923, RGALI, Moscow.

———. *Film Form.* New York: Harcourt, Brace and World, 1949.

———. *Izbrannye proizvedeniia.* 6 vols. Moscow: Iskusstvo, 1964–1971.

———. "Pis'mo Tynianovu." In *Iurii Tynianov. Pisatel' i uchenyi: Vospominaniia, razmyshleniia, vstrechi,* edited by Veniamin Kaverin, 176–181. Moscow: Molodaia gvardiia, 1966.

———. "O detektive." In *Prikliuchencheskii fil'm: puti i poiski*, 132–160. Moscow: VNIIK, 1980.

———. *Iz tvorcheskogo naslediia S. M. Èizenshteina*. Edited by Leonid K. Kozlov. Moscow: VNIIK, 1985.

———. "Chet-nechet: Razdvoenie edinogo." In *Vostok—Zapad*, 234–278. Moscow: Nauka, 1988.

———. "Nachahmung als Beherrschung." *Film und Fernsehen* 1 (1988): 34–37.

———. "Psikhologiia kompozitsii." In *Iskusstvoznanie i psikhologiia khudozhestvennogo tvorchestva*, edited by A. Ia. Zis' and M. G. Iaroshevsky, 267–299. Moscow: Nauka, 1988.

Eisenstein, Sergei M., and S. I. Iutkevich, eds. *D. U. Griffit*. Moscow: Goskinoizdat, 1944.

Eliade, Mircea. *Myth and Reality*. Translated by Willard R. Trask. New York: Harper and Row, 1968.

———. *Images et symboles: Essais sur le symbolisme magico-réligieux*. Paris: Gallimard, 1979.

———. *Aspects du mythe*. Paris: Gallimard, 1988.

Eliot, T. S. *The Waste Land*. In *Collected Poems, 1909–1935*. New York: Harcourt, Brace, 1930.

———. "Traditsiia i individual'nyi talant." In *Zarubezhnaia èstetika i teoriia literatury XIX–XXvv*, 169–176. Moscow: MGU, 1987.

Éluard, Paul. *Poèmes*. Paris: Gallimard, 1951.

Emerson, Ralph Waldo. *The Works of Ralph Waldo Emerson*.Vol. 2, *English Traits and Representative Men*. London: Henry Frowde, The World's Classics, 1903.

———. *Essays and Other Writings*. London: Cassel, 1911.

———. *The Complete Writings of Ralph Waldo Emerson*. New York: Wm. H. Wise, 1929.

Epstein, Jean. *Écrits sur le cinéma*. Vol. 1. Paris: Seghers, 1974.

Èstetika amerikanskogo romantizma. Edited by A. N. Nikoliukih. Moscow: Iskusstvo, 1977.

Fabricius, J. *The Unconscious and Mr. Eliot*. Copenhagen: Nyt Nordisk Forlag Arnold Busk, 1967.

Faverty, Frederic Everett. "The Source of the Jules-Phene Episode in 'Pippa Passes.'" *Studies in Philology* 36 (1939): 97–105.

Feaver, William. *The Art of John Martin*. Oxford: Clarendon Press, 1975.

Fell, John L. *Film and the Narrative Tradition*. Norman: University of Oklahoma Press, 1974.

Fenollosa, Ernest. *The Chinese Written Character as a Medium for Poetry*. Edited by E. Pound. San Francisco: City Lights Books, 1969.

Forsh, Ol'ga. "Sumasshedshii Korabl'." *Lazur'*, no. 1 (1989): 227–330.

Foucault, Michel. *Les Mots et les choses*. Paris: Gallimard, 1966.

———. *The Order of Things: An Archeology of the Human Sciences*. Edited by R. D. Laing. New York: Random House, 1970.

———. *The Archeology of Knowledge and the Discourse on Language*. New York: Barnes and Noble, 1972.

Francastel, Pierre. *L'Image, la vision et l'imaginaire: L'objet filmique et l'objet plastique*. Paris: Denoël, Gonthier, 1983.

Freidenberg, Ol'ga M. *Mif i literatura drevnosti*. Moscow: Nauka, 1978.

Fried, Michael. "Antiquity Now: Reading Winckelmann on Imitation." *October* 37 (1986): 87–97.

Gance, Abel. "Le Temps de l'image est venu!" In *L'Art cinématographique*. Vol. 2, 83–102. Paris: Librairie Félix Alcan, 1927.

———. "Blaise Cendrars et le cinéma." *Mercure de France* 1185 (1962): 170–171.

———. "Témoignage d'Abel Gance." In *Cendrars. Oeuvres complètes*. Vol. 2, xx–xxi. Paris: Le club français du livre, 1969.

———. "Vremia izobrazheniia prishlo!" In *Iz istorii frantsuzskoi kinomysli: Nemoe kino, 1911–1933*, 64–73. Moscow: Iskusstvo, 1988.

Gandolfo, Antonino. "*The Sands of Dee:* Analisi di un dramma marino di D. W. Griffith." *Griffithiana* 34 (1979): 25–30.

Garin, Èrast. "Obogashchenie literatury." *Literaturnaia gazeta,* January 15, 1935.

Gasparov, Mikhail L., and E. G. Ruzina. "Vergilii i vergilianskie tsentony (Poètika formul i poètika reministsentsii)." In *Pamiatniki knizhnogo èposa*. Moscow: Nauka, 1978.

———. "Pervochtenie i perechtenie: k tynianovskomu poniatiiu suktsessivnosti stikhotvornoi rechi." In *Tynianovskii sbornik. Tret'i tynianovskie chteniia*, 15–23. Riga: Zinatne, 1988.

Gaudreault, André. *Du littéraire au filmique: Système du récit*. Paris: Méridiens, Klincksieck, 1988.

Geduld, Harry M., ed. *Focus on D. W. Griffith*. Englewood Cliffs, N.J.: Prentice-Hall, 1971.

Geiger, N. "Louis Boulanger: Sa vie, son oeuvre." In *Louis Boulanger: Peintre-graveur de l'époque romantique (1806–1867)*. Dijon, 1970.

Genette, Gérard. *Introduction à l'architexte*. Paris: Seuil, 1979.

Gerhardt, Mia Irene. *Iskusstvo povestvovaniia: Literaturnoe issledovanie "1001 nochi."* Moscow: Nauka, 1984.

Gide, André. *Journal, 1889–1939*. Paris: Gallimard, 1951.

Giuliano, E., and R. C. Keenan. "Browning without Words: D. W. Griffith and the Filming of 'Pippa Passes.'" *Browning Institute Studies* 4 (1976): 125–159.

Godard, Jean-Luc. *Introduction à une véritable histoire du cinéma*. Paris: Albatros, 1980.

———. *Jean-Luc Godard par Jean-Luc Godard*. Paris: Ediitons de l'Etoile, Cahiers du cinéma, 1985.

Gogol, Nikolai. *Tales from Gogol*. Translated by Rosa Portnova. London: Sylvan Press, 1945.

———. *Sobranie sochinenii*. Vol. 3. Moscow: Khudozhestvennaia literatura, 1959.

Golding, John. *Cubism: A History and an Analysis, 1907–1914*. New York: George Wittenborn, 1959.

Goll, Ivan. *Die Chapliniade: Filmdichtung von Iwan Goll*. Dresden: Rudolf Koemmerer Verlag, 1920.

———. *Ivan Goll*. Paris: Seghers, 1956.

———. "Das Kinodram." In *Gefangen in Kreise*, 223–225. Leipzig: Reclam, 1982.

Gómez de la Serna, Ramon. *Kinolandiia*. Leningrad: Novinki vsemirnoi literatury, 1927.

———. *Movieland*. Translated by Angel Flores. New York: Macaulay, 1930.

———. "L'Enterrement du Stradivarius." *Les Cahiers de la cinémathèque* 30–31 (1980): 163.

Goodman, Ezra. *The Fifty-Year Decline and Fall of Hollywood.* New York: Simon and Schuster, 1961.

Görres, Joseph. "Aforizmy ob iskusstve." In *Èstetika nemetskikh romantikov,* edited by Alexsandre V. Mikhailov, 58–202. Moscow: Iskusstvo, 1987.

Gourmont, Remy de. *Physique de l'amour: Essai sur l'instinct sexuel.* Paris: Mercure de France, 1903.

———. "The Dissociation of Ideas." In *Selected Writings,* translated and edited by Glenn S. Burne. Ann Arbor: University of Michigan Press, 1966.

———. *La Culture des idées.* Paris: UGE, 1983.

Graham, Cooper C., S. Higgins, E. Mancini, and J. L. Vieira. *D. W. Griffith and the Biograph Company.* London: Scarecrow Press, 1985.

Greene, Naomi. "Artaud and Film: A Reconsideration." *Cinema Journal* 23, no. 4 (1984): 28–40.

Griffith, D. W. "Cinéma, miracle de la photographie moderne." *Cahiers du Cinéma* 187 (1967): 18–21.

———. "The Movies 100 Years from Now." In *Film Makers on Film Making,* edited by Harry M. Geduld, 49–55. Bloomington: Indiana University Press, 1969.

———. "L'Avenir du film à deux dollars." *Positif* 262 (1982): 21.

———. "Le Cinéma et les bûchers." *Positif* 262 (1982): 20–21.

———. "Le Théâtre et le cinéma." In *D. W. Griffith,* edited by P. Brion, 87–89. Paris: L'Équerre, Centre Georges Pompidou, 1982.

Gubern, Roman. "Contribution à une lecture de l'iconographie griffithienne." In *David Wark Griffith,* edited by J. Mottet, 117–125. Paris: L'Harmattan, 1984.

Gunning, Tom. "Note per una comprensione dei film di Griffith." *Griffithiana* 5–6 (1980): 13–23.

———. "De la fumerie d'opium au théâtre de la moralité: Discours moral et conception du septième art dans le cinéma primitif américain." In *David Wark Griffith,* edited by Jean Mottet, 72–90. Paris: L'Harmattan, 1984.

———. "Présence du narrateur: L'héritage des films Biograph de Griffith." In *David Wark Griffith,* edited by Jean Mottet, 126–147. Paris: L'Harmattan, 1984.

———. "D. W. Griffith and the Narrator-System: Narrative Structure and Industry Organization in Biograph Films 1908–1909." Ph.D. diss., New York University, 1986.

Gura, Phillip. *The Wisdom of Words: Language, Theology and Literature in the New England Renaissance.* Middletown, Conn.: Wesleyan University Press, 1981.

Hagan, J. "Cinema and the Romantic Tradition." In *Film before Griffith,* edited by Jonh L. Fell, 229–235. Berkeley: University of California Press, 1983.

Hamp, Pierre. *Le Rail.* Paris: Nouvelle Revue Française, 1921.

———. *Rel'sy.* Moscow: Zemlia i fabrika, 1925.

Hansen, Miriam. "Rätsel der Mütterlichkeit: Studie zum Wiegenmotiv in Griffith's 'Intolerance.'" *Frauen und Film* 41 (1986): 32–48.

———. "The Hieroglyph and the Whore: D. W. Griffith's 'Intolerance.'" *South Atlantic Quarterly* 88 (1989): 361–392.

Hanson, Brian. "D. W. Griffith: Some Sources." *Art Bulletin* 54 (1972): 493–515.

Hart, James, ed. *The Man Who Invented Hollywood: The Autobiography of D. W. Griffith.* Louisville, Ky.: Touchstone Publishers, 1972.

Hartlaub, Gustav Friedrich. *Zauber des Spiegels: Geschichte und Bedeutung des Spiegels in der Kunst.* Munich: R. Piper, 1951.

Heath, Stephen. "Narrative Space." *Screen* 17, no. 3 (1972): 68–112.

Heckscher, William S. "Bernini's Elephant and Obelisk." In *Art and Literature: Studies in Relationship,* edited by Egon Verheyen, 65–96. Durham, N.C.: Duke University Press; Baden-Baden: Verlag Valentin Koerner, 1985.

Hedges, Inez. *Languages of Revolt: Dada and Surrealist Literature and Film.* Durham, N.C.: Duke University Press, 1983.

Heidegger, Martin. "The Thing." In *Poetry, Language, Thought,* translated by Albert Hofstadter, 163–186. New York: Harper and Row, 1971.

Henderson, Robert M. *D. W. Griffith: His Life and Work.* New York: Oxford University Press, 1972.

Hibbard, Howard. *Bernini.* Harmondsworth, England: Penguin Books, 1978.

Hislop, Codman, and W. R. Richardson, eds. *"Trial without Jury" and Other Plays by J. H. Payne.* Princeton, N.J.: Princeton University Press, 1940.

Hoffmann, E. T. A. *Novelly.* Moscow: Khudozhestvennaia literatura, 1978.

———. "Klein Zaches genannt Zinnober." In *Hoffmans Werke.* Vol. 1. Berlin: Aufbau Verlag, 1990.

Hogg, James. "Robert Browning and the Victorian Theatre. The Experimental Dramatist: The Closet Plays." *Salzburger Studien zur Anglistik und Amerikanistik.* Vol. 1, part 2. Salzburg, 1981.

Hood, Thomas. "The Sea of Death." In *The Complete Poetical Works of Thomas Hood,* edited by Walter Jerrold, 279–280. Westport, Conn.: Greenwood Press, 1980.

Hoog, Michel. *R. Delaunay.* Paris: Flammarion, 1976.

Hudnut, Joseph. *Architecture and the Spirit of Man.* Cambridge, Mass.: Harvard University Press, 1949.

Hugo, Victor. *Les Orientales. Les Feuilles d'automne. Les chants du crépuscule.* Paris: Hachette, 1872.

———. *La Légende des siècles.* Edited by Jacques Truchet. Paris: Gallimard, 1950.

———. *Les Châtiments.* Edited by Franz André Burget. Paris: Gallimard, 1964.

———. *Les Contemplations.* Paris: Gallimard, Librairie Générale Française, 1965.

———. *Poésie.* Vol. 2 of *Oeuvres Complètes.* Edited by Jean Gaudon and Sheila Gaudon. Paris: Robert Laffont, 1985.

———. *Les Châtiments.* Paris: Nelson, n.d.

———. *Les Rayons et les ombres.* Paris: Hetzel, n.d.

Iakubinskii, Lev P. *Izbrannye raboty: Iazyk i ego funktsionirovanie.* Moscow: Nauka, 1986.

Iampolski, Mikhail. "Problema vzaimodeistviia iskusstv i neosushchestvlennyi mul'tfil'm Fernana Lezhe 'Charli-kubist.' " In *Problema sinteza v khudozhestvennoi kul'ture,* edited by Boris V. Raushenbakh, 76–97. Moscow: Nauka, 1985.

———. "'Smyslovaia veshch' v kinoteorii OPOIAZa." In *Tynianovskii sbornik: tret'i tynianovskie chteniia,* 109–119. Riga: Zinatne, 1988.

Icart, Roger. "A la découverte de 'La Roue.'" *Les Cahiers de la cinémathèque* 33–34 (1981): 185–192.

Irwin, John T. *American Hieroglyphics: The Symbol of the Egyptian Hieroglyphics in the American Renaissance.* New Haven, Conn.: Yale University Press, 1980.

Iutkevich, Sergei I. *O kinoiskusstve.* Moscow: Iskusstvo, 1962.

Ivanov, Viacheslav V. *Ocherki po istorii semiotiki v SSSR* . Moscow: Nauka, 1976.

———. "Fil'm v fil'me." *Tekst v tekste. Trudy po znakovym sistemam* 14 (1981) 19–32.

Jaffé, Aniela. "Symbolism in the Visual Arts." In *Man and His Symbols,* edited by C. G. Jung et al. London: Aldus Books, Jupiter Books, 1964.

Jakobson, Roman. *Essais de linguistique générale.* Paris: Editions de Minuit, 1963.

———. *Raboty po poètike.* Moscow: Progress, 1987.

Jennings, W. C. "Diderot: A Suggested Source of the Jules-Phene Episode in 'Pippa Passes.'" *English Language Notes* 1 (1964): 32–36.

Jenny, Laurent. "La Stratégie de la forme." *Poétique* 27 (1976): 257–281.

Joyce, James. *Ulysses.* New York: Random House, 1961.

Kauffman, Stanley, and B. Henstell, eds. *American Film Criticism from the Beginnings to "Citizen Kane."* New York: Liveright, 1972.

Kayser, Walter. "La Doctrine du langage naturel chez Jacob Boehme et ses sources." *Poétique* 11 (1972): 337–366.

Kingsley, Charles. *Poems.* New York: Thomas Y. Crowell, 1899.

Klee, Paul. *Théorie de l'art moderne.* Paris: Denoël, Gonthier, 1971.

Kleiman, Naum, and Marina Nesteva. "Vydaiushchiisia khudozhnik-gumanist." *Sovetskaia muzyka* 9 (1979): 68–78.

Klimenko, E. I. *Tvorchestvo Roberta Brauninga.* Leningrad: LGU, 1967.

Kozintsev, Grigorii. *Sobranie sochinenii.* Vol. 2. Leningrad: Iskusstvo, 1983.

Kozlov, Leonid. "Gipoteza o nevyskazannom posviashchenii." *Voprosy kinoiskusstva* 12 (1970): 109–133.

Krauss, Rosalind. "Originality as Repetition: Introduction." *October* 37 (1986): 35–40.

Kristeva, Julia. *Sémeiotikè: Recherches pour une sémanalyse.* Paris: Seuil, 1969.

Krolop, Kurt. "Dichtung und Satire bei Karl Kraus." In *Kraus K. Vor Walpurgisnacht: Ausgewählte Werke.* Vol. 3, 651–691. Berlin: Volk und Welt, 1977.

Kuntzel, Thierry. "Le Travail du film, 2." *Communications* 23 (1975): 136–189.

Kyrou, Ado. *Luis Buñuel.* Paris: Seghers, 1962.

———. *Luis Buñuel: An Introduction.* Translated by Adrienne Foulke. New York: Simon and Schuster, 1963.

Lagny, Michèle. "Histoire et cinéma: Des amours difficiles." *CinémAction* 47 (1988): 73–78.

Lang, Andrew. *Custom and Myth.* London: Longmans, 1898.

Langen, August. "Zur Geschichte des Spiegelsymbols in der deutschen Dichtung." *Germanisch-Romanische Monatschrift* 10–12 (1940): 269–280.

Langlès, Louis. *Monuments anciens et modernes de l'Hindoustan, décrits sous le double rapport archéologique et pittoresque.* Vol. 2. Paris: Didot, 1821.

Laplanche, Jean, and J. B. Pontalis. "Fantasme des origines, origine du fantasme." *Les temps modernes* 215 (April 1964): 1833–1868.

Latini, Brunetto. "Livre du Trésor." In *Bestiaires du moyen age.* Paris: Stock, 1980.

Lawder, Standish D. *The Cubist Cinema.* New York: New York University Press, 1975.

Léger, Fernand. *Fonctions de la peinture.* Paris: Gonthier, 1965.

———. "Présentation du 'Ballet mécanique.'" *Europe* 508–509 (1971): 64–65.

———. "Moskva, Èizenshteinu." *Iskusstvo kino* 1 (1973): 86.

Leiris, Michel. *Mots sans mémoire.* Paris: Gallimard, 1969.

Leroy, Claude. "Cendrars, le futurisme et la fin du monde." *Europe* 551 (1975): 113–120.

Lévesque, Jacques-Henry. *Blaise Cendrars.* Paris: Editions de la Nouvelle Revue Critique, 1947.

Levinton, Georgii A. "Istochniki i podteksty romana 'Smert' Vazir-Mukhtara'." In *Tynianovskii sbornik: Tret' i tynianovskie chteniia*, 6–14. Riga: Zinatne, 1988.

Lévi-Strauss, Claude. *La Pensée sauvage*. Paris: Plon, 1962.

Levy-Bruhl, L. *Pervobytnoe myshlenie*. Moscow: Ateist, 1930.

———. *How Natives Think*. New York: Washington Square Press, 1966.

Lindsay, Jack. *A Short History of Culture*. London: Victor Gollancz, 1939.

Lindsay, Vachel. *Collected Poems*. New York: Macmillan, 1925.

———. *The Art of the Moving Picture*. New York: Liveright, 1970.

———. *Letters of Vachel Lindsay*. Edited by M. Chenetier. New York: Burt Franklin, 1979.

Locke, John. *An Essay Concerning Human Understanding*. London: Routledge and Sons, n.d.

Lotman, Iurii M. *Analiz poèticheskogo teksta. Struktura stikha*. Leningrad: Prosveshchenie, 1972.

———. "Tekst v tekste." *Tekst v tekste. Trudy po znakovym sistemam* 14 (1981): 3–18.

———. "Simvolika Peterburga i problemy semiotiki goroda." *Semiotika goroda i gorodskoi kul'tury. Peterburg. Trudy po znakovym sistemam* 18 (1984): 30–45.

———. "Neskol'ko myslei o tipologii kul'tur." In *Iazyki kul'tury i problemy perevodimosti*. Moscow: Nauka, 1987.

Lotman, Iurii M., and Iurii G. Tsiv'ian. "SVD: Zhanr melodramy i istoriia." In *Tynianovskii sbornik: Pervye tynianovskie chteniia*, 46–78. Riga: Zinatne, 1984.

Lovey, Jean-Claude. *Situation de Blaise Cendrars*. Neuchâtel: À la Baconnière, 1965.

Lyotard, Jean-François. *Le Postmoderne expliqué aux enfants*. Paris: Galilée, 1986.

Lytton, Edward Bulwer. *Bulwer's Plays: Being the Complete Dramatic Work of Lord Lytton*. Edited by John M. Kingdon. New York: Robert M. DeWitt, 1875.

———. *Zanoni: A Rosicrucian Tale*. Preface by Paul M. Allen. Blauvelt, N.Y.: Steinerbooks, 1981.

Maier-Meintshel, A. "Vermeer Del'ftskii i Grigorii Teplov: Pis'mo kak motiv izobrazheniia." In *Veshch' v iskusstve*, 82–89. Moscow: Sovetskii khudozhnik, 1986.

Malevich, Kazimir S. "Pis'ma k M. V. Matiushinu." In *Ezhegodnik rukopisnogo otdela Pushkinskogo doma na 1974*, 177–195. Leningrad: Nauka, 1976.

Maliavin, V. V. "Kitaiskie improvizatsii Paunda." In *Vostok-Zapad*, 246–277. Moscow: Nauka, 1982.

Mancini, Elaine. "La Teoria cinematografica di Hugo Munsterberg in relazioni ai primi film di Griffith." *Griffithiana* 5–6 (1980): 62–72.

Marie, Michel. "Le Rasoir et la Lune: Sur le prologue de 'Un chien andalou.'" In *Cinémas de la modernité: Films, théories*, 187–198. Paris: Klincksieck, 1981.

———. "La Scène des fantasmes originaires." In *Ce que je vois de mon Ciné*. Paris: Meridiens, Klincksieck, 1988.

Martin, Jay. *Always Merry and Bright: The Life of Henry Miller*. London: Sheldon Press, 1979.

Massa, Ann. *Vachel Lindsay: Fieldworker for the American Dream*. Bloomington: Indiana University Press, 1970.

Matthews, J. H. *Benjamin Péret*. Boston: Twayne, 1975.

Matthiessen, Francis Otto. *American Renaissance: Art and Expression in the Age of Emerson and Whitman*. London: Oxford University Press, 1957.

Maupassant, Guy de. *Chroniques*. Vol. 3. Paris: UGE, 1980.

McFarlane, James. "The Mind of Modernism." In *Modernism, 1890–1930,* edited by M. Bradbury and J. McFarlane, 71–83. Harmondsworth, England: Penguin Books, 1976.

Merritt, Russell. "Rescued from Perilous Nest: D. W. Griffith's Escape from Theater into Film." *Cinema Journal* 21 (1981): 2–30.

Metz, Christian. *Essais sur la signification au cinéma.* Vol. 1. Paris: Klincksieck, 1975.

———. *Langage et cinéma.* Paris: Albatros, 1977.

———. *Le Signifiant imaginaire.* Paris: UGE, 1977.

Michelson, Annette. "'Anemic Cinema': Reflections on an Emblematic Work." *Artforum* 12 (1973): 64–69.

Miller, Henry. *A Devil in Paradise.* New York: New American Library of World Literature, 1956.

———. *Un diable au paradis.* Paris: Buchet-Chastel, 1965.

Miller, Perry, ed. *The Transcendentalists: An Anthology.* Cambridge, Mass.: Harvard University Press, 1967.

Montesanti, Fausto. "Pastrone e Griffith: Mito di un rapporto." *Bianco e nero* 5–8 (1975): 8–17.

Montesquiou, Robert de. *Diptyque de Flandre. Triptyque de France.* Paris: UGE, 1986.

Münsterberg, Hugo. *The Film: A Psychological Study. The Silent Photoplay in 1916.* New York: Dover, 1970.

Muratova, Kseniia. *Srednevekovyi bestiarii.* Moscow: Iskusstvo, 1984.

Nakov, Andrei B. "De la peinture sans référant verbal." *Hommage à Fernand Léger: XXe siècle.* N spécial (1971): 48–52.

"Nemaia kniga." In *Vozniknovenie i razvitie khimii s drevneishikh vremen do XVII veka.* Moscow: Nauka, 1980.

Nerval, Gerard de. *Oeuvres.* Vols. 1–2. Paris: Garnier, 1958.

The Notebooks of Leonardo da Vinci. Edited by Edward MacCurdy. Scarborough, N.Y.: Plume Books, 1960.

O'Dell, Paul. *Griffith and the Rise of Hollywood.* New York: A. Barnes, A. Zwemmer, 1970.

Painter, George D. *Marcel Proust, 1871–1903: Les années de jeunesse.* Paris: Mercure de France, 1966.

———. *Marcel Proust, 1904–1922: Les années de maturité.* Paris: Mercure de France, 1966.

Panofsky, Erwin. *Meaning in the Visual Arts.* Garden City, N.Y.: Doubleday Anchor Books, 1955.

———. "Style and Medium in Moving Pictures." In *Film: An Anthology,* edited by D. Talbot, 15–32. Berkeley: University of California Press, 1959.

———. *Idea.* Paris: Gallimard. 1989.

Parrot, Louis. *Blaise Cendrars.* Paris: Seghers, 1953.

Pater, Walter. *The Renaissance: Studies in Art and Poetry.* New York: Macmillan, 1900.

Peirce, Charles Sanders. *Philosophical Writings of Peirce.* Edited by Justus Buchler. New York: Dover, 1955.

Péret, Benjamin. *Il était une boulangère.* Paris: Editions du Sagittaire, 1925.

———. *Mort aux vaches et au champ d'honneur.* Paris: Eric Losfeld, 1967.

———. *Oeuvres complètes.* Vol. 1. Paris: Eric Losfeld, 1969.

Phillips, Leona Rasmussen. *D. W. Griffith: Titan of the Film Art (A Critical Study)*. New York: Gordon Press, 1976.

Physiologus: Frühchristlicher Tiersymbolik. Berlin: Union Verlag, 1987.

Pleynet, Marcelin. *Lautréamont par lui-meme*. Paris: Seuil, 1967.

Poe, Edgar Allan. *Poetical Works*. New York: Thomas Y. Crowell, 1892.

———. *Poetry*. Vol. 3 of *The Works of Edgar Allan Poe*. Edited by John H. Ingram. London: A & C Black Standard Edition, 1899.

———. *Tales*. Vol. 2 of *The Works of Edgar Allan Poe*. Edited by John H. Ingram. London: A & C Black Standard Edition, 1899.

Pound, Ezra. *Ezra Pound: A Critical Anthology*. Edited by J. P. Sullivan. Harmondsworth, England: Penguin Books, 1970.

———. *Ezra Pound and the Visual Arts*. New York: New Directions, 1980.

Prawer, S. S. *Caligari's Children: The Film as Tale of Terror*. Oxford: Oxford University Press, 1980.

Prokof'ev, Valery N. "Prostranstvo v zhivopisi Dega." In *Sovetskoe iskusstvoznanie 82 (2)*, 101–119. Moscow: Sovetskii khudozhnik, 1984.

Proust, Marcel. *La Prisonnière*. Paris: Gallimard, 1977.

Pruitt, J. "I Film Biograph 1908–1910: Fotografia e illuminazione." *Griffithiana* 5–6 (1980): 48–61.

Ramirez, Gabriel. *El cine de Griffith*. Mexico: Ediciones Era, 1972.

Ramsaye, Terry. *A Million and One Nights*. New York: Simon and Schuster, 1926.

Richer, Jean. *L'Alchimie du verbe de Rimbaud*. Paris: Didier, 1972.

Riffaterre, Michael. "Sémiotique intertextuelle: L'Interpretant." *Revue d'Esthétique* 32, nos. 1–2 (1972): 128–150.

———. "Le Tissu du texte: Du Bellay, Songe, VII." *Poétique* 34 (1978): 193–203.

———. *La Production du texte*. Paris: Seuil, 1979.

Ritter, Johann Wilhelm. *Fragmente aus dem Nachlasse eines jungen Physikers: Ein Taschenbuch für Freunde der Natur*. Leipzig: Kiepenheuer, 1984.

Rodenbach, Georges. *Bruges-la-morte*. Translated by Philip Mosby. Paisley, U.K.: Wilfron Books, 1986.

Rogin, Michael. "The Great Mother Domesticated: Sexual Difference and Sexual Indifference in D. W. Griffith's 'Intolerance.' " *Critical Inquiry* 15 (1989): 510–555.

Roheim, Geza. *Spiegelzauber*. Leipzig: Internat. psychoanalytischer Verlag, 1919.

Ropars-Wuilleumier, Marie-Claire. *Le Texte divisé: Essai sur l'écriture filmique*. Paris: PUF, 1981.

Roudaut, Jean. "Un geste, un regard." *La Nouvelle Revue Française* 172 (1967): 835–840.

Rudnitskii, Konstantin L. *Russkoe rezhissërskoe iskusstvo, 1898–1907*. Moscow: Nauka, 1989.

Sadoul, Georges. *French Film*. London: Falcon Press, 1953.

———. "Fernand Léger ou la cinéplastique." *Cinéma* 35 (1959): 73–82.

———. *Histoire générale du cinéma*. Vol. 5. Paris: Denoël, 1975.

Schapiro, Meyer. "Nekotorye problemy semiotiki vizual'nogo iskusstva: Prostranstvo izobrazheniia i sredstva sozdaniia znaka-obraza." In *Semiotika i iskusstvometriia*, 136–163. Moscow: Mir, 1972.

Schickel, Richard. *D. W. Griffith: An American Life*. New York: Simon and Schuster, 1984.

Schlesinger, Arthur. *The Rise of the City.* New York: Macmillan, 1933.

Schmalenbach, Werner. *Fernand Léger.* Paris: Cercle d'art, 1977.

Sèpman, Inna. "Tynianov-stsenarist." In *Iz istorii Lenfil'ma.* Vol. 3, 51–77. Leningrad: Iskusstvo, 1973.

Shklovskii, Victor. "Gorod nashei iunosti." In *Vospominaniia o Iu. Tynianove,* edited by Veniamin Kaverin, 5–37. Moscow: Sovetskii pisatel', 1983.

———. *Kak my pishem.* Moscow: Kniga, 1989.

———. *Gamburgskii schet (1914–1933).* Moscow: Sovetskii pisatel', 1990.

Shpet, Gustav G. *Sochineniia.* Moscow: Pravda, 1989.

Shub, Èsfir. *Zhizn' moia—kinematograf.* Moscow: Iskusstvo, 1972.

Sitney, P. Adams. "Image and Title in Avant-Garde Cinema." *October* 11 (1979): 97–112.

Skobelev, A. V. "K probleme sootnosheniia romanticheskoi ironii i satiry v tvorchestve Gofmana ('Kroshka Tsakhes')." In *Khudozhestbennyi mir È. T. A. Gofmana,* 247–263. Moscow: Nauka, 1982.

Sokolov, M. "Granitsy ikonologii i problema edinstva iskusstvovedcheskogo metoda (k sporam vokrug teorii È. Panofskogo)." In *Sovremennoe iskusstvoznanie Zapada o klassicheskom iskusstve XIII–XVII,* 227–249. Moscow: Nauka, 1977.

Solomon-Godeau, Abigail. "The Legs of the Countess." *October* 39 (1986): 65–108.

Sophocles. "Antigona." In *Antichnaia drama,* 179–228. Moscow: Khudozhestvennaia literatura, 1970.

———. *Sophocles: Antigone.* Edited and translated by Andrew Brown. Wiltshire, England: Aris and Phillips, 1987.

Soupault, Philippe. "Enfin Cendrars vint . . . ou tel qu'en lui-même enfin." *Mercure de France* 1185 (1962): 84–87.

———. *Poèmes et poésies.* Paris: Grasset, 1973.

———. *Ecrits de cinéma, 1918–1931.* Paris: Plon, 1979.

———. *Vingt mille et un jours.* Paris: Belfond, 1980.

Souriau, Etienne. *La Correspondance des arts.* Paris: Flammarion, 1969.

Spitzer, Leo. "Explication de texte applied to Walt Whitman's poem 'Out of the cradle endlessly rocking.' " In *Essays on English and American Literature,* 14–36. Princeton, N.J.: Princeton University Press, 1962.

Starobinski, Jean. *Les Mots sous les mots: Les anagrammes de Ferdinand de Saussure.* Paris: Gallimard, 1971.

Stepanov, Nikolai. "Zamysly i plany." In *Vospominaniia o Iu. Tynianove,* 231–247. Moscow: Sovetskii pisatel', 1983.

Survage, Léopold. "Le Rythme coloré." In *Cinéma: Théorie, lectures,* 275–277. Paris: Klincksieck, 1978.

Swedenborg, Emanuel. *Heaven and Its Wonders and Hell: From Things Heard and Seen.* New York: American Swedenborg Printing and Publishing Society, 1921.

Symons, Arthur. *An Introduction to the Study of Robert Browning.* London: Dent, 1906.

Szymczyk-Kluszczynska, Grazyne. "Antonin Artaud et l'idée du cinéma sans film." Unpublished ms., 1989.

Tennyson, Alfred Lord. "Enoch Arden." In *The Poems of Tennyson in Three Volumes.* Vol. 2, edited by Christopher Ricks. Essex: Longman House, 1987.

Thompson, Ch. "'Le Feu du ciel' de Victor Hugo et John Martin." *Gazette des Beaux-Arts* 65, no. 1155 (1965): 247–256.

Thoreau, Henry David. *The Works of Thoreau*. Boston: Houghton Mifflin, 1937.

———. *The Portable Thoreau*. Harmondsworth, England: Penguin Books, 1947.

Toddes, Eugenii. "Poslelslovie." In *Podporuchik Kizhe*, 164–200. Moscow: Kniga, 1981.

Tommasino, R. "Griffith: Una catalisi trasgressiva." *Filmcritica* 254–255 (1975): 173–176.

Tsiv'ian, Iurii G. "K istorii idei intellektual'nogo kino." In *Iz tvorcheskogo naslediia S. M. Èizenshteina*, 107–111. Moscow: VNIIK, 1985.

———. "Paleogrammy v fil'me 'Shinel'.'" In *Tynianovskii sbornik: vtorye tynianovskie chteniia*, 14–27. Riga: Zinatne, 1986.

———. "'Chelovek c kinoapporatom' Dzigi Vertova: K rasshifrovke montazhnogo teksta." In *Montazh. Literatura, iskusstvo, teatr, kino*, edited by Mikhail Iampolski, 78–98. Moscow: Nauka, 1988.

Tynianov, Iurii. *Problema stikhotvornogo iazyka*. Leningrad: Academia, 1924.

———. *Podporuchik Kizhe*. Screenplay. Archive of the Central Museum of Film, 1927.

———. *Poruchik Kizhe*. Screenplay. Archive of Veniamin Kaverin, 1933.

———. *Podporuchik Kizhe*. Moscow: Goslitizdat, 1954.

———. *Smert' Vazir-Mukhtara. Podporuchik Kizhe*. Voronezh: Voronizhskoe knizhnoe izdatel'stvo, 1963.

———. *Pushkin i ego sovremenniki*. Moscow: Nauka, 1969.

———. *Poètika. Istoriia literatury. Kino*. Moscow: Nauka, 1977.

———. *Kiukhlia. Podporuchik Kizhe. Voskovaia persona. Maloletnii Vitushishnikov*. Moscow: Khudozhestvennaia literatura, 1989.

———. "Obez'iana i kolokol." *Kinostsenarii* 3 (1989): 130–144.

———. *Lieutenant Kijé. Young Vitushishnikov*. Translated by Mirra Ginsburg. New York: Marsilio Publishers, 1992.

Tzara, Tristan. *L'Homme approximatif*. Paris: Gallimard, 1968.

Ulmer, Gregory L. *Applied Grammatology: Post(e)-Pedagogy from Jacques Derrida to Joseph Beuys*. Baltimore: Johns Hopkins University Press, 1985.

The Upanishads. Translated by Eknath Easwaran. 5th ed. Tomales, Calif.: Nilgiri Press, 1995.

Vanoye, Francis. "Le Cinéma de Cendrars." *Europe* 566 (1976): 183–196.

Varilä, A. "The Swedenborgian Background of William James's Philosophy." *Annales Academiae Scientorum fennicae*. Dissertationes humanorum litterarum 12. (Helsinki), 1977.

Vernet, Marc. *Figures de l'absence*. Paris: Editions de l'Etoile, 1988.

Villiers de l'Isle-Adam. *Oeuvres Complètes*. Vol. 3. Paris: Mercure de France, 1922.

Vinogradov, Viktor. *Izbrannye trudy: Poètika russkoi literatury*. Moscow: Nauka, 1976.

Virgil. *The Aeneid of Virgil*. Translated by C. Day Lewis. New York: Oxford University Press, 1952.

Virmaux, Alain, and Odette Virmaux. *Les Surréalistes et le cinéma*. Paris: Seghers, 1976.

Voloshin, Maksimilian. *Liki tvorchestva*. Leningrad: Nauka, 1988.

Warburton, William. *Essai sur les hiéroglyphes des Egyptiens.* Paris: Aubier, Flammarion, 1977.

Weber, J. -P. *La Psychologie de l'art.* Paris: P.U.F., 1958.

Whitman, Walt. *Complete Prose Works.* New York: Mitchell Kennerly, 1914.

———. *The Complete Poems.* Edited by Francis Murphy. London: Penguin, 1977.

———. *Leaves of Grass: The "Death-bed" Edition.* New York: Modern Library, 1993.

Willey, Basil. *The Seventeenth Century Background.* New York: Columbia University Press, 1958.

Williams, Linda. "The Prologue to 'Un Chien andalou': A Surrealist Film Metaphor." *Screen* 17, no. 4 (1976–1977): 24–33.

———. *Figures of Desire: A Theory and Analysis of Surrealist Film.* Urbana: University of Illinois Press, 1981.

Winn, James Anderson. *Unsuspected Eloquence: A History of Relations between Poetry and Music.* New Haven, Conn.: Yale University Press, 1981.

Wölfflin, Heinrich. *Renaissance und Barock.* Leipzig: Koehler und Amelang, 1986.

Wordsworth, William. *The Prelude: Or Growth of a Poet's Mind.* London: Oxford University Press, 1933.

———. *The Prelude.* Harmondsworth, England: Penguin Books, 1978.

Worringer, Wilhelm. *Abstraktion und Einfühlung.* 9th ed. München: R. Piper, 1919.

———. "Abstraktsiia i odukhotvorenie." In *Sovremennaia kniga po èstetike,* 459–475. Moscow: Izd. Inostrannoi literatury, 1957.

Yates, Frances A. *The Art of Memory.* Harmondsworth, England: Penguin Books, 1969.

Yoder, R. A. *Emerson and the Orphic Poet in America.* Berkeley: University of California Press, 1978.

The Zohar. Translated by Harry Sperling and Maurice Simon. London: Soncino Press, 1984.

Zola, Émile *Rugon-Makkary.* Vol. 1. Moscow: Pravda, 1957.

———. *Les Rougon-Macquart: Histoire Naturelle et Sociale d'une famille sous le Second Empire.* Vol. 1. Edited by Henri Mitterrand. Paris: Gallimard, 1960.

———. *Le Roman expérimental.* Paris: Garnier, Flammarion, 1971.

Zorkaia, Neia. "Tynianov i kino." *Voprocy kinoiskusstva* 10 (1967): 258–295.

Index

"Abbot Vogler" (Browning), 62
A B C du cinéma (Cendrars), 150, 156
Abel, Richard, 20
Abélard, 186
abstraction, 251; avant-garde, 127, 134;
  Eisenstein and, 228–39, 279n43, 280n66
Abstraktion und Einfühling (Worringer), 231
Adam, 12
"Adamic" language, 89, 99, 106, 120
Addams, Jane, 93
Adorno, Theodor, 229, 279n36
Aeneid (Virgil), 32–35
African fetish/dance, 151–52, 155
After Many Years (Griffith), 52, 83, 84,
  93–94, 98–99
L'Age d'or (Buñuel and Dali), 162, 184
aggression, 119–20
Ahuramazda (Ormuzd), 24
"Alchemical Theatre" (Artaud), 21
alchemy, 21–25, 172
alcoholism, 40, 60
Alcott, Amos Bronson, 88
Aleksandr Nevsky (Eisenstein), 229, 232, 240,
  243
alembic (alchemical still), 23–24
Alexandrian, Sarane, 268–69n66
allegory: avant-garde, 133–34, 136; of death,
  237; De Quincey, 114; Griffith, 73, 76,
  77, 120; Méliès, 14. *See also* hieroglyphs
Allin, Alex, 20
"Allotropies" (Breton), 170
Les Altantes (Gance), 269n77

Altman, Rick, 56
Aman-Jean, Pierre, 14
ambivalence: and *Lieutenant Kizhe*, 210; in
  search for origins, 81; surrealist, 173,
  178, 179
anagrams, 16–25, 100, 101, 153; alchemy
  and, 21–24; and hieroglyphs, 27; hy-
  pograms, 17; logograms, 17; sounds, 16,
  21–25, 26; surrealist, 178; trans-sense
  and, 201. *See also* paragrams
analogies: Eisenstein and, 221–22, 228, 230;
  surrealist, 185, 187–89, 250, 273n79
analysis, 7, 15; Eisenstein and, 225, 228,
  231–33, 237; graphological, 233; self-,
  237. *See also* psychoanalytic interpretation; theory
anatomy, 223–24, 239. *See also* body
androgyny, 2, 3, 181
Ane en putrefaction (Dali), 180
Anemic Cinema (Duchamp), 153
"L'Âne pourri" (Dali), 185
angels, 117; Apocalypse spirit, 115; of death,
  33, 73; in heavenly city, 109
animal images. *See* bestiaries; insects; *individual animals*
"Annabel Lee" (Poe), 107–8
anomalies, 247, 251; avant-garde, 125, 146,
  166; cinematic language, 74, 83, 100–
  104, 121; normalizing, 30, 83, 101, 121,
  125, 247; parallel shots, 93–94; and quo-
  tation/misquotation, 30, 34–35, 51, 52,
  58, 79, 201. *See also* inversion; negation

Compositor: Binghamton Valley Composition, Inc.
Text: 10/12 Baskerville
Display: Baskerville
Printer and Binder: Maple-Vail Book Manufacturing, Inc.